THE GLOBAL BUSINESS: FOUR KEY MARKETING STRATEGIES

Erdener Kaynak, PhD
Editor

SOME ADVANCE REVIEWS

"What emerges from this book is the message that each culture and subculture is relevant to the subject of marketing. . . . If world trade is to survive and flourish, we all need to know more about the differences in marketing globally rather than the similarities. This book is a welcome impulse for all of us."

Pat Joynt, PhD
Professor, Norwegian School of Management;
Visiting Professor at the University of Wisconsin, Madison

"Stimulating and balanced. . . . The chapters have excellent geographic representation, with all major countries and market types given coverage. Each contribution is eminently readable and reflects contemporary thought in its area. Most importantly, this collection demonstrates the growing maturity and development of the international marketing discipline and shows that despite the wide disparity in backgrounds and perspectives of individual scholars, a unified philosophy of the area is emerging."

John S. Hill, PhD
Professor, International Business
University of Alabama

T0383198

"Offers a most valuable selection of recent articles for courses in International Marketing and Comparative Marketing. There is a good balance of consumer behavior, strategic marketing, and national marketing studies — including developing and command economies — that remain fresh in their findings and suggest fruitful research implications."

Jean J. Boddewyn, PhD
Professor of Marketing and International Business
Baruch College (CUNY)

"A high-quality collection of [chapters] which can be quite helpful to managers, government officials, and scholars. Administrators and expert staff in intergovernmental organizations also will find much helpful material. The book's coverage of the Third World is particularly useful."

Thomas V. Greer, PhD
Professor
University of Maryland, College Park

The Global Business
Four Key
Marketing Strategies

INTERNATIONAL BUSINESS PRESS
Erdener Kaynak, PhD
Executive Editor

New, Recent, and Forthcoming Titles:

International Business Handbook edited by V. H. (Manek) Kirpalani

Sociopolitical Aspects of International Marketing edited by Erdener Kaynak

How to Manage for International Competitiveness edited by Abbas J. Ali

International Business Expansion into Less-Developed Countries: The International Finance Corporation and Its Operations by James C. Baker

Product-Country Images: Impact and Role in International Marketing edited by Nicolas Papadopoulos and Louise A. Heslop

The Global Business: Four Key Marketing Strategies edited by Erdener Kaynak

Multinational Strategic Alliances edited by Refik Culpan

Market Evolution in Developing Countries: The Unfolding of the Indian Market by Subhash C. Jain

The Global Business
Four Key
Marketing Strategies

Erdener Kaynak, PhD
Editor

International Business Press
An Imprint of The Haworth Press, Inc.
New York • London • Norwood (Australia)

Published by

International Business Press, an imprint of The Haworth Press, Inc., 10 Alice Street, Binghamton, NY 13904-1580

Library of Congress Cataloging-in-Publication Data

The global business : four key marketing strategies / Erdener Kaynak.
    p. cm.
Includes bibliographical references and index.
ISBN 1-56024-248-5 (alk. paper) – ISBN 156024-249-3 (pbk.: alk paper).
    1. Export marketing – Management. 2. Intercultural communication. I. Kaynak, Erdener.
HF1416.G55 1992
658.8′48 – dc20   91-34596
                                                      CIP

CONTENTS

List of Illustrations

TABLES

Chapter 9

Chapter 11

Chapter 12

Chapter 13

FIGURES

Chapter 10

Chapter 12

Chapter 20

ABOUT THE EDITOR

Erdener Kaynak, PhD, is a member of the marketing faculty at the School of Business Administration at The Pennsylvania State University at Harrisburg. He has held key teaching and administrative positions in Europe, Asia, and North America.

Professor Kaynak has extensive consulting and advising experience in international marketing in Europe, Latin America, the Middle East, and the Far East. He was Director of International Programs and served on the Board of Governors of the Academy of Marketing Science. In this capacity, he organized two World Marketing Congresses.

Dr. Kaynak has authored and co-authored many books and articles on international marketing and cross-cultural/national consumer behavior. Currently, Dr. Kaynak serves on several marketing journal review boards and is Executive Editor, International Business, for The Haworth Press, Inc. He is also editor of the *Journal of Global Marketing*, the *Journal of International Consumer Marketing*, the *Journal of International Food & Agribusiness Marketing*, the *Journal of Teaching in International Business*, and the *Journal of Euromarketing*, all published by The Haworth Press, Inc.

Foreword

As more business battles cross borders, managers must broaden their view of products, markets, and competition. Doing business in a global economy requires perseverance, dedication, and a lot of new learning—including how to find the right country in which to build a plant, how to coordinate production schedules across borders, how to market products and how to absorb research wherever it occurs. The managers must learn what sort of people to hire, how to inculcate a global mentality in the ranks, and when to sell standardized products instead of customizing them for local market needs and expectations.

Only a few managers are capable of handling the competitive rigors of the new global marketplace. Companies, even those long accustomed to doing business overseas, find it extremely difficult to make their managers look beyond their own fiefdoms to consider the resources, capabilities, and needs of the company as a whole in order to serve the global marketplace properly. In most cases, these managers struggle to reorient their subordinates to be global planners and strategists.

Briefly, the need of American business for more global expertise requires no elaboration. Its implications for developing appropriate study material are far reaching. *The Global Business* provides a collection of readings that contribute immensely toward gaining better insights into perspectives of managing a global corporation. The book comprises a good blend of theory and application. The book is especially useful:

   a. To increase the capabilities to deal effectively with major challenges which face global enterprises in the 1990s and beyond. In most cases, these changes are rooted in diverse competitive, socio-political, and organizational phenomena.

   b. To provide the means to identify, order, and analyze the key
      global trends and the changes they bring.
   c. To offer a better understanding and appreciation of the analyti-
      cal, political, and human skills so essential to the success of
      global business today and in the future.
   d. To enhance the understanding of global competition and how
      and when to respond to the competitive threats and opportuni-
      ties.
   e. To examine the moral and ethical issues which global situa-
      tions raise and which force value clarifications.

The readings included in the book are authored by recognized
leaders in the field. As companies consider challenges of global
business, *The Global Business* should serve as an exceedingly useful resource material for academicians, businesspersons, and public
policy makers alike.

Subhash C. Jain

Preface

Globalization of firms of all sizes and from a variety of industries is a watch word which must be reckoned with in today's competitive world markets. As the world becomes smaller and smaller, it is becoming more and more evident that business firms will increasingly face stronger competition. For instance, it was stated by the Chairman and CEO of Proctor & Gamble Company that virtually every U.S. business today is touched in some way by global competition.[1] By making strong commitments to their globalization policies, U.S. firms will have an opportunity to market their products and services around the world more effectively and efficiently. This global competition is being fuelled by economic, technological, legal/political, and social changes taking place around the globe. Many of these changes and transformations are taking place within the confines of the triad: North America, Europe, and East Asia. These emerging trading blocs and the countries therein do offer certain opportunities and threats for U.S. companies.

This book of readings on global marketing contains five sections. Section one describes global marketing theory and practice conceptually and analytically by offering managerially-oriented case stories and company practices in various global markets. Section two is devoted to the treatment of cross-cultural consumer marketing issues. For successful global marketing, a consumer-oriented approach is of prime importance. As such, this section examines various consumer and buyer behavior issues within a global environment by pinpointing that understanding and adapting to world consumer needs and wants become a necessity. In addition to understanding customer needs worldwide, companies will also have to be tuned with the global marketing environment. To this end, sec-

---

1. Procter & Gamble Company Annual Report, 1990, p. 5.

tion three examines strategy development activities of global firms in various global markets. Section four tries to apply global marketing strategies to Third World countries, whereas section five tries to apply them to socialist countries of Eastern Europe, the U.S.S.R. and the P.R.C.

As with the global marketing strategy and practice itself, this book is need and action-oriented. To this end, it offers practically oriented managerial guidelines for the benefit of global marketers, public policy makers at all levels, and students of marketing and researchers and scholars of marketing on a global scale by drawing parallels among marketing policies, strategies, and practices. In this endeavor, the book primarily tries to answer the following questions:

- What are the best methods of operating in global markets?
- Is there such a thing as global consumer? If so, what are his/her characteristics?
- What are the decision-making rules in global markets?
- Does domestic marketing strategy differ in any way from global marketing strategy?
- What is a global firm and how do they act and behave?
- What are the emerging patterns and developments in global marketing theory and practice today?
- What does the future hold for global firms?

During the preparation of this manuscript, the author received the help and encouragement of many individuals. It is too difficult to name them all here one by one. First, I would like to take this opportunity to extend my sincere thanks and appreciation to the contributors of this volume. Their individual chapters will make a great impact on the growing body of global marketing theory and practice. I extend my warmest thanks and appreciation to The Haworth Press, Inc. of New York and London. In particular, I gratefully acknowledge the assistance, cooperation, and support of the Haworth Book Division personnel. I also appreciate the professional assistance of the editorial staff who did an outstanding job of bringing the manuscript to publication.

As always, my family was a constant source of help and encouragement. They supported me morally and spiritually and offered me greater strength. Special thanks also go to Mrs. Fiona Hostetler for her word processing assistance. Needless to say, I am solely responsible for any errors or omissions in this volume.

Erdener Kaynak

SECTION I.
GLOBAL MARKETING:
INTEGRATIVE STATEMENT

It is predicted that global trade between developed and developing countries will grow at an accelerating rate in the years to come. Countries and firms that are highly successful in today's global trade are the ones which have recognized fully the changing global marketing methods, patterns, and techniques and are making proper adjustments to them. Future success and growth in global markets will hinge upon how well global companies react to changes and developments taking place in the global business environment. One can purposefully state that global firms will have to be future-oriented, predicting future occurrences in the best way possible. Otherwise, their market niche will be threatened.

The importance of globalization of companies is growing. The chapter by Kaynak introduces readers to the globalization process with a focus on the marketing processes and activities involved. It describes the different global marketing strategies, the stages of globalization, and makes suggestions to future research in the area.

Convinced that global firms are in the process of replacing internationals, this lead chapter analyzes the variations in the three major global marketing strategies: (1) monolith marketing; (2) multidomestic marketing; and (3) sub-global or modular marketing. It describes the advantages of going global, but also presents the barriers restricting the globalization of many firms. This introduction to global marketing is designed to help marketers develop a better understanding of the impact globalization will have on the firm's present and future marketing strategies and decisions.

1

Chapter 1

Global Marketing:
Theory and Practice

Erdener Kaynak

SUMMARY. With the increased advances in technology of communication and transportation, the world is becoming an ever-smaller market for companies to tap. This article examines the three interrelated global marketing strategies: multidomestic, sub-global, and monolith. It is pointed out that in their organization progress in world markets, companies show distinct characteristics. The stages followed as well as the policies and strategies utilized by global companies are explored conceptually and diagnostically.

INTRODUCTION

Globalization of companies is continually growing in response to the changing environment of international trade. For instance, North American and European companies are increasingly marketing their products among the newly emerging economies of the Far East, and the companies mainly from Japan and the neighboring East Asian countries are penetrating markets of the West. This accelerating trend is a result of global consumer convergence in socio-economic, demographic characteristics, habits, and culture. These forces are leading international companies to be more consumer-driven rather than geography-driven. For instance, Honda globalized by convincing middle-class American customers that riding motorcycles could be fun. To this end, the company adopted con-

This chapter was first published in the *Journal of Global Marketing*, Vol. 1(1/2), Winter 1987.

sumer preferences around the physical and aesthetic characteristics of Honda products. The company mainly appeals to its customers with higher quality product lines which are in harmony with the needs and expectations of their target markets (Hout, Porter & Rudden, 1982, p. 103).

Despite its increased importance, it is pointed out that only a small number of large-sized European and North American companies are truly involved in global marketing and its use generally is product specific. For instance, global marketing can work best for fast food and beverages, automobiles, airlines, packaged goods, manufactured goods, and consumer goods of general use (Agnew, 1986, p. 22). Manufacturers of these products in their search for internationalization adapt to global marketing techniques and strategies. Ohmae (1985) argues that universal products can be developed and marketed. An internationally oriented company would have a greater chance of securing consumer acceptance by developing and introducing products which are used and demanded on a universal scale, and their products will have "universal selling appeals." Companies like Seiko, Sony, Canon, Matsushita, Casio, and Honda are some of the company examples from the Far East which develop and market products worldwide according to a global perspective (Kotler, 1986).

Another group of companies utilize pan-regional marketing techniques which are developed for specific countries by taking into account individual socioeconomic, technological, and cultural characteristics. It is pointed out by Ohmae (1985) that there must be certain distinctions between products of global use which are truly universal in appeal (i.e., Singer Sewing Machines, Coca-Cola, and Exxon) and those that require local adaptations because of apparent nuances in certain regional and/or individual markets. For instance, many American companies have failed to realize that Japanese consumers have varying, distinct taste patterns which make some of the U.S. global products unacceptable unless they are "changed" somehow. Such standardized products offered by American merchandisers include oversize cars with left wheel drive, devices measuring inches, appliances and equipment not adapted to lower voltage and frequencies, office equipment without Japanese alphabet capabilities, and clothing not available in smaller dimensions. The most interesting case was that of Mattel's Barbie doll:

> Barbie doll which did very poorly in Japan until Mattel gave the manufacturing license to Takara, a Japanese toy and doll specialist. Takara did some market research and found that most Japanese disliked Barbie. Her breasts were far too big . . . her legs were exaggeratedly long. So Takara made the appropriate modifications of Barbie's anatomy, converted her California blue eyes to brown as well, and found instant success in the market. Two million dolls were sold in just two years. Explaining the cultural preferences that should be obvious to any smart marketer . . . What sells in America does not necessarily sell in Japan. But the sound concept can be transferred with intelligent interpretation, adaptation, and translation. (Thackray, 1985, p. 43)

Whether pan-regional or global marketing, internationally oriented companies are moving in the direction of global coordination of their marketing strategies, tactics, and organizational structures (*Advertising Age*, 1987, p. 16). For instance, in the last decade overseas sales of Midvale Corporation, as a percentage of total revenues have increased drastically. The company expansion abroad had been easy at first with increased globalization. The number and size of foreign subsidiaries had increased and the company started experiencing great difficulties in controlling its global operations. The company tried to fully integrate their global operations into the corporate structure while allowing the global operations to grow as fast as in the past (Dickson, 1983).

GLOBALIZATION TREND

Two forces shape the world trade today. These are technology and globalization. The company which thinks globally will replace the present multinational companies, if they are not converted to global companies. The global corporation will systematically converge the above mentioned two forces producing higher quality, greater reliability, and more standardized products at optimally lower prices, thus expanding its markets and profits. For those who fail to adapt to globalization, Darwin's law of natural selection will proceed with its course (Levitt, 1983).

The purpose of utilizing different types of marketing strategies on a global scale is to increase the firm's ability to produce a higher quality product at a lower cost on a world scale. This approach has resulted in "low cost producer" strategy being adapted as a viable strategic option by many companies. In particular, packaged goods markets are saturating around the world. To be able to compete on a cost basis, packaged goods manufacturers have created what is called world brands. It is hoped that this kind of strategy will bring about the opportunity for international economies of scale as the basis of long-term strategic global security (*The New York Times*, 1984, p. 6F).

In recent years, international firms are adopting an approach which puts companies through certain stages in their globalization efforts. The companies pass through five distinct stages, each of which requires a different set of strategic options. At stage I, the firm is a domestic marketer, at stage II, it is an exporter, at stage III, the firm is a multinational, at stage IV, pan-regional, and finally at stage V, it is a global company (Figure 1). Let's discuss the characteristics of each of these last three stages in the globalization process of firms.

MULTIDOMESTIC, SUB-GLOBAL, AND MONOLITH MARKETING

In recent years, there has been a rapidly expanding marketing management literature analyzing the developments for the planning and execution of global marketing strategies. There is a trend toward a more global view of marketing management. The underlying assumption here is that marketing strategies are most efficient when they are standardized rather than localized for each foreign market a company enters.

The nature of globalization of marketing strategy would show variations in diverse world markets. In a pure sense (monolith marketing), global standardization might mean the offering of identical product lines, at identical prices, through identical channels of dis-

FIGURE 1. Firm Organizational Progress to World Brands

	I DOMESTIC MARKETER	II EXPORT MARKETER	III MULTINATIONAL MARKETER	IV PAN-REGIONAL MARKETER	V GLOBAL MARKETER
STAGE OF PROGRESS	Company operates in its own country	Company starts to export	Company opens marketing companies overseas with their own manufacturing	Company coordinates marketing and production across different countries	Company centralizes production, distribution, and marketing by continents
	HOME COUNTRY ORIENTATION	STRAIGHT EXTENSION	LOCALIZED	MODULAR	GLOBAL
STRATEGY	Home Markets	Close Markets	Emergent Markets	Accelerating Global Markets	Competitive Global Markets

tribution systems while being supported by identical promotional/ advertising strategies in a number of world markets (Kollat, Blackwell, & Robeson, 1972, p. 178). Another strategy on the opposite end of the spectrum is a completely localized one (multi-domestic). Under this strategy, there is no common strategic marketing decision variable. Each strategic variable or a combination of it is manipulated for the market realities of a foreign market. In today's world, markets of neither of these extremes (monolith versus multidomestic) are desirable by consumers and companies alike. As a result, an "in-between" type of global marketing strategy (subglobal or modular) is utilized by many companies from North America, Europe, and the Far East. If this is the case, the strategic questions one has to answer will be: (a) Which variables of the global marketing strategy can be standardized and to what extent? (b) To what extent can channels of distribution, pricing, advertising, packaging design, and brand name be standardized? (c) What organizational arrangements should be utilized for different global marketing strategies? (d) Would certain regions/industries/countries/ product classes necessitate for a particular global marketing strategy? Now let's look at varying characteristics of each global marketing strategy in more detail (see Figure 2).

Multidomestic (Multinational) Strategy

Companies pursuing this strategy ignore similarities and concentrate on differences in their operational policies and programs (Farley, 1985, p. 12). The multinational corporation treats the world as if it were comprised of different and diverse markets. The multidomestic company utilizes separate marketing strategies in each market it operates while viewing the competitive challenge separately from one market to another. Each subsidiary in a foreign market maintains strategically independent operations (Hout, Porter & Rudden, 1982, p. 103).

People working in the local marketing unit need to be participants in the local culture, aware of the specific tastes and wants of their consumers in order to be able to intelligently interpret and adapt concepts into specific products. A concept is applicable to a number

FIGURE 2. Multidomestic, Sub-Global, and Monolith Global Marketing Strategies

MULTIDOMESTIC

Decentralized
Differentiated
(Polycentric)

LOCALIZED
MARKETING

- Diversity of response patterns
- Heterogeneity of needs
- Products have varying appeals
- Looks for differences
- Market heterogeneity
- Capitalizes on consumer satisfaction

SUB-GLOBAL

Thinking Globally
and Acting Locally
(Regiocentric)

MODULAR
MARKETING

- Insures international brand consistency

MONOLITH

Centralized
Standardized
(Ethnocentric/Geocentric)

GLOBAL
MARKETING

- Uniformity of response patterns
- Homogeneity of needs
- Harmonized consumer needs and attitudes
- Looks for similarities
- Products have universal appeal
- Capitalizes on competitive advantage
- Market homogeneity
- Common brand name, packaging, and communications

of foreign countries; a product is usually applicable to one or even to parts of one.

Sub-Global (Modular) Strategy

This is marketing module by module rather than trying to serve the whole world at once. Module can be country, a target group, a region, or a product class. A module may be geographic, economic, cultural, or it may be demographic in nature. The one requirement is that it must be small enough and sharply defined enough to be the means by which a concept can be converted into a product seen by people as meeting their individual demands. The important question is how can a module be independent, free to answer the needs of its local consumers, and be responsive to the expectations of its international headquarters to answer to global marketing guidelines? (Hauter, 1983, p. 622). For instance, the bouillon cube takes on many forms, shapes, and flavors around the world, and serves a large number of needs mostly as a flavor contributor. It comes as a cube or as a powder. It is sold in chicken or beef flavor in the U.S.A., Germany, or Switzerland. In Mexico, it comes in tomato or shrimp varieties. In Argentina you can get a corn bouillon, a chili variety in Kenya, a mutton variety in Ireland, and pork in Thailand. All of these are performing the one basic function of contributing flavor to food—there is only one single product concept (Hauter, 1983, p. 622).

Most industrialized societies of the West share the same aspirations. In general, some emotions such as love, hunger, pain, sex, and thirst are so basic that as a result they are universally applicable. However, the symbols for sex, hunger, pain, or thirst may vary tremendously from country to country. This leads to a policy of applying basic appeals globally, but the execution of that appeal may vary considerably from country to country (Matthei, 1975). This strategy of thinking globally but acting locally in international markets is termed modular marketing—strategic concepts with local implementation.

This approach necessitates aggregating a number of multi-domestic markets in which a company is operating. Through this approach, regional or developmental classifications are utilized. Under regional, the world is divided into different regions like Latin America, Europe, Asia, and Africa. In terms of developmental classification, the world is divided into developed, developing, and underdeveloped nations. It is pointed out that the degree and intensity of homogeneity among countries is sufficiently high for a standardized marketing strategy to be successful in achieving the desired corporate goals for each national market (Hovell & Walters, 1972, p. 75).

A cultural convergence is taking place around the world. At present, television and motion pictures are creating elements of shared culture among the peoples of the globe. This cultural convergence is facilitating the establishment of global brand characters. It is predicted that this cultural convergence and the resultant world brands will increase geometrically with the development of L-SAT high-power TV satellites throughout Europe. This will hopefully diminish cultural barriers, hence more uniform demand for products and brands among consumers of the world.

What will work is a careful balance between corporate, for strategic direction, and local, for tactical execution. What is required is a network of local strategic business units, operating autonomously and independently, but under a common set of global strategic, financial, and ethical guidelines (Hauter, 1983).

Global (Monolith) Marketing Strategy

This strategy assumes that all buyers of the world are alike. A company's mass produced product at home which is successful in its home country, could be mass marketed on a global scale.

The markets of the world have become increasingly homogenized (monolith). This has resulted in response to advances taking place in communication and transportation technologies. These technological developments have made products of the "developed" world desirable throughout the globe. It is pointed out that developments in communications and transportation have created certain commonalities among nations, creating homogenized tastes, preferences, and motivations of people which open the door for global corporations to create awareness and market on an international scale (Levitt, 1985, p 15).

The major reason for global marketing strategies is to create economies of scale with the resultant low-cost producer company business system. The pronounced economies of scale may arise through R&D materials purchasing, manufacturing, distribution, and advertising. Through these scale economies, company brands would be able to gain a competitive advantage world wide which will also lead to higher return on investment and long-term franchise building across the globe (Figure 3).

To be able to market world brands effectively, company management needs to think globally instead of domestically or one country at a time. Management of some world brand companies like Colgate-Palmolive, Nabisco biscuits, Gillette razors, Campbell soup, or Singer sewing machines may think in terms of geographic clusters such as Europe, Latin America, and the Far East instead of individual countries.

On a global basis, the world brand marketer must be able to cope with a series of differences available among different nations of the world. These are languages, products, product usage, competition, target groups, socioeconomic, cultural, and technological differences. The success of a world brand will hinge upon how well a company resolves these apparent differences among the nations the company is trying to operate (Lenrow, 1984, p. 40).

Zenith Electronics had been one of the unchallenged leaders in the U.S. television market up until the 1960s. During the late 1960s and early 1970s, cheaper foreign imports began pouring in, which negatively affected the competitive position of Zenith. Zenith decided to provide uniform, standardized products in order to cut its per unit cost of production to create a competitive advantage over its global rivals. Zenith has created production and assembly units in Taiwan, Japan, Korea, and Canada that perform complementary production (a mass producer of components or parts) and support functions (assembly work, warehousing, and distribution on a mass scale). Each SBU (Strategic Business Unit) serves as a link in the overall input-output business strategy of Zenith's global operations (Carpenter et al., 1986, pp. 24-25).

Although global marketing offers certain economic advantages, a variety of barriers such as differences in socioeconomic, cultural, technological, media variables, trade barriers, regulation, tariffs,

FIGURE 3. Company Economic Progress to World Brands

PRESSURE OF COST INFLATION IN STATIC DOMESTIC/FOREIGN MARKETS

NEED TO BE LOW COST PRODUCER AND MARKETER TO WIN HIGHER MARKET SHARE

COMPANY SEARCH FOR MORE EFFICIENT BUSINESS STRUCTURE

CREATION OF ECONOMIES OF SCALE

DEVELOPMENT OF WORLD MARKETS

Source: Adapted from "The Opportunity for World Brands," The New York Times, June 3, 1984, p. 6F.

and restrictions may make implementing a global marketing strategy difficult (*Marketing News*, 1987, p. 1). These barriers force companies to utilize decentralized organizational structures which brings more pan-regional direction to the organization as practiced by Nabisco Brands, Ritz crackers, Planters peanuts, Oreo cookies, and Colgate-Palmolive. The concept of globalization, it is argued, would apply only to certain products and some products are difficult to market globally with an equal success. For instance, butter and butter-related products are consumed heavily in Europe, but are met with heavy resistance in North America because of health consciousness among the populace and the availability of low-cholesterol food products. This shows that a product like butter may not be marketed globally with the same marketing strategy and tactics (Davidson and Haspeslagh, 1982).

FUTURE RESEARCH AVENUES
IN GLOBAL MARKETING MANAGEMENT

Management of international companies is expected to have a global frame of reference in making corporate and divisional marketing decisions. It is pointed out that this will encourage efficiency through standardization, better products, and more diverse markets to sell corporate/divisional products and/or services (Levitt, 1983). Consumer needs will also be better fulfilled by globalized companies through the creation of lower priced, higher quality, and reliable products. Besides these, consumers around the world try to satisfy their intangible needs from products available globally. Consumers buy products for their perceived value or benefit in addition to their quality, reliability, and monetary value. What may be needed perhaps is a balanced approach between standardized global strategy and that of localized multinational strategy which may lead companies to the use of modular marketing strategies in world markets.

Today intense involvement of an increased number of North American, European, and Far Eastern companies in international trade has paved the way for corporate and divisional decision makers to learn more about how to operate on a global scale more effectively. Most of the studies conducted, so far, deal with ad hoc adjustments on a country-by-country basis and are predominantly descriptive and exploratory in nature. What is now needed is the development of normative or prescriptive models and constructs dealing with the overall adjustment of the multinational company to global market conditions and realities. To strengthen the global marketing discipline, researchers are encouraged to study the following areas of inquiry:

a. What characteristics of international firms, products, global markets, and industries influence the globalization process? How can an international company assess its global marketing opportunities? How do global firms make decisions on the best modes of entry? What are some of the environmental factors that an international firm must consider in its effort to become global in its foreign markets? What trends will take place to tell North American and West European companies whether global markets will grow or decline? How can we operationalize these relationships?

b. How would global companies show sensitivity to the long-run interest and desires of consumers and develop flexibility in product design, modification, improvement, and consumer choice?

c. How can one integrate an international dimension into different components of the marketing curriculum to make it globally oriented? To this end, there are some endeavors on the part of AACSB (American Assembly of Collegiate Schools of Business) to globalize U.S. business administration curriculum at both graduate and undergraduate levels.

d. The problems faced by the global marketers in world markets are very complex. In most cases, these problems are related to the task of comparing the marketing systems in those global markets the company is interested in with the methods and techniques of marketing applicable at home, so that the appropriate marketing strategies and decisions are in line with the global market environment. How could the global marketing analysis provide us with an understanding of the interaction between marketing and its many environments in foreign markets?

e. There is an urgent need for the determination of relationships between environmental elements and mechanistic and behavioral concepts and techniques associated with the global marketing processes and functions. In this relationship, special consideration should be given to the cause-and-effect nature of the interactions, and the relative importance and strength of each of the environmental elements in its interaction with the global system of marketing.

f. Global marketing studies can be undertaken at both micro and macro levels. The former explains the workings of individual firms within global markets whereas the latter looks at the whole production-distribution-consumption system of a foreign market. What are the differences between global marketing viewed as a microsystem and global marketing viewed as a macrosystem? What analytical techniques can be utilized to measure the impact of each system on operations and practices of international firms?

g. What are the structural and institutional aspects of global marketing behavior? Would the structural and functional prerequisites of a global marketing system vary from one country to another? With increased levels of socioeconomic and technological development, would differences in buying and consumption behavior among different societies disappear and would nations of the world move toward a convergence? If this is the trend, what would be the prerequisites of it?

h. In global marketing which particular component of global markets does one need to examine within the context of a marketing system? To this end, how can one determine the marketing system to be compared; determine the unit of analysis used in the comparison process; and determine the relevant dimensions of the analysis?

REFERENCES

Advertising Age (1987, January 12). "Global Marketing Marches On."

Agnew J. (1986, October 24). "Cultural Differences Probed to Create Product Identity." *Marketing News*.

Carpenter, R.E., Kinard, J., Van Mullen, F., and Wright, P. (1986). "Product-Market Decisions: Dancing on the Razor's Edge." *Planning Review* (January), 14(1), pp. 24-26 & 46.

Davidson, W.H. and Haspeslagh, P. (1982). "Shaping a Global Product Organization." *Harvard Business Review* (July-August), 60(4), pp. 125-132.

Dickson, D.N. (1983). "Case of the Reluctant Multinational." *Harvard Business Review* (January-February), 61(1), pp. 6-8 & 12-18.

Farley, L.J. (1985, October 11). "Global Approach Seeks Similarities in Markets." *Marketing News*.

Hauter, E.D. (1983, August 1). "Organizing for International Marketing." *Vital Speeches of the Day*, 49(20), pp. 620-624.

Hout, T., Porter, M.E., and Rudden, E. (1982). "How Global Companies Win Out." *Harvard Business Review* (September-October), 60(5), pp. 98-108.

Hovell, P.J. and Walters, P.G.P. (1972). "International Marketing Presentations: Some Options." *European Journal of Marketing*, 6(2), p. 229.

Kollat, E., Blackwell, R. and Robeson, A. (1972). *Consumer Behavior*. Englewood Cliffs: Prentice-Hall.

Kotler, P. (1986). "Megamarketing." *Harvard Business Review* (March-April), 64 (2), pp. 117-124.

Lenrow, M.M. (1984, November 1). "Mapping New Strategy for World Brands." *Advertising Age*, pp. 40-43.

Levitt, T. (1983). "The Globalization of Markets." *Harvard Business Review* (May-June), 61(3), pp. 92-102.

Levitt, T. (1985, March 15). "Global Companies to Replace Dying Multinationals." *Marketing News*.

Marketing News (1987, January 16). "Differences, Confusion Slow Global Marketing Bandwagon."

Matthei, H. (1975, August 29). "How to Sell the Global Village." *Campaign*, pp. 17 & 19.

The New York Times (1984, June 3). "The Opportunity for World Brands." p. 6F.

Ohmae, K. (1985). *Triad Power: The Coming Shape of Global Competition*. New York: The Free Press.

Thackray, J. (1985). "Much Ado About Global Marketing." *Across the Board* (April), 22(4), pp. 38-46.

SECTION II.
CROSS-CULTURAL
CONSUMER MARKETING

Understanding consumers' wants and needs as well as their socioeconomic, demographic, and psychological characteristics is even more important in international markets than it is in the domestic market. In particular, cross-cultural and cross-national issues are of immense interest to international decision-makers in both industry and government. Knowledge of these issues enables managers to select the right target markets and develop appropriate international marketing strategies. In this section, cross-cultural and cross-national issues are examined in a comparative manner by drawing case examples from a variety of countries and regions throughout the world.

The first chapter by Cheron, Padgett, and Woods investigates two alternative approaches to global business strategies: "global marketing" and the "marketing module." It presents a method of cross-cultural comparisons that provides a comprehensive framework for evaluating whether a firm should blindly follow a global marketing strategy which uses the same marketing mix in all nations or whether a firm should modify its marketing mix to suit the local conditions of each individual country market. In doing this, the authors explore the local differences (i.e., differences in the purpose for which the product is used) which may influence product choice and purchasing decisions between nations. According to the authors, "it would be desirable to determine, prior to actual marketing commitment, whether a global or modular approach is more likely to succeed in a given situation."

This study further seeks to "improve the tools used to evaluate the marketing strategies by presenting a measuring instrument that can be used across nationalities on a global basis." It demonstrates that differences between cultures in purposes for purchasing can be identified on a product by product basis, and also that different cultures share basic personality traits but may express them differently. The method presented by the authors provides one with a means of gathering information on whether significant cultural differences exist between prospective nations in a company's marketing plans.

An issue of increasing importance in the area of cross-national consumer behavior concerns the validity of the interpretations made about consumer characteristics on the basis of consumer behavior data collected in cross-national settings. This problem arises because of differences in certain "significant" consumer features of the various environments within the various nations under study (e.g., the number and types of goods available may vary across the nations under study, or the amount and cost of information may vary). In the second chapter in this section, by Olshavsky, Moore, and Lim, several specific examples of this basic problem of interpretation are presented. The implications of these interpretations for theory development and marketing management strategies are also illustrated.

It is argued that identification of a valid interpretation of observed similarities and differences in the behavior of consumers in different nations is impossible without a theory of consumer behavior that takes into account the impact of the environment upon behavior. All existing theories are found to be deficient in this respect. Newell and Simon's original version of information processing theory is advocated as the one theoretical perspective that is capable of providing a solution to this problem.

Two basic assumptions characterize Newell and Simon's theory: (1) the consumer is an adaptive system, meaning that behavior is determined by an interaction that occurs over time between characteristics of the consumer and characteristics of the environment; and (2) the consumer is an information processing system, meaning that strategies are first selected and then executed in an attempt to achieve certain goals.

It is the authors' position that, developed to a sufficient level of detail, Newell and Simon's theory can eventually provide a theoretical perspective that will lead to the generation of testable hypotheses concerning observed similarities and differences in consumer behavior in different nations, and that this theory can provide a basis for making valid interpretations concerning the nature of consumer characteristics in these different nations.

The chapter by Chadraba and Czepiec is designed to help marketing managers to decide whether market standardization or customization is more appropriate when introducing new products, particularly in developed Western European countries. The chapter analyzes whether three European nations can be segmented on a psychological variable — the perceived product value.

It develops a simple inexpensive technique for segmenting nations on perceived product value, and applies the mechanism to Austria, France, and Switzerland. University students from these three countries were asked to indicate their valuation of five readily available consumer goods and 12 proposed product modifications. The respondents' perceptions of value of the base product and the modifications are compared within each country. There is considerable similarity in each of the countries about the type of added feature that is considered a valuable improvement. The respondents' perceptions are compared across the three countries, controlling for product ownership. There is much more homogeneity in value judgments among owners than non-owners. The respondents' value perceptions are compared across nation pairs, once again, controlling for product ownership. The Swiss and French display the most similarity, followed by the French and Austrians.

The magnitude in value perception, particularly among product owners, supports the need for psychological segmentation of nations. It also encourages the development of more standardized marketing strategies when introducing new products in developed international markets.

In their empirical study, Chasin, Holzmuller, and Jaffe state that the country of origin may influence consumer perception of product classes or categories and specific brands. Marketers planning to sell their products abroad must be aware of the extent to which country image may influence consumers' choice of a foreign made good.

Many studies have examined the country image effect, but most have considered it to be a single cue, or information source upon which respondents evaluated products. In reality, consumers utilize multiple cues or information sources. For example, does prior use or familiarity with a product brand reduce the effect of the country of origin cue? Does stereotyping differ by product class? Is there a home country bias in country of origin ratings, i.e., do consumers tend to rate local products more favorably that foreign products? The present paper answers these questions.

Two samples of American and Austrian purchasers of six industrial goods were asked to rate their home products against those made in several Eastern European countries and the United States (in the case of Austrians) and Austria (in the case of Americans). They were also asked if their purchasing preferences would change when either price or quality of the products was varied.

Results showed that both groups of respondents exhibited stereotyping of Eastern European goods. This finding confirms earlier studies that showed negative perceptions of Eastern European goods. The extent that ethnocentrism affects the perception of country image was inconclusive. While the American respondents consistently rated their products more favorably than Austrian-made goods, Austrian respondents showed very little home-country bias. As for product purchasing experience, buyer familiarity did not affect the way respondents evaluated the products.

Marketing strategies were suggested to reduce stereotyping. A suggested strategy, at least insofar as Eastern European countries are concerned, is to realize image advantages that accrue from joint ventures with Western partners by, when possible, emphasizing the trade name and imputed Western technology as much as possible.

Chapter 2

A Method for Cross-Cultural Comparisons for Global Strategies

Emmanuel J. Cheron
Thomas C. Padgett
Walter A. Woods

SUMMARY. An easy and inexpensive-to-use measure is proposed to compare the relative importance of purposes for purchasing in different cultures. Following a description of the instrument, a simple scoring procedure is presented. The reliability of the measurement method is evaluated and its validity is also discussed. Results of a pilot survey conducted in the U.S. and in Canada (Quebec) are reported to illustrate the procedure. Strategic implications of some of the findings are suggested.

INTRODUCTION

In recent months we have witnessed a substantial increase in publicity about "global marketing" (Rudolph, 1985; Chase, 1984; Levitt, 1983; Lenroe, 1984; Ohmae, 1985). Advocates of "global marketing" have asserted that products and brands can be marketed on a worldwide basis utilizing the same marketing mix in all nations, irrespective of cultural differences.

An alternative view is that of the "Marketing module"; a strategy designed from the outset to be modified to suit local conditions. Eric Hauter (1984) is quoted as saying that marketers must "think globally and act locally." This is done by modular marketing

This chapter was first published in the *Journal of Global Marketing*, Vol. 1(1/2), Fall/Winter 1987.

"Which combines strategic concepts with local implementation and involves market module by module . . . rather than trying to gobble up the whole globe in one gulp."

Among local differences which may influence product choice are differences in the purpose for which the product is used. These purposes may differ in different cultures. Fragrances, for example, may be used for making oneself more attractive to others, or for helping to avoid offending others or for personal enjoyment. Woods, Cheron, and Kim (1985), reported a study in which it was found that American (U.S.), French Canadian and Korean women differed in the purposes for which they used a number of products common to all cultures. Cultural differences were identified which appeared to influence different purchasing between nations. Some common purposes were also identified.

It would be desirable to determine, prior to actual marketing commitment, whether a global or a modular approach is more likely to succeed in a given situation. To proceed with a marketing strategy on the basis of one assumption or the other, rather than knowledge of whether significant cultural differences exist, can lead to unnecessary failures such as those reported over the years. The study by Woods, Cheron, and Kim (1985) has shown that attitudes of consumers in such diverse countries as the United States, French Canada and Korea can be directly compared. What is left is to improve the tools used and to develop a measuring instrument that can be used across nationalities on a global basis. The present study has undertaken to do this.

METHOD

Five products from the study by Woods, Cheron, and Kim (1985) were selected for study: coffee, perfumes and colognes, carbonated beverages, toothpaste, and musical recordings. The relative importance of purposes for purchasing products was measured through a forced choice paired comparison method. Items used in the pairings were derived or developed from findings in the study. The six most frequent purposes were identified for each product. These six purposes are listed in the tables in the findings section. Pairings of each item to every other item produced 15 pairs for comparisons for each product (N(N − 1)/2).

The 15 pairs were presented to each respondent who indicated the most important one in each. Forced choice paired comparisons was selected as the method which best satisfied the objectives. Rank ordering was eliminated because it appears to be less discriminating and reliable (Kuder, 1939). Likert-type scales were eliminated because they demand no discriminations between items; any item in an array of items can be rated independently of other items and all items can be rated equally. In the real world of shopping, consumers are forced to choose among items and brands on the basis of whatever differences are more important.

The same reasoning led to the elimination of paired comparisons with ties (Rao & Kupper, 1967). The graded pairs method was eliminated because it was judged to be a likely source of complication for respondents and would add to the analytic burden (Scheffe, 1952).

Analysis is a second practical consideration. A method that imposes a heavy analytic burden (as is the case with most paired comparison methods) will not be used in applied research. The scaling methods commonly used impose such a burden (Bradley & Terry, 1952; Thurstone, 1927).

Additive methods (de Leeuw, Young, & Takane, 1976; Takane, 1982) are less burdensome and permit the use of unscaled responses. These methods usually assume comparative responses with no zero base. An equally tenable assumption is that judgments leading to purchasing are absolute and any choice in an array of choices potentially has a zero value. This would be the case if any item in the array was never ranked "more important" than any other item, just as it would be if a particular brand lacked any feature of sufficient importance to attract any buyer(s). The forced choice method and additive analysis was chosen on the basis of this reasoning and these assumptions.

One consideration which arises in the evaluation of differences in purposes for purchasing is the possible influence of certain presumably pervasive personality traits. Three such characteristics relating to consumer behavior have been identified and reported in research. These three personality dimensions are (i) innovativeness, (ii) activity level (active-sedentary), and (iii) inner-outer directedness. In light of the potential influence of these dimensions, the research also undertook to identify and appraise their relevance to purposes for purchasing. This was done by obtaining responses to ten items (see Table 7) on a seven point scale. These items were factor analyzed to validate the presence of the hypothesized personality traits. Then, correlations between scores on the ten personality items and scores on the importance measures for the five products were computed.

The Sample

The sample was stratified by culture and by age. The total sample was composed as follows:

	United States	Canada (Quebec)	Total
Age Under 26	49	52	101
Age Over 39	51	65	116
Total	100	117	217

Within each subsample respondents were selected by "random convenience." Plots or locations were chosen at random in suburban Chicago, Illinois for the U.S. sample. Within plots, respondents were chosen at the convenience of the interviewer. The Canadian sample was drawn from the population of the city of Rimouski, Quebec, on the basis of interviewer convenience. The choice of Rimouski ensures a highly homogeneous French Canadian sample not different from the rest of the province of Quebec with respect to consumption patterns (Cheron, 1981).

Scoring Procedure

Scores for the paired comparisons were derived for each respondent for each item by cumulative summation. Since there are six purposes (items) being compared, each respondent has six scores for each product (a score for each item). The score for the item is the number of times that item is chosen over each of the other items.

Thus the individual's score on any product for item A = ΣA > B, C, D, E, F. The individual's scores for F = ΣF > A, B, C, D, E. Individual scores are summed and sample means are derived as follows:

$$i = \sum_{j=1}^{n} \frac{\text{individual scores}}{n} \qquad \text{(Formula 1)}$$

where n = number in sample and i = any item

Mean scores can be transformed to standard scores by dividing by n minus 1.

$$\text{Standard Score} = \sum_{j-1}^{n} \frac{\text{individual scores}/n}{N-1} \qquad \text{(Formula 2)}$$

where n = number of items being compared

The mean scores can be compared directly across samples. They provide a basis for further analysis such as by ANOVA.

The total score for any individual on any product will always be equal to the number of pairs or item compared. For each of the products in this study, there are 15 pairs (N(N − 1)/2). Thus the mean score for any total sample on all items will always be identical to the number of each individual's scores. Total scores for all items cannot, therefore, be used as a basis of comparisons between subsamples. Comparisons must be made on the basis of the order of importance (magnitude) of the item scores within samples or differences in the order of importance and magnitude of differences across samples.

Mean scores are the primary measure used in comparing the two cultures. These were computed by Formula 1, above. Significance of differences between cultures and between importance of purchases have been tested by use of Scheffe's method (Neter & Wasserman, 1974). Means scores and significance data are provided in Tables in the findings section.

Reliability and Validity Assessment

Three further considerations should be noted regarding the method. Firstly, the semantic meaning, but not the literal translation of the language from that of one culture to another — the purpose of use, the core concept and not the way the concept is stated — is what is being compared. Use of the same questionnaire format allows ignoring the comparability problem evoked by Jaffe and Nebenzahl (1984).

Secondly, the method does not lend itself to standard or traditional methods of reliability measurement. Reliability, in the sense of consistency of response among the items is the issue (Parameswaran et al., 1979). The individual who chooses A over B and B over C should be expected to demonstrate consistency by selecting A over C.

Kendall (1962), provides a method for examining inconsistency in a paired comparison. A value (d) is computed which represents the number of times an individual's response was inconsistent with a previous response. For this study, a value of zero indicates perfect consistency, and a value of 8 would indicate no consistency at all. Kendall also provided a theoretical distribution of d values for the assumption that the responses are random. Using the Kolmogorov-Smirnov One-Sample Test a comparison was made between the theoretical distribution under Kendall's randomness assumption and the actual distribution for all comparisons for the five products combined for the sample as a whole (15 comparisons for 5 products by 217 respondents) (Siegel, 1956). The hypothesis that the responses were random was rejected at .01, indicating that the respondents were reasonably consistent. This conclusion is reinforced by examination of the distribution of the actual d scores in Figure 1, which shows that 67.8% of respondents were perfectly consistent (d scores of zero), and only about 10% had more than two inconsistencies.

Finally, the method should be valid; it should facilitate prediction of differences in purchasing. To assess validity a convenience sample of 281 individuals, including grocery shoppers and college students, were administered the portion of the original test dealing with toothpaste. In addition, the brand of toothpaste that they normally purchased was determined. Brands used were separated into two categories according to whether the advertising emphasized cavity protection (Crest and Colgate), or non-protective benefits such as breath protection (all other brands). If a relationship could be found between brands purchased and purposes for purchasing, it would demonstrate that the method had power to predict. To measure these relationships, a Chi-Square test was used to test the hypothesis that individuals preferring brands that emphasize protection would rate protection higher among the six purposes than individuals preferring brands that emphasize other benefits (Hamburg, 1976). The results were significant at .05, and supported the hypothesis. The group using Crest and Colgate selected the protection purpose more often, and the other brands group selected the appearance purpose more often.

FIGURE 1. Distribution of Kendall's D Value for the Combined Sample

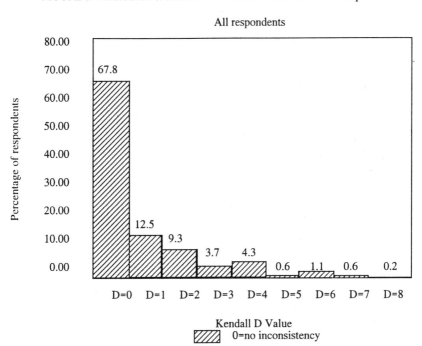

All respondents

FINDINGS

Differences in Purposes for Purchasing

The relative ranking of items within and between the comparison samples (U.S. vs. Quebec) is the central consideration. Regardless of the magnitude of differences between countries on particular items, if the order of importance is the same, the same marketing mix should apply to both cultures. But when the order of importance of items differs significantly between cultures a modular approach should be considered.

Given this perspective we may now consider each of the five products. For coffee (Table 1), the order of importance is almost identical in the two cultures. Nor are there any differences in order of importance between the older and the younger samples. Thus, to the extent that women represent the coffee market in the two countries, a global strategy is indicated. This is true even though Quebec women and older women place greater importance than American or younger women on taste.

A slightly different situation was found for toothpaste (Table 2). Quebecoise place significantly more importance than Americans on the "feel better" aspect and less importance on appearance benefits. The lack of any difference in importance attributed to these two benefits by Americans argue for giving priority to "feeling good" over appearance in global promotion. Appearance is of greater importance to younger females; thus, the importance of age segments by country would have to be considered.

The findings for perfumes (Table 3) suggests that although a basic global umbrella emphasizing personal enjoyment and attractiveness enhancement might be used, care will be required in dealing with secondary appeals and nuances. Modular executions of thematic materials will be required. This is indicated by the differences in the rankings on "pleasing others" and "avoid offending others" in the two cultures. Differences of this nature were noted in the study by Woods, Cheron, and Kim (1985). Such differences may derive from fundamental cultural differences in ways of relating socially.

The implications for carbonated beverages (Table 4) are quite

TABLE 1. Mean Paired Comparison Scores for Coffee

U. S.		Canada		Age Under 26		Age 39 or Older	
Taste enjoyment	3.56*	Taste enjoyment	4.32*	Taste enjoyment	3.76	Taste enjoyment	4.15
Gives a lift	3.00	Gives a lift	2.95	Gives a Lift	2.94	Gives a Lift	2.99
Habit	2.48	Habit	2.50	Social Use	2.53	Habit	2.47
Have on Hand	2.40	Social Use	2.40	Habit	2.52	Social Use	2.23
Social Use	2.31	Have on Hand	2.26	Have on Hand	2.46	Have on Hand	2.21
Please Others	1.26*	Please Others	0.57*	Please Others	0.79	Please Others	0.94

*Differences between cultures are significant at level .05.

Means not linked by vertical lines differ significantly at level .05. The differences are significant if > .68 for U. S., .61 for Canadian, .61 for the younger group and .55 for the older
group, using Scheffe's test.

TABLE 2. Mean Paired Comparison Scores for Toothpaste

U. S.		Canada		Age Under 26		Age 39 or Older	
Protect	4.14	Protect	4.48	Protect	4.29	Protect	4.35
Appearance	2.77*	Feel better	3.17*	Feel better	2.90	Feel Better	2.93
Feel better	2.63*	Appearance	2.23	Appearance	2.62	Not offend	2.52
Not offend	2.46	Not offend	2.11	Not offend	2.14	Appearance	2.24
Enjoy taste	1.67	Enjoy taste	1.61	Enjoy taste	1.62	Enjoy taste	1.65
Habit	1.33	Habit	1.40	Habit	1.43	Habit	1.31

*Differences between cultures and age groups on the same purpose are significant at .05.

Means not connected by a vertical line differ significantly at .05. The differences are if > .62 for U. S., .56 for Canadian, .58 for the younger group and .53 for the older group, Scheffe's test.

TABLE 3. Means of Paired Comparison Scores for Perfumes/Colognes

U. S.		Canada		Age Under 26		Age 39 or Older	
Enjoy fragrance	3.88*	Enjoy fragrance	3.59*	Enjoy fragrance	3.91	Feel Better	3.78
Feel better	3.32	Feel better	3.52	Attraction	3.02**	Enjoy fragrance	3.59
Attraction	3.04	Attraction	2.85	Feel better	3.00*	Attraction	2.88
Please others	2.33*	Not offend	1.83*	Please others	2.23	Please others	1.94
Not offend	1.34*	Please others	1.81*	Not offend	1.53	Not offend	1.62
Habit	1.08	Habit	1.40	Habit	1.30	Habit	1.18

*Differences between cultures and age groups for same purpose are significant at level .05.

**Attraction is significant at .10.

Means not linked by vertical lines differ significantly at level .05. Differences are significant if > .63 for U. S., .64 for Canadian, .60 for the younger group and .56 for the older group, using Scheffe's test.

TABLE 4. Mean Paired Comparison Scores for Carbonated Beverages

U. S.		Canada		Age Under 26		Age 39 or Older	
Enjoy taste	3.45	Quench thirst	3.85*	Enjoy taste	3.78*	Quench thirst	3.44
Quench thirst	2.94*	Enjoy taste	3.32	Quench thirst	3.38	Enjoy taste	3.03
Have on hand	2.66*	Social medium	2.35	Social medium	2.46	Have on hand	2.58
Social medium	2.15	Gives lift	2.19	Gives lift	2.16	Gives lift	2.12
Gives lift	2.08	Have on hand	2.09*	Have on hand	2.14	Social medium	2.06
For family	1.70*	For family	1.49*	For family	1.08*	For family	1.76

* Differences between cultures and age groups on the same purpose are significant at .05.

Means not connected by a vertical line differ significantly at .05. The differences are significant if > .62 for U. S., .58 for Canadian, .65 for the younger group and .61 for the older group, using Scheffe's test.

complex. Some differences are found which suggest that American women, and older women, are more concerned with having these beverages on hand for the use by family or others than for self use.

This market has been characterized by English (1983) as a young (under 35) market. Given the purported age differences we should pay more attention to the younger groups. Even among the younger groups the sample may not be sufficiently youthful. The report by English (1983) indicates that over 50 percent of all soft drinks sold in the U.S. are consumed by teenagers (18 and under).

The problem is compounded by the rapidly segmenting market — diet segments, flavor segments and noncaffeinated segments. It will obviously be necessary to develop a profile that accounts for these newly developing differences across markets.

A more complex pattern emerges for musical recordings. The order of importance of the six items is quite different for the two cultures (Table 5). Each purpose is found to differ to a significant degree across cultures. Use of music for relaxation plays a major role in each culture. However, the most important use in the U.S. is for stimulation. Use for escape is considerably more important in Canada. This finding confirms the earlier finding by Woods, Cheron, and Kim (1985).

When age groups are compared the order of importance is the same for older as for younger women. But younger women place greater importance on escape. Considering culture and age it appears that escape is more specifically identified with Canadian affiliation than with younger age.

Fundamental Psychological Dimensions

In the factor analysis performed to examine the presence of the personality traits, it was assumed that the overall variance could be separated between a common and a unique portion. The common variance, only, was decomposed into "factors." Varimax rotation of the matrix of factor loadings led to the identification of four identifiable dimensions. As can be seen in Table 6, the analysis conducted with all the respondents (N = 217) reveals, first: an active-sedentary propensity (43% of common variance), second: an innovative psychological dimension (17.5% of common variance),

TABLE 5. Mean Paired Comparison Scores for Musical Recordings

U. S.		Canada		Age Under 26		Age 39 or Older	
Stimulation	3.79*	Relax	4.17*	Relax	3.60	Relax	3.98
Relax	3.38*	Escape	2.99*	Stimulation	3.32	Stimulation	3.39
Habit	2.49*	Stimulation	2.98*	Escape	2.74	Escape	2.38
Social medium	2.19*	Social medium	2.70*	Social medium	2.69	Social medium	2.27
Escape	2.03*	Habit	1.56*	Habit	1.94	Habit	2.03
Please others	1.12*	Please others	0.60*	Please others	0.70	Please others	0.96

* Differences between cultures on the same purpose are significant at .05.

Means not connected by a vertical line differ significantly at .05. The differences are if > .62 for U. S., .58 for Canadian, .57 for the younger group and .53 for the older group, using Scheffe's test.

TABLE 6. Percentages of Common Variance Explained by Psychological Dimensions After Varimax Rotation

Psychological dimensions / Factor Analyses	All data N=217	U.S. data N=100	CDN data N=117	Age Under 26 N=101	Age Over 39 N=116
Active-Sedentary propensity	43.0%	32.9%	53.0%	32.2%	47.7%
Innovativeness	17.5%	22.1%	14.4%	24.2%	16.6%
Inner-Outer directedness	13.3%	15.5%	7.2%	19.1%	----
Participatory-Non participatory	15.8%	----	25.4%	----	21.0%
Total common variance explained	89.6%	70.5%	100%	75.5%	85.3%
Total communality	3.43	3.95	3.50	3.92	3.14
Total uniqueness	6.57	6.05	6.50	6.08	6.86

third: an inner-outer directedness (13.3% of common variance), fourth: a participatory-non participatory dimension (15.8% of common variance). Computation of the total communality indicated a variance of 3.43. Since the variance of the ten initial variables were standardized to unity, the total variance amounted to 10 and the total uniqueness was 6.57. This relatively high degree of uniqueness indicated a relatively low degree of redundancy in the measuring instrument.

The stability of this structure was tested with four additional factor analyses on various subsets of the data. Each subset met the rule of including about ten times more observations than variables. This practical rule provides enough degrees of freedom for parameters estimation in statistical optimization techniques such as factor analysis.

The results in Table 6 indicate a stable presence of the first two psychological dimensions. For the ''age over 39'' group, the inner-outer directedness is absent. With respect to the participatory-nonparticipatory dimension, it is not apparent in the U.S. data and the ''age under 26'' group. In spite of the differences observed among the four subsets of data, total uniqueness remains high across the different factor analyses, confirming a rather low degree of redundancy in the measurements of attitudes toward daily activities.

Factor analyses confirmed the presence of the fundamental personality dimensions in the two cultures. A comparison of scores on the ten items which contributed to the factors reveals a significant overall difference (at level .01) between cultures as indicated by Hotellings multivariate T-squared test (Table 7). Examination of differences on specific items indicates that the two cultures differ significantly in innovativeness in foods and dress. Americans are found to be more innovative with foods, Quebecoise in clothing.

Comparison of the two age groups in Table 7 indicates a significant overall difference (at level .01) as shown by the multivariate T-squared test. Consistent with fashion innovation theory, the younger sample is more innovative than the older one (item 2). Younger people are also found to be more active (less sedentary) than older people (items 3 and 4). This is consistent with previous findings (Hunsicker & Woods, 1983). Younger people also appear

TABLE 7. Comparison of Mean Scores of Ten Trait Scales

Activity	U.S.	CDN	T	2 tail prob.	Under 26	Over 39	T	2 tail Prob.
1. *New Foods; try first/don't try	4.65	3.77	4.21	0.000	4.28	4.04	1.09	0.278
2. Clothing; try first/don't try	3.63	4.29	-2.81	0.006	4.59	3.43	5.28	0.000
3. Active/sedentary	4.28	4.22	0.30	0.762	4.58	3.93	3.12	0.002
4. Sports; play/watch	3.77	4.89	-4.32	0.000	4.90	3.92	3.73	0.000
5. Play Games/Watch T.V.	4.37	3.29	4.49	0.000	3.60	3.93	-1.32	0.190
6. Play Games/Attend Concerts	3.27	2.77	1.68	0.094	2.67	3.30	-2.17	0.031
7. Go out/Stay home	4.91	4.23	2.47	0.014	4.58	4.47	0.38	0.706
8. Foods; Please self/Please others	5.79	6.07	-1.45	0.149	5.66	6.22	-3.02	0.003
9. Foods; Please self/Please others	3.33	3.47	-0.51	0.609	3.48	3.34	0.55	0.586
10. Groups; Lead/Follow	4.08	4.43	-1.46	0.146	4.43	4.13	1.30	0.195
N =	99	124			108	115		

Comparisons are of U. S. to Canadian groups and younger (under 26) to older (over 26) age groups.
Scores are on a 7 point scale, the modpoint of which is 4.0.

Hotellings T - squared for U.S. vs Canadian groups = 104.39   F = 10.01
Hotellings T - squared for age groups = 54.67   F = 5.24

*The above entries are read; New foods, try first is high (7) and don't try is low (1) end of 7 point scale.

to be more indulgent than older ones in pleasing themselves in dress (item 8).

Personality Traits Compared to Purposes for Purchasing

Space does not allow a complete report on the relationship of personality traits. We leave this task for a later paper and report only sufficient data to indicate the influence of these variables on purpose for purchasing. This is done by comparing two of the personality items: item 2, fashion innovativeness and item 10, social leader-follower to two product scores: perfumes and musical recordings.

Comparisons of the leader-follower dimension are provided in Table 8. The only significant correlation (at level .10) between leadership scores and purposes for purchasing perfumes is with "prevent offending." This low, negative value ($r = -.145$) suggests that followers are somewhat inclined to use perfumes in order to prevent offending others. The possibility that this characteristic influences purchasing of other products has to be considered. Comparison of leader-follower scores to the musical recordings scores revealed two low but significant correlations. "Escape" positively correlates ($r = .161$) while "pleases others" negatively relates. The negative correlation indicates that followers are somewhat inclined to use music to please others. We noted that followers use perfumes to avoid offending; however, the "please others" category for perfumes showed no correlation. This suggests that "prevent offending" and "please others" are based on different dynamics; yet both are characteristic of followers. This relationship is probably a fruitful area for further research. The uses of music for escape appears to be somewhat associated with self-perception of leadership. The small but positive correlation of .161 supports this interpretation.

Correlations between innovativeness in clothing and purposes for using perfumes are provided in Table 8. In these comparisons the only significant correlation is that between innovation and use of perfumes by habit. How this relationship should be interpreted is an

TABLE 8. Correlations Between Leader-Follower and Innovator Scores and Purposes for Use Scores for Two Categories

Perfumes/colognes			Musical Recordings	
Purpose	r (L-F)	R (IN)	Purpose	r (L-F)
Fragrance enjoyment	0.045	-0.063	To relax	0.086
Stimulation, lift	0.034	-0.086	For stimulation	0.076
Improve attractiveness, image	0.005	-0.008	For escape	0.161*
Please others	0.089	0.024	As social medium	-0.041
Prevent Offending	-0.145*	-0.023	Habit	0.132*
Habit	-0.020	0.137*	To please others	-0.171*

*Correlation coefficient significant at level .10.

open question. It may be that the use of perfume is a matter of routine for those seeking to be fashionable.

DISCUSSION AND CONCLUSION

This exploratory study has demonstrated that differences between cultures in purposes for purchasing can be identified on a product by product basis; this can be done through easy to administer and inexpensive methods. The availability of this method should be of material assistance in obtaining information for the development of strategies aimed at global or intercultural markets.

As an example, the findings reveal that the most important purpose in using coffee is taste enjoyment and not the caffeine lift that we had supposed. This relative ranking cuts across the two cultures and the two age groups. This indicates the feasibility and the desirability of a global strategy.

The findings also indicate that different cultures share basic personality traits but may express them differently. Since coffee has been identified as a dominantly enjoyment product, a global strategy appropriate to enjoyment products is necessary (Hunsicker & Woods, 1983). Enjoyment products must offer variety and should emphasize sales promotion and merchandising with limited advertising support. However, since Quebeçoise are less innovative in foods, a slower rate of adoption of new varieties (brands and flavors) should be expected in Quebec than in the U.S. This appears to be a strategy which has been used successfully in these markets.

The method itself, while simple and inexpensive, might be made even less expensive by adapting it to telephone interviewing, for which the paired comparison procedure is particularly advantageous. In countries where telephones are widely available, data could be collected rapidly, with the possibility of adequate geographic representation at reduced cost.

REFERENCES

Bradley, R.A., and Terry, M.E. (1952). "The Rank Analysis of Incomplete Block Designs I; The Method of Paired Comparisons." *Biometrika*, 39, pp. 324-345.

Chase, D. (1984, June 25). "Global Marketing; the New Wave." *Advertising Age*, pp. 49 +.

Cheron, E.J. (1981). *Style de vie de la consommation rimouskoise*, Rimouski: Department des sciences de l'administration, Université du Quebec à Rimouski.

de Leeuw, J., Young F.W., and Takane, Y. (1976). "Additive Structure in Qualitative Data; An Alternative Least Square Method with Optimal Scaling Features." *Psychometrika*, 41, pp. 471-503.

English, M.M. (1983, August 1). "Teens—The Soft Drink Generation." *Advertising Age*, p. 32.

Hamburg, M. (1976) *Statistical Analysis for Decision Making* (pp. 432-437). New York: Harcourt, Brace & World, Inc.

Hauter, E. (1984, April 27). "Modular Marketing Cracks International Markets." *Advertising Age*, p. 10.

Hunsicker, F.L., and Woods, W.A. (1983). "A Model for Integrating Strategic Resources with Consumer Market Parameters." In R.W. Darden, K.B. Monroe, and W.R. Dillion (eds.) *Research Methods in Causal Modeling, Proceedings Series*, American Marketing Association.

Jaffe, E.D., and Nebenzahl, I.D. (1984). "Alterative Questionnaire Formats for Country Image Studies." *Journal of Marketing Research* (November), 21, pp. 463-471.

Kendall, M.G. (1962). *Rank Correlation Methods*, 3rd ed., London: Charles Griffin & Company Limited.

Kuder, G.F. (1939). "The Stability of Preference Items." *Journal of Social Psychology*, 10, pp. 41-50.

Lenroe, M.M. (1984, November 1). "Mapping New Strategy for World Brands." *Advertising Age*, pp. 140-43.

Levitt, T. (1983). "The Globalization of Markets." *Harvard Business Review* (May-June), 61(3), pp. 92-102.

Neter, J., and Wasserman, W. (1974). *Applied Linear Statistical Models: Regression, Analysis of Variance, and Experimental Designs* (pp. 477-480). Homewood, IL: Richard D. Irwin, Inc.

Ohmae, K. (1985). *Triad Power: The Coming Shape of Global Competition*. New York: Free Press.

Parameswaran, R., Greenberg, B.A., Bellenger, D.N., and Robertson, D.H. (1979). "Measuring Reliability: A Comparison of Alternative Techniques." *Journal of Marketing Research* (February), 16, pp. 18-25.

Rao, P.V., and Kupper, L.L. (1967). "Ties in Paired Comparison Experiments; A Generalization of the Bradley-Terry Model." *Journal of the American Statistical Association*, 62, pp. 192-204.

Rudolph, A. (1985, May 27). "Standardization Not Standard for Global Marketers." *Marketing News*, p. 3.

Scheffe, H. (1952). "An Analysis of Variance of Paired Comparisons." *Journal of the American Statistical Association*, 47, pp. 381-400.

Siegel, S. (1956). *Nonparametric Statistics for the Behavioral Sciences*. New York: McGraw-Hill.

Takane, Y. (1982). "Maximum Likelihood Additivity Analysis." *Psychological Review*, 34, pp. 283-286.

Thurstone, L. L. (1927). "A Law of Comparative Judgement." *Psychological Review*, 34, pp. 283-286.

Woods, W.A., Cheron, E.J., and Kim, D.M. (1985). "Strategic Implications of Differences in Purposes for Purchasing in Three Global Markets." In E. Kaynak (ed.) *Global Perspectives in Marketing*. (pp. 155-170), New York: Praeger.

Chapter 3

An Information Processing Interpretation of Cross-National Consumer Characteristics

Richard W. Olshavsky
David J. Moore
Jeen-Su Lim

SUMMARY. The identification of a valid interpretation of the similarities and differences in the behavior of consumers in different nations is impossible without a comprehensive theory of consumer behavior that explicitly takes into account differences in the characteristics of the consumer, the marketplace, the social environment, and the physical environment of these nations. Newell and Simon's version of information processing theory is advocated as the one theory that is capable of providing a solution to this basic problem of cross-national research.

INTRODUCTION

One issue of increasing importance in the area of consumer behavior concerns the validity of the interpretations made of cross-national data. Anderson and Engledow (1977) have pointed out that in several cross-national studies a "homogeneous response" approach to data interpretation has been adopted. In this approach a representative sample from the particular nation of interest is selected and conclusions from the data are generalized to the entire

---

This chapter was first published in the *Journal of Global Marketing*, Vol. 1(4), Summer 1988.

population (e.g., Green & Langeard, 1975; Hempel, 1974; Lorimer & Dunn, 1970). In the light of previous studies that have demonstrated that consumer behavior patterns within nations are characteristically heterogeneous (see e.g., Frank, Massy, & Wind, 1972) there seems to be little justification for such generalizations about an entire nation. Indeed, a homogeneous response interpretation of cross-national data encourages the researcher to overlook the important within-nation differences in consumer behavior and to highlight "differences rather than similarities *between* countries" (Douglas, 1976, p. 12).

A more defensible approach to cross-national studies is the "heterogeneous response" approach. Instead of viewing an entire nation as one homogeneous unit, this approach identifies within each nation certain groups that may exhibit greater cross-national similarity (Katona, Strumpel, & Zahn, 1973). For example, Thorelli, Becker, and Engledow (1975) compared subscribers to magazines of independent product testing agencies to "average" consumers (nonsubscribers) in both Germany and the U.S.A. The study concluded that there exists, "a rather homogeneous cross-cultural elite of affluent and information sensitive consumers" across national boundaries (p. 141). As a sequel to this study, Anderson and Engledow (1977) analyzed this same group of "super-consumers" (i.e., information seekers) and found significant cross-national similarities in attitudes and behaviors.

THE BASIC PROBLEM

While the "heterogeneous response" approach has the virtue Of recognizing the differences that exist in consumer behavior within a nation and of stressing similarities among nations, this approach and the "homogeneous response" approach suffer from another, more basic type of problem. This problem concerns the fundamental difficulty of making a valid interpretation of the behavior of consumers in different nations unless the differences in certain "significant" features that characterize these nations have been explicitly taken into account. "Significant" features are those that are hypothesized to determine or cause consumer behavior.

A study by Douglas (1976) nicely illustrates this basic problem.

Douglas compared the shopping patterns of housewives in the U.S.A. and France. She concluded:

> In brief, while cross-national differences are, on the surface, greater than within country differences between working and non-working wives, a closer examination shows that observed differences probably reflect differences in the retail environment rather than in underlying attitudes and preferences. Consequently, focus on apparent differences in behavior between national samples may tend to be misleading, especially where this leads to negative conclusions concerning the feasibility of influencing or changing these patterns. (Douglas, 1976, p. 19)

In Douglas' study, the data *do* reveal differences in the behavior of consumers in these two nations, but these differences may simply reflect the different distribution structures that characterized France and the U.S.A. at the time of the study (van Raaij, 1977). The interpretation of these differences for theoretical or marketing management purposes is therefore very difficult.

Another illustration of the basic problem can be found in the Thorelli and Sentell (1974, 1982) summary report of one of the most comprehensive studies of consumer shopping practices ever conducted in Thailand (or perhaps in any less developed country). The study examined the patterns of information search among Thai consumers in various regions of the country. On the basis of their data, these researchers made the following interpretation for the whole of Thailand, and even for other less developed countries:

> There is strong evidence that information search, relatively speaking, plays a greater role in the buying process among consumers in the less developed countries than in the industrialized world. (Thorelli and Sentell, 1979, p. 326)

While there may be strong evidence for greater information search among Thai consumers, it is difficult to interpret these findings because of the differences that exist between Thailand and other more developed countries along many "significant" features (Thorelli and Sentell acknowledge and list many differences in potentially significant features). For instance, if less information is

available in the marketplace in Thailand or if the available information is of less quality, then greater search by Thai consumers may
simply reflect these environmental differences. Consequently, information search may not play a greater role in the buying process.
This latter interpretation is based upon the possibility that more
search occurs because more search is necessary to obtain *the same
amount of usable information*.

In the remaining portion of this paper, the nature and implications of this fundamental problem are explicated further by means
of a more detailed example. Then a theoretical framework is presented that is advocated as being more useful than existing theories
in guiding the interpretation of data from past cross-national studies
of consumer behavior and in guiding the design of future cross-
national studies.

FURTHER EXPLICATION OF THE BASIC PROBLEM

The nature of the basic problem will be described in greater detail
by the use of a specific study involving Korean consumers.

The Korean Refrigerator Buyer

This example involves one of the few published reports on the
extent of search for information by consumers in Korea (Whang &
Min, 1978). The product studied was refrigerators. With the cooperation of the manufacturers, a list of consumers in Seoul who purchased a refrigerator in the past two months was obtained. From
this list 250 names were randomly selected; of the 250 contacted,
233 interviews were usable. This study employed the personal in-
terview method. The questionnaire contained several different measures of the extent of information seeking. Only a few of these
measures will be reported on here (Jacoby et al., 1974).

Table 1 presents a distribution of the extent of search as measured
by "the number of brands considered," "the number of stores visited," and "the number of sources used." Table 2 presents the
types of external sources of information referred to and the relative
frequency of use of each type.

The Within-Nation Interpretation. The theorist or the practitioner

working within Korea would have little difficulty using these data
to guide theory development or marketing management decisions.
Specifically, it may be concluded that the majority of refrigerator
buyers considered only one brand, visited only one store, and used
several information sources. Also, it may be concluded that ''the

TABLE 1

Distribution of the Extent of Search
(Korean Study)

Number of Brands Considered			Number of Stores Visited			Number of Information Sources Used		
#	%	N	#	%	N	#	%	N
1	62.9	146	1	57.9	135	0	24.9	58
2	16.4	38	2	17.6	41	1-2	20.2	47
3	16.4	38	3	15.5	36	3-4	31.3	73
4-5	4.3	10	4-5	9.0	21	5-6	15.9	37
						7 or more	7.7	18

Source: Whang and Min (1978)

TABLE 2

Type of Information Sources Consulted
(Korean Study)

Type of Information Sources	% Consulting this Source	N
Neighbor	28.2	91
Family	43.3	140
Colleagues (co-workers)	5.0	16
Retail Outlets	9.0	29
Church and Other Social Clubs	14.6	47

Source: Whang and Min (1978)

family" and "neighbors" are the most frequently used sources (Dommermuth, 1965).

The Cross-National Interpretation. The theorist seeking to develop a theory general enough to encompass consumer behavior across nations cannot easily provide a meaningful interpretation of these data. Likewise the marketing manager of a multi-national company headquartered in some country other than Korea cannot easily interpret these data to guide marketing strategy in Korea without great risk of a marketing blunder (Ricks, Fu, & Arpan, 1974).

The interpretation of these data in a cross-national fashion is very difficult because of the differences that distinguish Korea from other nations in several potentially significant features. Consider, for example, the data presented in Tables 3 and 4; these findings are abstracted from a recent study involving American appliance purchasers using comparable measures of search (Wilkie & Dickson, 1985). What kinds of interpretations could be made concerning the observed *differences* in extent of external search behavior of Korean versus American consumers for refrigerators? It can be said, of course, that American consumers considered more brands, visited more stores, and used a greater number of sources of

TABLE 3

Distribution of the Extent of Search
(USA Study)

Number of Brands Considered			Number of Stores Visited			Number of Information Sources Used		
#	%	N	#	%	N	#	%	N
1	32	138	1	37	160	0	15	65
2	26	113	2	19	82	1	27	117
3	26	113	3	19	82	2	25	108
4 or more	16	69	4 or more	25	108	3	19	82
						4 or more	13	56

Source: Adapted from Wilkie and Dickson (1985, p. 8).
Compare also Dommermuth (1965); Newman and Staelin (1972).

TABLE 4

Type of Information Sources Consulted
(USA Study)

Type of Information Sources	% Consulting This Source	N
Appliance Salesperson	59	255
Newspaper Ad	39	169
Friend or Relative	38	165
Catalog	35	152
Brochures/Labels	28	121
Consumer Reports	20	87
Appliance Repairperson	14	61
Magazine Ad	12	52
T.V. Ad	10	43

Source: Adapted from Wilkie and Dickson (1985, p. 13).

information than Seoul consumers. And it can be said that Korean consumers made greater use of "personal" or noncommercial sources than American consumers.

But, no meaningful cross-national interpretations can be made unless and until the many differences that exist between Korea and America are taken into account. Some selected examples will now be listed. First, consider the nature of the marketplace with respect to the number of alternatives available. In Korea (specifically in Seoul) only four brands of refrigerators are available and imported brands are very few and are not available for public purchase. In America (specifically in Chicago), at least 13 brands are available for public purchase. Second, consider the types of information available about refrigerators in-store. In Seoul, in-store information is mostly obtained through the salesperson and direct observation of the product. In Chicago, the same types of information are available, but in addition other types of in-store information are available such as point of purchase materials and catalogs that systematically display the available brands, models and product characteristics. Third, consider the accessibility and availability of information in the social environment from friends and family. The average number of persons per household in Korea is 4.9, compared with 2.9 in the U.S. In addition, houses tend to be located closer to each other, thus affording far more social interaction and information exchange among family members, neighbors, and friends. Fourth, the channels of distribution differ. In Seoul, the exclusive dealership method is used, in Chicago it is not, except for a few brands. Further, there is greater physical distance between stores in Seoul, and this limits the number of stores that could be visited during a shopping trip. Fifth, the transportation system and auto ownership per household differ. In Seoul, there is greater reliance upon mass transit and less family car ownership than in Chicago.

Now that differences in some of the potentially significant features of these two nations have been described, it is possible to illustrate the basic problem that arises in interpretation and the implications of these interpretations for international marketing strategies. Consider two hypothetical interpretations, A and B. According to Interpretation A, Korean consumers are assumed to be impulsive buyers; that is, their purchases are made after consulting only one brand in the first store visited. On the basis of this interpretation, a logical marketing strategy would be: (1) heavy mass media exposure to create high brand awareness, (2) extensive distribution to increase the availability of the brand in as many stores as possible, and (3) heavy emphasis on point-of-purchase displays and in-store selling by sales personnel.

According to Interpretation B, Korean consumers are not impulse buyers, rather they engage in deliberate and extensive information search before visiting the store (i.e., store choice is tantamount to brand choice, given the exclusive dealership arrangements in Korea). Valuable and extensive information is acquired from family members, reference groups, newspapers, magazines, and other mass media. On the basis of this interpretation, a logical marketing strategy would be: (1) provide consumers with adequate information to consider and compare among the existing brands, (2) limit any expenditure on in-store promotional displays and sales personnel, and (3) adopt a selective distribution system.

The choice between Interpretation A and Interpretation B, or between these interpretations and any other interpretations a researcher might devise, is at the heart of the basic problem facing cross-national researchers. The implications of these interpretations for theory and managerial strategy is a separate, but closely related problem.

A THEORETICAL FRAMEWORK
FOR CROSS-NATIONAL RESEARCH

One solution that has been proposed for this basic problem is the use of "life-styles." "Understanding and interpreting differences between countries requires examination of the overall pattern and of the interrelationships between the various aspects of lifestyle." (Douglas & Urban, 1977, p. 47). We believe that Douglas and Urban are on the right track, but that their proposed solution does not go far enough.

What is needed to solve the basic problem of interpretation is a theory that explicitly identifies and specifies the influence of "significant" variables relating to the determination of consumer behavior. Only with such a theory can a valid interpretation be made concerning the differences and similarities that arise in consumer behavior across nations (Moore, 1981). According to Kaynak and Savitt (1984) there is an urgent need for a truly comprehensive comparative marketing theory that can be tested and applied across multiple nations and cultural settings.

Unfortunately, no theory of consumer behavior currently exists that is adequate to the task. Sheth and Sethi's (1977) theory of cross-national consumer behavior is primarily an extension of existing theories of diffusion and adoption. As such, this theory ignores the significant role of the characteristics of the task environment in determining consumer behavior. Other comprehensive theories of consumer behavior (Bettman, 1979; Engel, Blackwell, & Kollat, 1978; Howard, 1977; Howard & Sheth, 1969) have similar problems. However, we believe Newell and Simon's (1972) original version of information processing theory represents a good starting point for the development of an adequate theory.

According to Newell and Simon's theory, man is viewed as but one instance of a general class of information processing systems. (The digital computer is another familiar instance.) The behavior of such an information processing system is determined by the individual's goals, strategies, and information processing constraints.

And, most importantly, the behavior of the organism is shaped by the environment in which the organism seeks his/her goal. That is, behavior is *adaptive* to the task environment:

> The task environment . . . determines . . . the behavior of the problem solver independently of the detailed internal structure of his information processing system. (Newell and Simon, 1972, p. 788)

To better illustrate Newell and Simon's assumption concerning the shaping of behavior by the environment, two "significant" aspects of the *task environment* facing decision makers in general and consumers in particular will now be briefly discussed: (1) the number of alternatives; and (2) the nature of the information available. Although many other variables (such as perceived similarity of alternatives, accessibility of information and cost of information) affect extent of search, these two variables should serve to illustrate how the behavior of the consumer is determined by the interaction that takes place over time between characteristics of the consumer and characteristics of the environment.

The total number of alternatives available to a decision maker at any given period of time can range from as few as two to several thousand. Laboratory studies (e.g., Payne, 1976; Lussier & Olshavsky, 1979) have demonstrated that as the number of alternatives increases, the amount of search increases (where search is defined in terms of the number of brands considered and the number of attributes considered). The number of alternatives was also found to have a significant effect on brand choice strategy in other empirical studies (Hansen, 1972; Hendrick, Mills, & Kiesler, 1968).

The *nature of information* that exists in the marketplace also influences the amount of search. Olshavsky and Smith (1980) have pointed out that information within the marketplace is comprised of the *amount*, *quality*, and *format* of the information about alternatives available to the consumer. For brand choice, typical sources of information in the marketplace would include: (1) the product itself (through direct observation in-store); (2) the package; (3) point-of-purchase displays (brochures, pamphlets, etc.) and (4) sales personnel. (Advertising, word-of-mouth, product knowledge that the consumer has already stored in his long-term memory and certain other sources of information are not classified as part of the marketplace (Newman & Staelin, 1972).)

The amount of information available in the marketplace is a significant factor in determining the amount of information search. Extended search is not possible if there is little or no information available in the marketplace or if the information is available but inaccessible for some reason. A number of studies have demonstrated the increased use of information as the amount of information increases (see Bettman, 1979 for a review). Other studies have demonstrated that format or the manner in which information is presented is an important determinant of consumer's use of information (Bettman & Kakkar, 1977; Russo, 1977; Russo, Staelin, Nolan, Russell, & Metcalf, 1986).

The Korean Study — Revisited

As previously described, many differences exist between the characteristics of Korean and American consumers and between the characteristics of Korean and American marketplaces. But clearly, Seoul and Chicago do differ with respect to the two "significant" features of the marketplace just described. Chicago is characterized by a greater number of alternatives and greater amount of information. Based on the Newell and Simon theory, any differences observed between the search behaviors of Seoul consumers and Chicago consumers are due, at least in part, to these structural differences in the marketplaces that characterize each city. Indeed, the differences relating to the extent of search are in the direction predicted. It is not meaningful therefore to conclude that Korean consumers are more impulsive than American consumers, that they value information less or any other interpretation relating expressly to consumer characteristics (e.g., attitudes, values, beliefs, or lifestyles) unless separate measures are made to document such differences.

CONCLUSIONS AND IMPLICATIONS

It is easy to make comparative statements concerning differences and similarities in consumer behavior across nations, but it is difficult to make valid interpretations of these data unless a comprehensive theory of consumer behavior is available (Kaynak & Savitt, 1984). In the absence of any existing theory, we are simply proposing that Newell and Simon's original statement of information processing theory provides a viable starting point because their theory explicitly takes into account the influence of both characteristics of the consumer and characteristics of the external task environment in the determination of behavior.

Given the highly structured and goal-given nature of the types of problems addressed by Newell and Simon (e.g., chess, logic theorem proofs, cryptarithmetic), the richness and complexities of consumer behaviors are presently beyond the scope of their theory. Their theory can be extended, however, to incorporate many characteristics of the consumer other than the basic information processing constraints (e.g., beliefs, attitudes, skills, values, life goals, disposable income and time). Likewise, the repertoire of strategies can be expanded to include all types of strategies used by consumers, including heuristics such as getting recommendations from a product testing organization, imitating friends, or using price as an index of quality. And the notion of a task environment can be expanded to encompass not only the marketplace but also the social environment (which would include all groups—religious, governmental, business, etc.) and the physical environment (which would include geological structures, climate, etc.). Olshavsky (1975; 1985a; 1985b; 1985c; 1987) has already provided many specific suggestions as to how this basic theory can be expanded and adapted to the explanation of consumer behavior in any nation. This work makes it clear that differences that arise in cross-national research such as kinship patterns, household size and composition, beliefs, attitudes, values, life goals, ownership and use of automobiles, physical proximity of retail outlets, size and composition of marketplaces, presence of governmental regulations, presence of product-testing organizations, climatic conditions, and many other variables can be encompassed systematically within an expanded version of Newell and Simon's basic information processing theory.

Future efforts should be directed toward the further development and formalization of Newell and Simon's theory. The resulting expanded theory should then be used to generate testable hypotheses regarding observable differences and similarities in consumer behavior across nations.

In the meantime, we suggest that any interpretations made of cross-national data should be made cautiously and preferably by someone highly familiar with the detailed differences between characteristics of the consumers and characteristics of the marketplace, the social environment, and the physical environment that comprise the nations involved.

REFERENCES

Anderson, Ronald and Jack Engledow. (1977). "A Factor Analytic Comparison of U.S. and German Information Seekers," *Journal of Consumer Research*, (March), pp. 185-196.

Bettman, J. R. (1979). *An Information Processing Theory of Consumer Choice*. Los Angeles: Addison-Wesley Publishing Co., Inc.

Bettman, James R. and Pradeep Kakkar. (1977). "Effects of Information Presentation Format on Consumer Acquisition Strategies." *Journal of Consumer Research*, 13 (June), pp. 48-70.

Dommermuth, W. P. (1965). "The Shopping Matrix and Marketing Strategy." *Journal of Marketing Research*, 2, pp. 128-132.

Douglas, Susan P. (1976). "Cross-National Comparisons and Consumer Stereotypes: A Case Study of Working Wives and Non-Working Wives in the U.S. and France." *Journal of Consumer Research*, (June), pp. 12-20.

Douglas, Susan P. and Christine D. Urban. (1977). "Life-Style Analysis to Profile Women in International Markets." *Journal of Marketing*, 41 (July), pp. 46-54.

Engel, James F., Roger D. Blackwell and David T. Kollat. (1978). *Consumer Behavior* (3rd Ed.). Hinsdale, IL: Dryden.

Frank, R. E., W. F. Massy and Yoram Wind. (1972). *Market Segmentation*. Englewood Cliffs, NJ: Prentice Hall.

Green, R. T. and E. Langeard. (1975). "A Cross-National Comparison of Consumer Habits and Innovator Characteristics." *Journal of Marketing*, (July), pp. 34-41.

Hansen, Flemming. (1972). *Consumer Choice Behavior: A Cognitive Theory*. New York: The Free Press.

Hempel, D. J. (1974). "Family Buying Decisions: A Cross-Cultural Perspective." *Journal of Marketing Research*, (August), pp. 295-302.

Hendrick, Clyde, Judson Mills and Charles A. Kiesler. (1968). "Decision Time as a Function of a Number and Complexity of Equally Attractive Alternatives." *Journal of Personality and Social Psychology*, 8, pp. 313-18.

Howard, John A. (1977). *Consumer Behavior: Application of Theory*. New York: McGraw-Hill.

_____and Jagdish N. Sheth. (1969). *The Theory of Buyer Behavior*. New York: McGraw-Hill.

Jacoby, Jacob, Donald E. Speller and Carol A. Kohn. (1974). "Brand Choice Behavior as a Function of Information Load: Replication and Extension." *Journal of Consumer Research*, (June), pp. 33-42.

Katona, G., B. Strumpel and E. Zahn. (1973). "The Sociocultural Environment." In Hans B. Thorelli (ed.), *International Marketing Strategy*. Hamondsworth, Middlesex, England: Penguin Books.

Kaynak, Erdener and Ronald Savitt. (1984). "The Future Directions of Comparative Marketing: An Agenda for Research Priorities." In Erdener Kaynak and Ronald Savitt (eds.), *Comparative Marketing Systems*. New York: Praeger Publishers, pp. 278-285.

Lorimer, E. S. and S. W. Dunn. (1970). "Four Measures of Cross-Cultural Marketing Effectiveness." *Journal of Advertising Research*, 8 (January), pp. 11-13.

Lussier, Denis and Richard W. Olshavsky. (1979). "Task Complexity and Contingent Processing in Brand Choice." *Journal of Consumer Research*, 6 (September), pp. 154-165.

Moore, David J. (1981). "Cross-Cultural Consumer Information Search: A Task Environmental Analysis." Paper presented at the *Academy of International Business*, Annual Meeting, Joint Session, McGill University International Symposium on Cross-Cultural Management, Montreal, Canada.

Newell, Allen and Herbert Simon. (1972). *Human Problem Solving*. Englewood Cliffs, NJ: Prentice-Hall.

Newman, Joseph W. and Richard Staelin. (1972). "Prepurchase Information Seeking for New Cars and Major Household Appliances." *Journal of Marketing Research*, 9 (August), pp. 249-257.

Olshavsky, Richard W. (1975). "Implications of an Information Processing Theory of Consumer Behavior," in Edward M. Mazze (ed.), "Marketing in Turbulent Times and Marketing: The Challenges and the Opportunities." *Combined Proceedings*, The American Marketing Association, pp. 151-155.

_____(1985a). "Toward a More Comprehensive Theory of Choice." in Elizabeth C. Hirschman and Morris Holbrook (eds.), *Advances in Consumer Research*, Vol. XII, Provo, UT: Association for Consumer Research, pp. 465-470.

_____(1985b). "Perceived Quality in Consumer Decision Making: An Integrated Theoretical Perspective," in Jacob Jacoby and Jerry Olson (eds.), *Perceived Quality – How Consumers View Stores and Merchandise*. Lexington, MA, pp. 3-29.

_____(1985c). "Toward a Theory of Cross-National Consumer Behavior." *Proceedings* of the 1984 Conference, Comparative Consumer Psychology, Division 23, American Psychological Association, Charles F. Keown and Arch G. Woodside (eds.). Published by the Division of Research, U. of South Carolina, Columbia, SC 29208, pp. 10-13.

_____(1987). "Toward A Unified Theory of Consumer Behavior." Marketing Theory, Russell Belk and Gerald Zaltman (eds.), *Proceedings* of the 1987 AMA Winter Educator's Conference, pp. 280-283.

_____David J. Moore and Jeen-Su Lim. (1987). "Inferring Consumer Characteristics from Cross-National Behavioral Data." Summer Marketing Educators' Conference, Michael R. Solomon and Susan P. Douglas (eds.), American Marketing Association.

_____and Michael Smith. (1980). "A Taxonomy of Brand Choice Environments." American Psychological Association, *Proceedings*, pp. 145-154.

Payne, John W. (1976). "Task Complexity and Contingent Processing in Decision Making: An Information Search and Protocol Analysis." *Organizational Behavior and Human Performance*, 16, pp. 366-87.

Ricks, David, Marilyn Y. C. Fu and Jeffrey S. Arpan. (1974). *International Business Blunders*. Columbus, OH: Grid.

Ricks, David A. (1983). *Big Business Blunders: Mistakes in Multinational Marketing*. Homewood, IL: Dow Jones-Irwin.

Russo, J. Edward. (1977). "The Value of Unit Price Information." *Journal of Marketing Research*, 14 (May), pp. 193-201.

_____Richard Staelin, Catherine A. Nolan, Gary Russell and Barbara L. Metcalf. (1986). "Nutritional Information in the Supermarket." *Journal of Consumer Research*, 13 (June), pp. 48-70.

Sheth, Jagdish N. and S. Prakash Sethi. (1977). "A Theory of Cross-Cultural Buyer Behavior," in Arch G. Woodside, Jagdish N. Sheth and Peter Bennet, (eds.), *Consumer and Industrial Buying Behavior*. New York: North Holland, pp. 369-86.

Thorelli, Hans B., Helmut Becker and Jack Engledow. (1975). *The Information Seekers – An International Study of Consumer Information and Advertising Image*. Cambridge, MA: Ballinger.

_____and Gerald D. Sentell. (1974). "Consumer Ecology in the LDC: The Case of Thailand." *Proceedings* of the Academy of International Business Asia-Pacific Dimensions of International Business, Honolulu, HI, pp. 324-32.

Thorelli, Hans B. and Gerald D. Sentell. (1982). *Consumer Emancipation and Economic Development: The Case of Thailand*. Contemporary Studies in Economic and Financial Analysis, Vol. 37. Greenwich, CT: JAI Press Inc.

van Raaij, Fred W. (1977). "Cross-Cultural Research Methodology as a Case of

Construct Validity," in H. Keith Hunt (ed.), *Advances in Consumer Research*, Vol. 6, pp. 693-701.

Whang, Eui R. and Buyng M. Min. (1978). "A Study of Brand Choice Behavior," *Research Bulletin*, Korean Institute for Research in the Behavioral Science, Vol. 11, No. 5, (March).

Wilkie, William L. and Peter R. Dickson. (1985). "Shopping for Appliances: Consumers' Strategies and Patterns of Information Search." Working paper, *Marketing Science Institute*.

Chapter 4

Euroconsumers?
A Three-Country Analysis
of the Feasibility
# of Product Value Standardization

Petr Chadraba
Helena Czepiec

SUMMARY. This study develops a simple, inexpensive technique for segmenting nations on a psychological variable, perceived product value. It successfully applies the mechanism to three European countries, Austria, France and Switzerland. Respondents' perceptions of the value of several base products and their proposed modifications are compared within nation pairs as well as across all three nations. The magnitude in common value perceptions, particularly among product owners, supports the feasibility of this variable as an effective segmentation tool. The results also encourage the development of more uniform marketing strategies when introducing new consumer products cross-nationally.

BACKGROUND

Successfully introducing new products into the European market depends in part upon determining the homogeneity of values among European consumers. If product values transcend national boundaries and Euroconsumers prevail, the situation calls for a standardized marketing strategy. Otherwise, a customized approach may be more effective.

Choosing correctly is very important. If nations can be treated as

This chapter was first published in the *Journal of Global Marketing*, Vol. 1(4), Summer 1988.

coalitions of marketing groups, multinational companies can achieve cost savings, consistency in image, and improved planning and control through a standardized marketing approach (Buzzell, 1968). Not surprisingly many companies therefore opt for standardization whenever possible (Sorenson & Wiechmann, 1975; Buzzell, 1968). However, companies can commit big blunders resulting in financial losses and even withdrawal from the market by blindly relying on a standardized approach (Ricks, 1983).

If the consumers of different nations have little in common, then multinational companies should individually tailor their marketing mixes. Customization has the potential to achieve greater brand loyalty, sales, and profits. On the other hand, it may waste valuable resources and still fail to achieve marketing success (Ricks, 1983).

In Europe, choosing between standardization and customization is particularly difficult. On the one hand, the individual countries strive fiercely to maintain their separate identities. On the other hand, they are bonded at every turn by economic and political agreements; by increased international travel of their citizens; and by improved communications.

This study is designed to help marketers choose correctly between standardization and customization by measuring the similarity in product values of respondents from three European countries. Past studies tried to measure the similarity among European nations based only on economic and demographic variables (Sethi & Holton, 1973; Sethi, 1971) or market size and growth rate (Cateora, 1983). These commonly developed dimensions for segmenting international markets (Buzzell, 1968; Farmer & Richman, 1980; Keegan, 1980; Cateora, 1983), however, have proven to be better checklists for determining market entry rather than aids for developing marketing strategies. Economic and demographic variables, although effective for identifying market potential and markets where investments should be made, are inadequate when trying to decide whether to use a standardized marketing mix. This is substantiated by the marketing mistakes made by companies using a standardized approach in countries which were economically and politically similar, but judging from the failures differed in consumer product preferences (Ricks, 1983). Nonetheless, marketers continue to use standardized approaches in markets they perceive as having similar market conditions (Sorenson & Wiechmann, 1975).

It has long been recommended that psychological factors, including values, be examined for segmenting foreign markets (Engel, Kollat, & Blackwell, 1978; Sommers & Kernan, 1967). It is assumed that by understanding values, it is possible to determine what products will generally be sold and what promotions will be most effective (Sommers & Kernan, 1967). The importance of psychological bases of segmentation is apparent from their successful use in segmenting markets for the U.S. market, which is characterized by multi-cultures. A core of attitudes, needs and values have been found useful for segmenting markets for individual products as well as classes of products. Few attempts, however, have been made to determine whether psychological variables can indeed be used to segment international markets. Sommers and Kernan (1967) argued that products succeeded or failed in four demographically similar countries depending on the countries' values. They ranked Australia, Canada, Great Britain, and the United States, on six value orientations developed by Parsons (1964) and Lipset (1963) to characterize nations. Unfortunately Sommers and Kernan (1967) categorized the countries based on intuition rather than on any systematically gathered empirical evidence. Also many of the values which served as the basis for their segmentation were not directly related to product usage.

Morello (1984) found that eight European countries could be segmented on consumers perceptions of the nations along the three dimensions, evaluation, potency and activity, developed by Osgood, Succi, and Tannenbaum (1957). These three dimensions have proven to be salient pan-cultural factors. Moreover, consumers' evaluations of the countries on these scales were highly correlated with their perceived quality of the products the countries produced.

METHODOLOGY

The purpose of this paper is to measure the extent of homogeneity of perceived product values among European consumers. It develops a mechanism for determining whether countries can be grouped along this psychological consumer attribute (Sorenson & Wiechmann, 1975) and applies the mechanism to three Western European countries. Perceived product value has been found to be an important determinant of product purchase (Olson, 1977). This study explores whether this particular psychological variable can produce more meaningful segments of economically similar and geographically proximate European countries. Respondents from France, Austria, and Switzerland were asked to indicate their perceived value of five readily available consumer goods and twelve proposed but not yet available product improvements. The three countries had been clustered previously on their demographic and economic similarities (Sethi & Holton, 1973; Cateora, 1983) and were selected in part because they might be viewed as candidates for a standardized marketing approach.

The respondents were students from the University of Vienna in Austria (N = 104); the University of Strasbourg in France (N = 105); and the University of Zurich in Switzerland (N = 105). The students were selected on a quota basis from business and economics classes within the schools. The respondents from the three samples were similar demographically. They were predominantly male (70%), had three years of college, and an average age of 23 years.

College students were used because they were readily accessible and permitted better control over several cross-national samples. Moreover, the students were considered to be an important market segment for the products being evaluated.

The products being evaluated were selected on the basis of their familiarity to participants in the study. The five base products (available in each country) and their variations (unavailable but possible product adaptations) are listed in Table 1. To ensure that the respondents were thinking of similar products, each of the items was carefully described in terms of the dimensions and the functions it could perform. Furthermore, the respondents were shown drawings of the items, carefully avoiding any brand identification. It was assumed that brand or trademark identification would influence the consumers' perceptions of product quality (Monroe, 1976; Jacoby, Szybille, & Busato-Schach, 1977).

The research questionnaires were translated into German and French. To ensure validity the questions were translated to the respective foreign language, then translated back to English by different translators (Brislin, Lonner, & Thorndike, 1973). Also the translated questions were tested for understanding on foreign exchange students from Austria, France, and Switzerland.

TABLE 1. List of Basic Products and Product Improvements

BASE PRODUCT	ADDED FEATURES
Pocket size camera	*Power telephoto zoom lens *Push-button film advance *Waterproof case
Pocket size calculator	*Time and date function *Permanent memory *Built-in cassette recorder
AM/FM digital clock radio	*Ceiling time projector *Heating element
High intensity desk lamp	*Electric pencil sharpener *Automatic timer
Extension cord	*Wide housing attachment *Spiral shape to double size

In order to measure perceived product value, the respondents were asked to assign a price (in local currencies) first to several base products and then to the same products with additional features not yet available on the market. The relative value of the added features was calculated accordingly:

$$V \text{ of } A \text{ (in percent)} = \frac{P \text{ of } (A + B) - P \text{ of } B}{P \text{ of } B} \times 100$$

where

A = added feature unavailable but possible product adaptation
B = base product available in each country
P = stated price
V = value perception

First the respondents' perceptions of the value of the base product and each of the product modifications were compared within each country. The Mann-Whitney U-test was used to determine whether each enhancement was perceived as being significantly different from the base product. The Mann-Whitney U-test was selected because it can compare rankings which are not influenced by skewed distribution. According to some authors, the test appears stronger than the T-test or chi-square especially when applied to ordinal data (Churchill, 1979). Since the U-test used ranking, it was possible to compare results cross-nationally without using some type of common monetary value.

Second, the respondents' perceptions of the value of the product modifications were compared across the three countries. The Kruskal-Wallis one-way analysis of variance by ranks test was used to determine if the modifications were perceived similarly. The perceptions of owners of the base products were compared separately from non-owners because preliminary analysis had suggested that the perceptions of these two groups might differ. The Kruskal-Wallis test was used because more than two samples were being compared.

Third, the value perceptions for each enhanced product within every pair of nations, France vs. Switzerland, France vs. Austria, and Switzerland vs. Austria, were compared using the Mann-Whitney U-test. The analysis for country pairs was repeated for owners versus non-owners.

FINDINGS

The respondents in each of the three countries expressed similar judgments about the type of added feature they would view as a valuable improvement over an existing product (Table 2). The Austrian sample valued all twelve modifications as significant improvements. The values expressed in monetary form for all of the product enhancements were different at the .05 level of significance from those of the base products and the mean ranks of added features were greater than the mean ranks of base products for the Austrian sample (Table 2). The Swiss respondents viewed all the modifications as significant improvements except for the AM/FM radio-time projector (Table 2). The French viewed all but three improvements, the calculator-time and date, AM/FM radio-time projector, and the desk lamp pencil sharpener, as being worth more than their respective base products (Table 2). The Austrians

TABLE 2. Change in Value Perceptions of Base vs. Modified Products

Mann-Whitney U-Test

| | Z-Values Base vs. Modified Products | | |
Product	Austria	France	Switzerland
Camera-zoom in	4.293	5.605	5.864
Camera-power advance	2.310	3.020	2.540
Camera-waterproof case	4.678	4.802	4.303
Calculator-time and date	2.797	1.264*	3.590
Calculator-permanent memory	4.109	3.479	5.937
Calculator-tape recorder	5.884	5.580	7.415
AM/FM radio-time projector	1.813	.926*	1.645*
AM/FM-heating element	2.750	1.795	2.002
Desk Lamp-pencil sharpener	2.060	.864*	1.822
Desk Lamp-timer	4.081	3.568	5.106
Extension Cord-attachable	5.087	2.664	2.924
Extension Cord-Spiral	5.510	5.424	4.850

*indicates no change in value perception at .05 level of significance

seemed to be most open to product innovations, while the French were the most skeptical.

Moreover, the owners of the base products in the three countries valued similarly six of the twelve product enhancements: camera-power advance; camera-waterproof case; AM/FM radio-time projector; AM/FM radio-heating element; desk lamp-timer; and extension cord-spiral (Table 3). Non-owners, on the other hand, held similar value perceptions of only the calculator-permanent memory and the calculator-tape recorder (Table 3). The owners may have had more homogenous views because they were more familiar with the products and their worth.

To determine whether any two of the countries could be segmented based on their value perceptions of the product innovations,

TABLE 3. Similarity in Value Perceptions in Austria, France, Switzerland Combined

Kruskal-Wallis
One-Way Analysis of
Variance by Ranks

	Chi-Square Scores	
Product	Owners	Non-Owners
Camera-zoom in		
Camera-power advance	1.680*	
Camera-waterproof case	5.157*	
Calculator-time and date		
Calculator-permanent memory		3.515*
Calculator-tape recorder		2.846*
AM/FM radio-time projector	2.049*	
AM/FM-heating element	3.038*	
Desk Lamp-pencil sharpener		
Desk Lamp-timer	7.094*	
Extension Cord-attachable		
Extension Cord-Spiral	6.834*	

*Chi-square less than 7.87 at 3 degrees of freedom shows similarity at .05 level of significance

the analysis was repeated for each pair of countries. Table 4 shows the Z values for each nation pair, controlling for ownership of the base product. The Swiss and the French respondents showed a large degree of similarity within both the owner and non-owner categorIes. The owner group valued similarly nine out of twelve features at the .05 level of significance and the non-owner group ranked eleven of twelve features similarly. Owners within the Swiss/Austrian pair perceived all twelve features similarly while non-owners perceived seven features alike. The French/Austrian pair showed the least level of common value perceptions. Owners

TABLE 4. Similarity in Value Perceptions Between Country Pairs

Z-Values based on
Mann-Whitney U-Test

Product	France vs. Switzerland		France vs. Austria		Switzerland vs. Austria	
	Owners	Non-Owners	Owners	Non-Owners	Owners	Non-Owners
Camera-zoom in	.352*	.917*	1.537*	.809*	.941*	.217*
Camera-power advance	.451*	1.433*	.366*	2.743	.518*	1.887*
Camera-waterproof case	.788*	1.120*	1.190*	3.002	1.828*	2.382
Calculator-time and date	5.260	.616*	6.184	4.122	.319*	3.014
Calculator-permanent memory	4.243	1.193*	4.014	1.673*	.499*	.422*
Calculator-tape recorder	2.851	.706*	3.075	.357*	.340*	.288*
AM/FM radio-time projector	.699*	1.865*	1.045*	4.831	.312*	2.867
AM/FM-heating element	1.034*	.471*	.493*	4.195	1.665*	4.173
Desk Lamp-pencil sharpener	.483*	2.197	2.550	5.343	1.483*	3.356
Desk Lamp-timer	.266*	1.730*	1.479*	1.766*	1.362*	.125*
Extension Cord-attachable	1.339*	1.209*	3.021	2.929	1.950*	1.855*
Extension Cord-Spiral	.456*	.560*	.630*	1.194*	.254*	.685*

*indicates similarity in value perception at .05 level of significance

viewed seven features similarly and non-owners only five features alike.

Incidentally, similarity in demographic or economic variables did not appear to be an indicator of similar value perceptions. The respondents in Austria and Switzerland ranked consistently high in similar value perceptions. The respondents in France and Austria ranked much lower even though they were expected to be the most similar based strictly on economic variables. Actual ownership of the goods for which the respondents were tested appeared to influence the degree of similarity in value perception. The magnitude of common value perceptions for all of the products increased dramatically when the respondents were grouped into owner and non-owner categories.

LIMITATIONS

While a step in the right direction, the study relies heavily on a single indicator of perceived product value. However, given its success, other psychological variables for segmenting nations should be examined.

The measure of product value is applied to only three countries. It should be tested on a larger number of countries to determine its effectiveness. The three countries in the sample are more likely to be similar than other European countries due to their geographic proximity, high level of intercountry travel, and somewhat common historical background. Furthermore, the perceived product value concept may be best suited for more developed countries, where most new products are variations of existing products similar to those included in the sample. It remains to be seen whether the concept will be applicable to less developed nations.

The findings also may be limited in generalizability because they are based on a sample of university students and involve a narrow range of consumer products.

MANAGERIAL IMPLICATIONS

Foreign markets can be segmented on psychological variables. Marketers need not rely only on economic and demographic characteristics. This study provides a simple, inexpensive technique for segmenting nations on perceived product value. The similarity in perceived value, for example, between the French and the Swiss and between the Austrian and Swiss consumers was too strong to ignore.

In the past psychological bases for segmentation may have been avoided in part because marketers suspected that similarities among nations would not be uncovered. Consequently they would be required to tailor individual marketing strategies for each nation. These findings indicate that similarities among nations do exist and may prove useful for designing uniform regional marketing strategies.

Since Europe as a geographic area represents the United States' largest trading partner, standardization can produce significant savings to American exporters. Segmenting countries on attitudinal variables like value perceptions gives international marketing managers the opportunity to realize a number of advantages besides the obvious economies of scale. The results suggest that when introducing new products marketing managers can determine whether the proposed products will be perceived significantly similarly in several national markets. This will enable the simultaneous introduction of new products in several markets thus improving response time to changes in demand. Even though the study dealt with new products, the findings can be generalized to other aspects of marketing strategy. First, this type of segmentation leads to the development of more efficient and effective promotional strategies. Advertising, for example, will be strengthened if the creative message incorporates the consumers' perceived product value. Furthermore, there will be less likelihood of confusion among consumers in adjoining national markets if a uniform appeal can be transmitted cross-nationally.

Second, if similarities in value perceptions exist firms may find it easier to target their products with uniform price strategies. By knowing which countries perceive features alike a company can establish a market price that reflects more accurately the perceived value of owning the product. Knowing how much an additional feature is worth to consumers in different countries helps companies determine more demand oriented pricing strategies.

Third, it may enable a more uniform product positioning strategy spanning several national markets. Besides resulting in economies of scale, uniform positioning strategies would further reduce consumers' product image confusion in areas where national and market boundaries overlap.

Lastly, the study indicates that common value perceptions increase with product ownership. Therefore, it is likely that the opportunities for marketing standardization will increase dramatically in the future as ownership of basic products continues to grow.

REFERENCES

Brislin, Richard W., Walter J. Lonner and Robert M. Thorndike. (1973). *Cross-Cultural Research Methods*. New York: John Wiley and Sons.

Buzzell, Robert D. (1968). "Can You Standardize Multinational Marketing?" *Harvard Business Review*, (November/December), pp. 102-113.

Cateora, Philip R. (1983). *International Marketing*, 5th ed., Homewood, IL: Richard D. Irwin.

Churchill, A. (1979). *Marketing Research*. Englewood Cliffs: Prentice-Hall.

Engel, James F., David T. Kollat and Roger D. Blackwell. (1978). *Consumer Behavior*, 3d ed., Hinsdale, IL: The Dryden Press.

Farmer, Richard N. and Barry M. Richman. (1980). *International Business*, 3d ed., Bloomington, IN: Cedarwood Press.

Jacoby, Jacob, George Szybille and Jacqueline Busato-Schach. (1977). "Information Acquisition Behavior in Brand Choice Situations." *Journal of Consumer Research*, 3 (March), pp. 209-216.

Keegan, Warren J. (1980). *Multinational Marketing Management*, 2d ed., Englewood Cliffs, NJ: Prentice-Hall.

Lipset, Seymour. (1963). "The Value Patterns of Democracy: A Case Study in Comparative Values." *American Sociological Review*, 28 (August), pp. 515-531.

Monroe, Kent B. (1976). "The Influence of Price Differences and Brand Familiarity on Brand Preferences." *Journal of Consumer Research*, 3 (June), pp. 42-49.

Morello, Gabriel. (1984). "The 'Made In' Issue: A Comparative Research on the Image of Domestic and Foreign Products." *European Research*, 12 (January), pp. 5-21.

Olson, Jerry C. (1977). "Price as an Informational Cue: Effects on Product Evaluations," Arch G. Woodside, Jagdish N. Sheth, and Peter D. Bennett, in *Consumer and Industrial Buying Behavior*, New York: North-Holland.

Osgood, C.E., G.J. Succi and P.H. Tannenbaum. (1957). *The Measurement of Meaning*. Urbana: University of Illinois Press.

Parsons, Talcott. (1964). *The Social System*. New York: The Free Press of Glencoe.

Ricks, David A. (1983). *Big Business Blunders: Mistakes in Multinational Marketing*. Homewood, IL: Dow Jones-Irwin.

Sethi, Prakash S. (1971). "Comparative Cluster Analysis For World Markets." *Journal of Marketing Research*, 8 (August), pp. 348-354.

_____and Richard H. Holton. (1973). "Country Typologies for the Multinational Corporation: A New Basic Approach." *California Management Review*, 15 (Spring), pp. 105-118.

Sommers, Montrose and Jerome Kernan. (1967). "Why Products Flourish Here, Fizzle There." *Columbia Journal of World Business*. (March/April), pp. 89-97.

Sorenson, Ralph Z. and Ulrich Wiechmann. (1975). "How Multinationals View Marketing Standardization." *Harvard Business Review*, (May/June), pp. 38-167.

Chapter 5

Stereotyping, Buyer Familiarity, and Ethnocentrism: A Cross-Cultural Analysis

Joseph B. Chasin
Hartmut H. Holzmuller
Eugene D. Jaffe

SUMMARY. This paper presents the results of a cross-cultural, comparative study of United States and Austrian buyer perceptions of industrial goods made in Eastern Europe. Many COMECON countries possess skilled workers and natural resources which afford them with comparative advantage in the manufacture of a range of consumer and industrial goods. However, in practice, trade with the United States and most Western European countries is limited by administrative trade restrictions. In the event that restrictions are removed, would trade between East and West increase substantially? In order to test the assumption that purchase experience with Eastern goods promotes a more favorable image (or less stereotyping), two studies of industrial goods buyers were completed, one in New York, the other in Vienna. Austrian respondents were selected because their buying experience with Eastern European goods was greater. Results show that despite the differences in trade proportions, stereotyping of Eastern European goods exists in both the United States and Austria.

Extensive research of country-of-origin influence on consumer perception of products and brands has been reported in the litera-

This chapter was first published in the *Journal of International Consumer Marketing*, Vol. 1(2) 1988.

ture. Most studies have used country-of-origin as a single cue, or
information source, upon which respondents evaluated products
(Rierson, 1967; Nagashima, 1970, 1977; Gaedeke, 1972; Darling
and Kraft, 1977; Bannister & Saunders, 1978; Bon & Ollivier,
1979; Halfhill, 1980; Niffenberger, White, & Marmet, 1980; Wang
& Lamb, 1980; Naranya, 1981; Cattin, Jolibert, & Lohnes, 1982;
Kaynak & Cavusgil, 1983; Festervard, Lumpkin, & Lundstrom,
1985). Later research efforts have extended the single design to
include additional cues, such as brand (Seaton & Vogel, 1985; Johansson & Nebenzahl, 1986), price (Johansson & Nebenzahl,
1987), and behavioral factors such as product or brand familiarity
(Johansson, Douglas, & Nonaka, 1985; Johansson, 1986; Johansson & Nebenzahl, 1987), risk perception (Hampton, 1977; Yavas &
Tuncalp, 1985; Lumpkin, Crawford, & Kim, 1985) and consumer
demographics (Wang, 1978; Forgas & O'Driscoll, 1984).

Additional classification typologies include the perception of
products made in developed versus developing countries (White,
1979), geographic area, e.g., Western versus Eastern European
countries (Chasin & Jaffe, 1979, 1987), cross-cultural, i.e., the
way Italian and Dutch consumers perceive products made in third
countries (Morello, 1984) and studies of hybrid products, e.g.,
"American" branded products made in Korea (Johansson & Nebenzahl, 1986). Most of the research cited above has consistently
found that "country-of-origin" effects hold for products in general,
classes of products and specific brands (Bilkey & Nes, 1982).
Moreover, many of these same studies show that country-of-origin
biases consumer perception of products and brands, sometimes resulting in a more favorable image of "home" products. What is
lacking in most of these studies, however, is an explanation of what
determines the stereotype or bias. For example, is the stereotype a
function of source country considerations such as the stage of economic development and political system? Or, is the stereotype related to the respondent's experience or knowledge of products or
particular brands made in the country?

In choosing between products or brands, consumers rely on two
sorts of cues (Olson & Jacoby, 1972), intrinsic (e.g., taste, performance, value) and extrinsic (e.g., price, brand, country-of-origin).[1]
Generally, consumers unfamiliar with a brand will rely more upon

extrinsic cues when making product evaluations. Another indicator of cue utilization is its predictive value (Cox, 1962; Olson & Jacoby, 1972), the degree to which the consumer *believes* a given cue represents a product characteristic. For example, a consumer may use country-of-origin as a proxy for product quality. In this case, the cue PV may be high. One explanation for the high PV in this instance may be owing to a lack of familiarity with the country's products. Where experience or familiarity is limited, the impact of the country-of-origin stereotype may be greater (Johansson, Douglas, & Nonaka, 1985, p. 389).[2]

Some recent research has identified the behavioral dimensions underlying country-image (Erickson, Johannson, & Chao, 1984; Johannson, Douglas, & Nonaka, 1985), but not much has been done to determine whether stereotyping varies by product class or brands (Czepiec & Gottko, 1984). The purpose of the present chapter is to (1) show whether stereotyping differs by product class, (2) whether purchase experience with a country's product class lessens the impact of stereotyping, and (3) whether there is a home-country bias in country-of-origin ratings.

RESEARCH METHODOLOGY

Studies by Chasin and Jaffe (1979, 1987) among samples of American purchasing agents, showed considerable stereotyping of products made in Eastern Europe, particularly the Soviet Union. Whether stereotyping decreased as buyer familiarity with the products increased could not be ascertained owing to the fact that few of the agents had purchasing experience with the analyzed product categories made in Eastern Europe. This lack of experience is indicative of the small volume of trade between the United States and Eastern European countries. To investigate the relationship between familiarity and stereotyping, it is necessary therefore to find a population which has experience with the purchasing of goods made in these countries. Austrian purchasing agents were selected for this purpose.[3] Austria imports 11 percent of her total imports from Eastern Europe as compared to less than 1 percent for the United States. Table 1 shows absolute trade figures for both the United States and Austria and the Eastern European countries studied.

Table 1

SURVEYED EASTERN EUROPEAN COUNTRY EXPORTS TO:

($ Millions)

	USA		AUSTRIA	
	1985	1986	1985	1986
Soviet Union	409	605	912	1,062
Hungary	239	247	414	565
Poland	244	261	232	369

The Survey Form and Respondent Tasks

The questionnaire form used was taken from Chasin and Jaffe (1987), translated into German and back-translated (Douglas & Craig, 1983, p. 187). The population of interest was defined as participants and influencers on the purchasing of industrial goods by the firm. All contacted potential respondents were personally screened and considered eligible for interviewing if they reported purchasing experience in at least one of the six industrial goods categories included in this study. The sample is considered to be a judgmental, non-probability type, yet sufficiently representative of the desired population.

Respondents had to complete the following tasks:

1. For each of the five countries, ratings of the country's industrial goods output on 11 product and marketing attributes using a 9 point visual scale in which the extremes of 9 and 1 were labelled as excellent/high and as poor/low.

   Product Attributes
   Product Reliability, dependability
   Product uniformity, consistency
   Materials quality, workmanship
   Fullness of product lines
   Product reputation, guarantees
   "Overall" rating of industrial goods

Marketing Attributes
Innovative, advanced technology
Field service, technical support
Credit extension, terms
On-time deliveries
Price, value for the money
Supplier contact, ample information

The respondents were told that these attributes represent "whatever they mean to you."

2. For the United States and the Soviet Union, ratings for each of six categories of industrial goods on these same attributes. These categories were selected because they were judged to be more promising in terms of possible trade between the countries.

Industrial Goods Categories
Chemical Products
Electrical Equipment
Farm Machinery and Equipment
Machine Tools
Scientific Precision Equipment
Textiles

The respondents were told that these product categories were defined by whatever products they thought "belonged to them."

3. Identification of the overall three most important and three least important attributes in affecting purchase decisions.
4. Determination of the willingness to consider the purchase of goods from the other countries at lower price levels when the quality of the goods was regarded as equivalent to Austrian made goods.
5. Determination of the willingness to consider the purchase of higher quality level goods from the Soviet Union when priced equivalently to Austrian made goods.
6. Determination of the current purchasing experience in the six product categories of the six countries studied.

Analytic Procedures

A total of 84 questionnaires were found to be usable. To improve comprehension of the response values, the 9 to 1 scale was linearly transformed to a 100 to 0 range. The maximum attribute score possible is 100, the minimum score is 0. Any mean rating over 50 represents above average (favorable) perception of the attribute; under 50, below average. Collectively, the set of attribute means forms a profile or image of a country's industrial goods capabilities.

This study consists of two sets of analyses. One involves measuring the country-of-origin images of the countries involved, including an attempt to determine whether there is an "ethnocentric effect," i.e., whether respondents consistently rate products made in their own country more highly. In this case, both the Austrian and American (Chasin & Jaffe, 1979) samples were analyzed for the presence of this effect. The American sample of 224 respondents was analyzed to determine how American purchasers rated products made in the United States versus those made in Austria. The same procedure was repeated for the Austrian sample. Significant differences between attribute means were calculated using "t" tests, and discriminant analysis was used to determine which attributes discriminate between U.S. and Austrian responses. Factor analyses were made on product dimensions and country image to extract common components.

The second analysis split the Austrian respondents into two groups; those having buying experience with goods made in the U.S.S.R. and those lacking such experience. Two separate product profiles were generated based on these groups and tests for significant difference were run.

FINDINGS

Stereotyping by Product Class

A number of studies have measured country-of-origin effects across product and product class (Nagashima, 1970, 1977; Hampton, 1977; Chasin & Jaffe, 1979). Chasin and Jaffe (1979,1987), e.g., found stereotyping of product classes evidenced by high correlations among product attributes.

In the present study, Austrian and American respondent perceptions of industrial products made in the U.S., Austria, Poland, Hungary and the U.S.S.R. were measured. The data in Table 2 show that the differences in U.S. and Austrian respondent ratings are most significant in the case of Poland, Austria, the U.S.S.R. and

Table 2

MEAN RATINGS OF INDUSTRIAL PRODUCTS MADE IN:

Attributes		USA	POLAND	AUSTRIA	HUNGARY	USSR	JAPAN
Sample:							
1	USA	80.6	45.0	59.9	45.1	47.5	40.6
	AUS	79.2	32.6a	79.2	47.1	45.1	
2	USA	75.5	48.8	62.1	48.1	50.8	40.6
	AUS	73.5	29.9a	79.4a	43.0	41.7a	
3	USA	69.5	49.8	57.5	47.5	47.7	39.9
	AUS	58.9a	56.5b	68.3a	58.3a	54.4	
4	USA	72.2	38.7	53.0	40.0	44.1	35.1
	AUS	68.8a	27.6a	73.5a	42.4	42.7	
5	USA	89.0	38.1	53.9	40.3	55.1	41.7
	AUS	88.6	17.9a	62.3a	30.0a	34.7a	
6	USA	81.7	35.0	50.1	37.0	40.6	36.8
	AUS	62.2a	20.0a	78.1a	30.0b	22.7a	
7	USA	80.0	46.0	59.5	46.3	50.5	40.7
	AUS	76.6	32.1a	77.3a	44.2	41.4a	
8	USA	81.2	41.4	56.7	41.6	43.4	40.0
	AUS	73.7a	27.3a	75.6a	38.5	34.9a	
9	USA	82.1	36.2	49.8	37.4	36.2	37.0
	AUS	65.3a	27.9a	83.8a	40.1	27.3a	
10	USA	83.7	34.4	48.4	36.3	37.3	34.5
	AUS	56.8a	21.3a	78.4a	33.6	31.5	
11	USA	87.8	35.9	51.5	38.7	45.2	39.8
	AUS	77.4a	24.5a	62.8a	32.8b	36.4a	
12	USA	83.1	41.5	57.4	43.4	46.6	39.3
	AUS	75.8b	27.9a	76.0a	40.6	37.7a	

a
  p=.o1
b
  p=.05

n
  USA=202
n
  AUS=77

the U.S. Discriminant analysis confirmed that American and Austrian respondents differ significantly in the ratings of industrial goods made in all five countries, although less so for Hungary and the U.S.S.R. (see Table 3). American respondents consistently rated Polish and Soviet industrial products more favorably than did Austrian buyers. However, the overall ratings given the two Western countries are significantly higher than those given to Socialist countries. From these findings, one may conclude that overall ratings of both the Socialist countries and the U.S. and Austria are stereotyped owing to the high correlations of individual country profiles. Because of this stereotyping it is necessary to determine if the components of country image are the same for all countries. That is, we must extract the number of dimensions underlying the images measured. Country profiles of each country separately were factor analyzed by principal components with varimax rotation. Rotation was stopped when eigenvalues dropped below 1.0.

Table 4 shows the rotated factor scores for the U.S., Poland and Hungary (the U.S.S.R. and Austria were dropped because only one factor emerged). Two factors — explaining about half of the total variance — are identified: "product quality-value" and "operational-service" characteristics. These two factors are nearly identical for all three countries indicating that although the concept of country image is multidimensional, the same dimensions comprise country-of-origin for at least three of the countries studied.

Overall country image gives the least amount of information to the marketer since it cannot tell him whether there is variation between product categories of a given country. Therefore, it is neces-

Table 3

DISCRIMINANT ANALYSIS OF US AND AUSTRIAN RATINGS

OF INDUSTRIAL GOODS MADE IN:

	USA	POL	HUNG	AUS	USSR
Cannonical Correlation	.61	.59	.46	.63	.50
Wilkes Lambda	.62	.65	.79	.60	.75
Chi-Squared	131.94	121.45	65.07	142.24	79.7
Significance	.01	.01	.01	.01	.01
% of "grouped" cases correctly classified	82.4	82.7	73.9	82.8	77.5

Table 4

FACTOR ANALYSES OF COUNTRY ATTRIBUTES

COUNTRY

Factor	USA I	USA II	POLAND I	POLAND II	HUNGARY I	HUNGARY II
Attributes						
Reliability	.82		.86		.87	
Uniformity	.78		.86		.86	
Quality	.82		.84		.83	
Innovativeness	.44		.67	.45	.64	.46
Full lines	.64		.76		.69	.41
Service	.74		.79		.71	.37
Credit/terms	.78		.80		.76	
On-time deliv.	.58		.67	.41	.76	
price/value	.36	.58	.36	.53	.40	.51
product reput.	.53	.56	.62	.56	.67	.45
supplier/info.	.75		.74	.36	.77	
Cumulative Variance:	51.4	54.0	54.6	56.6	54.2	56.4

Factor I = product quality – value

Factor 2 = operational – service

sary to determine what variation, if any, exists across products or between brands. For this purpose, six industrial product categories were selected for analysis among the U.S., Austria and the U.S.S.R. Of the five Socialist countries mentioned previously, the U.S.S.R. was selected because it has the largest manufacturing capacity of industrial goods. Both American and Austrian respondents were asked to evaluate their own industrial products in each of the six categories along with those of the Soviet Union. The results show that in all product categories, both U.S. and Austrian products are rated significantly (p = .01) higher than U.S.S.R. products.[4] Moreover, there is little variability within and between product categories, suggesting a halo effect, or stereotyping.

Looking at individual product attributes, "price" was the only descriptor of country image where the difference between the Austrian and U.S. perception of U.S.S.R. products across all categories had the least variability. This suggests that price may be an important extrinsic cue in a person's decision to consider or purchase a product, in the absence of other cues, such as brand, or when there is a lack of familiarity with the product or brand.

When asked what price they would be willing to pay for goods made in the U.S.S.R. (if equal in quality to equivalent U.S.-made goods), 37 percent of Austrian buyers of U.S.S.R. goods replied the "same price." The figure for nonbuyers of U.S.S.R. goods was 17 percent. Moreover, 54 percent of Austrian nonbuyers would purchase U.S.S.R. goods (of equal quality to equivalent U.S.-made goods) if they were priced from 11 to 25 percent lower than U.S.-made goods. In comparison, 38 percent of buyers would want a price differential of the same amount.

Table 5 also shows that the higher volume of Austrian-Soviet trade compared to U.S.-U.S.S.R. trade is not associated with a more favorable U.S.S.R. country image. On the contrary, Austrian respondent perception of Soviet-made industrial goods is significantly (p = .01) lower than U.S. respondents on all variables except "price" across all six product categories.

Product Purchasing Experience and Country-of-Origin

The possibility that buyer familiarity or level of awareness with a seller's product or brand or of the seller would effect the direction of country-of-origin was raised by Han and Qualls (1985) and Johansson (1986). Two recent studies (Johansson, Douglas, & Nonaka, 1985; Johansson & Nebenzahl, 1986) showed that contrary to intuition, country stereotyping occurs among buyers who are more, rather than less, familiar with a product.

In the present study, 25 percent of the Austrian respondents had some buying experience with one or more of the six product categories made in the U.S.S.R.. The product ratings along the 12 descriptors of this group were tabulated separately. The same procedure was followed for the nonbuyers. A comparison of the product profiles of both groups is given in Table 6. The results show that there are only three significant differences (p = .05) between both groups, relating to only one descriptor ("on-time delivery") on three product categories (chemicals, farm equipment and textiles). These findings show that buyers do not have more positive or negative perceptions of those products than nonbuyers. In the case of goods made in the U.S.S.R., purchase experience is not an explanatory factor of country image.

Table 5

MEAN RATINGS OF PRODUCTS MADE IN THE USSR

Attributes	Sample:	CHEM	ELEC	FARM	TOOLS	SCIEN	TEXT
1	USA	60.4	57.7	52.5	57.1	65.4	51.4
	AUS	46.8a	40.5a	49.4a	48.5a	44.9a	37.7a
2	USA	60.5	57.9	54.2	56.5	63.9	49.6
	AUS	43.6a	37.1a	43.0a	41.7a	42.2a	31.4a
3	USA	52.7	50.1	47.1	49.9	53.4	45.5
	AUS	56.6	52.8	56.8a	54.7	54.2	50.9
4	USA	46.7	45.4	45.1	45.1	50.3	43.9
	AUS	41.1	39.0	41.7	39.4	38.4a	34.1a
5	USA	59.6	55.7	49.4	52.5	65.8	45.7
	AUS	36.4a	32.6a	36.0a	37.1a	38.4a	35.0a
6	USA	47.7	47.5	43.1	46.1	54.4	40.9
	AUS	27.8a	24.2a	29.2a	25.9a	29.2a	22.7a
7	USA	59.5	57.7	51.6	55.2	63.4	49.4
	AUS	42.6a	37.1a	43.0a	42.0a	41.4a	34.1a
8	USA	48.3	46.9	43.5	47.5	54.6	42.0
	AUS	34.7a	30.5a	35.6a	35.8a	36.7a	29.7a
9	USA	43.8	44.5	41.3	44.3	50.3	40.8
	AUS	28.0a	25.8a	30.3a	28.4a	28.8a	23.9a
10	USA	43.6	43.7	43.7	45.3	47.8	41.2
	AUS	33.9a	35.8a	37.1	35.2	34.3a	33.0a
11	USA	52.4	49.2	45.7	48.4	55.8	42.6
	AUS	35.0a	32.0a	36.7a	36.6a	37.7a	29.2a
12	USA	53.3	51.4	47.6	50.8	58.6	45.6
	AUS	40.2a	36.7a	39.6a	40.3a	39.6a	29.9a

a
p=.01

b
p=.05

n
USA=200
n
AUS=66

Table 6

**MEAN RATINGS OF INDUSTRIAL PRODUCTS MADE IN THE USSR
by AUSTRIAN BUYERS and NON-BUYERS**

		CHEM	ELEC	FARM	TOOLS	SCIEN	TEXT
Attributes							
1	Buyers	51.8	40.4	53.6	45.2	42.9	41.1
	Non-Buyers	45.8	41.4	48.3	51.4	46.9	37.2
2	Buyers	43.5	33.3	47.0	40.4	40.4	34.5
	Non-Buyers	45.0	39.4	42.2	43.6	44.4	30.6
3	Buyers	58.3	51.8	60.1	53.0	52.4	48.2
	Non-Buyers	56.7	53.6	56.1	56.1	55.6	53.1
4	Buyers	50.0	45.8	52.4	46.4	44.0	44.0
	Non-Buyers	37.5a	36.4	37.2a	36.7	36.4	30.0a
5	Buyers	36.9	29.2	36.3	33.9	35.7	26.8
	Non-Buyers	37.5	34.1	36.4	39.7	40.6	24.7
6	Buyers	28.6	23.2	33.3	25.6	25.6	26.8
	Non-Buyers	29.2	26.1	28.6	27.5	31.9	21.4
7	Buyers	43.5	33.9	47.0	39.3	38.7	33.9
	Non-Buyers	43.9	38.9	42.2	44.7	43.6	34.7
8	Buyers	39.3	30.4	41.1	34.5	37.5	35.1
	Non-Buyers	37.5	30.8	33.6	37.8	37.5	28.1
9	Buyers	30.4	25.6	36.3	31.0	29.2	30.3
	Non-Buyers	28.6	27.5	28.3	28.9	29.2	21.9
10	Buyers	35.1	24.5	39.9	33.9	32.7	34.5
	Non-Buyers	34.4	37.5	38.9	36.7	35.8	33.1
11	Buyers	33.3	29.8	39.3	36.3	33.9	35.1
	Non-Buyers	37.7	33.1	36.1	38.3	40.3	26.7
12	Buyers	40.4	34.5	42.9	36.9	36.9	32.7
	Non-Buyers	41.4	38.3	35.9	43.1	41.4	29.4

a
$p=.o5$
n= Buyers, 21
Non-buyers, 45

Ethnocentrism and Country-of-Origin

Research (White, 1979; Johansson, Douglas, & Nonaka, 1985)
has shown that country-of-origin stereotypes have an ethnocentric,
or "home-country" bias. Accordingly, domestic-country products
will invariably be perceived as superior or preferable to those made
abroad. Some evidence has found the contrary (Nagashima, 1970;

Halfhill, 1980). Intuitively, one would expect that given sufficient information, purchasing agents—especially those familiar with given products—would be able to differentiate between home-country and foreign-made products on parameters of quality, etc. As U.S. and Austrian respondents were asked to rate domestic products as well as those made abroad, it is possible to show at least three relationships: (1) how U.S. respondents rate domestic products versus how Austrians rate Austrian products, (2) U.S. respondent ratings of domestic products versus U.S. ratings of Austrian-made products and (3) Austrian ratings of U.S. products versus Austrian ratings of Austrian products. For each product category and descriptor, cells a versus d show relationship (1) from the preceding, cells a versus b represent relationship (2), and cells c versus d show relationship (3) (see Table 7).

Relationships (2) and (3) represent the ethnocentric, or home-country bias. Looking at the U.S. data first (relationship 2), we find a consistent ethnocentric bias across all product categories and for all descriptors. In every comparison, U.S.-made products were rated significantly (in most cases, p = .01) higher than Austrian-made products.

The Austrian data show little ethnocentric bias, but rather differentiate between product categories and descriptors. U.S.-made textiles were rated significantly (p = .01) higher than Austrian-made products of the same category on four descriptors, and U.S.-made scientific equipment was rated higher on three descriptors. Austrian farm equipment and textiles were rated higher on six descriptors, tools on five, and chemicals on four descriptors.

Looking across product categories by descriptor, another pattern emerges. The U.S. is stronger on innovativeness, full product lines (product-quality variables), while Austria is stronger on field service, credit, price, and supplier contact (distribution and price variables). Intuitively, these findings make sense as Austrian suppliers may be expected to provide better service than exporters and as apparently believed, at more favorable price/terms.

What can explain the home-country bias of the American respondents? Again, one may list those variables that affect ratings of products made in different countries cited in the literature review.

Table 7

HOW USA, AUSTRIAN RESPONDENTS RATE INDUSTRIAL PRODUCTS MADE IN THE

USA AND AUSTRIA

Attributes		CHEM		ELEC		FARM		TOOLS		SCIENT		TEXT	
		USA	AUS	USA	AUS	USA	AUS	USA	AUS	USA	AUS	USA	AUS
1	USA	82	61	82	63	81	61	81	66	84	66	74	62
	AUS	79	76	79	82	77	82	78	82	83	78	68	78
2	USA	79	60	80	63	80	63	78	66	83	64	73	63
	AUS	77	78	76	81	76	82	75	80	82	77	68	78
3	USA	72	63	72	62	73	58	71	61	75	60	67	60
	AUS	58	67	60	68	60	67	61	67	65	66	59	67
4	USA	73	59	72	61	72	60	71	60	74	63	70	59
	AUS	71	75	72	76	70	73	73	76	73	75	67	76
5	USA	87	57	85	60	81	58	81	61	89	59	73	60
	AUS	87	64	85	69	83	70	80	73	88	70	71	69
6	USA	80	55	79	57	77	57	77	60	81	59	71	56
	AUS	70	76	69	79	65	78	67	80	71	76	63	75
7	USA	80	59	81	63	79	61	78	66	83	64	73	62
	AUS	77	77	78	81	76	80	76	80	82	76	68	78
8	USA	79	61	80	63	78	60	79	63	82	61	71	61
	AUS	74	74	70	75	70	76	70	78	74	74	62	73
9	USA	81	57	79	58	78	57	77	60	80	60	72	56
	AUS	67	77	65	80	63	80	64	80	71	76	62	76
10	USA	78	61	79	61	77	59	79	60	78	58	75	60
	AUS	58	72	59	74	59	72	61	75	60	71	57	72
11	USA	85	58	85	59	81	58	82	59	84	56	77	57
	AUS	86	65	82	73	80	68	78	72	83	67	74	71
12	USA	81	59	81	63	79	61	78	62	83	62	72	66
	AUS	75	74	74	76	71	77	73	73	80	75	66	73

Cell Legend:

	USA	AUS
USA	a	b
AUS	c	d

n=USA, 224
    AUS, 74

However, as only three percent of American purchasing agents had any experience with Austrian-made products compared to 23 percent of Austrians with U.S.-made goods experience, a plausible explanation is that country-of-origin was substituted for product experience.

CONCLUSIONS AND IMPLICATIONS

Four major findings of this study may be summarized as follows:

1. Buyer perception of goods made in Eastern Europe is stereotyped by both Austrian and American respondents. The country-of-origin effect is generalized and not specific to any product category.
2. Following conclusion (1), the United States and Austrian respondents' bias may be more related to personal dogmatism and influenced more by their attitudes toward the political and/ or social systems of the countries (cf. Tongberg, 1973). The bias towards the country is primary, the product evaluation is secondary. In this case, country-of-origin may in fact be an intrinsic cue.
3. The hypothesis that familiarity with a product reduces stereotyping is rejected. American respondents with little or no familiarity with U.S.S.R. products did not employ country-of-origin as a surrogate for product knowledge any more than Austrian respondents, whose familiarity was greater.
4. Ethnocentrism may influence country image where the strength of other cues, such as product attributes, are limited.

Possible marketing strategies for sellers of products made in Eastern Europe are indeed limited owing to the stereotypes found in this study. However, some possibilities exist to reduce the stereotype effect:

1. The most obvious strategy is to mount a public relations campaign on an industry level supported by advertising to point out that some product categories are indeed superior. The problem with this sort of effort is that those having negative stereotypes will not pay much attention. Moreover, unless detente becomes a reality, country image may be difficult to improve.
2. A more interesting and realistic possibility is for Eastern European countries to consider the marketing advantages accruing from joint-ventures with Western partners. Such agreements

made with the Western partner's technology and know-how (and possibly brand name) may improve country image. Knowledge of Renault's technological agreement with Romania for the production of Delta automobiles may improve the Delta's product image. Sufficient examples of cooperative ventures between Western and East European countries exist to provide the framework for additional studies of country image in this respect.

NOTES

1. Johansson (1986, p. 9) suggest conditions under which country-of-origin may be an intrinsic product attribute.
2. A second cue value refers to how confident a consumer is in his or her ability to perceive the cue. In the case of country image studies, the consumer would have to know the country of manufacture to have high confidence.
3. The purchasing involvement by product category and country of the Austrian respondents is shown in the Appendix. For a similar presentation of the American sample, see Chasin and Jaffe, 1979.
4. The ratings of U.S.S.R. product categories are shown in Table 5; those of the U.S. and Austria, in Table 7.

REFERENCES

Bannister, J.P. and Saunders, J.A. (1978). "UK Consumers' Attitudes Towards Imports: The Measurement of National Stereotype Image." *European Journal of Marketing*, Vol. 12, pp. 562-70.
Bilkey, W. and Nes, E. (1982). "Country-of-Origin Effects on Product Evaluations." *Journal of International Business Studies* (Spring/Summer), pp. 89-99.
Bon, J. and Ollivier, A. (1979). "L'Influence de l'Origine d'un Produit sur son Image a l'Etranger." *Revue Francaise du Marketing*, Cahier 77, pp. 101-114.
Czepiec, H. and Gottko, J. (1984). "Import of Consumer Orientations on Perceptions of Hybrid Product Quality." Paper presented at the Academy of International Business Conference, Cleveland, Ohio (October 17-20).
Chasin, J. and Jaffe, E. (1979). "Industrial Buyer Attitudes Toward Goods Made in Eastern Europe." *Columbia Journal of World Business*, 14 (Summer), pp. 74-81.
———(1987). "Industrial Buyer Attitudes Toward Goods Made in Eastern Europe: An Update." *European Management Journal*, 5:3.
Cattin, P., Jolibert, A. and Lohnes, C. (1982). "Cross-Cultural Study of 'Made-In' Concepts." *Journal of International Business Studies*, (Winter), pp. 131-41.

Cox, D. (1962). *Risk Taking and Information Handling in Consumer Behavior.* (Cambridge, MA.: Harvard University Press.

Darling, J. and Kraft, F. (1977). "A Comparative Profile of Products and Associated Marketing Practices of Selected European and Non-European Countries." *European Journal of Marketing,* 11:2, pp. 519-31.

Douglas, S. and Craig, C. (1983). *International Marketing Research.* New York: Prentice-Hall, 1983.

Erickson, G., Johannson, J. and Chao, F. (1984). "Image Variables in Multi-Attribute Product Evaluations." *Journal of Consumer Research,* 11 (September), pp. 694-99.

Festervard, T., Lumpkin, J. and Lundstrom, W. (1985). "Consumers' Perceptions of Imports: An Update." *Akron Business and Economic Review,* 16:1, pp. 31-6.

Forgas, J. and O'Driscoll, M. (1984). "Cross-Cultural and Demographic Differences in the Perception of Nations." *Journal of Cross-Cultural Psychology,* 15:2 (June), pp. 199-222.

Gaedeke, R. (1972). "Consumer Attitudes Towards Products 'Made In' Developing Countries." *Journal of Retailing,* 49 (Summer), pp. 13-24.

Halfhill, D. (1980). "Multinational Marketing Strategy: Implications of Attitudes Toward Country of Origin." *Management International Review,* 20:4, pp. 26-30.

Hampton, G. (1977). "Perceived Risks in Buying Products Made Abroad by American Firms." *Baylor Business Studies* (October), pp. 53-64.

Han, C. and Qualls, W. (1985). "Country of Origin Effects and Its Impact Upon Consumers' Perception of Quality," in *Historic Perspective in Consumer Research: National and International Perspective,* Association for Consumer Research.

Johannson, J. (1986). "Deducing the Determinants and Effects of 'Made In' Labels." Unpublished manuscript.

_____, S. Douglas and Nonaka, I. (1985). "Assessing the Impact of Country-of-Origin on Product Evaluations: A New Methodological Perspective." *Journal of Marketing Research,* 22 (November), pp. 388-96.

_____ and Nebenzahl, I. (1986). "Multinational Production: Effect on Brand Value." *Journal of International Business Studies,* Fall, pp. 101-126.

_____(1987). "Country-of-Origin, Social Norms, and Behavioral Intentions," in S. Cavusgil (ed.), *Advances in International Marketing,* 2 (June), pp. 65-79.

Kaynak, E. and Cavusgil, S. (1983). "Consumer Attitudes Towards Products of Foreign Origin: Do They Vary Across Product Classes?" *International Journal of Advertising,* 2, pp. 147-57.

Lumpkin, J., Crawford, J. and Kim, C. (1985). "Perceived Risk as a Factor in Buying Foreign Clothes." *International Journal of Advertising,* 4, pp. 157-71.

Morello, G. (1984). "The 'Made In' Issue: A Comparative Research on the Image of Domestic and Foreign Products." *European Research* (June), pp. 5-21.

Nagashima, A. (1970). "A Comparison of U.S. and Japanese Attitudes Toward Foreign Products." *Journal of Marketing,* 34 (June), pp. 68-74.

_____(1977). "A Comparative 'Made In' Product Image Survey Among Japanese Businessmen." *Journal of Marketing*, 41 (July), pp. 95-100.

Naranya, C. (1981). "Aggregate Images of American and Japanese Products: Implications on International Marketing." *Columbia Journal of World Business* (Summer), pp. 31-5.

Niffenberger, P., White, J. and Marmet, G. (1980). "How British Retail Managers View French and American Products." *European Journal of Marketing*, 14(8), pp. 493-498.

Olson, J. and Jacoby, J. (1972). "Cue Utilization in the Quality Perception Process," in M. Venkatesan (ed.), *Proceedings of the Third Annual Conference of the Association for Consumer Research*, pp. 167-79.

Rierson, C. (1967). "Attitude Changes Toward Foreign Products." *Journal of Marketing Research*, 4 (November), pp. 385-7.

Seaton, B. and Vogel, R. (1985)."Brand, Price and Country of Manufacture As Factors in the Perception of Product Quality." Paper presented at the Academy of International Business Annual Meeting, New York City (October 17-20).

Tongberg, R. (1973). "An Empirical Study of the Relationships Between Dogmatism and Attitudes Toward Foreign Products." *Proceedings of the American Marketing Association*, pp. 87-91.

White, P. (1979). "Attitudes of U.S. Purchasing Managers Toward Industrial Products Manufactured in Selected Western European Nations." *Journal of International Business Studies* (Spring-Summer), pp. 81-90.

Wang, C. (1978). "The Effect of Foreign Economic, Political and Cultural Environment on Consumers' Willingness to Buy Foreign Products." Unpublished Ph.D. dissertation, Texas A & M University.

_____ and Lamb, C. (1980). "Foreign Environmental Factors Influencing American Consumers' Predispositions Toward European Products." *Journal of the Academy of Marketing Science* (Fall), pp. 345-356.

Yavas, V. and Tuncalp, S. (1985). "Saudi Arabia: Perceived Risk in Buying 'Made-in-Germany' Label." *Management International Review*, 25:4, pp. 58-65.

APPENDIX

Attributes given in Tables 2, 5, 6 and 7 are listed in order of importance to the purchase decision as follows:

1. Reliability/dependability
2. Materials quality/workmanship
3. Price value for the money
4. On-time delivery of quantity ordered
5. Innovativeness/advanced technology
6. Field service, technical support
7. Uniformity/consistency
8. Product reputation, guarantees
9. Supplier contact, ample information
10. Credit extension/terms
11. Full product line available
12. Overall rating

Significant Differences to TABLE 7

Attributes	CHEM	ELEC	FARM	TOLLS	SCIEN	TEXT
1	a=.01	a=.01	a=.01	a=.01	a=.01	a=.01
						d=.01
2	a=.01	a=.01	a=.01	a=.01	a=.01	a=.01
						d=.01
3	a=.01	a=.01	a=.01	a=.01	a=.01	a=.05
	d=.01	d=.01	d=.05	d=.05		d=.01
4	a=.05	a=.01	a=.01	a=.01	a=.01	a=.01
						d=.01
5	a=.05	a=.01	a=.01	a=.01	a=.01	a=.01
	d=.01	d=.01	d=.05	d=.05	d=.01	
6	a=.01	a=.01	a=.01	a=.01	a=.01	a=.01
	d=.05	d=.01	d=.01			d=.01
	a=.01	a=.01	a=.01	a=.01	a=.01	a=.01
7	a=.01	a=.01	a=.01	a=.01	a=.01	a=.01
					d=.05	d=.01

Significant Differences to TABLE 7 (continued)

8	a=.01	a=.01	a=.01 d=.05	a=.01 d=.01	a=.01	a=.01 d=.05
9	a=.01 d=.01	a=.01	a=.01 d=.05	a=.01 d=.01	a=.01	a=.01 d=.01
10	a=.01 d=.01	a=.01 d=.01	a=.01 d=.01	a=.01 d=.01	a=.01 d=.01	a=.01 d=.01
11	a=.01 d=.01	a=.01 d=.01	a=.01 d=.01	a=.01 d=.05	a=.01 d=.01	a=.01
12	a=.01	a=.01	a=.01 d=.05	a=.01	a=.01	a=.01 d=.05

```
a = cells a - b
d = cells c - d
```

Current Purchasing Involvement of Austrian Respondents

	Ever Buy	USA	POLAND	HUNGARY	USSR
Chemicals	44%	16%	8%	3%	4%
Electrical Equip.	39	12	9	10	16
Farm Machinery	35	4	4	3	23
Machine Tools	33	20	12	14	18
Scientific Equipment	31	18	14	10	12
Textiles	27	15	15	14	12

Note: Percentages are based on multiple responses. The first line is read as follows: 44% of the Austrian respondents bought chemical products in any of the surveyed countries; 16% bought chemical products in the U.S.; 8% in Poland; 3% in Hungary; 4% in the U.S.S.R., and so on.

SECTION III:
CROSS-NATIONAL MARKETING PLANNING AND STRATEGY DEVELOPMENT

The globalization of business has been accompanied by an expansion of corporate facilities in foreign markets. The chapter by Leontiades considers, first, the identification of new locations for such international expansion. Since the location of new facilities is itself a major decision, location analysis is subsequently used to gain insight into global competitor strategy.

The problem of analyzing and interpreting international locations has received relatively little attention in literature. The few articles available consider new site possibilities on a country by country basis; each country is considered as an individual unit. The objective is to select the best national site. Whatever the usefulness of this approach for the firm just embarking on international expansion, it has scant relevance to the global firm. For these companies, the problem is not one of interpreting national sites individually. Such firms typically have a network of existing plants and other facilities abroad. Analysis has to relate the firm's network of existing sites to multiple new site possibilities. In considering the latter, note must be taken of international links which may make national boundaries less relevant than regional groupings such as the European Community.

A simple technique using portfolio analysis is adapted from the strategic planning literature and applied to the task of site location for the global firm. An expansion of this technique is used to interpret the global and regional distribution of competitor facilities. The international network of locations is mapped against the firm's own international network. The overview thus provided of the competitor site locations can yield valuable information on changes in competitor global strategy and areas of competitor vulnerability as well as indications of particular strengths and competence.

A sample of 50 multinational corporations (MNCs) with over 550 subsidiaries was taken by Keegan, Still, and Hill to investigate the transfer of marketing skills and products between developed and less-developed countries. Past studies indicate that many MNCs standardize their approach because of cost savings, economies of scale, mobile consumers, strong U.S. images, and to capitalize upon consumer similarities worldwide. However, some MNCs adapt their products when marketed to Lesser-Developed Countries (LDCs) based on consumer tastes, purchasing patterns, and country guidelines and rules. Also, product transfers have been found to be related to the degree of market similarity or target market similarities between the nations.

The chapter empirically presents the findings of a study of product and promotion theme transfers and adaptations between the U.S./U.K. and (LDCs). To this end, it investigates four main hypotheses concerning the absorption level of modern consumer products in LDCs, the adaptation level of transplanted products for culturally-diverse LDC consumers, the adaptation level of promotional themes in LDCs, and the interdependence between product and promotion themes in LDCs. The study resulted in three important findings: (1) economic and cultural gaps do not deter MNCs from transferring modern consumer products to LDCs; (2) most MNCs substantially adapt most modern products before marketing them in LDCs; and (3) although many modern themes are transferred into LDCs without substantial change, results suggest interdependence between marketing adaptation and standardization decisions.

It is pointed out by William C. Moncrief that selling has been perceived as a unidimensional concept by many academicians, students, and practitioners. In reality, sales jobs may differ considerably based on the set of activities that are typically performed. Empirical evidence from the U.S. has shown that there is an extensive list of sales activities performed by industrial salespeople. The focus of this chapter is the examination of sales activities in an international setting. Specifically, 90 companies in Germany and Denmark were questioned concerning their sales forces. The results were then compared to 53 U.S. companies which have been described in a previous study.

A list of 400 companies was chosen, from both Germany and Denmark, to be included in the study. All companies were drawn from SIC codes 20-39 which is classified as manufacturing. The questionnaires were mailed to the companies in their native languages, and 57 from Denmark and 36 from Germany responded.

The results of the study indicated a number of activities that are frequently performed by almost all salespeople; these included closing a sale, monitoring the competition, overcoming objections, and providing feedback to customers and management. There were other activities that were very infrequently performed, such as providing maintenance, making deliveries, stocking shelves, and installing equipment.

Further, it was found that German responses were much more similar to those from the U.S. than were those from the Danish companies. There were also a number of activities that the Germans performed more frequently than their U.S. counterparts, such as setting up point of purchase, training, work from a bid, and work with distributors. The U.S. salespeople travelled much more frequently than their European counterparts. In addition, U.S. salesforces prospect more heavily, work with orders more frequently, and conduct inventory more often. Almost all activities were performed less frequently by the Danes than by either the German or the U.S. salespeople. The Danes were much less likely to travel, entertain, or prospect.

The results of the study indicate that there are clear differences in which, and how frequently, sales activities are performed. The differences are not European versus U.S. The U.S. and German responses were much more similar than were the German versus Dane responses. Clearly there needs to be much more research on sales activity differences in an international setting.

The study by Crawford and Lamb confirms that the source of the product is important to the buying decision. Some countries are more preferred than others. It is evident that factors within the country impact the buyer. The degree of political freedom, the level of economic development, and the culture to which the country belongs each appear to contribute to the buyer's portrait of a particular country as a purchasing source. Stereotypical behavior is to be expected in industrial buying situations. There is a strong preference for dealing with the developed countries as opposed to the developing ones. There is an equally strong preference for those countries of the same cultural heritage (European) although the Japanese have apparently overcome this barrier for many of their products.

These findings suggest that manufacturers in the developing world have an uphill battle before them in trying to gain access to the U.S. market for industrial products. There is no strong latent support for them as "deserving" sources of supply. Indeed, given the choice with other things being equal, the industrial buyer in the U.S. is more than likely to opt for products from the developed world.

Over the last two decades there has been an intense debate in the business literature about whether or not it would be profitable to standardize marketing in general and advertising in particular across borders. The success of companies like Coca Cola, McDonalds, IKEA, Benetton, etc., has certainly contributed to the increased interest in a standardized approach to international marketing. At the same time the increased interest in cross-cultural research has provided a more detailed picture of the differences and similarities between cultures. Furthermore, 1992 and the coming of the European economic integration and its large single market with multiple cultures has made the issue even more interesting. Very few companies, however, have adopted a completely standardized approach, despite the obvious cost advantages available.

Wells has presented some valuable ways to look at different cultures, which helps explain why the completely standardized approach to advertising management is not the most predominant approach. Wells discusses cultures in terms of high- and low-context cultures. Examples of the high-context cultures are the Asian cultures like Japan and China as well as the Arab culture. Examples of the low-context cultures are the German, the Scandinavian, and the North American cultures. In a high-context culture the meaning of the message cannot be understood if it is isolated from the context in which it occurs. The context can be the people who use the product, the way they talk and dress, the scenery in the commercial.

Applied to the field of advertising it is logical to expect that people from a high-context culture will be able to understand nonverbal communication in a different way than people from a low-context culture, i.e., the former would be able to get more information from a nonverbal commercial rich in cues. To test whether this was true or not Rita Martenson tested six European commercials on five different cultural groups of which one was a mixture of cultures. Results clearly confirmed Wells' observations that high-context cultures (here Asians) perceived nonverbal advertising to be much more informative than low-context cultures (here Swedes). The findings in this exploratory study are so clear as well as important for the practitioner that they deserve additional attention in the future, particularly to provide a deeper understanding of the reasons for these perceptual differences between cultures.

Chapter 6

Global Location Strategy

James C. Leontiades

SUMMARY. The essence of global strategy is the worldwide mobilization of the firm's resources behind global objectives. Global companies see national markets as part of a single world market. This perception fundamentally affects their strategy, including questions of geographic location, i.e., where to locate the firm's plants and other facilities.

In general, methods for evaluating geographic location have not received a great deal of attention in the literature. Those that have been forwarded focus on an individualistic country-by-country evaluation of potential sites which is at odds with the more integrative view of world markets currently adopted by global companies.

This article applies and adapts portfolio screening as developed in the corporate strategy literature to the special problem of international site location. It provides a simple yet effective method for viewing the global geographic positioning of the firm relative to world markets.

Secondly, geographic analysis is further developed as a tool for identifying and interpreting global competitive strategy.

A key part of any global marketing strategy concerns the geographic location of the firm's plants and facilities. To an extent greater than is sometimes realized, the globalization of business has progressed through the ability of companies to establish subsidiaries and other operating units within foreign markets. This is certainly true of the post-World War II expansion of American firms. European companies, at one time constrained from locating abroad due

---

This chapter was first published in the *Journal of Global Marketing*, Vol. 1(4), Summer 1988.

to a shortage of foreign exchange, have for many years now embarked on an aggressive program of expansion through foreign direct investment. Until recently, the Japanese were the major exceptions to this trend, preferring to base their facilities within Japan, reaching foreign markets through exports. They are now the growth leaders in establishing facilities in foreign markets, not only for manufacturing plants but also with reference to banks and other service industries.

Yet the problem of analyzing and interpreting potential site locations on an international scale has received surprisingly scant attention. In particular, there has been little practical guidance in the literature regarding the first subject addressed in this article, location decisions faced by management within firms pursuing a global strategy. The distinguishing feature of such strategies is that they take a wholistic view of the world, mobilising the firm's various resources and facilities behind global objectives.

The global firm is not so much interested in "country location" as it is in the global distribution of its worldwide system of plants, offices and other facilities. Geographic location is but one aspect, though a critical one, of the firm's strategy for positioning itself in the global marketplace relative to its customers and competitors.

Historically, multinational firms have established their foreign facilities in foreign markets as a means of gaining greater access to customers. Location within the target market may be viewed as part of the firm's overall international marketing strategy, since the establishment of locally based facilities within the target market may and very likely will influence tariffs and other entry barriers, the firm's cost structure and through that its pricing policies, delivery times, even its national image in that country as well as its own integral management attitudes.

Conceptually the solution is simple. The company's new facility (whether it is a plant, office or research center) should be located in that part of the world which maximizes its contribution to the firm. Since most global companies will already have existing plants and operations in other parts of the world, the location of the new plant should be the one which maximizes contribution to the firm's existing international network of facilities. In principle this contribution can be defined in financial terms as the net increase in revenue arising from the establishment of the new facility, expressed as a proportion of the resources invested in it.

Putting this prescription into effect raises some practical problems. Financial analysis, while useful in *evaluating* the various national site possibilities, once the firm's strategy for making use of those sites has been formulated, does little to help management *identify* the major strategic options.

Also, it has come to be increasingly recognised that financial analysis may incorporate hidden or unrealistic assumptions. For example, return on investment (ROI) estimates of new facilities often assume without saying so that each national operation is a self-contained unit. This is convenient but, as already noted, increasingly unrealistic as regards global companies which operate their various plants and facilities as part of a globally or regionally integrated network. The contribution of the new facility is not independent of the firm's existing network of plants and their geographic distribution.

The more immediate problem with the financial evaluation method is the sheer expense of making financial estimates for each possible national site candidate. In his research on the foreign investment decision process in major multinationals, Yair Aharoni (1966) found that "even the most cursory investigation of each of more than 150 countries in the world is practically impossible."[1]

The difficulties of any in-depth detailed search, financial or otherwise, has meant that many firms arrive at location decisions with little or no systematic search. Perhaps the most effective and widely used method is "try it and see." By that we refer to the general introduction of firms to most countries through exporting.

In their research on companies which have established facilities abroad, Johanson and Vahlne (1977) show that they have typically begun their operations in a particular foreign country through exports. This involves minimal risk of company resources and, perhaps for that reason, is also frequently characterized (e.g., Simmonds and Smith, 1968) by little in the way of systematic search and evaluation of national site possibilities. Investment in foreign facilities tends to come later, after the firm has already gained a certain amount of knowledge and experience about a foreign market through exporting. However, in a fast-changing economic climate this "try it and see" approach leaves much to be desired. Increasingly, firms are leaping into new markets with little or no prior export experience. Furthermore, even with well-established export bases in all potential candidate countries, there will be occasions when a new facility will so change the firm's prospects in a particular country (or countries) that past experience based on exporting is of little relevance.

For these reasons many firms have felt the need to engage in a systematic search for new plant locations which requires some form of screening. The aim of screening is to quickly and cheaply reduce the number of national sites to be investigated to a very small number, usually on the basis of desk research. Once this is done, these countries can be subjected to a much more detailed investigation—involving on-site inspection, the development of a strategy suited to that site, and finally a financial projection of likely returns.

TRADITIONAL SCREENING METHODS

The use of screening techniques has been recommended by a number of researchers investigating the procedures companies use to identify new national locations. Goodnow (1985), based on his research with some 40 multinational firms, recommends the use of a "screening devise to delimit the countries for detailed examination."[2] To fill this need, with special reference to the mode of entering a foreign market, he recommends a computerized screening system based on an extensive list of screening criteria, including national population, per capita gross national product, currency reserves, etc.

Wind and Douglas (1972) recommended a two-stage screening process aimed at segmenting international market opportunities. An initial screen is suggested to identify those countries "which on the basis of national market characteristics, legal and political constraints provide potentially attractive market opportunities."[3] Further screening is used to group the various countries according to specific customer characteristics.

In an extensive research project on American multinational companies, Robert Stobough (1969) found that the great majority continued to use a crude form of ROI analysis to identify potential location sites. However, the 20% of his sample representing the more sophisticated investors used a rating scale method, analogous to that shown in Figure 1. The general approach for developing and applying such rating scale screening procedures is as follows:

1. Screening criteria are chosen which are considered to be indicative (correlated with) the potential of a country as a national location. "Potential" may refer to profitability, growth, risk, etc., depending on the firm's own priorities and objectives.
2. Each country is rated according to its performance on each of these criteria, usually on a numerical scale from one to ten, e.g., if high per capita gross national product is considered favourable, countries with a high per capital GNP would be rated towards the top of the scale.
3. A numerical weight, usually calibrated from one to ten or one to five, is applied against each criteria rating, to reflect its overall importance.[4]
4. The weighted ratings are calculated for each country. Those with the highest score are selected for more intensive examination, usually involving on the spot examination and a projection of risk and financial returns.

The general procedure is by no means specific to international site location. Medical screening is widely used to identify high risk medical conditions. New product ideas are screened to select the most promising possibilities. But actually applying the rating scale approach to facilitate international site location reveals a number of pitfalls.

As part of their training at the Manchester Business School, graduate students work closely with companies planning international expansion. The author had the opportunity to work with over 90 such companies. About half of these involved some form of screening for international site location. The following specific problem areas in applying the screening method described above were identified.

FIGURE 1
Rating Scale for Screening National Environments

SCREENING CRITERIA	National Rating (1-10)	X Weight (1-10)	= Combined Score
Political stability	_____	_____	_____
Government attitude to foreign companies	_____	_____	_____
Repatriation of capital	_____	_____	_____
Repatriation of earnings	_____	_____	_____
Investment incentives	_____	_____	_____
Tariff protection	_____	_____	_____
Ownership restrictions	_____	_____	_____
Controls on foreign managers	_____	_____	_____
Taxation provisions	_____	_____	_____
Exchange rate stability	_____	_____	_____
Per capita gross national product	_____	_____	_____
Gross national product	_____	_____	_____
Prospect for economic growth	_____	_____	_____
Rate of inflation	_____	_____	_____
Size of product market	_____	_____	_____
Product market growth rate	_____	_____	_____
Industry capacity utilisation	_____	_____	_____
Industry legislation	_____	_____	_____
Distribution system	_____	_____	_____
Competitor concentration	_____	_____	_____
Buyer concentration	_____	_____	_____
Industrial relations	_____	_____	_____
Availability of necessary supplies	_____	_____	_____
Industrial standards	_____	_____	_____
Labour costs	_____	_____	_____
Raw material costs	_____	_____	_____
TOTAL COMBINED SCORE	. . . .		_____

1. Neglect of Regional/Global, Political, and Other Linkages

Since each country is rated and assessed individually, there is no provision for identifying linkages and relationships between countries which may be relevant. For example, it may be optimal to locate a plant in one of the countries of the European Community even though individually it receives a low rating scale score if, from there, the product can be shipped tariff free to other European countries with superior market opportunities. Hence the proliferation of plants in Ireland shipping their products tariff free to France, the United Kingdom, West Germany, and other members of the Community. Analogous cross-national commonalities in industrial standards, legislation, etc., on a regional or global basis, are increasingly to be found and may have an important bearing on location decisions.

2. Weakness in Identifying Regional/Global Strategic Possibilities

The country-by-country evaluation of the present approach to country screening may overlook regional and global strategic considerations in the distribution of the firm's overall network of facilities. In an increasing number of global industries, particularly those in the high technology areas, long-term growth and even survival require that the firm is able to directly compete in certain key national market locations, even though these may not be considered optimal when considered strictly on their own merits (Hout, Porter, & Rudden, 1982). A screening method which permits the analyst an overview of global demand and locational possibilities is required in such cases.

3. Failure to Take Sufficient Account of Firms' Ability to Compete

Traditional screening methods are frequently biased toward interpreting market potential in terms of national market "attractiveness." There is typically a heavy emphasis on criteria such as total gross national product, per capita GNP, economic growth, size of product/market, and political climate and similar criteria which bias the result toward the selection of the larger, faster growing national markets considered "attractive" in terms of overall demand for that industry. [See Stobough (1969); also Wind and Douglas (1972) reference (cited previously) to "potentially attractive market opportunities."]

Yet it is observable that many firms do quite well in smaller, less prosperous national markets while some companies who actually establish operations in the larger, more prosperous countries have been known to fail. No matter how attractive and generally favorable the economic and political environment offered by a particular country, it is of little avail if the company in question is not able to compete there successfully. Traditional screening methods, relying as they do on a single rating scale, tend to confuse two quite separate and distinct sets of national characteristics: those which refer to the general attractiveness of a particular national market and those which refer to the ability of a new foreign company to compete there successfully.

Portfolio Screening

The portfolio concept differs from the above method in that it views the firm's national site options as part of a broader strategy. Figure 2 illustrates a very simple example as applied by the Cadbury-Schweppes company in the mid-1970s to review the geographic distribution of the world market for chocolate products. Figure 2 reveals at a glance the virtual absence of the firm from some of the world's major national markets. It should also be noted (but is not indicated in Figure 2) that areas of high market share coincide with the firm's plant locations. In an increasingly global market for its products, could the company afford not to establish a stronger presence in these countries? The answer had more to do with interpreting Cadbury-Schweppes' future position in world markets considered collectively, as a portfolio of investment possibilities, than an evaluation of national markets each considered in isolation. Shortly after this review, Cadbury-Schweppes switched the focus of its global marketing initiatives to North America,

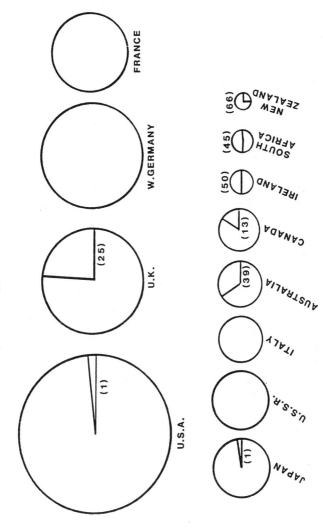

FIGURE 2

Cadbury-Schweppes Share of
World Markets for Chocolate Confectionery - 1976

(Cadbury-Schweppes Share in Brackets)

FRANCE

W.GERMANY

(25) U.K.

(1) U.S.A.

(66) NEW ZEALAND

(45) SOUTH AFRICA

(50) IRELAND

(13) CANADA

(39) AUSTRALIA

ITALY

U.S.S.R.

(1) JAPAN

Source : Cadbury-Schweppes

107

where it quickly established its own production and distribution facilities in the United States through the purchase of the Peter Paul confectionery company. This was followed by a 30% stake in the Dr. Pepper soft drinks company. Export operations in Europe were also significantly strengthened. Both moves were part of a broader international strategy which shifted the company's orientation away from its historic geographic focus on the British domestic market and Commonwealth countries.

The method described above has the virtue of simplicity and it can be effective in providing a global perspective, something traditional screening does not do. However, the very important matter of the firms competitive capability in prospective new markets is still missing. Figure 3 introduces this competitive aspect through the adaptation of a portfolio technique used by the Shell company (Robinson, Hichens, & Wade, 1978) to screen for new business opportunities. This technique is adapted here to the particular requirements of geographic analysis for identifying new plant sites. In subsequent sections in this chapter this method is further developed to take account of regional linkages between different national locations and to position the firm relative to global competitors.

Figure 3 uses two rating scales to assess different national locations in terms of both attractiveness and the firm's ability to compete there. The national attractiveness rating of each national location is based on the more traditional screening criteria indicative of the political and economic climate, including such variables as total size of the product market (or markets), GNP, national economic growth as well as market growth rates, per capita income levels, political stability, exchange rate volatility and analogous variables, the precise selection depending on the strategy, objectives and situation of the firm carrying out the screening.

What constitutes "attractiveness" with reference to national location may therefore vary from one company to another. However, there is considerable agreement among researchers (Goodnow, 1985; Wind and Douglas, 1972; Stobough, 1969) that both economic and political/institutional criteria are important. Examples of these are indicated in Figures 1 and 3.

FIGURE 3

Portfolio Screening of
National Location Opportunities

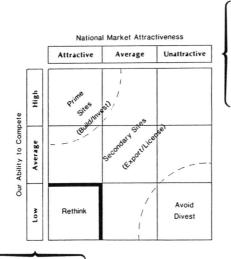

ATTRACTIVENESS

• Political Stability
• Repatriation of Capital and Income
• Exchange Rate Stability
• Total Gross National Product
• Per Capita Gross National Product
• Prospects for Economic Growth
• Size of Product-Market
• Growth of Product-Market
• Investment Incentives
• Industrial Relations

ABILITY TO COMPETE

• Government Attitude to Foreign Firms
• Capacity Utilization
• Competitor Technology
• Competitor Concentration
• Competitor Market Power
• Availability of Distribution Channnels
• Adverse Legislation and Regulations
• Buyer Concentration
• Wage and Raw Material Costs
• Availability of Supplies

Note : The national market may be defined as the national market for a given industry or, where that is too broad, as the national market for a specific product (the national product-market).

Assessing Ability to Compete

Since traditional screening methods for national location stress "attractiveness," the above criteria will appear familiar. The following measures aimed at assessing national markets from the standpoint of the firm's ability to compete are either omitted altogether from traditional screening methods or lumped in with the attractiveness criteria. We begin by identifying four general categories which each company will want to consider in searching for the specific criteria of ability to compete that are most representative of its particular situation. In essence the objective here is to ascertain entry barriers from the perspective of a foreign company.

Government Attitude Toward New Foreign Entrants

Screening criteria in this category have reference to the government's attitude toward foreign firms newly entering the country in question. A country may have a generally favorable political climate in terms of government stability, industry legislation, and regulations governing the repatriation of capital and income and still be unwelcoming to new foreign companies and/or particular companies entering specific industries, e.g., telecommunications and defence industries.

Each company will have its own priorities and interests which will dictate the specific measures most appropriate for its situation, but examples of those which can be used to indicate the government's attitude toward new foreign entrants include:

1. Measures of foreign direct investment flows, both incoming and outgoing.
2. Industry regulations and standards which favor domestic companies.
3. Legislation which restricts the transfer of foreign managers, technicians, technology or components.

Fortunately, information of a political nature that would have one day been extremely difficult to gather on an international scale is now becoming widely available through the development of government agencies and private sources, and in particular specialised news services and private publication services such as Business International.

Likely Competitor Response
to New Foreign Entry

How likely are firms already operating in this market to respond adversely against a new foreign company? The rate of capacity utilization in the industry within the country in question provides a useful indicator. If the firms in the territory are already operating at near full capacity they will have limited resources (and motivation) to divert against a new competitor. Particularly if the market in question is also growing rapidly, they will feel less threatened, when operating at high levels of capacity utilization, than in a situation where plant is already underutilized and customers are hard to find.

The degree of industry concentration is another possible screening criterion within this overall category. In highly fragmented industries the cohesiveness and industrial organization required to mount a concerted response against new competition is generally less than in highly concentrated industries dominated by a few large firms (Porter, 1984). Estimates of buyer concentration can similarly prove useful, particularly if there is an oligopsony/oligopoly situation in the country, linking a few buyers closely to a small number of sellers.

Competitive Strength of Firms
Already in the Market

It is important to assess not only the probability of local competitor reaction against new market entry but also the likely effectiveness of such response. Clearly, the technological capability of competitors already operating within the territory in question will be important in those industries where technology is a major competitive variable, particularly if the new entrant is in possession of a technology not presently to be found there.

"Market power" refers to the ability of local competitors operating within the region or territory being screened to influence other firms or agencies in a way which may adversely affect the new entrant's possibilities of success. Such power cannot be directly measured but can often be ascertained from external evidence, such as ownership or managerial links (e.g., cross-membership on boards of directors) between upstream suppliers and potential competitors or between these competitors and downstream outlets.

Availability of Supplies and Infrastructure

Ability to compete is also likely to depend on the availability of certain supplies and infrastructure (Farmer, 1981). The examples cited in Figure 3 under this category are "availability of supplies," "wage and raw material costs" and "availability of distribution channels."

Plotting the position of each country on a matrix such as that in Figure 3, according to the results of *both* sets of screening criteria, enables management to interpret the distribution of national site possibilities in terms of the attractiveness of the market as well as the firm's ability to compete there. Those locations which rate high in terms of both (upper left hand corner of Figure 3) represent the prime sites and clear candidates for closer consideration. However, it should also be noted that certain of the secondary sites may represent a better "fit" with reference to the firm's overall strategy and the geopolitical considerations mentioned above. A better view of where and how the new facility may fit in with the firm's existing plants may be gained by indicating on the matrix of those countries which are already the sites of existing company facilities.

Questions can be raised regarding the geographical proximity and concentration of the firm's present locations and how they relate to any proposed new site. The accessibility and possibility of product transfer between the new location and existing locations in other countries can also be considered. Of particular importance will be those countries classified in the lower left hand corner of Figure 3, countries representing attractive markets but where the firm is for one reason or another poorly placed to compete. Can anything be done to improve competitiveness in these areas? Should the firm consider divestment or reduction of its commitment in certain countries, i.e., right side of Figure 3 and particularly the lower right hand corner?

Further insight into such questions may be gained by plotting the location of competitor facilities along with the firm's own global network as in Figure 4. Having classified the various national sites according to its own screening criteria into the various "boxes" on the matrix, it is a simple matter to indicate which countries already provide sites for its own international facilities and those of its competitor or competitors.

In Figure 4, Brazil, China and Australia represent the prime sites which emerge from the screening process as possible new national locations (though the firm will also want to consider the possibility of further expansion in existing locations). It is also evident from Figure 4 that the company in question is poorly placed to compete in the U.S.A., West Germany, and Mexico even though its competitor already has established itself in two of these countries. But this initial perception can prove deceptive, since there are also a number of possible regional linkages which have to be considered. In Figure 4 the various national sites being reviewed are coded to indicate their regional trade group affiliation. The company carrying out the analysis should consider that its existing plants in the United Kingdom, France, Ireland, Italy, and Greece already provide access to the West German and other European Community markets. In addition, regional trade preferences between the European Community and the European Free Trade Area open up other possibilities which can easily be hidden in the more traditional approach. The lack of facilities by the company carrying out the analysis in any of the countries which are members of the Latin American Integration Association is worth noting, particularly in evaluating Brazil as a potential site.

The relevant regional groupings to be considered are not necessarily confined to trade groups. In an increasing number of cases various regional legal and product standards associated with particular industries are a vital element of competitive strategy and location decisions. During the 1960s, the strategy of the television producers turned about the division of the world's markets into three regions using different technical television standards, PAL, SECAM, and NTSC. These were probably more important than any national or regional barriers in their impact on corporate strategy for this industry.

FIGURE 4

Classification of Potential and Existing Plant Sites

National Market Attractiveness

		Attractive	Average	Unattractive
Our Ability to Compete	**High**	UK* (EC) Brazil (LA) China † Australia	Canada Argentina † (LA) Ireland* (EC) New Zealand Hong Kong Finland (EF)	Malasia* (AS) Norway (EF) Turkey* Morocco Denmark (EC)
	Average	France * † (EC) Venezuela †(LA) Japan Spain (EC)	Italy * † (EC) Sweden* (EF) Belgium (EC) Holland (EC) Saudi Arabia Switzerland (EF)	Peru (LA) Nigeria * Greece * (EC) Tunisia Portugal (EC)
	Low	USA † W. Ger. † (EC) Mexico (LA)	Thailand (AS) Philippines * (AS) S. Korea	India * Paraguay (LA) Chile (LA) Uganda

Note : Country where firm already has existing facilities indicated by asterisk. † indicates country where firms major competitor has facilities. Membership in major regional trade groups indicated within parentheses. (AS) = Association of Southeast Asian Nations , (EC) = European Community, (EF) = European Free Trade Area, (LA) = Latin American Integration Association.

Relevance of the Portfolio Concept to Global Location

A number of authors have cast doubt on the applicability of the portfolio concept for firms pursuing a global strategy. Hout, Porter, and Rudden (1982) and Porter (1986) point out that truly global firms are run with a high degree of interdependence and not as a portfolio of different (and independent) businesses. This statement, and particularly the reference to "independent," refers to the fact that the portfolio concept as used in the corporate strategy literature finds its clearest application in firms comprised of separate, independent businesses, so that the competition of the firm's portfolio of business may be altered without bringing the whole enterprise to a halt.

Doubts concerning the applicability of the portfolio concept stem from the interdependence which characterizes many of today's global competitors. Business activities in one part of the world are functionally dependent on those in another, e.g., unit A supplies unit B which supplies unit C, so that the firm's freedom to "drop and add" to its portfolio is severely curtailed.

But one must be careful to distinguish the type of portfolio at issue. As applied here, portfolio analysis is used to refer to geographical locations, not the business activities themselves. New activities may be initiated in new locations and old ones shifted from existing locations without necessarily disrupting the interrelated functioning of the enterprise.

IBM closed down operations in India and recently opened up a new plant in Mexico. It is demonstrably true that even the most highly integrated global competitors have a choice to make regarding locations, i.e., they alter their geographic portfolio. Not to do so would mean that such companies remained within their traditional borders. The evidence today is that just the opposite is happening.

Location as a Tool for Strategic Analysis

Devising a global strategy implies an attempt to understand competitor behavior and strategy on a world scale. Since the particular countries and regions where firms have chosen to locate their facilities represent major decisions and are an integral part of corporate strategy, the global distribution and pattern of such facilities can yield valuable clues and indications as to competitor strategy and objectives. In short, the geographical positioning of competitor facilities is itself worthy of analysis for the insight it provides into competitor thinking. Figure 4 shows at a glance that the firm's major competitor has more facilities positioned within the more attractive world markets.

An inspection of locational patterns can also yield further information, on the following subject areas.

Changes in Global Strategy

Traced over time, the changes in the geographic distribution of a competitor's facilities provide strong indications as to changes in his global strategy. The fact that facilities generally require a long lead time before they are completed means that early notice of new investments can often give advance warning on competitor strategy.

In 1984, Cable and Wireless, the British telecommunications firm, made a major commitment to the Pacific region when it invested 442 million dollars to purchase the Hong Kong telephone company. The same year saw the firm expand rapidly into the North American area. C&W formed a joint venture with the Missouri-Kansas-Texas railroad subsidiary of Katy Industries, laying optical fibre cable to link commercial centers in the American Southwest. Also during 1984, C&W was active in optical fibre telecommunications links between Washington and New York. This gave C&W a unique geographic positioning relative to its competitors, while most of the major communications firms, with the exception of Sweden's Ericsson, had their major facilities and operations clustered near their home markets and contiguous territories. C&W was busy developing operations that linked major commercial centers in the Pacific, North America, and Europe. Its distinctive geographic spread clearly anticipated global strategy. This was described a few years later by C&W as a plan to build a "digital highway" linking the world's major financial centres.

Like most strategies, this was the subject of evolutionary change. The point is that the general direction of such change was signalled by changes in the location of C&W facilities, long before the new digital highway strategy was announced.

Areas of Vulnerability

Foreign investments expose companies to risks, such as those associated with exchange rates, political and economic circumstances, which may provide opportunities for competitors able to identify particular areas of vulnerability brought about by such risks.

A case in point is provided by Midland Bank, one of Britain's largest banking institutions. Its acquisition of the American Crocker bank in 1981 turned out disastrously and Midland had to subsequently divest itself with substantial losses on property and development loans. More recently, Midland had to set aside reserves of nearly 1.5 billion dollars as bad debt provisions in connection with loans to Third World countries. Both of these losses were highly publicized and provided an opportunity which the National Bank of Australia was quick to capitalize on. For several years NBA had been seeking acquisitions in Europe to expand its retail banking network outside the Pacific region. With demand for banking facilities increasing rapidly, acquisition opportunities proved very scarce. But Midland's overseas difficulties signalled just such an opportunity. NBA spotted it and took advantage of Midland's circumstances to acquire one-fifth of its retail network.

Competence

Geographic location can also help to identify areas of competitor competence, since the type of expertise a company needs to succeed is subject to change from one part of the world to another. Ericsson, the Swedish telecommunications company referred to earlier, required expertise in producing products suitable for the developing countries which comprised its major area of foreign operations for many years, i.e., small modularized telephone exchanges and the managerial skills needed to deal with the particular needs and aspirations of governments in developing countries. Now that Ericsson has made a major bid to enter the French telecommunications market in conjunction with the French firm Compagnie Générale de

Constructions Téléphoniques (CGCT), a different product mix and different managerial skills will be required.

Marketing and the specific type of marketing competence required to succeed may also vary with geography. A different marketing approach and techniques are required to succeed in China and the East bloc countries as opposed to free market economies. A company successful and heavily committed to one of these groups reflects a certain type of competence which has implications for its global strategy.

In conclusion, global location analysis can provide useful insights regarding competitor strategy and vulnerability by addressing the following questions:

1. What is the global pattern and emphasis (particularly with reference to new locations) of the competitor's major international facilities? Are these consistent with past strategy or do they signal a major change of direction?
2. What particular high risk areas of the world is the competitor committed to and what are the possible adverse consequences of such risks for the competitor?
3. Does the location of competitor facilities point to a particular competence or set of competencies in technology, political relations, marketing in less developed countries, etc.?

SUMMARY

This chapter has addressed two different situations in relation to global location strategy: firstly, the question of new facilities location. The screening methods suggested by the literature proceed on a country-by-country basis, developing a score which rates each national location individually. These methods fail to differentiate clearly between the general attractiveness of a particular national location and the firm's ability to compete there. The portfolio approach presented here makes this distinction. Also, it provides the manager with an overview of the various site options, enabling him to identify patterns and linkages which cross national boundaries, such as:

1. The global distribution of the firm's existing facilities.
2. The location and geographic pattern of competitor facilities.
3. Regional and trade group linkages relevant to global strategy and site location.

Secondly, location analysis of competitor plants and facilities is used to provide a method for the early detection of competitor changes in global strategy, vulnerabilities and competence.

NOTES

1. Aharoni, Y. (1966, p. 79).
2. Goodnow, J.D. (1985, p. 23).
3. Wind, Y. and Douglas, S.P. (1972, p. 18).
4. For a fuller discussion of weighting schemes and associated problems, see Hofer and Schendel (1978, pp. 73-78) and Leontiades (1985, pp. 96-98).
5. See Hout, Porter, and Rudden (1982, p. 106) and Porter (1986, p. 19).

REFERENCES

Aharoni, Y. (1966). *The Foreign Investment Decision Process*. Boston, Harvard Business School.

Farmer, D. (1981). "Source Decision Making in the Multinational Company Environment." *International Journal of Physical Distribution and Materials Management*, II, (2/3), pp. 5-15.

Goodnow, J.D. (1985). "Developments in International Mode of Entry Analysis." *International Marketing Review*, Autumn, pp. 17-30.

Hofer, C.W. and Schendel, D. (1978). *Strategy Formulation: Analytical Concepts*. St. Paul: West Publishing Co.

Hout, T., Porter, M. and Rudden, E. (1982). "How Global Companies Win Out." *Harvard Business Review*, September-October, pp. 98-108.

Johanson, J.T. and Vahlne, J.E. (1977). "The Internationalization Process of the Firm — A Model of Knowledge Development and Increasing Foreign Market Commitments." *Journal of International Business Studies*, Spring-Summer, pp. 23-32.

Leontiades, J.C. (1985). *Multinational Corporate Strategy — Planning for World Markets*. Lexington, Lexington Books.

Porter, M.E. (1984) (ed). *Competition in Global Industries*. Boston: Harvard Business School.

Robinson, S.J.Q., Hichens, R.E. and Wade, D.P. (1978). "The Directional Policy Matrix — Tool for Strategic Planning." *Long Range Planning*, II, pp. 8-15.

Simmonds, K. and Smith, H. (1968). "The First Export Order: A Marketing Innovation." *British Journal of Marketing*, Vol. 2, Summer 1986, pp. 93-100.

Stobough, R.B. (1969). "How to Analyze Foreign Investment Climates." *Harvard Business Review*, September-October, pp. 100-108.

Wind, Y. and Douglas, S.P. (1972). "International Market Segmentation." *European Journal of Marketing*, 6(1), pp. 17-25.

Chapter 7

Transferability and Adaptability of Products and Promotion Themes in Multinational Marketing — MNCs in LDCs

Warren J. Keegan
Richard R. Still
John S. Hill

SUMMARY. A great deal has been written about the transferability and adaptability of products and promotion themes, but little empirical data have been reported. The research reported here analyzed MNC's records in transferring products and promotion themes from base markets to markets in LDCs. Data analysis includes checks on consistency of subsidiary adaptation or standardization for products and promotion themes.

The transfer of marketing skills and products between nations has long been a major characteristic of Multinational Corporations (MNCs). In international marketing, few topics have been as controversial as the standardization or adaptation of marketing mixes. Products and promotions, in particular, have received much attention.

But to view product and promotion transfers strictly in an adaptation-standardization context is to ignore that they are parts of a complex marketing process. Little attention has been given, at least em-

This chapter was first published in the *Journal of Global Marketing*, Vol. 1(1/2), Fall/Winter 1987.

pirically, to three pertinent questions. First, to what extent are products transplanted from one market into another? Products have to be transferred between nations before any standardizing or adapting occurs. Second, what is an adapted product? Products have multiple components — packaging, labeling, ingredients and the like — a change in any component is an adaptation, and "degree of adaptation" better describes product change than does the dichotomous "adaptation-standardization." Third, when products are transferred, what proportion of their promotion themes undergo substantial change? This article presents the findings of a study of product and promotion theme transfers and adaptations between the U.S./U.K. and Lesser-Developed Countries (LDCs).[1]

Interest in marketing-mix transfers focused initially on conceptual frameworks laying out conditions under which marketing mixes were either adapted or standardized. Buzzell (1968) investigated this central premise in his now-classic "Can You Standardize Multinational Marketing?" Britt (1974) suggested a framework for international marketing decision making, in which the degree of change introduced into marketing mixes (and particularly advertising appeals) depended upon intermarket differences in consumption patterns, psychosocial characteristics, and cultural criteria.

Empirical studies of marketing mix (decision variables) standardization/adaptation, show that standardized offerings predominate in the international marketplace. Sorenson and Wiechmann's (1975) study of 27 U.S. MNCs in Europe showed a low degree of adaptation of American consumer packaged goods sold in European markets. Ward (1973) reached similar conclusions after studying 93 European products sold in the U.S. Michell (1979), focusing upon the effects of differences in economic development between home-markets and recipient countries, found exports of British products had high standardization (86%) to developed countries and lower standardization (52%) to LDCs, while advertising messages showed lower standardization overall, with 52% in developed markets and 44% in LDCs.

Product adaptations have received much attention in the literature, but have been the focus of little empirical research. Kramer (1964), Fayerweather (1970), and Terpstra (1978) all have noted that standardization, not adaptation, has dominated MNC product strategies overseas. One barrier to empirical research has been in defining "product adaptation." However, numerous product components are identified in the literature;[2] for example, see Robinson (1961), Root (1966), Deschampsneuf (1967), Thomas (1969), Fayerweather (1970), Majaro (1977), and Terpstra (1978). Among these components are: operating instructions, delivery, credit, maintenance, product quality, constituents, labeling, sizing, warranty, packaging protection, packaging aesthetics, brand name, and product features. A few reported studies have recognized multiple components in determining the degree of change introduced into products. Sorenson and Wiechmann (1975), for example, used three components—product characteristics, brand name, and packaging; Ward (1973) chose five—use/operations, styling, quality, packaging and labeling.

Promotion theme standardization and adaptation has been the subject of many commentaries. First, Elinder (1965), then Fatt (1967), argued the feasibility of global theme standardization, this in sharp contrast to those advocating individual approaches and adaptations to markets (Lenormand, 1964; Green, Cunningham, & Cunningham, 1975). The adaptionist viewpoint has been reinforced by Ryans and Fry (1976), who found little support among international advertisers for simple direct advertising transference in Europe; and by Dunn (1976), who found evidence of strengthening national identity in Europe and decreasing intermarket message standardization. Nevertheless, Sorenson and Wiechmann (1975) reported over 70 percent standardization of basic messages by American firms selling in European markets.

WHY DO MNCs STANDARDIZE OR ADAPT?

Marketing mix standardization and adaptation issues are meaningful only in terms of MNC organizational goals. MNCs seeking to standardize marketing mix elements do so for diverse reasons. Significant research and development cost savings flow from not having to "reinvent the wheel" (i.e., totally redesigning products). Other scale economies are available to firms servicing markets through exports. In fact, many MNCs test-market new products by importing them first, because until products are proven successful in a new market, they are unwilling to commit on-site production resources. The test-market process, then, often unwittingly encourages MNCs to standardize offerings from market to market.

Scale economies are available to multinational promoters running the same advertisements in multiple markets (except for translation and dubbing). Pepsi estimates that global standardization saves it over $8 million a year in production expenses.

Some MNCs take advantage of mobile consumers such as tourists and businessmen, whoenjoy the consistency of product offering as they move from country to country. Gillette, Kodak, and Hilton hotels are companies for which uniformity of product or service offering internationally is a definite "plus."

For American MNCs, a strong U.S. image can be advantageous overseas. Levi's jeans, Wrigley's chewing gum, Marlboro cigarettes, and Kentucky Fried Chicken benefit from their identification with U.S. lifestyles. These "country-of origin effects" come in several forms such as the Western cowboy image (Marlboro, Levi's, Stetson hats); American consumption habits (hamburgers, Coca-Cola, bourbon); and U.S. service efficiency (Hertz, Avis, and Pan-Am).

But perhaps the most potent argument for standardized products and promotions is to capitalize upon consumer similarities worldwide. In most markets, there are consumer segments whose purchasing motives and product-use habits are sufficiently alike internationally to make marketers comfortable in standardizing product and promotion offerings. Gerber, Heinz, and Carnation target baby segments globally. Fisher-Price, in spite of numerous country-level legal restrictions, aims its toys at essentially the same consumer groups worldwide. The fashion and record industries target teenagers in many markets to take advantage of similar behavior patterns. Pharmaceutical companies standardize offerings in countries sharing the same health problems (headache remedies, upset stomachs, sexual diseases, etc.). Finally, standardization is advisable for elitist products for high-income consumers. Automobile manufacturers such as Rolls-Royce, Mercedes-Benz, and BMW easily take their offerings virtually unchanged to most markets. French champagne, Dutch bulbs, Russian caviar, and British Scotch whisky are specialty products, for which adaptation strategies would be downright foolish.

In spite of the temptation to standardize, many MNCs adapt products and promotions. This is especially true for products not possessing characteristics such as strong American images. Some companies change some product components (such as sizing or ingredients) without altering product appearances (Still & Hill, 1984), thereby preserving image. At the other extreme, some products are completely redesigned to fit customer tastes, purchasing patterns, and to stay within country-specific rules on labeling, measurement unit and sizing guidelines. Companies with on-site manufacturing in a market and extensive distribution find that more adaptations are required to appeal to rural inhabitants and consumers at the lower end of the socioeconomic spectrum.

Given the wide variety of product and promotion alternatives, and the importance of LDCs in world marketing, a perspective on the strategies MNCs currently use in developing markets is important. Let's now examine the standardization-adaptation issue from the MNC viewpoint in LDCs.

TRANSFER AND ADAPTATION OF CONSUMER PRODUCTS AND PROMOTION: A CONCEPTUAL FRAMEWORK

Figure 1 is a conceptualization of the process of product and promotion transfer and adaptation. The act of transplanting products from one market to another reflects management's perceptions of the degree of market similarity. It is reasonable to expect that countries at similar levels of economic development should have similar product mixes. As market differences increase, less frequent product transfers among markets are likely.

Although some products made in the U.S./U.K. are marketed in LDCs, the cultural diversity of LDCs should result in a preponderance of locally-developed products. Through transferring products, head-offices and subsidiaries seek to reap the advantages of standardization (cost savings, uniform global images and the like). Even when subsidiaries determine that transferred products and pro-

FIGURE 1. Transfer and Adaptation Process of Consumer Nondurable Products: A Conceptual Framework

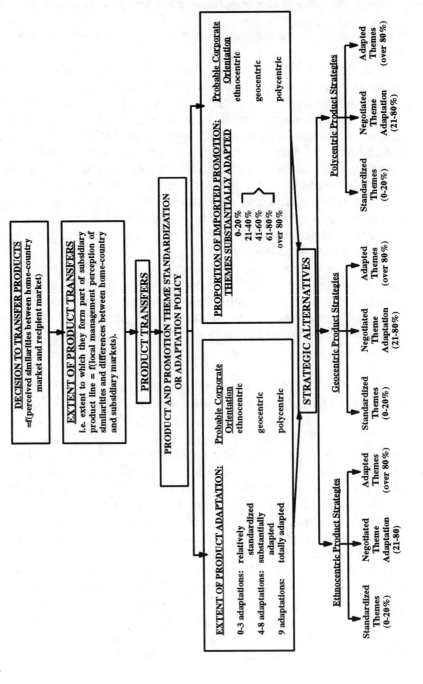

motion themes require substantial adaptations, these are often more economical than developing totally new locally-oriented products.

It is possible to make certain changes in products without compromising their standardized images. Adaptations to accommodate local legal requirements, packaging protection changes to counter adverse climates, and pack size adaptations to adjust to consumers' buying behavior—all can occur without substantially altering a brand's global image. However, firms seeking the advantages of standardization generally do not change such product components as brand names, packaging aesthetics, or major constituents because these adaptations require parallel promotion changes. Products with up to three adaptations are considered here as "relatively standardized" (see Figure 1).

Firms not desiring uniform global images either make sufficient product changes to gain local market acceptance or redesign the product concept to fit local conditions. As shown in Figure 1, products with from four to eight changes are described as "substantially adapted." Those with nine changes (i.e., completely redesigned) are "totally adapted."

The extent of change in transferred promotional themes reflects the strength of home office influence on overseas marketing practices, since the extent and nature of marketing transfers are related to company goals and policies. Given, for example, the often-great cultural and economic gaps between advanced home countries of MNCs and LDCs, firms that, outwardly at least, seldom adapt home-country promotional themes may be searching for standardization opportunities. These opportunities occur when product use patterns are the same between markets; or when target market similarities are apparent (teenage markets, for example). Conversely, in situations where company subsidiaries adapt most incoming themes, as happens, for example, in the Unilever organization, MNC top management encourages adaptations by field managements. In these cases, host-country orientations are either essential (as in culturally-diverse LDCs), or else MNCs need locally-oriented marketing strategies to maintain low profiles in politically-volatile environments.

Nevertheless, not all MNCs have clear-cut standardization or adaptation orientations. Many adapt or standardize to the degree believed necessary for market success. In some cases, the home-country office develops prototype promotional campaigns and forwards them to subsidiaries or affiliates for consideration (Peebles et al., 1978). During the ensuing dialogue, efforts are made to capture the advantages of theme standardization but only insofar as purchasing motives, products, media availability, and the like do not necessitate drastic changes in home country themes. In situations where subsidiaries use themes they think best for their individual markets, a geocentric orientation dominates.

The decision to standardize or adapt *both* products and promotion themes raises the question of interdependence among marketing mix elements. If marketing mix changes are consistent, there is parallelism in product and promotion-theme adaptations. That is, ceteris paribus, MNCs should standardize or adapt *both* products and promotions simultaneously. However, some marketing theorists visualize situations in which product and promotion changes are entirely independent. Keegan's strategic alternatives (1969), for example, postulated adapted products with standardized themes, and standardized products with adapted themes.

HYPOTHESES

Because this study focused upon marketing transfers between developed countries and markets in LDCs, there was doubt that MNCs were transferring and standardizing marketing mix elements of culturally-sensitive consumer products (Ward 1973, p. 13) across markets with wide economic and cultural differences. It is, therefore, posited that:

1. Multinational product lines in LDCs are incapable of absorbing more than 40 percent of modern consumer products.
2. Transplanted products are adapted heavily to meet the needs of culturally-diverse LDC consumers.
3. Most promotion themes transferred into LDCs require substantial adaptation, because of cultural and economic gaps between home-country markets and LDC markets.
4. Strong interdependence exists between product and promotion adaptations. Thus, extensive product adaptations should parallel substantial promotional theme changes, and standardization moves should encompass both products and promotions.

STUDY DETAILS:
RESEARCH DESIGN AND METHODOLOGY

Sample. The total sample consisted of 50 MNCs with over 550 subsidiaries in LDCs. The sample was drawn from the *Directory of American Companies Operating in Foreign Countries.* The major qualification for inclusion was that consumer nondurables were the MNC's major products. Industries represented included food and drink, pharmaceuticals, cosmetics, and general consumer goods.

Method of Contact. Telephone calls were made to headquarters of randomly selected MNCs to identify management responsible for international marketing operations and to determine MNCs' willingness to participate. Nineteen MNCs agreed to participate. Eighteen were U.S.-based and one was from the United Kingdom. Participating MNCs chose either to have questionnaires sent to their international headquarters in the United States or direct to their LDC subsidiaries.

Respondents and Response Rates. The 19 MNCs were: CPC International, Colgate-Palmolive, Canada Dry Corporation, Cheeseborough-Pond's, General Foods, Kraft Foods, Unilever, The Pillsbury Company, Pfizer, Revlon, Quaker Oats, Royal Crown Cola, Seven-Up Corporation, Mead-Johnson, Standard Brands, Warner Lambert, Helena Rubinstein, Johnson and Johnson International, and Eli Lilly. Thirty-six questionnaires were returned from MNC international headquarters in the United States; and of the 74 questionnaires mailed to LDCs, 31 were returned (41.9% response rate) of which 25 were usable. Sixty-one responses were computer-analyzed.

Headquarters Responses vs. Subsidiary Responses

Since international marketing VPs and managers either chose to receive questionnaires at their international divisions in the U.S. or to have them mailed directly to their overseas subsidiaries, we wondered whether this decision correlated with the degree of promotion theme standardization or adaptation. Table 1 shows the results.

TABLE 1. Respondent Country of Origin by Proportion of Substantially Adapted Themes

Respondent Country of Origin	PROPORTION OF SUBSTANTIALLY ADAPTED THEMES (in percentages)					No. of Subsidiaries
	0-20	21-40	41-60	61-80	Over 80	
U.S./U.K.- answered	20	3	7	3	3	36
Foreign- answered	7	5	3	3	7	25
No. of Subsidiaries	27	8	10	6	10	61

Twenty of 27 U.S.-based respondents substantially adapted less than 20% of incoming themes and 7 of 10 foreign-based respondents changed over 80% of themes. This suggests that decisions on site of questionnaire response are significant indicators ($p < 0.09$) of an MNC's international orientation toward promotion theme adaptation. Corporations providing details of LDC marketing strategies from their U.S. international headquarters were likely to standardize themes between markets. MNCs having their LDC subsidiaries answer questionnaires granted subsidiaries more freedom to change incoming U.S./U.K. promotion themes.

A similar test was conducted to determine whether the number of product adaptations was related to the country from which the completed questionnaire was mailed. No significant differences were found between the two groups of respondents.

Countries Represented. Data were obtained from: Indonesia, Malaysia, Philippines, Thailand, Sri Lanka, India, Argentina, Venezuela, Brazil, Chile, Colombia, Ecuador, Peru, Uruguay, Costa Rica, Guatemala, Jamaica, Mexico, Panama, Zimbabwe, Nigeria, and Egypt.

Information collected included:

1. "Approximately how many products does your subsidiary have in its product lines?"

   1-10   11-24   25-49   50-74   75-100   Over 100

2. "What proportion of the products you now market were first sold in the U.S./U.K.?"

   0-20%   21-40%   41-60%   61-80%   Over 80%

   Using the median values of the responses (5 products for 1-10 products, 17 for 11-24, etc; and 10% for 0-20%, 30% for 21-40%, etc.), we estimated the proportion of MNC product lines in LDCs which originated in the U.S. or U.K.

3. Respondents were asked to select three transplanted U.S./U.K. products and provide details on which of nine product components were changed to suit market conditions: brand name, packaging protection, packaging aesthetics, measurement units, product features, labeling, usage instructions, pack sizes and product constituents.

4. "Of those products marketed in this LDC as well as in the U.S./ U.K., approximately what proportion of the messages that promote them have substantially different promotional themes than their U.S./U.K. counterparts?"

   20-20%   21-40%   41-60%   61-80%   Over 80%

FINDINGS

Transferability of Modern Products into LDCs

Terpstra (1981), summarizing state-of-the-art-knowledge of intermarket product transfers, commented:

> The conventional wisdom about international product policies—*unsupported by solid empirical evidence* (emphasis added)—is that firms tend to extend abroad the same products as they sell at home.

Using respondent answers on product line size and the proportion of those lines that had originated in the U.S./U.K., it was found that about 1200 of the 2200 products (54.4%) sold by the 61 subsidiaries had been transferred from home-country markets (U.S. or U.K.) into LDCs. In other words, over half the items in LDC lines are "international products"—that is, their commercial appeal extends over multiple markets. This left nearly 45% of LDC products that were either especially created for LDC markets or transferred from third-party markets (i.e., countries other than U.S./U.K. or the LDC itself). MNCs evidently diagnose LDC market needs and then either develop products in the LDCs or transplant product ideas from other markets. The implication is that MNC managements' thinking goes beyond transferring declining products from home-markets into LDCs in order to extend product life cycles.

Surprisingly, MNCs selling consumer packaged goods — most with good marketing reputations — perceived few problems transferring products between markets so economically and culturally dissimilar as the U.S./U.K. and LDCs. But two important factors encourage the marketing of "modern" products in LDCs. First, almost all LDCs have pockets of expatriates and prosperous local inhabitants with high-income lifestyles which mesh nicely with modern products. Second, the "demonstration effect" (Nurkse, 1953) is a strong influence in many LDCs and numerous poorer consumers buy modern products as a way to identify with the consumption society. Some modern products, then, become status symbols, as refrigerators were in Mexico in the 1950s (Fayer-weather, 1970).

Even though many modern products are transferred relatively unchanged from one developed country to another, it would be surprising to find these products being sold in LDCs without further adaptations. Hence, we analyzed the extent to which transplanted MNC products undergo change for sale in LDC markets.

Extent of Adaptation of Modern Consumer Nondurable Products in Developing Markets

Each of the 61 responding subsidiaries provided details on adaptations made to three ex-U.S./U.K. products marketed in their LDC. We analyzed changes made to 174 products, this out of a total of 1200 U.S./U.K. products transferred into LDCs by our sample.

In all, the 174 products sold in LDCs had 718 adaptations, an average of 4.13 changes out of a possible nine. As shown in Table 2, 15 products (8.6%) were transferred totally unchanged into

TABLE 2. Extent of Adaptation of U.S./U.K. Products in LDC Markets

Number of Adaptations	Number of Products	Percent Total	Corporate Orientation
0	15	8.6	
1	27	15.5	
2	15	8.6	Ethnocentric
3	9	5.2	
4	18	10.3	
5	21	12.1	
6	39	22.4	Geocentric
7	22	12.7	
8	3	1.7	
9	5	2.9	Polycentric
Totals	174	100.0	

LDC markets. Thus, over nine products out of 10 had one or more components adapted.[4] Significantly, 103 out of 174 products (59.2%) were substantially adapted (four to eight changes). MNC marketers shape products to local needs, even if this means sacrificing appearance or other features considered important in the home-country market.

Firms changing three or fewer components believe they reap many of the advantages of standardization, probably for one of three reasons. First, their products have universal appeal (such as Coca-Cola or Pepsi). Second, they are moving toward greater standardization (Kodak or Gillette). Third, consumers prefer some products with strong modern images (Max Factor cosmetics).

Interestingly, only five products had all nine components changed, total redesigning and retaining only the core product idea. Well-known examples of these types of product "inventions" include the hand-cranked washing machine sold in India, and Ford's "Model T for Asia," the Fiera (Keegan, 1980).

Promotion Theme Transferability and Adaptability

What themes are used to promote these 1200 transferred products in LDCs? Our findings (see Table 3) show that nearly half of the sample (28 of 61 subsidiaries) substantially adapted 20% or less of

TABLE 3. Proportion of Adapted Promotion Themes

Percent	0-20	21-40	41-60	61-80	Over 80	Total
Number of Subsidiaries	28	7	11	5	10	61
Percent	45.9%	11.5%	18.0%	8.2%	16.4%	100%

imported themes. This negates the hypothesis that most themes require substantial adaptation when moving from advanced to developing markets. Only 10 of the 61 subsidiaries reported LDC markets as highly or totally unreceptive to modern themes. The strong orientation towards standardization in promotion themes traces either to MNCs exclusively targeting affluent consumer groups in LDCs or to expectations that many consumers in LDCs respond more readily to modern than to locally-oriented themes.

Supporting Peeble et al.'s (1977) contention that promotion theme adaptations are negotiated rather than subjected to absolute standardization or adaptation policies, 24 of the subsidiaries – the middle group – adapted between 20 and 80 percent of the incoming themes. For these MNCs, dialogs probably occur between headquarters and the field to ensure suitability of transferred themes.

Extent of Uniformity
Among Promotion Theme Adaptations

How much consistency characterizes MNC adaptation strategies in their product and promotion elements? Do subsidiaries with heavily adapted products adapt imported themes, or is product adaptation unrelated to promotion theme adaptation? We cross-tabulated the degree of product change with subsidiaries' records of imported theme adaptation (See Tables 4a, b, and c). Table 4a shows the initial cross-tabulation of subsidiary promotion adaptation policies against the respective product adaptation strategies. While our units of analysis are responses at the subsidiary level, results may not indicate overall subsidiary marketing strategies, since subsidiary examples of product adaptation strategies are not usually uniform. That is, a subsidiary may substantially adapt between zero and 20% of incoming promotion themes, but its three product examples might have respectively two, three and six adaptations. Cross-tabulations are aggregated indications of LDC marketing strategies, and are not particularized for individual subsidiaries.

When these results are placed into our conceptual framework (see Table 4b), it was not possible to draw conclusions as to possible statistical associations between product and promotion adaptations.

TABLE 4a. Cross-Tabulation of Number of Product Changes Made by Subsidiaries by Proportion of Substantially-Adapted Promotion Themes

Proportion of Adapted Themes	TOTAL NUMBER OF ADAPTATIONS PER PRODUCT										
	0	1	2	3	4	5	6	7	8	9	Total
0-20%	15	19	8	1	5	1	20	10	0	0	79
21-40%	0	0	3	0	4	6	4	4	0	0	21
41-60%	0	5	3	2	4	7	6	3	0	0	30
61-80%	0	2	0	0	4	1	6	2	0	0	15
Over 80%	0	1	1	6	1	6	3	3	3	5	29
Total	15	27	15	9	18	21	39	22	3	5	174

TABLE 4b. Collapsing of Product Adaptation and Promotion Theme Adaptation Responses into Framework Categories

Promotion Theme Adaptation Strategy	PRODUCT ADAPTATION STRATEGY			Total Number of Products
	Relatively Standardized 0-3 Adaptations	Substantially Adapted 4-8 Adaptations	Totally Adapted 9 Adaptations	
Standardized 0-20% Adaptation	43	36	0	79
Negotiated 21-80% Adaptation	15	51	0	66
Adapted Over 80% Adaptation	8	16	5	29
Total Number of Products	66	103	5	174

TABLE 4c. Alternative Classification of Product and Promotion Theme Adaptations
(to examine statistical relationships using chi-square contingency table tests)

PROMOTION THEME ADAPTATION STRATEGY	PRODUCT ADAPTATION STRATEGY Number of Applications			
	0-3	4-6	7-9	Total
0-20% Adaptation (observed)	43	26	10	79
Expected Frequencies*	(30)	(35.4)	(13.6)	
21-80% Adaptation (observed)	15	42	9	66
Expected Frequencies*	(25)	(29.6)	(11.4)	
Over 80% Adaptation (observed)	8	10	11	29
Expected Frequencies*	(11)	(13)	(5)	
Totals	66	78	30	174

*Frequencies expected if no relationship exists between the two variables
RESULTS: A chi-square score of 27.48 was recorded where 14.86 would indicate a
significant relationship at the 0.005 level for 4 degrees of freedom.

This was because chi-square contingency table tests are not valid where observed frequencies are zero or where theoretical frequencies for 20% of cells were five or less. Consequently, the data was rearranged to conform to required conditions for contingency table tests. Table 4c shows the results. A definite relationship between product and promotion theme adaptability exists at the 0.001 level. The observed and expected frequencies show — particularly in the 0-20% and over 80% promotion theme adaptation categories — that in general product and promotion theme adaptations go hand-in-hand.

When the data are placed in our original conceptual framework (using 0-3,4-8 and 9 adaptation product categories), further conclusions are possible. For 43 of 66 relatively standardized products, subsidiaries had substantially changed less than 20 percent of imported themes. The desire to standardize, often formalized in explicit policy, generally results in uniform nonadaptation of both products and promotions. Consistency in adaptation strategies was also apparent. The five totally redesigned products were from subsidiaries consistently adapting modern themes to LDC market conditions.

Products with four to eight adaptations show the most diversity in promotion theme strategies. Roughly one-half (51 of 103) were from subsidiaries with no definite theme standardization or adaptation tendencies—that is, these subsidiaries adapted from 21 to 80 percent of imported themes. A second group (36 products) were from subsidiaries with records of standardized themes, indicating that Keegan's "product adaptation-promotion extension" strategy is feasible in LDCs. This may indicate that either theme adaptations are not needed in "relatively advanced" LDCs or product adaptations do not affect advertised sales features. The third group (16 products) were from subsidiaries adapting over 80% of incoming themes. Inappropriateness of modern themes may stem from products being sold in culturally-diverse LDCs, sales feature changes, corporate directives to localize market offerings, or anti-American sentiments (in Central America, for example).

CONCLUSIONS AND IMPLICATIONS
FOR FUTURE RESEARCH

This study resulted in three important findings. First, economic and cultural gaps between modern markets (like the U.S. or U.K.) and LDCs do not deter MNCs from transferring modern consumer products between them. Second, the MNCs in our sample substantially adapt most modern products before marketing them in LDCs, suggesting that universal products (like Coca-Cola and Colgate Toothpaste) are the exceptions rather than the rule. However, this finding may not hold for less culturally-sensitive products, such as consumer durable and industrial products. Third, although many modern themes are transferred into LDCs without substantial change, the extent of theme adaptation parallels the degree of product adaptation, suggesting interdependence between marketing adaptation and standardization decisions.

Several directions for future research are indicated. We need to know more about transfers between advanced markets (e.g., the U.S. and Europe) and more about the origins of LDC product lines.

What proportion of products in LDCs come from home-country markets? From third-party markets? How many are developed for exclusive sale in particular LDCs? The details of the product transfer process within MNCs needs researching, inasmuch as product transfers occur before transfers of other marketing-mix elements. Room exists, too, for studies of transfers of industrial and consumer durable goods from advanced countries to LDCs. Finally further studies of theme-adaptation strategies are needed, especially relating to product sales platform changes versus adaptations to creative contexts of promotions.

NOTES

1. The authors use lesser-developed country, developing country, and emergent country interchangeably.
2. Here we use the broader definition of "product" analogous to Kotler's (1980) "augmented product" including warranties, services and the like.
3. MNCs view the entire world as a potential market, and use the best marketing strategy for each market, regardless of origin (Wind, Douglas, and Perlmutter (1973).
4. For details as to which of the nine components were adapted most, see Richard R. Still and John S. Hill, (1984) "Adapting Consumer Products to Lesser-Developed Markets," *Journal of Business Research*, Vol. 12, No. 1.

REFERENCES

Britt, Steuart Henderson. (1974). "Standardizing Advertising for the International Market." *Columbia Journal of World Business*, 9, No. 4 (Winter), pp. 39-45.
Buzzell, Robert D. (1968). "Can You Standardize Multinational Marketing?" *Harvard Business Review*, Vol. 46, No. 6 (November-December), pp. 102-113.
Deschampsneuf, Henry. (1967). *Marketing Overseas*. London, England: Pergamon Press, Ltd.
Dunn, S. Watson. (1976)."Effect of National Identity on Multinational Promotional Strategy in Europe." *Journal of Marketing*, Vol. 40, No. 4 (October), pp. 50-7.
Elinder, Erik. (1965). "How International Can European Advertising Be?" *Journal of Marketing*, Vol. 29, No. 2 (April), pp. 7-11.
Fatt, Arthur C. (1967). "The Danger of 'Local' International Advertising." *Journal of Marketing*, Vol. 31, No. 1 (January), pp. 61-2.

Fayerweather, John. (1970). *International Marketing*. Englewood Cliffs, New Jersey: Prentice-Hall, Inc., 2nd Edition.

Green, Robert T., William H. Cunningham, and Isabella C. M. Cunningham. (1975). "The Effectiveness of Standardized Global Advertising." *Journal of Advertising*, Vol. 4, No. 3 (Summer) pp. 25-8.

Keegan, Warren J. (1980). *Multinational Marketing Management*. Englewood Cliffs, New Jersey: Prentice-Hall, Inc., 2nd Edition.

_____. (1969). "Multinational Product Planning: Strategic Alternatives." *Journal of Marketing*, Vol. 33. No. 1 (January), pp. 58-62.

Kotler, Philip. (1980). *Marketing Management: Analysis, Planning and Control*. Englewood Cliffs, New Jersey, Prentice-Hall, Inc., 4th Edition.

Kramer, Roland L. (1964). *International Marketing*. Cincinnati, Ohio: South-Western Publishing Company.

Lenormand, J. M. (1964). "Is Europe Ripe for the Integration of Advertising?" *The International Advertiser*, Vol. 5, No. 1 (March), pp. 12-14.

Majaro, Simon. (1977). *International Marketing: A Strategic Approach to World Markets*. London, England: George Allen & Unwin, Ltd.

Michell, Paul. (1979). "Infrastructures and International Marketing Effectiveness." *Columbia Journal of World Business*, Vol. 14, No. 1 (Spring), pp. 91-101.

Nurske, Ragnar. (1953). *Problems of Capital Formation in Undeveloped Countries*. New York: Oxford University Press.

Peebles, Dean M., John K. Ryans, Jr., and Ivan R. Vernon. (1978). "Coordinating International Advertising—A Programmed Management Approach that Cuts Through the 'Standardized vs. Localized' Debate." *Journal of Marketing*, Vol. 42, No. 1 (January), pp. 28-34.

_____. (1977). "New Perspective on Advertising Standardization." *European Journal of Advertising*, Vol. 11, No. 8, pp. 568-76.

Robinson, Richard D. (1961). "The Challenge of the Underdeveloped National Market." *Journal of Marketing*, Vol. 25, No. 6 (October), pp. 19-25.

Root, Franklin R. (1966). *Strategic Planning for Export Markets*. Scranton, Pennsylvania: International Textbooks Company.

Ryans, John K., Jr. and Claudia Fry. (1976). "Some European Attitudes on the Advertising Transference Question: A Research Note." *Journal of Advertising*, Vol. 5, No. 2 (Spring), pp. 11-13.

Sorenson, Ralph R. and Ulrich S. Wiechmann. (1975). "How Multinationals View Marketing Standardization." *Harvard Business Review*, 53, No. 3 (May-June), pp. 38-54, pp. 166-7.

Still, Richard R., and John S. Hill. (1984). "Adapting Consumer Products to Lesser-Developed Markets." *Journal of Business Research*, Vol. 14, No. 1 (March), pp. 12-17.

Terpstra, Vern. (1978). *International Marketing*, Hinsdale, Illinois: The Dryden Press, 2nd Edition.

_____. (1981). "On Marketing Appropriate Products in Developing Countries." *Journal of International Marketing*, Vol. 1, No. 1, pp. 5-13.

Thomas, Michael J. (1969). "Product Planning for Export Markets," in Michael J. Thomas (Ed.), *International Marketing Management*. Scranton, Pennsylvania: International Textbooks Company.

Ward, James J. (1973). *The European Approach to U.S. Markets: Product and Promotion Adaptations by European Multinationals*. New York: Praeger Publishers, Inc.

Wind, Yoram, Susan P. Douglas, and Howard V. Perlmutter. (1973). "Guidelines for Developing International Marketing Strategies." *Journal of Marketing,* Vol. 37, No. 2 (April), pp. 14-23.

World Trade Press Publication (1975). *Directory of American Companies Operating in Foreign Countries*. New York: Simon and Schuster.

Chapter 8

A Comparison of Sales Activities in an International Setting

William C. Moncrief

SUMMARY. This study examines sales activities of industrial salespeople. Data were gathered from 34 companies in Germany and 57 companies in Denmark. The results indicate very significant differences among the two countries. In addition, the sales activities of the two countries are compared to 51 American companies based on a previous study.

The nature and scope of a salesperson's work responsibilities vary across job types, industries, and possibly even countries. Sales activities are one way to view sales jobs. A sales activity can be described as an overt action that may include complex mental task elements. These overt actions work in conjunction with one another to accomplish tasks that are fundamental elements to the job (Wallace, 1982).

One perception that college students, potential sales recruits, and many business managers make is that most salespeople perform the same set of sales activities. In reality, selling is not a unidimensional concept. Sales job activities differ considerably. Empirical evidence from the U.S. has shown that there is an extensive list of sales activities performed by industrial salespeople (Lamont & Lundstrom, 1974; Walker, Churchill, & Ford, 1979; and Moncrief, 1986a and 1986b). In addition, the frequency of performance of

This chapter was first published in the *Journal of Global Marketing*, Vol 1(1/2), Fall/Winter 1987.

these activities varies considerably based on sales job type (Moncrief, 1986b). Given differences in frequency of performance of sales activities in the U.S., it is likely that sales activities will differ based on a comparison with other countries.

Although sales activities are discussed or mentioned in almost every sales and sales management text, research examining the concept of sales activities has been sparse. Lamont and Lundstrom (1974) were among the first to attempt to identify the activities of a salesperson. The authors, using salespeople from a single firm in the building industry, identified 60 items describing all aspects of the sales position. These 60 items were factor analyzed and produced the eight descriptions that are found in column 1 of Table 1.

Moncrief (1986a) followed up the Lamont and Lundstrom study by surveying 1393 sales representatives from 51 companies. The 51 Moncrief companies represented 15 different 3 digit SIC groups and 36 industries. The Moncrief questionnaire consisted of 121 sales activities derived from personal interviews, focus groups, sales management texts, and the literature. The 121 sales activities were factor analyzed and produced 10 factors which can be seen in column 2 of Table 1.

The Lamont/Lundstrom and Moncrief studies produced some similar results. Both studies have a selling factor comprised of basic selling activities. Service was also an important factor with both studies, as was information management. The remaining factors,

TABLE 1
A COMPARISON OF FACTORED SALES ACTIVITIES

Lamont & Lundstrom (1974)*	Moncrief (1986a)**
1. Direct Selling	1. Selling Function
2. Customer Service	2. Servicing the Product
3. Working with Managers	3. Servicing the Account
4. Personal Integrity	4. Information Management
5. Customer Relations	5. Working with Others
6. Keeping Abreast of Market	6. Conferences/Meetings
7. Meeting Sales Operations	7. Training/Recruiting
8. Maintaining Customer Relations	8. Entertaining
	9. Out of Town Travel
	10. Working with Distributors

*Sampled from a building firm
**Sampled from 51 manufacturing companies

although different, had many similarities of individual activities. The differences in the two studies may be explained by a set of specific one-company activities versus a broader multi-company sales activities list.

The focus of this study is the examination of sales activities in an international setting. Specifically, 90 companies in two European countries (Germany and Denmark) were queried concerning the sales activities of their salesforces. The results of this study compare sales activities of Germany and Denmark to activities of American companies. In addition, the study will examine differences that occur among the German and the Danish corporations.

THE STUDY

The first part of this section discusses the activity list that was used in the study. This is followed by an examination of the sample used in the German and Danish studies, along with a discussion of the companies used in the Moncrief study. The section concludes with a discussion of the survey instrument.

The Activities

The activities used in the study were obtained from the Moncrief (1986a) study. The Moncrief activities were chosen because of their generation from a multi-company, multi-industry sample. Moncrief originally generated 121 activities but reduced these activities to 10 factors comprised of 55 activities. In order to make this study more manageable, the list of 55 activities was reduced to 36 based on subjective judgment. The present study was more concerned with the ten factors developed by Moncrief, rather than the individual 55 activities. Many of the Moncrief activities were able to be condensed into a single item representing the factor name. For example, Moncrief named one of his factors "Entertaining" which was comprised of taking clients to lunch, taking clients for a drink, party with client, and fish, golf with client. This study uses only one activity which was entertain clients. There were other "factors" that were treated in a similar manner to condense the list of activities. In addition, there were a few activities that were added that did not load on one of the factors but which Moncrief stated was important in describing different sales jobs. The list of the final 36 activities can be found in Table 2.

The Sample

This study defined industrial selling as non-retail and non-service. Service and retail sales activities are very broad categories and thus may not be comparable to industrial sales activities. The combination of retail/service with industrial sales jobs may result in non-meaningful and/or uninterpretable results.

Two systematic stratified samples were drawn from SIC categories 20 to 39, with each of the 20 SIC categories defined as a stratum. The number of companies per stratum was determined by the proportion of total companies listed in the stratum. The samples consisted of 400 firms from Germany and 400 firms from Denmark. The sample frame was a list of the two thousand leading companies from Germany and two thousand leading companies from Denmark. The sample frame classifies every company by SIC code. The headings of the German/Danish SIC codes matched the same labels used in the U.S. A systematic drawing was used to ensure that a mixture of large and small companies were included.

A graduate student from Denmark wrote a letter to the vice-president of sales or marketing of each of the Danish corporations. The letter explained that he was a Dane working on a graduate degree in the U.S. He asked permission to survey the company on a number of sales issues (including the sales activity section). In addition to the Danish student's signature, the Danish consulate officer in the Dallas area and the Dean of the School of Business signed the letter endorsing the project. The same process was repeated using a German graduate student for the German corporations.

A large number of companies responded stating that they did not have a field salesforce and thus were unable to respond. Others felt that the information was proprietary and that it was inappropriate for them to respond. There were also several questionnaires that were returned for lack of a correct address. Because of time constraints and cost, no further attempt was made to include those com-

TABLE 2
PERCENTAGE OF RESPONDENTS WHO PERFORM THE ACTIVITY

ACTIVITY	RESPONDENTS		
	N = 34* German %	N = 57 Danish %	N = 51 U. S. %
1. Make Closure of Sale 88.8	100.0	82.5	85.0
2. Monitor Competition	100.0	82.5	93.2
3. Make Sales Presentations	90.9	86.0	96.7
4. Overcome Objections	100.0	78.9	96.9
5. Study Trends & Needs	96.8	80.7	
6. Attend Conferences/Meetings	100.0	78.9	81.1
7. Prepare Sales Presentations	90.9	82.5	94.4
8. Provide & Receive Feedback	92.9	80.7	95.4
9. Fill Out Reports	100.0	71.9	NA
10. Read Co. & Trade Literature	93.3	75.4	96.6
11. Travel Overnight	96.8	68.4	92.9
12. Entertain Clients	93.7	64.9	96.3
13. Work with Management	100.0	61.4	96.6
14. Estimate & Submit Bids	96.7	63.2	67.3
15. Plan Daily Routine	96.7	63.2	97.4
16. Write Letters–Memos	89.7	64.9	NA
17. Attend Seminars	96.7	59.6	NA
18. Look up Prices	75.0	66.7	NA
19. Conduct Demonstrations	60.6	70.2	NA
20. Train Customers	61.3	63.2	33.6
21. Work With support People	71.4	52.3	NA
22. Handle Credit	71.0	49.1	63.1
23. Work with Distribution	77.8	45.6	59.3
24. Keep Office in Order	66.7	47.3	NA
25. Set up Point of Purchase	63.3	49.1	37.9
26. Test Product	63.3	42.2	31.8
27. Correct & Followup Orders	48.4	36.8	76.7
28. Conduct Customer Inventory	36.7	42.1	54.4
29 Train/Recruit Others	40.0	41.4	45.3
30. Prospect	41.4	36.8	94.3
31. Expedite Orders	43.3	33.3	82.9
32. Install Equipment	41.4	31.6	29.7
33 Stock Product	31.0	32.3	23.9
34. Provide Local Ad	40.0	28.1	30.8
35. Deliver Products	37.9	26.3	27.9
36 Provide Maintenance	20.7	21.7	27.9

*N = Number of companies responding. The U.S. response is from
Moncrief 1986a and represents 1393 salespeople from 51 companies.

panies. There were a total of 93 usable questionnaires returned, 57
from Denmark and 36 from Germany.

The representativeness of the sample was not as comprehensive as
that of Moncrief (1986b). Whereas Moncrief had 15 of the 20 SIC
categories represented, the present study only contains 8 of 20 SIC

categories. However, German/Danish companies were not as numerous in many of the SIC categories as were the U.S. counterparts.

The Survey Instrument

The survey instrument was an eight page questionnaire that included the sales activities section and other sales information that was used by the students in coursework. The entire instrument was written in German or Danish. The graduate students translated the English intent into German or Danish. The foreign language department of the University then translated the German/Danish back to English to ensure a proper decoding process. If the interpretation was different at any point, the document was changed until the question was decoded as intended. The questionnaire language was then tested using the local consulates in Dallas.

The sales activities were listed on a single page using a five-point scale of frequently/infrequently. Each respondent was asked if the average salesperson for that corporation performed that activity. If the activity was performed, the level of frequency was indicated with 1 labeled as "infrequently" performed and 5 labeled "frequently" performed.

The respondents in this study were typically sales managers or sales executives. Sales managers or higher were a necessity because of other information needed in the study but not reported here. The Moncrief (1986b) study interviewed salespeople, or sales managers that were still actively selling. This presents a problem for comparison of the two data sets. Salespeople's responses to their activity performance may very well differ from the perceived notions of management. However, management's perceptions should be relatively accurate in providing direction of differences between U.S. and Danish/German responses to activity differences. Comparing Danish and German differences will obviously be unaffected by the sample. The relative similarities of German and U.S. activities presented in the results would lead one to believe that management was able to indicate frequency of performance for activities. However, the reader does need to be aware of the differences in sample respondents.

RESULTS

Activity Performance

Table 2 lists the 36 activities that were used in the study and the percentage of the respondents from each country that perform the activity. The table is divided into three columns; the first and second present the German and Danish responses to the activity, and the last provides the 1393 U.S. responses from the Moncrief study.

As expected, there were common activities such as closing a sale, monitoring the competition, overcoming objections, studying trends and customer needs, providing feedback and receiving feedback performed by a large majority of the salespeople. Other activities, such as providing maintenance, delivering the products, providing local advertising, stocking the products, and installing equipment, were performed by relatively few of the respondents.

German to U.S. Comparisons

Comparing German and Danish sales activities (see Table 2) to the U.S. results provides some interesting contrasts and some similarities. The German responses were much more similar to the U.S. than they were to the Danish responses. However, there were some interesting differences. The German corporations (61.3%) were more likely to report that their salespeople train their customers more than the U.S. corporations (33.6%). The Germans were also more likely to set up displays, including point of purchase (63.3%), than were their U.S. counterparts (37.9%). Given the lack of food corporations represented in the study, the point-of-purchase response is surprising. The Germans did have a number of responses from the leather and glassware industries which might need point-of-purchase.

Testing the product was done by the majority of the German respondents but less than a third of the U.S. respondents (63.3% to 31.8%). German corporations also appear to work from a bid approach (96.7%) to only 67.3% for the American companies. Other activities with a higher German performance than their counterparts in the U.S. include: attend conferences, work with distributors, and make closure on a sale.

A couple of possibilities present themselves as to why some of these differences may occur. "Providing closure" would seem to be an unusual difference. However, in the Moncrief taxonomy of sales jobs, Moncrief reports that the most common job type in the U.S. was a Missionary job. The Missionary job has as a characteristic the lack of closure on a sale. Missionary salespeople do not take orders. The orders are placed with distributors. It is possible that the Missionary job type is not as prevalent in Europe. An alternative explanation could also be traced to the difference of a sales manager responding that the average salesperson provides closure, whereas a variety of salespeople in reality might not provide closure. The testing difference could be due to the heavy concentration of technical products in the German sample. However, the Germans use of the bid system is very high when compared to the U.S. companies regardless of industries represented.

There were some interesting results from the opposite perspective. The U.S. responses had very high performance scores on "prospecting" (94.3%). Virtually all of the American respondents spend some time prospecting for new customers. The German response was only 41.4%, less than half the American response. The Danish response was even less than the German (36.8%). The prospecting activity would appear to be a major difference in the way Europeans and the U.S. salesforces spend some of their sales time. The U.S. was also much more order oriented than were their counterparts in Germany. A large majority (76.7%) of the U.S. respondents indicated that they correct or follow up orders. Only 48.4% of the Germans responded in a similar manner. Eighty-three percent of the U.S. respondents indicated they expedite orders, while only 43.3% of the Germans perform this activity. The other major difference is that U.S. salespeople are more likely to conduct customer inventory (54.4% to 36.7%). The rest of the activities were basically performed similarly by the German and U.S. salespeople.

The results indicate that the German and U.S. companies have a degree of similarity in their sales activities The U.S. companies seem to spend more time looking for new customers and then providing more post-purchase service. The Germans appear to be somewhat more presale oriented such as preparing bids, testing the product, and training their salespeople. It would be very interesting for future research to determine if the Germans would classify with the same five job types found by Moncrief. There are indications that the job types might differ.

Comparing Danish Activity Performance to German/U.S.

The Danish sales activities were performed less frequently than either the Germans or Americans on all items but training customers, conducting demonstrations, and stocking the product. However, even these activities were only slightly greater in performance. The Danes were more likely to help customers with their inventory and were more likely to conduct demonstrations in their sales pitch. On the other hand, the Danes were much less likely to spend a night on the road (Denmark = 68.4%, Germany = 96.8%, and the U.S. = 92.9%). The Danes were also much less likely to entertain clients/customers. In fact, the Danes scored considerably lower than the Germans on almost all of the top 20 activities listed in Table 2. They did score higher than the Americans on training customers (also slightly higher than the Germans).

The activity list created by Moncrief (1986a) seems to be somewhat appropriate for German sales corporations, but not well suited for the Danish corporations. It would seem that the daily activities of the Danish salespeople have not been adequately detailed.

Sales Activity Frequency of Performance

Table 3 provides a comparison of the frequency of performance of each of the 36 sales activities. The German and Danish means are based on a 1-5 scale, with 5 being "frequently" performed. The U.S. means are from the Moncrief (1986a) study that was based on a 1-7 scale, with 7 labeled "frequently" performed. The t-statistic tests significant differences between the German and Danish means on the sales activities. Table 3 also provides a ratio that will help compare the German/Danish means to the U.S. means. The ratio was derived by dividing the mean score into the maximum scale score. For example, the Germans had a mean of 3.03 on "making sales presentations." Dividing 3.03 by 5 (maximum answer on the scale) provides a ratio score of .606. The U.S. mean on the same

THE GLOBAL BUSINESS

TABLE 3
SALES ACTIVITY FREQUENCY OF PERFORMANCE
GERMAN VS. DANISH*

ACTIVITY	German** Mean	Ratio	Danish Mean	Ratio	T-test	U.S. Mean	Ratio***
1. Make Sales Presentations	3.03	.606	3.22	.644	NS	5.43	.775
2. Conduct Demonstrations	1.61	.322	2.05	.410	NS	2.97	.424
3. Make Closures of Sales	4.41	.882	3.56	.712	.000	4.28	.611
4. Overcome Objections	3.93	.786	2.86	.572	.029	5.01	.717
5. Prepare Sales Presentations	2.80	.560	2.75	.550	NS	4.37	.624
6. Entertain Clients (lunch, drinks)	1.91	.382	1.25	.250	.096	4.58	.654
7. Test Equipment	1.50	.300	.68	.136	.014	.98	.140
8. Supervise Equipment Installation	1.17	.234	.56	.112	.000	.89	.127
9. Perform Equipment Maintenance	.41	.082	.49	.098	NS	.73	.104
10. Make Delivery of Product	1.07	.214	.42	.084	.001[a]	.64	.091
11. Train Customers to Use Product	1.77v	.354	1.77	.354	NS	2.20	.314
12. Inventory Customer Stock	1.23	.246	1.11	.222	NS	2.14	.306
13. Set up Point of Purchase	2.00	.400	1.09	.218	.097[a]	1.53	.219
14. Handle Local Advertising	.73	.146	.54	.108	NS	1.11	.159
15 Stock Shelves	.83	.166	1.07	.214	NS	.75	.107
16. Expedite Orders	1.73	.346	1.09	.218	NS	3.35	.475
17. Correct and Follow-up Orders	1.35	.270	1.10	.220	NS	2.50	.357
18. Fill Out Reports	3.22	.644	2.56	.512	.001[a]	4.82	.736
19. Train/Recruit Other Sales Reps.	.73	.146	.54	.108	NS	1.33	.190
20. Attend Conferences/Meetings	2.20	.440	1.61	.322	.007	2.11	.301
21. Handle Credit Investigation	1.81	.362	1.07	.214	NS	1.77	.253
22. Estimate and Submit Bids	3.50	.700	2.35	.470	.014	2.87	.410
23. Look up Prices	2.21	.442	2.42	.484	NS	4.23	.604
24. Travel Overnight	2.00	.400	1.84	.368	.014	3.97	.567
25. Study Trends and Clients' Needs	2.58	.516	2.87	.574	NS	4.33	.619
26. Work with Distributors	2.74	.548	1.30	.260		2.96	.423
27. Produce Prospects for Clients	.93	.186	.82	.164	NS	4.51	.644
28. Attend Seminars	1.65	.333	1.01	.202	NS	1.33	.196
29 Write Letters-Memos	2.20	.440	1.77	.354	NS	3.69	.527
30. Keep Office in Order (file, etc.)	1.50	.300	1.18	.236	NS	4.33	.619
31. Plan Daily Routine	3.30	.660	2.05	.410	.059[a]	5.81	.830
32. Work with Support People	2.32	.464	1.74	.348	NS	3.79	.541
33 Work with Management	2.90	.580	1.84	.368	.011	2.35	.336
34. Provide and Receive Feedback	2.89	.578	2.70	.540	NS	4.81	.687
35. Read Company and Trade Literature	2.47	.494	2.10	.420	NS	5.21	.744
36. Monitor Competition	3.61	.722	2.77	.554	.073	4.33	.619

*The higher the mean the more frequently the performance of the activity.
**German and Danish are a 1-5 scale. The U. S. is based on a 1-7 scale. The higher the ratio the more frequently the activity is performed.
***The ratio is determined by dividing the mean into the maximum answer on the scale.
[a]The differences were not significant when comparing a subset of SIC 35.

activity is 5.43 divided by 7 or a ratio of .775. It is important that the reader understand that this procedure cannot accurately compare the two groups. However, it does allow the comparison of direction and some conclusions can be speculated.

German/Danish Activity Frequency Compared to American

The U.S. salespeople were more frequently making sales presentations than were the Germans or Danes. However, the Danes scored higher than the Germans. The Americans and the Danes also scored higher than the Germans on conducting demonstrations. However, Activity 3 (closure of sale) was significantly more frequently performed by the Germans than either of the other two groups. In fact, the German mean was higher on a 5-point scale than was the U.S. mean on a 7-point scale. Entertaining clients appears to be much more a U.S. phenomenon than a European one. The U.S. mean/ratio was considerably higher than the German or Dane ratio. The U.S. salespeople also seem to more frequently spend the night on the road, which should not be unexpected.

The Germans scored higher frequencies on technical sales activities such as testing equipment, installing the product, and delivering the product. The Germans also more frequently worked with displays. In somewhat of a surprise, the Germans had a much higher frequency score on "submitting bids" than did the other two. The German score was significantly different from the Danish mean, and the Danish ratio was much higher than the U.S. ratio, leading to the conclusion that the Europeans may work more on a bid basis than a repeat purchase/brand loyalty approach. The Germans were also more frequently working with their management than were either the Danes or the Americans. The German mean was higher than the U.S. and the ratio was much higher. One caveat should be made here. The U.S. study was of salespeople, and in the present study, the respondents were sales managers. Managers may perceive a closer working relationship than does the typical salesperson.

The U.S. had higher ratios on a number of items. The U.S. corporations tended to more frequently fill out reports, check manuals for prices, work with distributors, write letters, keep office in order, and provide and receive feedback. There were a few other activities that had a considerably higher ratio than did the European counterparts. Planning daily routine received a ratio of .830 for the U.S. companies, compared to .660 for the Germans and .410 for the Danes. Reading company and trade literature also had high frequency for the U.S. (.744) and much lower for the Germans (.494) and the Danes (.420). It would appear that the U.S. salespeople spend more time on routine, nontraditional selling functions than do their counterparts in Germany and Denmark.

Comparison of German/Danish Subsets

One possible explanation for the differences in sales activities by country is based on the country's industry composition. Moncrief (1986a) found that industry does have some effect on activity composition but stated that job types and thus activities varied within an industry. Two competing companies might perform the same or a similar set of activities but at different frequencies of performance. However, it was important to take a subset of the German/Danish data and compare on a similar industry to determine if the industry was accounting for the differences in activity performance. SIC 35 was chosen as a subset because of a heavy representation in both the German and Danish samples. The results indicated that of the 14 significant differences found in Table 3 on the full data samples, only four became nonsignificant when compared on SIC 35. Making deliveries, setting up point-of-purchases, filling out reports, and planning daily routine became nonsignificant when compared on SIC 35. The other 10 activities remained significantly different. These results would seem to indicate that the industry does have some importance in determining activities, but differences seem to be explainable at least in part by the country being surveyed.

Company SIC Categories

Table 4 indicates the SIC classifications of the participating corporations and description of that SIC category. The U.S. corporate breakdown was based on the Moncrief (1986a) article. One obvious conclusion from examining the industry composition is the

TABLE 4
INDUSTRY SIC COMPOSITION

SIC	DESCRIPTION	GERMAN		DANISH		U. S.	
		N	%	N	%	N	%
20	Food	0	0.0	0	0.0	1	1.96
21	Tobacco	0	0.0	0	0.0	0	0.00
22	Textile	0	0.0	0	0.0	1	1.96
23	Apparel	0	0.0	0	0.0	4	7.84
24	Wood Products	0	0.0	0	0.0	0	0.00
25	Furniture	0	0.0	0	0.0	0	0.00
26	Paper Products	0	0.0	0	0.0	0	0.00
27	Printing	0	0.0	0	0.0	2	3.92
28	Chemicals	0	0.0	0	0.0	1	1.96
29	Petroleum	0	0.0	0	0.0	0	0.00
30	Rubber Products	0	0.0	0	0.0	3	5.88
31	Leather Products	19	17.9	30	17.8	2	3.92
32	Stone, Glass, Concrete	4	7.1	0	0.0	3	5.88
33	Primary Metals	2	3.5	0	0.0	5	9.86
34	Fabricated Metals	5	8.8	0	0.0	5	9.80
35	Machinery, Non-Electrical	13	22.9	8	23.4	8	15.68
36	Electrical Machinery	1	1.8	2	5.8	8	15.68
37	Transportation	3	5.3	1	2.9	3	5.88
38	Measuring Instruments Medical, Optical, Watches	18	31.6	14	47.0	4	7.84
39	Miscellaneous	0	0.0	2	5.9	1	1.96
		34		57		51	

N = Number of Companies

lack of German and Danish representation in SIC 20-30. The sample was drawn from a complete list of all German/Danish corporations. There were samples from most of these categories included but their numbers were small. There were also five SIC categories not represented in the U.S. sample.

A second interesting observation was the percentage of companies represented by SIC 38, classified as measuring instruments, medical, optical and watches. SIC 38 comprised 31.6% of the Danish sample and 47% of the German sample. However, only 7.84% of the U.S. sample was located in SIC 38.

The second more represented SIC category was SIC 35 (machinery, nonelectrical). The Germans had 22.9% of their sample in SIC 35; the Danes had 23.4% and the U.S. 15.7%. Leather products (SIC 31) was the third most common category for both the Germans and the Danes. Electrical machinery (SIC 36), followed by primary metals (SIC 33) and stone, glass, and concrete (SIC 32), were the next most common for the U.S.

DISCUSSION

This study was exploratory in nature, designed to examine how sales activities might differ across countries. The results of the study indicate that some activities, as might be expected, are shared by most salespeople. However, there are situation specific scenarios in which sales activities may differ considerably.

Sales activities are the fundamental aspect of every sales job. The concept of sales activities was important enough that Walker, Churchill, and Ford (1979) included sales activities and job types in their widely cited sales management model, even though at that time no one had compiled an activity list or empirically created sales job types. Sales management and selling texts refer to sales activities to attempt to convey that selling is not universally the same. Sales jobs do differ, and thus sales activities must differ. One question that this study examines is how sales activities differ internationally.

The results of this study indicate that there are clear differences in which sales activities are performed and how frequently. One original premise for this paper was to combine the German and Danish answers and compare them to the U.S. responses. However, the German respondents as a whole were more similar to the U.S. sales activities than they were to the Danes. This is perhaps the most interesting result of the study. The Germans are more notable in the international selling arena than are the Danes. The similarities of the U.S. and German activities might indicate that selling in an international multi-nation market may not be as diverse as might be expected. Certainly, there are still differences in sales activities between the U.S. and Germany and the differences need to be examined in more detail in future research.

The Danish results were difficult to interpret. Basically, the Danes performed fewer of the listed activities than did their counterparts (and when performed, they were typically performed less frequently). The industry composition of the German and Danish respondents was very similar as can be seen in Table 4, therefore the difference should not be attributable to industries. A possible explanation for the differences is that selling is less forceful in Denmark or the list of selling activities is not appropriate for the Danes.

However, there were clear differences among the three groups. Most notable was the lack of prospecting by both the Germans and the Danes. The modal U.S. response to prospecting was very frequent, whereas the German/Danes was not. Over 90% of U.S. and German respondents travelled whereas the travelling activity among Danes was rather low. The frequency of overnight travel was much higher for the U.S. The Denmark response was not surprising. However, the rate of overnight travel for the German respondents was somewhat surprising. One would expect the territories in the U.S. to be much larger in land mass and thus require a great deal more travel.

The German respondents more frequently had a tendency to perform technical activities, possibly because of a heavy representation in the machinery and more complex product categories. The U.S. corporations were more diverse in the type of companies represented and thus more nontechnical activities occurred with a higher frequency.

Directions for Future Research

There clearly needs to be more research performed examining differences in international selling. Moncrief (1986b) identified five sales job types based on sales activity responses from 51 U.S. companies. The five job types include an order taker, a simple rebuy scenario; an institutional seller, who sells a product to institutions or other manufacturers; a missionary salesperson, who concentrates on selling goodwill and rarely physically takes an order; a trade servicer, who sells and services products to a reseller; and a trade seller, who performs presales activities with a minimum of postsales service. It would be interesting to examine selling in other countries to discover if the same job types would emerge. Based on the exploratory work in this study, it would appear that the job types might not be the same. Even though German and U.S. sales activities were similar, the frequency of performance was not.

Based on answers of the Danish respondents, the 121 Moncrief activity list may not be comprehensive enough for an international study. The expansion of the activity list would have to be the first step in determining if the sales job types are indeed different in an international market. The expansion of the list would take a comprehensive study examining salespeople in multiple countries. The Moncrief activity list was developed from focus groups. Focus groups might not be realistic for a study of this magnitude. The activity list would then become the basis of developing the job types or testing the existing job types.

This study used two European countries of different status in the international market. However, it would be even more interesting to examine the Japanese sales forces which might have sales activities that most resemble the sales activities of the U.S. It would seem logical that the more international oriented the country the more similar the sales processes. The size of the country's GNP, the primary target markets, philosophical and political issues, primary industries, population, and geographic proximity will all be issues that may affect the frequency of performance of sales activities.

In conclusion, this study has certain limitations that must be mentioned. The German and Danish studies were obtained simultaneously with the same basic research instruments, while the comparison to the U.S. was accomplished through a previous study with a different questionnaire. The samples were also different, with the current study surveying managers and the U.S. study surveying salespeople. However, the study does indicate some interesting similarities and differences that should be examined in future research. As countries become more involved in the international market, it will become increasingly more important to determine how we sell, and what might be the most effective way to sell. Sales activities are the key to the selling process and the fundamental center of managing the selling process.

REFERENCES

Lamont, Lawrence M. and William J. Lundstrom. (1974). "Defining Industrial Sales Behavior: A Factor Analytic Study." *Proceedings*, American Marketing Association, Ronald C. Curham, ed., pp. 493;498.

Moncrief, William C. (1986a). "Ten Key Activities of Industrial Salespeople." *Industrial Marketing Management*, 15, pp. 309-318.

_____. (1986b). "A Taxonomy for Industrial Salesforce Job Activities." *Journal of Marketing Research*, August, Vol. 23, pp. 261-270.

Walker, Orville C., Gilbert A. Churchill, Jr., and Neil M. Ford. (1979). "Where Do We Go from Here? Selected Conceptual Empirical Issues Concerning the Motivation and Performance of the Industrial Salesforce." *Critical Issues in Sales Management: State of the Art and Future Research Needs*. Gerald Albaum and Gilbert A. Churchill, Jr., eds., Eugene, Oregon: University of Oregon.

Wallace, Mark J., A. Fredric Crandall and Charles H. Fay. (1982). *Administering Human Resources*. New York, NY: Random House, p. 182.

Chapter 9

The Role of Environmental Factors in the Purchase of Foreign Industrial Products

John C. Crawford
Charles W. Lamb

SUMMARY. This study examined the influence of selected environmental factors on industrial buyers' willingness to buy products of foreign origin. A national sample of U.S. purchasing managers reported distinct preferences for products from certain countries related to the cultural realms to which these countries belong, their level of political freedom, and their stage of economic development.

INTRODUCTION

Despite some evidence to the contrary (Johansson, Douglas, & Nonaka, 1985), the results of most studies suggest that consumers, business people, and professional purchasing managers have stereotypes about imported products based upon their country of origin (e.g., Schooler, 1965; Reierson, 1966; Nagashima, 1970; Greer, 1971; Dornoff, Tankersley, & White, 1974; Gaedeke, 1973; White & Cundiff, 1978; Wang & Lamb, 1980; Crawford & Lamb, 1981; Kaynak & Cavusgil, 1983; Barker, 1987). These stereotypes or biases may influence consumers' and purchasing agents' willingness to buy products that are produced in foreign countries, since source country stimuli do appear to affect perceptions of quality.

This chapter was first published in the *Journal of International Consumer Marketing*, Vol. 1(3) 1989.

While the existence of this so-called "bias phenomenon" has clearly been established, there is considerable debate as to the form it takes and to its antecedents. One view (Scott, 1965), is that the level of like or dislike of a particular country correlates with product preferences. Another, is that tradition, history and other non-product factors pertaining to the country of origin may bias the consumer for or against a particular country's products (Barker, 1987). Other studies (e.g., Schooler, 1965; Anderson & Cunningham, 1972), have attempted to use socioeconomic and psychological characteristics as antecedents to bias in consumer studies, with mixed results. As far as the industrial buyer is concerned, certainly, no such varied and systematic investigations have been conducted to identify what factors account for the products of some countries being perceived more favorably than the products of other countries.

The purpose of the study reported here was to assess whether industrial buyers' willingness to buy foreign products is influenced by the environment that exists within a product's country of origin. It is generally recognized that the buyer is usually only one of several people who influence and decide on the purchase of industrial products (Sheth, 1973). This multiple buying influence is a common occurrence in industry and is well documented in the literature. Nonetheless, the buyer occupies a key position in being able to select the supplier and negotiate the terms of the agreement in many buying situations. This places him in a position of much greater significance than most of the other officials influencing the buying of industrial goods (Webster & Wind, 1972). The industrial buyer is, therefore, a key executive in the buying process and an understanding of the factors which influence his decision making is a major concern of this study.

Better understanding of the industrial buyer requires some conceptual scheme for the analysis of buyer behavior and its determinants. Wind (1967), for example, hypothesized that a buyer's behavior is a function of five sets of variables; the buyer's own characteristics, interpersonal influences, organizational variables, inputs from sources of supply, and environmental variables. In dealing with foreign suppliers the foreign environment is of the utmost importance (Wind, 1967).

Three environmental factors, economic development, political freedom, and culture have been identified as being most important in determining the environment of any foreign country (Fayerweather, 1965), and these were selected for this study. It was hypothesized that U.S. industrial buyers' willingness to buy foreign products is affected by: (1) the stage of economic development reached by the country of origin, (2) the level of political freedom existing in the country, (3) the cultural realm to which the country belongs, and (4) the possible interactive effects of these factors.

The reason for selecting these particular variables to investigate was that the results of previous studies (e.g., White & Cundiff, 1978; Bilkey & Nes, 1982) suggest that industrial buyers may generalize their knowledge or perceptions about foreign countries to the quality of products produced in these countries, and that environmental differences among countries might, at least partially, explain buyers' favorable predispositions toward the products of some countries and unfavorable predispositions toward the products of other countries.

VARIABLES AND RESEARCH DESIGN

Variables Analyzed

The dependent variable in the study was professional purchasing managers' willingness to buy products made in each of 35 foreign countries assuming that price, quality, and services were acceptable.

Foreign country of origin was treated as an independent variable. The 35 countries included in the study were mainly significant exporters (over $200 million yearly) to the U.S. However, several countries not meeting this requirement were included to ensure an adequate representation of the major cultural groupings of the world and a cross-section of the political and economic categories within the major cultural groupings.

State of Economic Development

The classification schemes used to operationalize this and the other two independent variables are based upon classification schemes that have been developed by authoritative sources. Several well-known methods of classifying countries include Rostow's (1960) "Five Stages of Economic Growth" approach, Wilcox, Hunter and Baratz' (1976) view of the world's nations as being at different points in the process of development, and the United Nations' *World Economic Survey* which assigns each member country to one of three categories: developed market economies, centrally planned economies, and developing economies. Not all countries are members of the U.N., however. There are numerous other classifying systems. For example, Howe and the staff of the Overseas Development Council (1974) categorized all of the countries in the world into four categories based upon their stage of economic development: (1) poorest developing, (2) other developing, (3) Organization of Petroleum Exporting Countries [OPEC], and (4) developed countries. Howe's classification scheme was chosen for the study because it encompasses all of the world's economies, which the other schemes do not. It was slightly modified in that OPEC countries were merged into the category of developing countries since they meet all but one of the criteria (per capita income) for this category in terms of stage of socioeconomic development. The resultant scheme was comprised of the following three stages of economic development: (1) poorest developing; (2) other developing; and (3) developed.

Political Freedom

One method of measuring a nation's political freedom is to rate its performance in the areas of civil liberties and political rights. Freedom House, a private organization that monitors the level of freedom in the world along these dimensions and publishes *The Comparative Survey of Freedom,* annually rates countries of the world as "not free," "partly free," or "free." Each of the countries involved in the study were categorized using this classification scheme. The level of freedom was used to assess the impact of country of origin on industrial buyers' willingness to buy from specific countries.

Cultural Realm

A frequently used criterion for classifying culture is obtained by sorting, objectively, the many diverse segments of the earth's population into a simple but meaningful framework of broad cultural realms. The term cultural realm signifies a large geographic area or region that has a fundamental unit in the composition, arrangement, and integration of significant traits which distinguishes it from other realms (Broek & Webb, 1973). In achieving this goal, however, the researcher has to recognize that many of the individual differences between (and within) countries are submerged, and that clustering countries together in one large cultural realm ignores the possibility that smaller clusters may exist which exhibit characteristics not shared by the larger whole (Hofstede, 1983). Two well-known schemes for establishing cultural realms (James, 1976; Broek & Webb, 1973) were combined and consolidated to produce a composite scheme comprising the following six cultural realms: (1) Africa; (2) Asia; (3) Australia/New Zealand; (4) Europe; (5) Latin America; and (6) the Middle East/North Africa.

Classification of Countries

As Table 1 illustrates, the 35 foreign countries included in the study were assigned to one of three stages of economic development, three levels of political freedom, and six cultural regions. Since no country can appear in more than one economic, political, or cultural category, the countries were "nested" within environmental groups. A nested factorial design (Winer, 1971, p. 359) was therefore used. The independent variables of the model were the environmental factor (fixed), country factor (fixed and nested within environment) and respondent factor (random). The dependent variable was purchasing managers' willingness to buy from different countries. Duncan's Multiple Range Test was used to determine which environmental levels produced these differences.

TABLE 1

Countries Classified By:

Cultural, Political and Economic Dimensions

Culture/	Political*	Economic+	Culture/	Political	Economic
AFRICAN			**EUROPEAN**		
Ethiopia	NF	PD	France	F	D
Ghana	NF	PD	Italy	F	D
Ivory Coast	NF	PD	Spain	F	D
Angola	NF	OD	Sweden	F	D
Nigeria	PF	OD	U. Kingdom	F	D
Zaire	NF	OD	W. Germany	F	D
S.Africa	PF	D	Turkey	F	OD
ASIAN			**MID. EAST**		
India	F	PD	Sudan	PF	PD
Thailand	NF	PD	Egypt	PF	OD
Indonesia	PF	PD	Libya	NF	OD
Singapore	PF	OD	S. Arabia	NF	OD
S. Korea	PF	OD	Israel	F	D
Taiwan	PF	OD			
Japan	F	D			
LATIN AMERICA			**AUST/ N.Z.**		
El Salvador	PF	PD	Australia	F	D
Haiti	NF	PD	New Zealand	F	D
Honduras	PF	PD			
Argentina	PF	OD			
Brazil	PF	OD			
Mexico	PF	OD			
Venezuela	F	OD			

* Political: F=Free; PF=Partly Free; NF=Not Free
+ Economic: D=Developed; OD=Other Developing; PD=Poor Developing

DATA COLLECTION

The sample for this study was randomly selected from the list of members of the National Association of Purchasing Managers, Inc. The original selection was designed, according to zip code, to cover a complete cross-section of the continental United States. A total of 1,090 questionnaires, which constituted a sample of 4.5 percent, was mailed to members of the association. Postcards encouraging a timely response were mailed to the sample one week after the initial questionnaires were mailed. Follow-up letters and questionnaires were sent to persons who had not responded two weeks after the initial mailing. Four hundred responses (37%) were returned. Of these, 376 (35%) were usable. An analysis of the response patterns was conducted to determine if the results needed to be adjusted to correct for non-response bias. Response patterns were analyzed to determine possible non-response bias. During the three-week period in which survey responses were received, records were kept of the weekly response pattern. Chi-square tests were used to determine whether a systematic relationship existed between the sex, age, years of experience, and education of early, middle and late respondents. Similar tests were applied to size of firm, product category and classification of industry. No significant differences (at the 0.05 level) were found. Responses of early versus late respondents were also compared on the assumption that the late respondents answered only after repeated prompting, and, but for this prompting, would likely have been non-respondents (Oppenheim, 1966). A Spearman rank-order correlation of $r_s = 0.98$ (significant at the 0.01 level) revealed a strong similarity of responses between early and late respondents. It is, thus, not unreasonable to assume that the non-respondents to the survey have the same demographic characteristics as the respondents.

Respondents were asked to indicate their willingness to buy products made in each of the 35 foreign countries included in the study. A Likert-type scale allowed respondents to record their responses, ranging from extremely unwilling (1) to extremely willing (5). The reliability of the instrument was estimated following a pilot study and after the main study. The results (Spearman-Brown split-half coefficient 0.92; Pearson rank-order correlation 0.94; Kendall rank-order correlation 0.87) show a fairly high degree of reliability.

RESULTS

The Impact of Stage of Development

Analysis of variance revealed that the main effect of stage of economic development on willingness to buy was significant. Duncan's Multiple Range Test was used to determine which level or levels of development caused this result. As Table 2 indicates, purchasing managers included in the study prefer products first

TABLE 2

Duncan's Multiple Range Test for Variables

Willingness to Buy and Economic Development

Grouping*	Mean+	No. of Countries	Development
A	3.92	11	Developed
B	3.43	15	Developing
C	3.23	9	Poor Dev.
		35	

* Groupings signify that means are significantly different at 0.01 level

+ On a scale: 1=extremely unwilling, to 5=extremely willing.

from the developed countries, second from the other developing countries and last from the poorest developing countries.

The Impact of Political Freedom

The main effect of the independent variable "political freedom" was also highly significant. The Duncan's test results shown in Table 3 illustrate that those countries classified as "free" were preferred over those that are "partly free," and the "partly free" countries are preferred to the "not free" countries as sources of supply. This finding supports the hypothesis that the industrial buyer's perception of a country's political climate influences his willingness to buy products from that country.

The Impact of Cultural Realm

The analysis of variance results also support the hypothesis that industrial buyers' perceptions of the cultural realm to which a country belongs influence willingness to buy from that country. Again the Duncan's test results in Table 4 indicate that buyers have a preference for products from the Australia/New Zealand cultural realm over all others, followed by a preference for products from the European cultural realm. Products from Asian and Latin American countries were less desirable than products from the European cultural realm. Africa and the Middle East were the least preferred origins of products.

It appears that the closer a cultural realm is to that of the United States the more preferred it is as a source of supply for U.S. industrial buyers. The two cultural realms that rated highest, Australia/ New Zealand and Europe, are those with strong cultural ties to the U.S. in terms of language, traditions, and heritage. Possibly, buyers feel more comfortable in dealing with suppliers from these realms than from others that do not appear to be as close in a cultural sense.

The Interactive Impact

It was hypothesized that there might be some interaction between culture, political freedom, and/or stage of economic development upon purchasing managers' willingness to buy. The interaction effects between economic development and political freedom, economic development and cultural realm, political freedom and cultural realm, and all three variables were statistically significant. Apparently, respondents' preferences are influenced by the combination of a country's stage of economic development, the political freedom that exists in the country, and the culture to which it be-

TABLE 3

Duncan's Multiple Range Test for Variables

Willingness to Buy and Political Freedom

Grouping*	Mean+	No.of Countries	Political
A	3.80	13	Free
B·	3.49	14	Partly free
C	3.11	8	Not free
		35	

* Groupings signify that means are significantly different at 0.01 level.
+ On a scale: 1=extremely unwilling, to 5=extremely willing.

TABLE 4

Duncan's Multiple Range Test for Variables

Willingness to Buy and Culture Realm

Grouping*	Mean+	No. of Countries	Culture
A	4.07	2	Aust/NZ
B	3.86	7	Europe
C	3.63	7	Asia
D	3.50	7	Latin Am.
E	3.31	5	Mid. East
E	3.13	7	Africa
		35	

* Groupings with same letter are not significantly different at 0.01 level

+ On a scale: 1-extremely unwilling to 5=extremely willing

longs. As Table 5 illustrates, buyers appear to distinguish countries not only on the basis, for example, of "free" or "not free," but also between Asian, European, and Latin American "free" and "not free" countries. A similar relationship appears to exist between other variables such as developed-free versus developed-not free countries. The significant interaction effects were expected since the variables economic development, political freedom and culture are often closely related and difficult to isolate. However, with one exception, "free" countries were preferred to those with some restraint on freedom for each level of economic development. The exception is that for the developing countries, the mean willingness to buy from "partly free" countries was greater than the mean willingness to buy from "free" countries. A possible explanation for this is that buyers are not familiar with the politic scenes of some of the developing countries and are unable to differentiate on this basis, or alternatively, that they are more tolerant of a lack of freedom in the developing world than in the developed world.

TABLE 5

Interactive Effect of Economic Development, Political Freedom

and Culture on Buyers' Mean Willingness to Buy

Development	Freedom	Culture	No. of Countries	Mean Willingness
Developed	Free	Asia	1	4.11
Developed	Free	Aust/NZ	2	4.07
Developed	Free	Europe	7	3.86
Developed	Free	Mid. East	1	3.78
Developed	P. Free	Africa	1	3.40
Developing	Free	Latin Am.	1	3.56
Developing	Free	Europe	1	3.26
Developing	P. Free	Asian	3	.74
Developing	P. Free	Latin Am.	3	.70
Developing	P. Free	Mid. East	1	3.64
Developing	P. Free	Africa	1	3.21
Developing	N. Free	Mid. East	2	3.08
Developing	N. Free	Africa	2	.99
Poorest Dev.	Free	Asia	1	3.34
Poorest Dev.	P. Free	Asia	1	3.40
Poorest Dev.	P. Free	Latin Am.	2	3.22
Poorest Dev.	P. Free	Mid. East	1	2.99
Poorest Dev.	N. Free	Asia	1	3.36
Poorest Dev.	N. Free	Africa	3	.11
			35	

Additional Findings

In addition to the impact of stage of economic development, political freedom and cultural realm, it was hypothesized that willingness to buy foreign products might be partly explained by the industry that an individual uses as his or her frame of reference, and perhaps also by the size of the firm. People employed in the fashion or perfume industry, for example, might be more willing to buy foreign products than people employed in the transportation industry based upon tradition and past experiences. Likewise, buyers for larger firms, particularly multinationals, might be more prone to purchase products from foreign countries on a reciprocal basis or because of a need to secure several sources of supply for their international operations.

To test the hypothesis that willingness to buy foreign products might be partly explained by the industry that an individual uses as his or her frame of reference, respondents were asked to indicate whether their principal industry was construction, transportation, mining, agriculture, retail/wholesale, manufacturing, or other. Firm size was categorized by asking respondents whether the firm employed less than 500 people, 500 to 999 people, or over 1,000 people. Analysis of variance revealed that neither industry nor firm size was significantly related to a purchasing manager's willingness to buy foreign-made products. Furthermore, no significant interaction between industry and size was found. In other words, there were no significant differences in respondents' willingness to buy products from various countries of origin based upon respondents' firm size or industry affiliation.

LIMITATIONS OF THE FINDINGS

The findings obtained are subject to several limitations and, in consequence, should be treated as suggestive and not objective. Attention is drawn to some important limitations.

Due to the large number of countries included in the survey it is reasonable to assume that not all the buyers were familiar with all of the countries. Thus, their indicated willingness to buy may be unrelated to their level of knowledge, possibly a neutral or favorable response was obtained in the absence of actual buying experience.

Because of the large non-response rate some caution must be observed in generalizing the results of the survey to all purchasing managers.

It is recognized that willingness to buy may also be influenced by certain "domestic" variables such as the unavailability of products from local suppliers or a desire to break the monopoly position of a domestic supplier. Willingness to buy may not result in an actual decision to buy, of course. A basic willingness to buy can be overcome by variations in price where their effect is to reduce the perceived risk of buying foreign products (Schooler & Wildt, 1968).

The instruction to respondents to assume that price, quality, and terms of delivery were the same for foreign and domestic goods introduced an equalizing factor not present in real life buying situations. Obviously, all of these elements are weighed carefully by the buyer in making his decision.

Finally, the choice of classification schemes to group the countries in the study into broad economic, political and cultural categories is always a subjective decision. While making the analysis more manageable, it clearly groups together nations which have unique characteristics and which if classified using other criteria might not be part of the same cultural set as defined herein.

CONCLUSIONS

The results of this study indicate that U.S. industrial buyers' willingness to buy foreign products depends to some degree upon their views of the country where the product originated. Figure 1 illustrates this point. It shows the influences of level of economic development, political freedom and cultural realm on industrial buyers' willingness to purchase foreign products. Although some cells do not contain any countries, each country in the world can be assigned to one of the 54 (3 × 3 × 6) distinct cells.

The shaded area represents the most favored mix of environments as far as the U.S. industrial buyer is concerned. The most preferred sources of supply are those countries which are developed (industrialized), free, and belong to the Australia/New Zealand cultural realm. These countries are in fact very close to the United States culturally, and have a common political and legal heritage. Thus, it appears that buyers prefer to deal with countries perceived as most like their own country. In general, the closer a country is to the shaded area in Figure 1, the greater the willingness of buyers to purchase products from that country.

The most acceptable countries are those which are politically free, developed and culturally close to the U.S., although each of these criteria has a different impact on the decision making process. In some situations political freedom outweighs economic and cultural effects. South Africa, for example, an industrialized economy, is rated as "partly free" and is the only developed country which

Figure 1
Environmental Segmentation Model

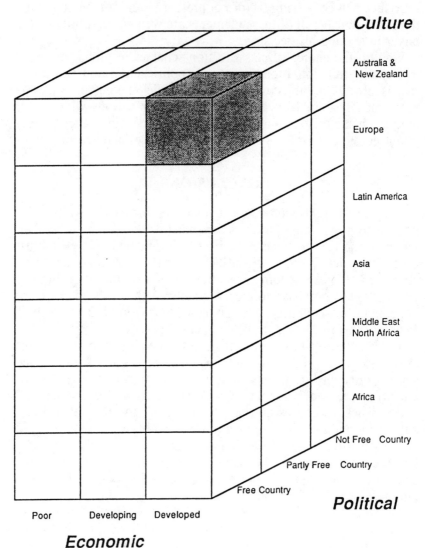

does not rank among the most preferred sources of supply. Japan, although not the most preferred culture, is a highly preferred source probably because its political freedom and industrial economy outweigh the cultural factor. Of course, there are likely many situation specific factors that also affect purchasing managers' willingness to buy from various countries of origin such as past experience, reciprocity arrangements, long run product availability, relative prices, quality differentials, differences in selling skills among salesmen, and the reputations of firms representing manufacturers from different countries.

In the absence of situation specific factors, U.S. buyers appear to stereotype countries and their willingness to buy is influenced by these stereotypes. A pronounced preference for developed and free countries exists. Failure to meet either of these criteria reduces a country's prospects of exporting to the U.S. Products from countries with positive stereotypes are more favorably regarded and would, therefore, have greater opportunities to enter the U.S. market.

These findings seem to be supported by the present flow of international trade, the bulk of which occurs between the industrialized nations, particularly those that are politically free. They also explain the apparent lack of acceptance of products from developing countries of the world by U.S. buyers.

REFERENCES

Anderson, W.T. and William H. Cunningham. (1972). "Gauging Foreign Product Promotion." *Journal of Advertising Research,* 12(1) (February), pp. 29-34.

Barker, A.T. (1987). "A Study of Attitudes Towards Products Made in Australia." *Journal of Global Marketing*, 1(1/2) (Fall/Winter), pp. 131-144.

Bilkey, W.J. and E. Nes. (1982). "Country-Of-Origin Effects on Product Evaluation." *Journal of International Business Studies,* (Spring/Summer), pp. 89-99.

Broek, Jan O.M. and J.W. Webb. (1973). *A Geography of Mankind.* New York: McGraw-Hill Book Company.

Crawford, J.C. and C.W. Lamb, Jr. (1981). "Source Preferences for Imported Products." *Journal of Purchasing and Materials Management,* (Winter), pp. 28-33.

Dornoff, D.J., C.B. Tankersley and G.P. White. (1974). "Consumer's Perceptions of Imports." *Akron Business and Economics Review*, (Summer), pp. 26-29.

Fayerweather, John. (1965). *International Marketing*. Englewood Cliffs, NJ: Prentice-Hall, Inc.

Gaedeke, R. (1973). "Consumer Attitudes Toward Products Made in Developing Countries." *Journal of Retailing*, (November), pp. 13-24.

Greer, T.V. (1971). "British Purchasing Agents and the European Economic Community: Some Empirical Evidence on International Industrial Perceptions." *Journal of Purchasing*, 7, pp. 56-63.

Hofstede, Geert. (1984). *Culture's Consequences*. Sage Publications, Beverly Hills, CA: Sage Publications.

Howe, James W. and the Staff of the Overseas Developmental Council. (1974). *The U.S. and the Developing World: Agenda for Action*. New York: Praeger.

James, Preston E. (1976). "World View of Major Culture Regions," in *World Regional Geography: A Problem Approach*, Fred E. Dohis and Lawrence M. Sommers, eds., New York: West Publishing Company.

Johansson, K. Johny, Susan P. Douglas and Ikujiro Nonaka. (1985). "Assessing the Impact of Country of Origin on Product Evaluations: A New Methodological Perspective." *Journal of Marketing Research*, 22 (November), pp. 388-396.

Kaynak, Erdener and S. Tamer Cavusgil. (1983). "Consumer Attitudes Towards Products of Foreign Origin: Do They Vary Across Product Classes?" *International Journal of Advertising*, 2 (April-June), pp. 147-157.

Nagashima, Akira. (1970). "A Comparison of Japanese and U.S. Attitudes Toward Foreign Products." *Journal of Marketing*, 34 (January), pp. 95-100.

Oppenheim, A.N. (1966). *Questionnaire Design and Attitude Measurement*. New York: Basic Books.

Reierson, C. (1966). "Are Foreign Products Seen as National Stereotypes?" *Journal of Retailing*, 42 (Fall), pp. 33-40.

Rostow, W.W. (1960). *The Stage of Economic Growth: A Non-Communist Manifesto*. Cambridge, MA: Cambridge University Press.

Schooler, Robert D. (1965). "Product Bias in the Central American Common Market." *Journal of Marketing Research*, 2 (November), pp. 394-397.

Schooler, Robert D. and Albert R. Wildt. (1968). "Elasticity of Product Bias." *Journal of Marketing Research*, 5 (February), pp. 78-81.

Scott, W.A. (1965). "Psychological and Social Correlates of International Images," in *International Behavior*, H.C. Kelman, ed., New York: Holt, Rinehart and Winston, pp. 99-100.

Sheth, Jagdish N. (1973). "A Model of Industrial Buyer Behavior." *Journal of Marketing*, 37 (October), pp. 50-56.

Wang, C.K. and C.W. Lamb, Jr. (1980). "Foreign Environmental Factors Influencing American Consumers' Predispositions Toward European Products." *Journal of the Academy of Marketing Science*, 11 (Winter), pp. 71-84.

Webster, Frederick E. and Yoram Wind. (1972). *Organizational Buying Behavior*. Englewood Cliffs, NJ: Prentice-Hall, Inc.

White, Phillip D. and Edward W. Cundiff. (1978). "Assessing the Quality of Industrial Products." *Journal of Marketing,* pp. 80-85.

Wilcox, C., H. Hunter and M.S. Barantz. (1976). *Economics of the World Today.* New York: Harcourt Brace Jovanovich, Inc.

Wind, Yoram. (1967). "The Determinants of Industrial Buyer's Behavior," in *Industrial Buying and Creative Marketing*, P.J. Robinson, C.W. Faris and Y. Wind, eds., Boston: Allyn & Bacon, Inc.

Winer, B.J. (1971). *Statistical Principles in Experimental Design.* 2nd ed. New York: McGraw-Hill Book Company.

Chapter 10

International Advertising in Cross-Cultural Environments

Rita Martenson

SUMMARY. Six European commercials were tested on 239 respondents belonging to five cultural groups, ranging from the high-context Asian group to the low-context Swedish group. Results clearly support Wells' proposition that high-context cultures perceive nonverbal communications elements as being more informative than a low-context culture does. These findings are important for the international advertiser and deserve much more exploration in order to determine more about how to manage nonverbal elements in cross-cultural communications.

INTRODUCTION

A review of earlier studies in international and global marketing shows that products tend to be more and more standardized worldwide. The development in advertising seems to be different; the more we know about advertising, the easier it becomes to adapt it to local market differences (Martenson 1987a, 1987b, 1988). In a recent study by the Management Centre Europe, it was found that the majority of respondents (246 from 17 countries) thought that a standardized international campaign in which local variations are accepted would be the best alternative for the international advertiser. Very few favored either of the extreme alternatives, completely standardized or completely locally adapted.

Lately, Wells (1987) has added some valuable insights to international advertising management. Wells has suggested that some cultures might be low-context cultures, where the meaning of a mes-

This chapter was first published in the *Journal of International Consumer Marketing*, Vol. 2(1) 1989.

sage can be isolated from the context in which it occurs and understood as an independent entity. According to Wells, one can rank cultures from high-context to low-context, starting with the Japanese, the Chinese, the Arab, the Greek, the Spanish, the Italian, the English, the French, the North American, the Scandinavian and ending with the German culture as being one of the most low context-oriented. As an example of how high-context advertising works, Wells quotes the president of DYR, Takashi Michioka, who put it in this way:

> . . . in Japan, differentiation among products does not consist of explaining with words the points of difference among competing products as in America. Differentiation is achieved by bringing out nuances and overall differences in tone, by dramatizing those differences in the people appearing in the commercial. The way they talk, the music, the scenery, etc. Rather than emphasizing the unique features and dissimilarities of the product itself.

Michioka's description of Japanese advertising is more or less what has come to be known as nonverbal advertising. Nonverbal commercials are supposed to communicate far beyond what is actually said or written in other commercials. Hecker (1987) has summarized the elements used to communicate the message:

- paralanguage (e.g., the tone, pace and number of voices)
- glance (e.g., eye contact or not with the audience)
- proxemics (e.g., who is touching whom, where, and how much)
- gestures (e.g., pointing, nodding, waving)
- body language (e.g., standing, running, leaning)
- facial cues (e.g., smiling, frowning, raised eyebrows)
- spokesperson characteristics — perception (familiarity and type), attributes ascribed to him/her (attractive, authoritative, trustworthy)
- dress (e.g., for suggestion of occupation, status, appropriateness)
- deception cues (e.g., exaggerated demonstrations)
- pitcher/catcher or teacher/learner relationships (who is interfacing with whom and their apparent relationship).

There are also a number of background elements which might affect how a message is perceived by different cultural groups:

- music (e.g., familiarity)
- semiotics (e.g., signs, symbols and artifacts that provoke certain associations)
- setting (e.g., indoor versus outdoor, country versus city, foreign versus domestic)
- sound effects (e.g., type and intention)
- tonality/mood (e.g., feelings projected by the commercial).

Earlier research has shown that cultural factors influence perception. Bagby (1957) found, for example, highly significant differences between what Americans and Mexicans reported on what they saw when looking at pictures with culturally familiar and unfamiliar scenes. Each group identified more easily with the culturally familiar scene. Bagby's results reflected genuine perceptual dominance of the scenes characteristic of one's own culture rather than just differences in reporting these scenes. If this is so also in advertising, then the global advertiser should adapt his global campaign to local markets, for example, in terms of the settings shown in the commercial. An example of a global campaign adapted to different geographical areas is the campaign for Camel. One part of the campaign is based on "wilderness," i.e., in this case showing settings from different types of jungles or local wildlife areas.

One of the difficulties in cross-cultural research is that certain cross-cultural differences are unconscious to the society. The cultural unconscious is the deep underlying attitude and value structure that is imprinted on each member of society from their first experience with something (Sills-Levy, 1987). These underlying values do not change rapidly, but rather last throughout the individual's lifetime. The archetype is common to everyone in a culture and tends to last as long as the culture itself. According to Sills-Levy, knowing the cultural unconscious of what a product or a service really means to consumers is to know its Archetype, which means what can be said about it, what should be said about it, what this product or service is not, and what cannot be said and should never, never be said about it.

All cultural variables are not relevant in the context of this chapter. Rather, this chapter has limited the discussion to its role in advertising, e.g., language and visual and auditory symbols. Symbols can often mediate between the individual and his surroundings, and they can focus his attention on some aspects of his environment and deflect it from others and they can also affect the way the world is classified in different categories.

PURPOSE AND METHODOLOGY

The purpose of this study was to see whether people from different cultures react differently to commercials from other countries. People from low-context cultures might, for example, have difficulties understanding the high-context technique, since it does not "get to the point," and vice versa. If Wells' interesting observations are true, then high-context respondents would be able to get more information out of nonverbal advertising than respondents from a low-context area in an advertising testing situation. More specifically, the Asian respondents in the study would be able to interpret nonverbal elements in the commercials much better than the other respondents in the study and the Swedish respondents would get the least information from these nonverbal commercials.

An interesting question in the study was how long a person belongs to one culture after having moved from one country to another. Jacobs and Campbell (1961) found that "significant remnants of the culture persisted for four or five generations beyond the last confederate." It is likely, however, that the cultural influence varies from one situation to another. Typically, the effects of the cultural background become more marked as a function of the complexity and ambiguity of the available information and of the opportunities that an individual has to engage in his own independent checking of what comes to him from social sources. It could easily be assumed that commercials have a low degree of complexity and ambiguity, and that therefore it would not be reasonable to assume that cultural effects would be present as long as five generations in this case. In this study it was assumed that it would take approximately three generations until a foreign culture would be completely assimilated with the "American culture," i.e., to be classified as being from the American cultural group the respondent would have to come from a family where three generations were born in the United States.

Two-hundred and thirty-nine persons (convenience sample) participated in this study. Sixty-one were Americans, 21 had Mexican origin, 109 had Asian origin, and 31 came from other cultural areas (e.g., Europe). The study was done in Los Angeles and participants had either full-time or part-time jobs with a few exceptions, and they attended a local university. Approximately six months later 17 Swedish students in Sweden participated in the study.

Respondents were shown six European nonverbal commercials, which had been produced for domestic markets in Europe, i.e., none of the commercials came from a global campaign. The first commercial was a spaghetti commercial from Italy, the second was a cigarette commercial from Germany, the third was an insurance commercial from Sweden, the fourth was a catsup commercial from England, the fifth was a chewing gum commercial from France and the sixth was a bank commercial from England. Each commercial was shown three times and reactions were measured immediately after as well as one week later (unaided and aided recall as well as other measures). Reactions were measured by 6-point Likert scales as well as by open questions that were later content-analysed. All the measures taken are not presented here.

The following scales were used to measure how much information different respondents got from each commercial:

- The commercial made it easier for me to choose what brand to buy the next time.
- I learned something from the commercial worth remembering.
- The commercial showed you the difference between this product/company and other products/companies on the market.

RESULTS

Results in this study should be seen as an indication only, particularly since the study is based on a convenience sample. Due to space limitations, this presentation does not go into detail to explain why there are cultural differences in the material. Rather, the focus is on the extent to which Wells' proposition on differences between high-and low-context cultures gets support or not from this study. No commercial was perceived to give very much information, which was not expected from a group of nonverbal commercials.

The spaghetti commercial showed the beautiful Italian nature and rich people played an important role. The commercial was very rich in cues; a well-dressed man, looking at expensive watch, driving expensive car to a luxury house, etc. The brand was rated highest by the Swedes and lowest by the Mexicans. Results clearly confirmed the cultural differences proposed by Wells. The Asian group thought that the commercial was much more informative than the Swedish group perceived it to be, exactly as predicted by Wells (see Figure 1).

In the cigarette commercial the setting was in a bar with dart playing. Lots of sound effects, but no people were shown. The

FIGURE 1. Amount of Information from Spaghetti Commercial

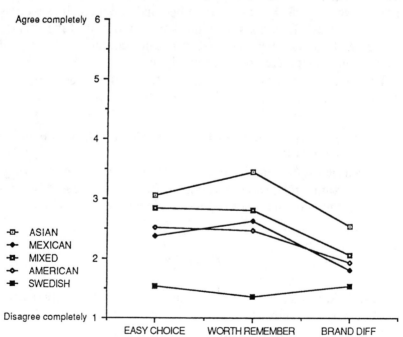

brand was rated highest by the Asians and lowest by the Swedes. This is probably more due to the product than to the commercial. Results clearly confirm Wells' idea that the Asian culture gets information from the context to a higher extent than the Scandinavian culture does (see Figure 2).

In the insurance commercial the setting is the wilderness where a couple has put up a tent for camping. Suddenly, a sports plane crashes on their car, when they least expect it. The Mexican group rated the company the lowest and the Swedish group rated this Swedish company significantly higher than all the other groups. The Mexican group had difficulties identifying themselves with the story and the setting of the commercial. Also this commercial gives support to Wells' observations, although the cultural differences are not as clear as in the other cases. This could be explained by the fact that people in general have huge difficulties seeing differences between different services companies (see Figure 3).

FIGURE 2. Amount of Information from Cigarette Commercial

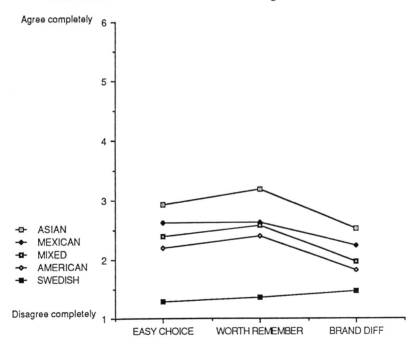

FIGURE 3. Amount of Information from Insurance Commercial

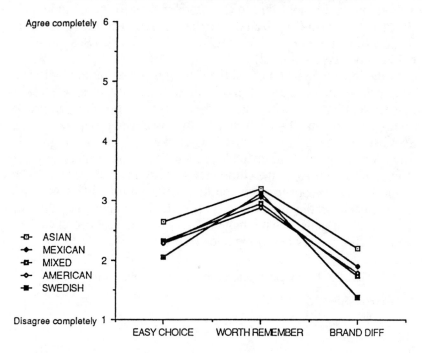

The catsup commercial was very short and a bowl of catsup was "filled" from the bottom with catsup. The commercial ended with: "born for each other." Americans and Mexicans thought that it was "gross" to show catsup with spaghetti. If catsup wasn't served with hamburgers it should not be served at all. Americans and Mexicans rated the brand the lowest and the mixed group rated it the highest. This is an excellent example of how food is perceived quite differently by different cultural groups. This commercial created more negative immediate feelings than any of the other commercials. Again, the Asian group considered the commercial more informative than the Swedish group. Strangely enough, the Swedish group thought that the commercial showed the difference between this brand and other brands to a higher extent than all other groups with the exception of the Asians (see Figure 4).

The chewing gum commercial showed teenagers chewing and

FIGURE 4. Amount of Information from Catsup Commercial

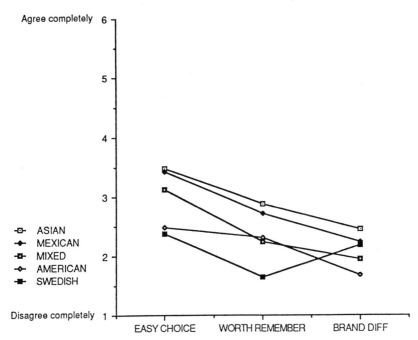

playing with chewing gum. The commercial had sexual undertones. Swedes gave this brand significantly lower evaluation than all the other groups. The Swedes were particularly disturbed by the sexual associations, which some perceived to be discriminating to women. The brand was rated highest by the Mexicans. This commercial was extremely popular among Asians. Whereas the Asians liked the sexy undertones, some Americans disliked seeing teenagers kissing. It is interesting to note that Americans and Swedes didn't really appreciate what they saw, but based on different grounds. Very clear cultural differences between the Asian and the Swedish groups support Wells' ideas (see Figure 5).

The bank commercial showed a punker in London who took a lot of effort to change his appearance to go to the bank, just to find out it was not necessary for such changes. The bank was rated the highest by the Swedes and lowest by the Mexicans. The setting was probably more unfamiliar to the Mexican group than to any of the

FIGURE 5. Amount of Information from Chewing Gum Commercial

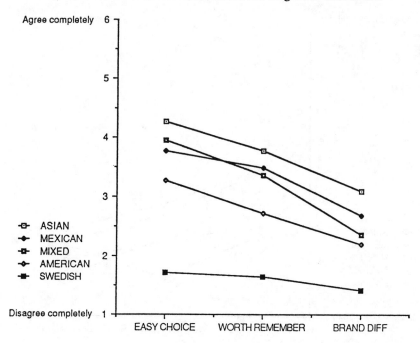

other groups. This commercial created more immediate positive feelings than any of the other commercials. Also this commercial gives support to the fact that high-context cultures find information from nonverbal elements to a higher extent than low-context cultures (see Figure 6).

CONCLUSION

This presentation has focused on the question of whether or not high-context cultures really get more information from nonverbal communication elements than low-context cultures do. Results of this exploratory study clearly confirm this observation. In 17 out of 18 evaluations the high-context group (Asians) rated the commercials higher or much higher in information than what the other groups considered the commercials to be. In 16 out of 18 evalua-

FIGURE 6. Amount of Information from Bank Commercial

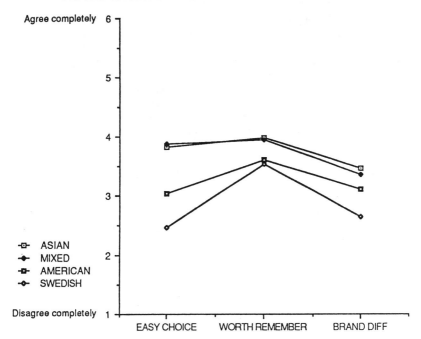

tions the low-context group (Swedes) rated the commercials lower or much lower than what the other groups considered them to be. It is unreasonable to expect more support for the notion that high-context cultures and low-context cultures do communicate in different ways. The present study has not provided any help in telling us how we should communicate to acknowledge these differences, and future studies should address this question in detail.

REFERENCES

Bagby, J.W. (1957). "A Cross-Cultural Study of Perceptual Predominance in Binocular Rivalry." *Journal of Abnormal Social Psychology*, 52.

Handbook of Social Psychology. Eds. Lindsey, G. & Aronson, E., Random House, New York, 1960.

Hecker, S. (1987). "Nonverbal Measurement of Response to Advertising." In

Broadening the Horizons of Copy Research. 4th Annual ARF Copy Research Workshop, New York.

Jacobs, R.C. & Campbell, D.T. (1961). "The Perception of an Arbitrary Tradition Through Several Generations of a Laboratory Microculture." *Journal of Abnormal Social Psychology,* 49.

Management Centre Europe (1987). *International Advertising.* Brussels.

Martenson, R. (1987a). "Advertising Strategies and Information Content in American and Swedish Advertising." *International Journal of Advertising.*

Martenson, R. (1987b). "Is Standardization of Marketing Feasible in Culture-Bond Industries?" *International Marketing Review.*

Martenson, R. (1988). *Swedish Marketing in the U.S.* Studentlitteratur & Chartwell-Bratt, Sweden.

Sills-Levy, E. (1987). "The Archetype Marketing Process." In *Marketing Insights Through Qualitative Research.* Second bi-annual ARF qualitative research workshop. New York.

Wells, W. (1987a). "Global Advertisers Should Pay Heed to Contextual Variations." *Marketing News,* February.

Wells, W.D. (1987b). "What's Global? What's Not?" Paper from Needham, Harper Worldwide, Chicago.

SECTION IV:
THIRD WORLD MARKETING

Global marketing practices take place in a volatile and, in most cases, unpredictable environment of the world. Global firms' main challenge today is one of making an optimum adaptation to changes and developments taking place in the global environment. Most of these changes are macro in nature which, at least in the short run, are beyond the control of the global firms. Understanding the characteristics and behavioral patterns of global consumers is a must. Furthermore, the effect and impact of legal-political, competitive, and technological environments of global markets need to be studied to maintain viable and profitable operation in ever changing world markets.

The central focus of the first chapter in this section by Ross and McTavish is how the developed nations can readily transfer and make operational managerial tools, concepts and techniques available to less-developed nations. On the basis of the views of marketing educators in developing countries, the chapter examines technological transfer of marketing concepts and techniques to these countries. It is the contention of the authors that education, knowledge, and technology transfer stimulate development in the Third World and thus aid in the maintenance of world stability and security.

In discussing the evolution of marketing, the competing conceptualizations of this discipline are noted. In developing countries generally marketing activities are often viewed with disdain and suspicion. The authors go on to explain the reasons behind these prejudices and give views and examples from previously published works. This study attempts to shed light on some of the issues in the universality of marketing principles debate on the question of the role of marketing in a developing country.

The research framework of this study investigates the applicability of micro and macromarketing concepts in the Third World. This is accomplished by obtaining the opinion of marketing educators on certain basic issues of the field and how these opinions relate to certain personal, institutional, and country characteristics. The first hypothesis set focuses on the relationship between educators' opinions and their personal characteristics. The second hypothesis set focuses on the relationship between educators' opinions and the characteristics of the institution to which the educators belong. The characteristics of the country in which the professor resides is the focus of the third hypothesis set.

The methodology utilized was a self-administered questionnaire administered to 120 professors of marketing, representing a wide cross section of professors from Africa, Asia, Latin America, and the Middle East. A five point scale was utilized to record opinions and the data were analyzed using the Kruskal-Wallis ANOVA, a non-parametric statistic.

The findings of the study show that few significant differences were observed among the groups based on personal characteristics. The institutional characteristics have relatively little impact on the opinions of marketing educators in developing countries. A test of the third hypothesis reveals that even when countries are grouped according to different dimensions, the results are remarkably consistent.

The implications of this study are three fold. First, the debate on transferability of marketing concepts and techniques to developing countries is more complex than is generally believed. The second implication of this study is that while all professors believe marketing theory and thought to be useful and beneficial to developing countries, the professors in the poorer nations are disenchanted with the actual application of marketing. The third implication seems to indicate that in the poorer developing countries marketing managers should be extremely cautious in their use of standard marketing tools. These implications suggest the need for more theorizing and research in the poorer countries of the world so that specific tools and concepts can be generated.

Multinational corporations need to improve their marketing performance in less developed countries (LDCs). The chapter by Dawson proposes creation of a separate strategic business unit, known as the SBU(LDC), to be responsible for all such operations. A strategic planning model for the SBU(LDC) is presented which parallels the typical corporate strategic plan but includes significant modifications as well as additional steps.

Broadening the corporate mission statement may be an essential key to sharpening the focus of a firm's approach to LDC markets. Objectives and goals for the SBU(LDC) need to be framed in long-run terms, and it is especially important that objectives be qualified as well as quantified. Market opportunity analysis is necessary to locate the most suitable and attractive market opportunities. A plan for segmenting the Third World marketplace is presented, based on alternative approaches to development being pursued by various nations.

Product strategies for LDC markets can range from devising wholly new technological solutions to making minor adaptations of existing products. A product strategy mix is presented, based upon innovation and adaptation of technology and products. The four strategy alternatives that result are discussed in detail.

Entry strategies for LDC markets are also discussed. A special responsibility of the SBU(LDC) is to evaluate the cultural, social, and economic ramifications of market entries through thoughtful impact analysis. It is the author's contention that important issues must be addressed in integrating the SBU(LDC) in the corporate framework. These include determining the scope of responsibility of the unit, its interrelationships with other organization components, staffing of the unit, and the nature of the corporate support required for its success.

It is well recognized that the nations of the world are deeply concerned about improving their economic development. Unfortunately, there are differing opinions as to the means by which this development can be enhanced. Dramatic new data reveal that trade plays an important part in improving development, as do reduced population growth, individualistic societies, and improvements in literacy.

Central to burgeoning literature on marketing in the Third World is the acknowledgment that the market environment of the Third World differs from that of the industrialized countries. Of the factors that underlie the differences, product-market (buyers' or sellers') and state control (moderate or high) are offered as instrumental. However, empirical assessment of the influence of the two factors is badly lacking in the current marketing literature. The chapter by Dadzie, Akaah, and Riordan therefore explores, in the context of selected African countries, (1) the incidence of product-market/ state control market typologies, and (2) differences in marketing activity performance across market typologies.

With respect to the first study objective, the results indicate that the product-market/state control environment under which firms in Africa operate is heterogeneous in character—spanning at least four market typologies, i.e., moderately controlled buyers' market, moderately controlled sellers' market, highly controlled buyers' market, and highly controlled sellers' market. Of the four, the moderately controlled sellers' and the highly controlled sellers' markets appear to be the predominant market types.

With respect to the second study objective, the results indicate that the incidence and regularity of marketing activity perfor- mance—particularly that of advertising and sales promotion, mar- keting management, channel design and evaluation, and pricing— varies as a function of the product-market/state control environment under which firms operate. This implies that the planning and/or execution of marketing strategies in the Third World, particularly in Africa, should derive from the peculiarities of the product-market/ state control environment under which firms operate.

The argument that marketing can improve efficiency and effec- tiveness of exchange systems in the developing world is gaining increased acceptance. Will marketing be such a catalyst? There is also a growing realization that sustained adoption of marketing practices requires not only positive state intervention to create a supportive environment, but entrepreneurial initiative as well. Will such initiative blossom out, and will it take the shape of aggressive expansion-minded capitalism that characterized the now developed world during its formative years? These are among the questions answered in the lead article.

There are important differences when one examines the situation in the industrial economies as opposed to that of the agricultural sector in the developing economies. While the risks posed by economic, political, and regulatory instability to industrial firms are formidable, manufacturing firms have also been the beneficiaries of considerable "infant industry" protection. Tariff and non-tariff protection of domestic industry has been employed throughout the developing world to considerable, though varying, extent. It has been commonly agreed that such protectionism has been most pronounced in Latin America. Economists have argued the unfavorable externalities of such protectionism in terms of inefficiencies and misallocations that it generates.

In marketing, we should be concerned with the consequences that the sheltered environment of import substitution poses for industrial enterprise. They include a high degree of industry concentration, a lessening of price oriented competition, and what some have referred to in general as "sellers' markets." Will the necessity be felt for marketing action in those cases, or will it be more beneficial for companies to leverage market power? Domínguez's chapter defines market power as the capacity to set supply terms that may be inferred from a company's privileged position in other markets. In other words, a position of power in some markets may be a determinant of success in another market.

Is acquired market power a greater determinant of success than marketing action? If we measure marketing intensity as reliance on traditional marketing mix tools to achieve success, then we could compare market power and marketing intensity as predictors of market success, argues Domínguez. His chapter measures success as market share and provides a justification for this proxy.

The results clearly show that market power is a stronger correlate of market success than is marketing intensity. Domínguez argues that the reason for this is the possibility of domination of internal markets by firms that have amassed power by their participation in other businesses. Leverage of this power is a more effective instrument for accomplishing business goals than the exercise of marketing strategy.

The lessons of the Venezuelan experience are twofold. First, the internal market structure of import substituting nations does not foster the adoption of marketing practices, simply because there are more effective means of attaining success. Second, heightened competition is an essential instrument for modernization of the industrial sector of LDCs. Nations that pursue a unidimensional policy of import substitution which effectively blocks foreign competition will inevitably create internal markets that are not as responsive to consumer needs. Until the macroenvironment is made to be more favorable to competition, important barriers exist to full adoption of the marketing concept as far as their domestic markets are concerned.

Schooler, Wildt, and Jones explore the concerted efforts of Third World countries to expand the autonomous exports of manufactured goods to high income countries through the example of Mexican microwave ovens. The authors find that "most Third World countries have neither patronage in, nor market access to, the highly competitive, difficult to penetrate, high income markets," and they point out that even well structured and implemented export expansion strategies from the Third World countries can meet a formidable set of market barriers in high income countries including non-availability of channels, established consumption patterns, and strong trade names. However, one barrier, consumer bias on the basis of product origin, is the main topic of this study, because this barrier is often left unrecognized.

In previous studies consumer bias has been found to directly affect the acceptability of foreign products and that the effect of the bias can be altered through circumventing strategies. Strategies developed in the past, however, have fallen short of their needed qualities. The strategies should be multifaceted and the strategies must be legal, affordable, and effective. This study illustrates a research approach to building a multidimensional marketing strategy which can overcome consumer resistance based on product origin without falling short of the qualities of being legal, affordable, and appropriate to the firms' resources and competitive dynamics in the industry. The research approach presented is designed to help Third World marketing managers test their potential multifactor strategies.

In his chapter, Hans B. Thorelli explores the "unique attempt at combining socialism and liberalism" in the People's Republic of China and its implications for other developing countries. Market socialism is a hybrid among economic systems which is in its experimental stages within the PRC. The PRC is the first to test the basic concept of an open market within the economy of essentially publicly owned means of production, and the results so far have been highly successful in agriculture, at least moderately successful in the distribution and services sectors, and seem to be very promising in industry, especially in the consumer goods area. This chapter presents the results of the PRC experiment by focusing on the major implications of the experiments for developing countries who are interested in learning from them.

The chapter is divided into three major areas of concern: (1) accelerating and governing forces, (2) cautions and constraints, and (3) the transferability of the Chinese experience into different settings. In the first area, the article portrays some dramatic changes in the PRC philosophy of motivation, total planning, marketing, private property, and pricing among others. However, when considering the cautions and constraints, the author explores the possibilities of inflation, inequality in earnings, unemployment, resistance, competition, consumer emancipation, and the interaction between economic and political freedom. The author then explores the transferability of these ideas to other developing countries who are in need of fresh approaches to socioeconomic development.

Chapter 11

Marketing:
Perspectives from the Third World

Christopher A. Ross
Ronald McTavish

SUMMARY. This exploratory study investigates the relationship between certain personal, institutional and country characteristics and the opinions of professors in developing countries on macro and micromarketing concepts and issues. The results indicate that the opinions of professors in the more affluent developing countries are similar to traditional marketing views while the opinions of professors in the poorer developing countries are more radical. The study also points out the implications of these results for academics and managers.

INTRODUCTION

Increasing interdependence among the countries of the world (Editorial Staff, 1984) makes it difficult to overemphasize the importance of Third World development to the maintenance of world stability and security. Consequently, improving the level of development and the standard of living of the peoples in the Third World continues to be one of the major preoccupations of various countries and international institutions.

In the search for tools which can aid developing countries, education, knowledge and technology transfers are often identified as being among the more promising means of stimulating development

This chapter was first published in the *Journal of Global Marketing*, Vol. 1(1/2), Fall/Winter 1987.

(Emlen, 1958). Management education, in particular, seems to hold considerable potential as a stimulus to development. A key issue, however, is the extent to which managerial tools, concepts and techniques from the industrialized countries can be readily transferred to and made operational in developing countries. This issue is the focus of this chapter. Based on the views of marketing educators in developing countries, this chapter seeks to answer the following question: To what extent are marketing concepts and techniques transferable to and applicable in developing countries?

MARKETING AND THE THIRD WORLD

Marketing as it is commonly understood has its roots in the industrialized countries of the world. Formalized as a discipline in the early 1900s, marketing evolved through many different conceptualizations until today it is seen as an organizational technology with goals that are typically associated with managerial efficiency. Competing conceptualizations of marketing do exist, for example, marketing as a social process, but the managerial orientation is what dominates the field and is therefore often the focus of the debate on the ease or difficulty of transferring marketing know-how to developing countries (Carter & Savitt, 1983).

But marketing activities are often viewed with disdain and suspicion in developing countries. Sentell (1981), for example, observes that marketing and distribution are often short-changed in development plans and that marketing institutions are viewed as nonproductive. Little attention is paid to the functions which connect production and consumption processes (Mittendorf, 1982). Consequently, there is a tendency to neglect private marketing enterprises (Samli & Kaynak, 1984). Duhaime, McTavish, and Ross (1985) also point out that in developing countries marketing is often perceived as the cause of elevated levels of expectations and Cavusgil and Yavas (1984) report that in Turkey management attitudes towards marketing can be characterized as indifferent or even hostile.

Many explanations exist for these prejudices against marketing in developing countries. One explanation is that in developing countries there exists a widespread view that middlemen are exploitive (Sentell, 1981; Samli & Kaynak, 1984). In other instances too the underlying principles of marketing are not completely understood.

Further, it is sometimes believed that marketing is a major tool used by industrialized countries to further their own economic interests in developing countries. Many planners in developing countries also take the position that marketing activities are wasteful and inconsistent with objectives of cost minimization or production efficiencies (Mittendorf, 1982).

The hostility and disdain towards marketing activities and institutions may partly explain the lack of available trained marketing personnel in developing countries. Mittendorf (1982) believes that the lack of marketing specialists is a major bottleneck in developing countries. Thus, as an aid to development, many researchers call for the training of specialists in the use of modern marketing concepts and techniques. The underlying assumption is that these concepts and techniques can be readily transferred to the Third World. Cundiff and Hilger (1979) make this assumption when they state that economic development requires the presence of experts among the business community "who are aware of current knowledge and thinking about marketing in the more highly developed nations" (p. 181).

There are a substantial number of scholars, however, who question the universal applicability of unadapted marketing techniques. Bartels (1983) contends, for example, that marketing is ". . . a discipline of domestic marketing theory . . . . It is not a discipline of globally derived principles that may be applied to the subset of national economies. It has not been a means by which underdeveloped economies may be helped to develop" (p. 35). El-Sherbini (1979) also believes that marketing concepts and techniques are ethnocentric and that limited contributions have been made to development. Meissner (1982) is unequivocal when he asserts that Western marketing technology is too big and too expensive for Third World countries. Shapiro's view, (1965), on the other hand, is that marketing techniques may be universally relevant if, with each application, due regard is given to existing social structures and value systems.

Some authors go beyond questioning the general orientation of marketing and raise specific issues. Ross and McTavish (1984), for example, question the extent to which the notion of the marketing manager having complete control over marketing mix variables is applicable to developing countries. Dholakia and Dholakia (1980) go even further. They argue that in the non-market economies of the Soviet bloc and in the partial market economies of the Third World, the traditional organizing framework of the 4 p's is not valid. Arndt (1979) suggests that one must go beyond the 4 p's and deal with politics, conflict resolution, negotiation and administrative procedures in marketing.

The debate on the validity or applicability of traditional marketing concepts to developing countries also hinges on the question of the extent to which marketing can stimulate development. Cundiff and Hilger (1979) identify two schools of thought: those who hold that marketing responds to the environment and thus plays an essentially passive role in development, the "determinists," and those who hold the view that marketing influences the environment and thus plays an active or stimulative role in development, the "activists."

The focus of the determinists' work is to compare the environment for marketing activity with the market system in various countries. Their core belief is that the marketing structures of a country are determined by the level of economic development. Bartels (1976), referring to this view of marketing as the adaptive function, argues that the determinists promote the hypothesis that marketing follows production. The activist school is exemplified by Drucker's (1958) article. In this work Drucker suggests that marketing is the most important multiplier of development. He believes that marketing makes possible economic integration and the fullest utilization of the productive capacity of an economy.

The present study is an attempt to shed light on some of the issues in the universality of marketing principles debate and on the question of the role of marketing in a developing country. The trajectory of development which the Third World takes has important implications for the entire world system (Dholakia, 1981). However, the lack of basic information and conceptual frameworks about existing less developed countries' marketing systems and the lack of trained professionals have been major constraints to development (Waines, 1963). What role can marketing play and what role should marketing play in this trajectory of development are thus important questions facing the whole marketing fraternity.

RESEARCH FRAMEWORK AND HYPOTHESES

The present study investigates the opinions of marketing educators in developing countries on the applicability of micro and macromarketing concepts to Third World countries. More specifically, one objective of the study is to obtain the opinions of marketing educators in developing countries on certain basic issues of the field. These issues cover both micro and macromarketing. The second objective is to relate these opinions to certain personal, institutional and country characteristics. The second objective can thus be captured in the following general form:

$$\text{Educators' opinions} = f (\text{Personal Characteristics, Institutional Characteristics and Country Characteristics})$$

In line with this formulation three hypothesis sets are presented.

Hypothesis Set H1

The first hypothesis set focuses on the relationship between educators' opinions and their personal characteristics. It seems reasonable to expect that educators' opinions regarding the applicability of marketing concepts and techniques to developing countries result from their socialization and exposure to the field of marketing and their experience in using marketing concepts either in teaching or business. Opinions should therefore be shaped by education, perspectives and personal experiences. For example, the number of years teaching marketing or age or the extent of business experience may allow time for reflection on some concepts and frameworks. Therefore Hypotheses Set H1 is as follows:

> The opinions of educators in developing countries, on macro and micromarketing issues, differ on the basis of their personal characteristics.

Hypothesis Set H2

The second hypotheses set, H2, focuses on the relationship between educators' opinions and the characteristics of the institution to which the educators belong. Institutional characteristics may have an impact on educators' opinions. The presence of a group of marketing professors as opposed to being alone in a department, for example, can encourage discussion and the emergence of new orientations on the part of the faculty member. If the group of business professors is part of a larger faculty as opposed to being an independent unit, the interchange of ideas with colleagues from non-business disciplines may take place. This cross-fertilization can again result in newer and different orientations among the business faculty. The formal statement of Hypothesis Set H2 thus reads as follows:

> The opinions of educators in developing countries, on macro and micromarketing issues, differ on the basis of the characteristics of the institutions to which they belong.

Hypothesis Set H3

The characteristics of the country in which the professor resides is the focus of the third hypothesis set. It is generally held that the culture, social conditions and value system of a country shape a person's view of the world. The case or difficulty of applying concepts and techniques within the particular country may therefore influence the marketing professor's views. It seems reasonable, therefore, to hypothesize that the overall level of development of the educator's country has an impact on opinions held, especially those which focus on the application of concepts. The formulation of Hypothesis Set H3 is as follows:

> The opinions of educators in developing countries, on macro and micromarketing issues, differ on the basis of the characteristics of the country in which they reside.

DATA COLLECTION AND ANALYSIS

One hundred and twenty professors of marketing in developing countries were selected from the 1983 AMA Membership Directory and from available university calendars. The sample represented a wide cross section of professors from Africa, Asia, Latin America and the Middle East. Forty-six usable questionnaires were returned giving a response rate of 38 percent. Table 1 outlines the personal, institutional and country characteristics considered in this study. The means, medians and standard deviations of these characteristics provide a profile of the professors, institutions and countries represented in the sample.

The questionnaire probed the professors' opinions on macro and micromarketing issues in developing countries and their opinions on teaching the Third World student. This article focusses only on opinions of macro and micromarketing. These opinions were measured with 5-point scales, ranging from 1 = "Strongly Disagree" to 5 = "Strongly agree." The personal and institutional characteristics shown in Table 1 were obtained from the respondents. The

TABLE 1. The Independent Variables

Personal Characteristics	Mean	Median	Standard Deviation
1. Years teaching marketing	10.0	9.6	6.0
2. Lived in a developed country (76%)	NA	NA	NA
3. Associate Professor or below (59%)	NA	NA	NA
4. PhD degree (49%)	NA	NA	NA
5. Age (years)	39.7	38.8	7.4
6. Years since last degree	8.7	8.5	5.0
7. Extensive business experience (60%)	NA	NA	NA
Institutional Characteristics			
1. Self-contained business school (52%)	NA	NA	NA
2. Possession of a marketing major (54%)	NA	NA	NA
3. Number of full-time marketing faculty	4.0	3.2	3.4
4. Percentage of courses devoted to cases	33.9	29.4	26.0
Country Characteristics			
1. Located in Africa, Latin America, Middle East, or Southeast Asia	NA	NA	NA
2. Per capita income in U.S. dollars	2364	1696	2868
3. Population in millions	97.0	28.0	191.0
4. Literacy rate (%)	64.0	65.5	24.7
5. Life expectancy in years	60.7	63.3	8.4
6. Urbanization (%)	47.6	43.8	25.5
7. Contribution of agriculture to GDP (%)	19.9	17.5	14.0
8. Contribution of industry to GDP (%)	36.0	36.6	13.3
9. Contribution of manufacturing to GDP (%)	19.1	18.5	8.5
10. Contribution of services to GDP (%)	43.4	41.5	9.3

country characteristics were obtained from Tables 1 to 3 of World Development Report 1983. The data were analyzed using Kruskal-Wallis ANOVA, a non-parametric test of differences.

RESULTS

Opinions of the Overall Sample

In general, the sample of marketing educators disagree that modern marketing concepts have little to offer developing countries (Var 1, $\bar{x} = 1.9$) and they agree that the managerial approach to teaching marketing is the most useful approach in developing countries (Var 2, $\bar{x} = 4$). They also agree that most business people in developing countries have little or no understanding of the marketing concept (Var 3, $\bar{x} = 3.9$), and that marketing concepts are applicable to both the profit and non-profit sectors (Var 4, $\bar{x} = 4.2$). Marketing educators also strongly disagree that marketing theory and practice can contribute little to economic development (Var 5, $\bar{x} = 1.3$). Uncertainty creeps in, however, when they give their opinion on the compatibility of marketing concepts with central economic planning (Var 7, $\bar{x} = 2.5$) and about the potential of the not-for-profit sector in development (Var 8, $\bar{x} = 2.5$). They are also uncertain about whether the minimization of consumer dissatisfaction or the maximization of satisfaction is more important (Var 11, $\bar{x} = 2.8$).

At a more micro level, marketing educators in developing countries are of the opinion that conditions of scarcity do affect marketing practice in a negative way (Var 23, $\bar{x} = 3.8$; Var 24, $\bar{x} = 3.7$; Var 26, $\bar{x} = 3.5$; Var 27, $\bar{x} = 3.6$; Var 28, $\bar{x} = 3.3$; Var 29; $\bar{x} = 3.6$). They agree that it is important for professors to be familiar with the problems of marketing primary products (Var 18, $\bar{x} = 4$) and that little is known about organizational buying behavior (Var 19, $\bar{x} = 3.9$). They are somewhat uncertain about the uniqueness of the problems of small enterprises in developing countries relative to the developed countries (Var 20, $\bar{x} = 3.1$) and about the absence of knowledge about the factors influencing export success (Var 15, $\bar{x} = 3.4$). Table 2 shows the opinions measured.

TABLE 2. Opinions Measured

THE SCOPE OF MARKETING

Var 1   Modern marketing concepts (e.g., brand loyalty, product positioning, product portfolio models) have little to offer developing countries.

Var 2   The managerial approach to marketing with the marketing manager seeking to optimize the elements of the marketing mix is the most useful approach to teaching marketing in developing countries.

Var 3   Most business people in developing countries have little or no understanding of the marketing concept.

Var 4   Marketing management concepts are applicable to both the profit sector and the not-for-profit sector (government, charities, etc.) in developing countries.

Var 5   Marketing theory and practice can contribute little to the economic development of the developing world.

Var 6   In developing countries, the consumer becomes less and less powerful as industrialization progresses.

Var 7   Marketing concepts are incompatible with central economic planning by the state.

Var 8   If marketing can play a role in development at all, its greatest potential lies in the not-for-profit sector.

Var 9   In a developing country, marketing has little value; the production of goods and services is the important thing.

Var 10   With increasing industrialization in developing countries, there is an increasing need for consumer protection agencies in these countries.

Var 11   The real marketing issue in developing countries is the minimization of consumer dissatisfaction rather than the maximization of consumer satisfaction.

MICROMARKETING

Var 12   The traditional marketing management framework with its emphasis on the 4 p's (product, place, promotion and price) is not well suited to the environment of developing countries because most of these variables are uncontrollable by the marketing manager.

Var 13   Because of scarcity conditions in most developing countries, it is difficult to measure the success or failure of a brand on its own merits.

Var 14   In developing countries, small enterprises — less than 50 employees — are the norm in the manufacturing sector.

Var 15   In developing countries, very little is known about the factors which influence the success of manufactured exports for the individual firm.

Var 16   In developing countries, pricing decisions must be tempered by notions of justice and equity.

Var 17   Because of situations of scarcity in most developing countries, there is a tendency for salespeople to have an allocation rather than a marketing philosophy.

Var 18   In developing countries, it is important that the marketing educator be familiar with the problem of marketing primary products.

Var 19   In developing countries, very little empirical knowledge is available about organizational buying behaviour.

Var 20   In developing countries, the marketing problems of small enterprises are unique relative to those in developed countries.

Var 21   In developing countries, managers find pricing decisions difficult because of government controls.

Var 22   Most developing countries import their capital equipment.

Var 23   Companies operating in situations of scarcity often experience a decline in marketing competence.

Var 24   In developing countries, seller's market conditions dominate for most products.

Var 25   In developing countries, even some distribution decisions are controlled by the government.

Var 26   Because of situations of scarcity, most managers do not know the true size of the market for their products.

Var 27   Because of situations of scarcity, there is a tendency to have little product variety.

Var 28   Because of situations of scarcity, there is a tendency for advertising creativity to deteriorate.

Var 29   Because of situations of scarcity, there is a tendency for product quality to deteriorate.

Test of Hypothesis Set H1

While the results presented so far assume that the sample is homogenous, the next three hypotheses assume that there may be differences among groups of professors. Because of the exploratory nature of the research, the relatively small size of the sample and the less stringent assumptions about the data that are necessary, Kruskal-Wallis ANOVA is used to test the three hypothesis sets in this study. The major assumption of the Kruskal-Wallis is that the variable under study has an underlying continuous distribution; the test requires that the variable be measured at least at the ordinal level. The sample was broken into two groups for each of the characteristics identified in Table 1. For continuous variables, the median was the dividing point for the groups. In the case of nominal variables, categories were combined to form natural groups.

Regarding opinions on the scope of marketing (Table 2, Variables 1 to 11), few significant differences are observed among the groups based on personal characteristics — hypothesis set H1. The professors with PhD degrees are in significantly more agreement with the statement that business people in developing countries have little or no understanding of the marketing concept. Another significant difference is that the respondents who have had their degree for a shorter period of time tend to be significantly more in agreement with the statement that marketing concepts are incompatible with central economic planning by the state.

More significant differences are observed when opinions on micromarketing are examined. The critical factor influencing these opinions seems to be the number of years teaching marketing. On a number of variables, professors with less than 9.6 years teaching experience have significantly different opinions from professors who have more teaching experience. Professors with less teaching experience tend to agree more that relatively little is known about factors influencing the export success of manufacturing firms. These same professors also agree that salespeople tend to have an allocation rather than a marketing philosophy, that the marketing competence of firms declines at items of scarcity, that a seller's market dominates for most products, that managers do not know the true size of the market for their products and that scarcity produces little product variety. Younger professors, as opposed to those with less experience, are in less agreement with the opinion that pricing decisions must be tempered by notions of justice and equity.

Overall, therefore, younger professors, those with less teaching experience and more recent graduates tend to be more hard-nosed and critical of micromarketing practice in developing countries, with teaching experience "explaining" much of the differences in opinions. The results of this hypothesis test, H1, are presented in Table 3.

Test of Hypothesis Set H2

Institutional characteristics have relatively little impact on the opinions of marketing educators in developing countries. Only two characteristics have any relationship and then with only two opinion

TABLE 3. Differences of Opinion Based on Educators' Characteristics

Operations	Groups	N	Mean Rank	x2	Sig.
VAR 03	PhD Degree	27	26.9	6.58	.010
	No PhD Degree	18	17.1		
VAR 07	<8.5 years since degree	21	25.1	3.95	0.47
	>8.5 years since degree	21	17.9		
VAR 12	Assistant Professor	15	26.6	10.71	.013
	Associate Professor	11	15.1		
	Professor	10	29.2		
	Administrator	8	16.8		
VAR 15	<9.6 years teaching	22	26.7	5.5	.019
	>9.6 years teaching	22	18.3		
VAR 16	<38.8 years old	21	18.9	4.11	.043
	>38.8 years old	24	26.6		
VAR 17	<9.6 years teaching	22	27.64	6.6	.010
	>9.6 years teaching	23	18.6		
VAR 23	<9.6 years teaching	22	26.6	3.93	.048
	>9.6 years teaching	23	19.6		
VAR 24	<9.6 years teaching	22	28.3	10.27	.001
	>9.6 years teaching	23	17.2		
VAR 26	<9.6 years teaching	22	26.8	4.17	.041
	>9.6 years teaching	23	19.4		
VAR 27	<9.6 years teaching	22	26.7	4.02	.045
	>9.6 years teaching	23	19.5		

statements. The professors from schools with marketing majors have significantly more disagreement with the view that the greatest potential for development lies with the not-for-profit sector than the professors from schools with no marketing majors. In addition, schools with less that three full-time marketing faculty have significantly more disagreement with the statement that even some distribution decisions are controlled by the government. On the whole, therefore, even if some opinions differ on the basis of whether the school has a marketing major or not and on the basis of the number of full-time faculty, it seems that institutional characteristics have far less relationship with opinions than personal characteristics and hypothesis set H2 cannot be accepted.

Test of Hypothesis Set H3

The test of this hypothesis set provides some revealing results (Table 4). Even when countries are grouped according to different dimensions, the results are remarkably consistent. Evidently part of the explanation for this result is the intercorrelation among the country characteristics (Table 5).

For the opinion that modern marketing concepts have little to offer developing countries (Var I) (even though the overall sample disagrees ($\bar{x} = 1.9$), there is a significant difference in opinion between the poorer developing countries and the relatively well-off countries of the sample. The more underdeveloped countries — Africa, those with low per capita incomes, literacy rates and life expectancy, less manufacturing and services as a percentage of G.D.P. — have less disagreement with the opinion than the rest of the sample.

A great deal of consistency among the groups also exists for some other opinions as well. Countries with greater life expectancy, less agriculture and more services as a percent of G.D.P., the better-off countries, have significantly more agreement than the rest of the sample that marketing's greatest potential for development lies in the not-for-profit sector. Professors from countries with low per capita incomes, literacy rates and life expectancy have significantly more agreement with the opinion that the real marketing issue is the minimization of consumer dissatisfaction. Again a similar pattern

TABLE 4. Differences of Opinion Based on Country Characteristics

Opinions	Groups	N	Mean Rank	x2	Sig.
VAR 01	Africa	10	35.60	16.53	.001
	Middle East; Pakistan; India	7	28.8		
	Latin America; Caribbean	15	17.8		
	Southeast Asia	14	18.3		
	≤$1696.25 per capita income	22	27.5	10.23	.001
	>$1696.25 per capita income	21	16.3		
	≤65.5% literacy rate	21	26.3	7.66	.006
	>65.5% literacy rate	21	16.7		
	≤63.3 years life expectancy	23	28.9	10.95	.001
	>63.3 years life expectancy	22	16.9		
	≤18.5% mfg. in GDP	20	23.9	4.05	.044
	>18.5% mfg. in GDP	20	17.1		
	≤41.5% services in GDP	20	24.4	5.25	.022
	>41.5% services in GDP	20	16.6		
VAR 03	Africa	10	33.4	6.172	.016
	Middle East; Pakistan; India	7	23.3		
	Latin America; Caribbean	15	23.7		
	Southeast Asia	14	16.3		
VAR 08	≤63.3 years life expectancy	23	19	4.63	.031
	>63.3 years life expectancy	22	27.2		
	≤17.5% agriculture in GDP	20	24.1	3.96	.047
	>17.5% agriculture in GDP	20	16.9		
	≤41.5% services in GDP	20	15.4	7.98	.005
	>41.5% services in GDP	20	25.6		

VAR 11	≤$1696.25 per capita income	22	26.1	6.30	.012
	>$1696.25 per capita income	21	17.2		
	≤65.5% literacy rate	21	25.8	5.51	.019
	>65.5% literacy rate	21	17.2		
	≤63.3 years life expectancy	23	27,9	6.58	.009
	>63.3 years life expectancy	22	17.9		
VAR 12	Africa	10	33.3	8.88	.031
	Middle East; Pakistan; India	7	24.1		
	Latin America; Caribbean	15	21.7		
	Southeast Asia	14	18.11		
	≤28.25 million people	23	17.6	5.02	.025
	>28.25 million people	18	25.4		
	≤$1696.25 per capita income	22	25.6	4.19	.041
	≤$1696.25 per capita income	21	18.2		
VAR 14	≤28.25 million people	23	24.2	4.12	.042
	>28.25 million people	18	16.9		
VAR 22	≤18.5% mfg. in GDP	20	23.8	3.85	.050
	>18.5% mfg. in GDP	20	17.2		
VAR 23	≤43.75% urbanization	21	26.5	5.93	.015
	>43.75% urbanization	22	17.8		
VAR 27	≤$1696.25 per capita income	22	26.3	6.301	.012
	>$1696.25 per capita income	21	17.6		
	≤63.3 years life expectancy	23	26.8	4.81	.028
	>63.3 years life expectancy	22	19		
	≤43.75% urbanization	21	26.5	6.37	.012
	>43.75% urbanization	22	17.7		

TABLE 4 (continued)

VAR 28	Africa	10	30.8	7.67	.053
	Middle East; Pakistan; India	7	29.1		
	Latin America; Caribbean	15	19.3		
	Southeast Asia	14	19.93		
	≤$1696.25 per capita income	22	25.8	4.61	.032
	>$1696.25 per capita income	21	18.1		
	≤63.3 years life expectancy	23	27.63	6.38	.009
	>63.3 years life expectancy	28	18.2		

TABLE 5. Spearman Correlation of Country Characteristics

		76	77	78	79	80	81	82	83	84
Population	76	x								
Per Capita Income	77	-.35	x							
Literacy Rate	78	-.17	.46	x						
Life Expectancy	79	-.30	.72	.88	x					
Urbanization	80	-.08	.59	.47	.55	x				
Percent Agriculture in GDP	81	-.02	-.64	-.41	-.50	-.29	x			
Percent Industry in GDP	82	-.56	.48	.26	.33	.37	-.12	x		
Percent Manufacturing in GDP	83	-.04	.10	.45	.40	.61	.17	.37	x	
Percent Services in GDP	84	-.37	.39	.62	.57	.58	-.09	.36	.68	x

Significant relationships are underlined

follows on the suitability of the 4 p's framework to developing countries: African countries and those with large populations or low per capita incomes have significantly less agreement than the rest of the sample on the suitability of this framework. It would seem, therefore, that professors from the poorer developing countries hold significantly different opinions from their counterparts in the richer developing countries and that these opinions are less conservative and more questioning of the traditional wisdom.

Professors from countries with low per capita incomes, low levels of life expectancy and urbanization are in significantly more agreement than the rest of the sample that salespeople have an allocation rather than marketing philosophy. The poorer countries also agree that government controls increase the difficulty of pricing decisions, that there is little product variety, and that advertising creativity deteriorates in times of scarcity. These differences of opinion reinforce the notion that the nature of a professor's views is related to level of development of the country of residence.

Opinions on micro and macromarketing issues also differ on some other dimensions, although there is less consistency among the categorizing variables. Professors from African countries believe that their businesspeople have the least understanding of the marketing concept; professors from smaller countries have significantly more agreement that small enterprises predominate; and the less urbanized the country the more the professors believe that the marketing problems of small enterprises are unique, that companies operating in situations of scarcity experience a decline in marketing competence and that even some distribution decisions are controlled by government. Hypothesis set H3 can therefore be accepted.

DISCUSSION AND IMPLICATIONS

For the sample as a whole, many of the opinions seem not to be surprising, for, in the main, the opinions of marketing educators are quite close to conventional marketing thinking in the industrialized countries. The exceptions are the opinions which focus on conditions of scarcity, a condition endemic to the Third World.

When the sample is categorized into groups, however, a different picture emerges. Of the eleven variables used to measure the scope of marketing, there are no differences between the groups whether classified along personal, institutional or country characteristics, for six of the variables. Thus, there is general agreement among professors of the developing world that the managerial approach to marketing is the best pedagogical approach to use. They also agree that marketing concepts are applicable to both the profit and non-profit sectors and that there is an increasing need for consumer protection agencies as industrialization develops. Furthermore, these educators disagree that marketing theory can contribute little to economic development, that the consumer becomes less powerful with industrialization and that marketing has little value.

But for the other five variables of the set measuring the scope of marketing, there are significant differences according to group, with the characteristics of the country having more significant relationships than the personal or institutional characteristics. In general, the professors from the poorer countries of the sample hold more radical opinions than their counterparts in the relatively richer countries. Put differently, professors from the relatively well-off countries hold opinions that are more in keeping with the opinions of their colleagues in the industrialized countries. Thus, the richer and more developed an economy, the more the professors support the view that marketing concepts can contribute to developing countries, that not-for-profit marketing can play an important role in development and that the maximization of consumer satisfaction is the critical issue.

When the variables dealing with micromarketing decisions are examined, two findings stand out. The first is that faculty with less teaching experience tend to be more critical and radical in their views about the marketing behavior of marketers in developing countries. It may well be that the less experienced professors simply lack the broad views of the older professors or else they are less patient with their perception of bad marketing practice among organizations.

The second finding, as in the case of macromarketing variables, is that professors in the poorer developing countries hold the more radical opinions. These professors, particularly in Africa but in other low income and less urbanized countries as well, believe that marketing concepts are not suitable to their particular circumstances, that the government controls pricing and distribution decisions and that marketing behavior is selling oriented rather than marketing oriented.

In general, therefore, this study suggests that the characteristics of the professor, particularly the number of years teaching, have an impact on opinions held, but that the characteristics of the environmental milieu have an even greater impact on opinions. Institutional characteristics seem to play only a small role.

One implication of this study is that the debate on the transferability of marketing concepts and techniques to developing countries is more complex than is generally believed. For the more advanced developing countries, the opinions of marketing educators seem to suggest easy transferability once the social structures and value systems are taken into account. This view is similar to that of Shapiro (1965). For the less well-off developing countries, however, more radical adaptation of marketing concepts or possible development of concepts specifically for these countries may be required.

Another implication of this research is that while all professors believe marketing theory and thought to be useful and beneficial to developing countries, the professors in the poorer countries are disenchanted with the actual application of marketing; specific concepts appear to be less useful.

This study also has implications for managers and businesses operating in the poorer developing countries. If one accepts the opinions of educators, it would seem that in the poorer developing countries marketing managers should be extremely cautious in their use of standard marketing tools. More emphasis needs to be placed on understanding the particular nature of the environment of these countries as well as on the marketing as opposed to the selling aspects of the operation. In spite of conditions of scarcity, managers should strive to maintain their standards of efficiency by continuing to emphasize meeting consumer needs and minimizing consumer dissatisfaction.

These implications suggest the need for more theorizing and research in the poorer countries of the world so that specific tools and concepts, grounded in the conditions of these countries, can be generated. For example, while marketing in the developed world is product driven, for the poor countries of this world it may well be that marketing can make its greatest contribution when it is distribution driven. The irony of this situation is that the professors and researchers in the poorer countries are those with the least resources for developing new approaches, concepts and techniques.

REFERENCES

Arndt, J. (1979). "Toward a Concept of Domesticated Markets." *Journal of Marketing* (Fall), 43, pp. 69-75.

Bartels, R. (1983). "Is Marketing Defaulting Its Responsibilities?" *Journal of Marketing* (Fall), 47, pp. 32-35.

Bartels, R. (1976). "Marketing and Economic Development." In P.D. White and C.C. Slater (eds.) *Macromarketing: Distributive Process from a Point of View* (pp. 211-217). Proceedings of Macromarketing Seminar, University of Colorado, Boulder, CO (August 15-18).

Carter, F.S., and Savitt, R. (1983). "A Resource Allocation Model for Integrating Marketing into Economic Development Plans." In E. Kaynak (ed.) *Managing the International Marketing Function: Creative Challenges of the Eighties* (pp. 79-88). Proceedings, World Marketing Congress, Halifax, N.S. (November 3-5).

Cavusgil, S.T., and Yavas, U. (1984). "Transfer of Management Know-How to Developing Countries: An Empirical Investigation." *Journal of Business Research,* 12, pp. 35-50.

Cundiff, E.W., and Hilger, M.T. (1979). "Marketing and the Production Consumption Thesis in Economic Development." In G. Fisk et al. (eds.) *Macromarketing: Evolution of Thought* (pp. 177-186). Proceedings of the Fourth Macromarketing Seminar, University of Colorado, Boulder, CO (August 9-12).

Dholakia, N. (1981). "The Future of Marketing in the Third World." In D.F. Mulvihill (ed.) *Marketing and the Future* (pp. 63-72). AMA Proceedings.

Dholakia, N., and Dholakia, R.R. (1980). "Beyond Internationalization: A Broader Strategy for Marketing Pedagogy" (pp. 30-32). In R.P. Bagozzi et al. (eds.) *Marketing in the 80s: Changes and Challenges,* AMA Educators Conference, Series 46.

Drucker, P.F. (1958). "Marketing and Economic Development." *Journal of Marketing,* (January), 22, pp. 252-259.

Duhaime, C.P., McTavish, R., and Ross, C.A. (1985). "Social Marketing: An Approach to Third World Development." *Journal of Macro-Marketing,* (Spring), 5 (1), pp. 3-13.

Editorial Staff (1984). "The Realities of Economic Interdependence." *Finance and Development,* (March), 21(1), pp. 28-32.

El-Sherbini, A.A. (1979). "Behavioral Adjustments as Marketing Constraints on Economic Development." In G. Fisk et al. (eds.) *Macromarketing: Evolution of Thought*. Proceedings of the Fourth Macromarketing Seminar, University of Colorado, Boulder, CO (August 9-12).

Emlen, W.J. (1958). "Let's Export Marketing Know-How." *Harvard Business Review,* (November-December), 36, pp. 70-76.

Meissner, F. (1982). "In Search of Appropriate Marketing Technology for the Third World." In R. Day (ed.) *Economic Analysis and Agricultural Policy* (pp. 320-334). The Iowa State University Press, Ames, IA.

Mittendorf, H.J. (1982). "The Role of FAO in Promoting Effective Agricultural Marketing Systems." Paper presented at the 23rd Annual Meeting of the GEWISOLA, Giessen, Germany (September 29-October 1).

Mittendorf, H.J. (1982). "Topics for Studies on Agricultural and Food Marketing in Developing Countries." *Quarterly Journal of International Agriculture* (April-June), 21(2), pp. 139-154.

Ross, C.A., and McTavish, R. (1984). "The Marketing Education Task in Third World Countries." *Journal of Marketing* (Spring), pp. 20-27.

Samli, A.C., and Kaynak, E. (1984). "Marketing Practices in Less Developed Countries." *Journal of Business Research,* 12, pp. 5-18.

Sentell, G.D. (1981). "Relationships Among Dualism, Development, Markets and Consumer Characteristics." *Thai Journal of Development Administration* (April), 21(2), pp. 309-335.

Shapiro, S.J. (1965). "Comparative Marketing and Economic Development." In G. Scharwtz (ed.) *Science in Marketing* (pp. 398-429), New York: John Wiley and Sons Inc.

Waines, W.J. (1963). "The Role of Education in the Development of Underdeveloped Countries." *The Canadian Journal of Economics and Political Science* (November), 29(4), pp. 437-445.

Chapter 12

Multinational Strategic Planning for Third World Markets

Leslie M. Dawson

SUMMARY. There are compelling reasons why multinational corporations (MNCs) must improve their marketing performance in less developed countries (LDCs). A solution to better performance may be creation of a separate strategic business unit, known as the SBU (LDC), to be responsible for all third world operations. A strategic planning model for the SBU(LDC) is presented; it parallels the typical corporate strategic plan but differs in significant respects. Planning steps discussed include mission and objectives, market opportunity analysis, target market evaluation, product strategy, entry strategy, marketing program, and impact analysis. Key issues involved in implementing the SBU(LDC) within the corporate framework are discussed.

INTRODUCTION

Most large corporations have adopted the practice of strategic planning. A strategic marketing plan differs from a traditional marketing plan in two key respects: (a) It focuses on long-term strategy for market development rather than short-term manipulation of marketing mix variables; (b) It is prepared at the level of strategic business units (SBUs) rather than for individual products or market segments.

Application of strategic planning to international marketing,

This chapter was first published in the *Journal of Global Marketing*, Vol. 1(3), Spring 1988.

however, has lagged: "Planning practices for multinational markets are far behind those for domestic markets . . . most marketing planning among multinationals is operational and short term" (Jain, 1984, p. 660).

Nowhere in the international marketplace does this observation hold more true than with respect to less developed countries (LDCs). This article explains why improved performance in LDC markets is critical to the future of multinational corporations (MNCs), and proposes creation of a separate business unit to be responsible for all such operations.

MULTINATIONALS AND THE THIRD WORLD

LDCs account for three-quarters of world population, but less than one-quarter of MNC sales revenue. The proportion of industrial nation manufactured and merchandise exports going to developing countries actually declined between 1964 and 1984, despite rapid population growth and steadily rising GNP in the latter nations (World Bank, 1986). Between 1980 and 1984, U.S. private industry earnings from direct investment in developing countries fell by more than 40% (U.S. Department of Commerce, 1986).

MNCs have been attracted to LDCs by trade incentives, inexpensive labor, and access to strategic materials, but the relationship has been a stormy one. MNCs have been the frequent victims of expropriation, expulsion, and damaging publicity. Nor have MNCs been blameless; often they have entered LDC markets with quick-strike, profit-skimming strategies that reflect scant regard for the welfare of host countries, and there have been instances of meddling in domestic political affairs. MNCs are often viewed as agents of economic exploitation, and on more than one occasion a boiling over of public resentment has prompted LDC governments to enact restrictive legislation aimed at multinationals.

From a short-term perspective, LDC markets do not appear attractive to MNCs. Mass markets with high purchasing power do not exist, risks are high in proportion to returns, and requirements for success do not match well with MNC operating practices and philosophies. Whereas standardization of products and marketing programs, formalized decision making, and rigid control have tended to be hallmarks of large enterprise, LDCs want flexible approaches, personalized attention, and above all, a significant "piece of the action."

Yet, there are compelling reasons to foresee that in the long-range future, markets of the Third World will become an increasingly critical key to the very survival of multinationals:

1. *Resource dependency.* LDCs occupy two-thirds of the world's land mass, and commensurately control the major global share of many strategic resources. LDCs, for example, control from 50 to 90% of the known recoverable stock of such strategic materials as aluminum, chromium, cobalt, copper, tin, titanium, tungsten, tantalum, and natural rubber (Schuh, 1986). While the distribution of global resources among rich and poor nations is nothing new, what *is* new is the inclination of Third World countries to use their resource bases more aggressively as bargaining chips in the arena of world power relationships. The long-term success of the OPEC cartel may be in doubt, but it stands as the best object lesson to date of the *potential* clout that LDCs can employ.

2. *Shifts in growth markets.* Third World countries are likely to constitute the world's true growth markets of the future. During the decade of 1973-1984, the real growth of gross domestic product in low-income nations averaged 5.3% annually, compared to 2.4% in the industrial market economies; the comparable ratio of private consumption growth was 5.1% to 2.6%. Over the same decade the 5 fastest growing economies of the world were Saudi Arabia, South Korea, Brazil, Turkey, and Algeria (World Bank, 1986).

3. *Moral imperative.* In the world today, according to the World Health Organization: at least 10 million die each year from too little food; over 500 million suffer irreversible effects of malnutrition; half the human race exists in conditions of chronic poverty. The economic power and dominance of multinationals almost certainly means that increasing pressure will be brought to bear upon them to contribute to a solution to the plight of the world's poor; not through charity, but through creative marketing approaches. Rich markets can no longer be so conveniently separated from poor markets; chronic world poverty threatens the very existence of all world institutions — multinationals included.

Simply stated, long-term self-interest and the survival instinct constitute sufficient reason for MNCs to apply the concept of strategic planning to their marketing efforts in Third World countries.

A STRATEGIC PLANNING MODEL

A solution for better performance in Third World markets would be to consolidate responsibility for all such operations in a separate strategic business unit, hereafter referred to as an SBU(LDC). The planning process for the SBU(LDC) should be derived from, and parallel, the corporate strategic plan. Figure 1 illustrates a strategic planning model for the SBU(LDC) including its relationship to the corporate plan.

At the corporate level, strategic planning attempts to create a fit between the organization and its changing environment. It follows the logic of developing a clear company mission statement, establishing appropriate goals and objectives, formulating growth strategy, and devising a business portfolio plan. The latter stage consists of identifying the key strategic business units that will comprise the

Figure 1. A Strategic Planning Model for the SBU(LDC)

CORPORATE LEVEL		SBU(LDC) LEVEL
Mission statement	---->	Mission statement
Objectives and goals	---->	Objectives and goals
Growth strategy	---->	Market opportunity analysis
Business portfolio plan	--->	Target market evaluation
		Product strategy
		Entry strategy
		Marketing program
		Impact analysis

enterprise. Such SBUs are thereafter treated as individual businesses; controlling their own resources, and planned independently of other units.

As shown, the SBU(LDC) emanates from the business portfolio plan stage as a separate and distinct operation. While the SBU (LDC) planning sequence follows the logic of the corporate plan, the unique aspects of LDC markets require significant modification of the corporate plan, as well as special additional steps. Each step of the SBU(LDC) planning sequence is described in detail in the discussion that follows.

MISSION STATEMENT

Firms having a strategic perspective will have formulated a mission statement to provide the enterprise with a clear sense of purpose and direction. Subject to continual review and change, mission statements answer such questions as, "What business are we in?" "Which customers should we serve?" and "How shall we satisfy customer needs?" Consistent with the corporate statement, business unit managers must answer similar questions for their organizational component. The mission statement for the SBU(LDC) will be derived from the corporate statement, but may reflect important differences. A broadening, or modification, of the corporate statement may in itself be an essential key to sharpening the focus of the firm's approach to LDC markets.

International Fragrances and Flavors (IFF) is a case in point. In its primary markets, IFF sells its products to industries that use them as ingredients in such consumer goods as condiments and cosmetics. Nominally, such final products fall in the convenience/luxury category. It thus might appear that IFF would have little to offer a developing country more concerned with raising basic living standards than with providing conveniences and luxuries to the few who can afford them. However, IFF took a fresh look at its mission as to how it might relate to LDC markets. It realized that its business could be as basic as satisfying two of the five senses, taste and smell—thus suggesting potential applications across the globe. One specific outcome of the new thinking was the development of a flavor attractant that draws nitrogen-fixing bacteria in the soil to the root system of crops, thereby substituting for high-cost nitrogen fertilizer. IFF realized that their potential "customers" were not only humans, but any living organisms. The result? A new product admirably suited to the needs of countries at the low end of the development scale.

OBJECTIVES AND GOALS

The mission statement must be translated into a set of actionable objectives and goals. The process is illustrated by the fertilizer division of International Minerals and Chemical Corporation, which first defined its global mission not as selling fertilizer, but "to fight world hunger" (Kotler, 1980). Next, the mission statement was translated into a hierarchy of objectives. First, world hunger is to be fought by increasing agricultural productivity. Agricultural productivity, in turn, is to be accomplished by developing high-yield fertilizers. But research and development require funding, so a third objective is profit improvement. Profits can be improved by increasing sales or reducing costs, so further objectives were established in each category.

Objectives for the SBU(LDC) need to be quantified in the same way as for other corporate units. At the same time, ROI and profit objectives may need to be framed in broader, or longer-run terms. In some markets, negative ROI may be acceptable, just as a firm tolerates losses early in a product's life cycle, or as a temporary phase of a market share battle. Negative returns in some SBU(LDC) markets may be acceptable for similar reasons, or for others such as preservation of a needed source of strategic materials.

Moreover, in the SBU(LDC) it is especially important that objectives be *qualified* as well as quantified. That is, in addition to specifying minimum requirements for ROI, for example, objectives must be framed in the context of acceptable means for their achievement. It may be found that there are alternative strategies for achieving the same ROI, but that great differences would ensue in the social/ cultural impact of the options under consideration.

To illustrate, consider the case of the Green Giant Company, a producer of canned and frozen vegetables. Much of the firm's product mix falls in the convenience category; quick to prepare but expensive. To the extent that Third World markets even seem worth considering for such goods, the likely target market would be the affluent minority. Perhaps the overprivileged class would be found sufficiently large to provide an acceptable profit return. Green Giant, however, takes a more enlightened view, having set the major goal of devising "strategies for profit in overcoming global malnutrition" (Kraar, 1980). The premise is that a food-producing MNC can act as a key catalyst in bringing together farmers, processors, agronomists, distributors, and farm implement manufacturers in an all-out effort to attack the world hunger crisis; and, with ingenuity, it can be done as an undertaking that will return profits equivalent to what could be achieved by simply selling the conventional product line.

MARKET OPPORTUNITY ANALYSIS

Within the Third World, profound differences divide regions and countries in such respects as culture, political orientation, race, religion, and receptivity to foreign enterprise. Within this confusing milieu, the SBU(LDC) must locate the most suitable and attractive opportunities to fulfill its mission and objectives. The single most important measure of opportunity is the match between market needs and the firm's product mix. To facilitate the opportunity search, some method of market segmentation is essential.

Numerous single-factor and multifactor constructs for grouping countries have been proposed (see Rizkallah, 1980). A common approach is to group countries by level of economic development; the World Bank, for example, employs 6 strata to classify the world's 128 nations. This approach provides helpful clarification when the terms "Third World" or "less developed countries" are used broadly, as in this discussion. Clearly, significant differences exist in needs, opportunities, and trade potentials between countries at the lowest rungs of the development ladder and those which have recently joined the ranks of major exporters of manufactured goods, such as South Korea and Taiwan. At the same time, much heterogeneity exists among nations classified at the same development level.

The author suggests that a systematic and useful way to differentiate opportunities in LDCs is to categorize such nations on the basis of their *approach* to, rather than level of, development. In traditional economic thinking, "development" has been construed as movement along a uniform, linear path leading to the Western stereotype of mass industrialization. Many Third World leaders, however, have concluded that the rich nations' concept of development is predicated upon goals neither attainable nor desirable on a global scale. In the current literature of development, alternative approaches have been proposed (e.g., Oshima, 1977; Pinches, 1977; Streeten, 1977; Wirada, 1983).

Table 1 illustrates how the Third World market may be segmented on the basis of four alternative development approaches, and includes current or recent examples of nations ostensibly committed to each course as evidenced by their stated development policies.

Basic Needs Countries

This concept disfavors forced-draft industrialization drives aimed at emulating the Western economies (Ghai, 1977; Lisk, 1977; Mathieson, 1981). The premise is that LDCs face problems never encountered by the rich nations, and that industrial growth in the former can occur only after agriculture has been placed on a firm foundation, peasant living standards raised, and income redistributed. Accordingly, development emphasis is shifted from industrial projects to raising agricultural productivity, developing light consumer goods industry, expanding small-scale local enterprise, and achieving mass dissemination of public health service and educational opportunities.

BN countries are especially good markets for simple, practical, inexpensive products or services that relate to basic human needs. Possible examples are meat substitutes, synthetic fabrics, alternative energy sources, protein-rich foods and beverages, contraceptives, generic drugs, housing materials, and educational hardware and software. BN countries are keenly interested in low-technology products that will raise small farm output, such as innovative farm implements, high-yield seeds, fertilizers, animal feed, fungicides, and insecticides.

At the same time, high-tech firms are by no means excluded from

Table 1

A Market Segmentation Model of Nations Based on Approach to Development

Approach	Cornerstones of Development Policy	Prominent Examples: Current or Recent
Basic Needs	Redistribution of income Health, education, welfare of masses Raising agricultural productivity Central planning and control	China, Colombia, Costa Rica, Gabon, Malawi, Mali, Peru, Sri Lanka, Tanzania

Appropriate Technology	Evolutionary progress toward
	  local/regional self-reliance
	Decentralized decision-making
	Small, simple, labor-intensive
	  manufacture and handicraft
	Rural agro-industrial culture
		Bangladesh, Bhutan,
		Ethiopia, Ghana, India,
		Indonesia, Philippines

Isolationism	Total economic self-sufficiency Freedom from superpower domination Fervent protection of values Rigid central planning and control	Albania, Algeria, Burma, China, Cuba, Iran, Kampuchea, Uganda

Indigenous Modernization	Greater "piece of the action" in
	  international economy
	Maximum exploitation of natural
	  resource base
	Preservation of national culture
	Selective industrialization and
	  modernization
		Brazil, Egypt, Jordan,
		Kenya, Lebanon, Liberia,
		Mexico, Saudi Arabia,
		Syria, Venezuela, Zaire

BN markets. Indeed, some frontier areas of technology hold great promise for application to developing countries to the extent that they are low-cost, energy-conserving, and readily adaptable to LDC rural concentrations, climates, and traditional skills. One such area is biotechnology, comprising a wide spectrum of processes such as the use of microbes to produce energy, the biochemical conversion of waste into fuel, fish farming, and the use of insects for productive work.

Appropriate Technology Countries

Whereas the BN model postpones heavy industrial development, the AT approach permanently repudiates it (Schumacher, 1973; Szecsey, 1979). The AT concept favors creation of an agro-industrial culture founded upon an intermediate level of technology that is rural, rather than urban, based. The core idea is to create many thousands of workplaces to maximize not national output, but work opportunity. Such workplaces are to be small, simple, labor-intensive, to use indigenous resources, and to produce for local market needs. While basic need satisfaction is a central concern, higher priority is given to achieving local self-sufficiency.

AT countries are particularly open to ideas for new, small-scale production technologies; examples are small factories in India that make building blocks from native red clay, the manufacture of "bamboocrete" as a roofing compound in small Indonesian plants, and the use of bamboo to make sanitary water pipes in Asian countries. The technique of "inventing backward" is especially applicable to AT markets; recent examples include hand- and foot-powered sewing and washing machines, solar cookers made of cardboard, and simple clay stoves to replace open fire cooking. AT countries also need innovative ideas for meeting energy, transportation, communication, education, and similar community needs; examples are windmill power systems and waterfall hydroelectric systems.

Isolationist Countries

Nations in this category have forsworn large-scale industrialization for a different motive (Amin, 1974; Chipeta, 1981; Waterlow, 1974). Wishing to be insulated from "destructive" intrusions of foreign influence, they act on the precept that meaningful progress can best be achieved by drawing a "poverty curtain" around their borders. Their prime goals are total self-sufficiency and freedom from dependence on the international economic system. Usually there are Marxist overtones to such a view, but nations pursuing this approach tend to be animated by a spirit of fierce independence and resolute resistance to superpower domination.

By definition, isolationist country opportunities for foreign firms are severely limited; however, they can be receptive to products, services, or processes that will, in the long run, contribute to their self-sufficiency. Examples might include processes or equipment that would improve efficiency in the extraction and processing of raw materials, or that might facilitate eventual domestic manufacture of goods presently imported (e.g., medicines; precision instruments; automotive parts).

Indigenous Modernization Countries

Nations in this category remain committed to the imperative of achieving industrial growth and concomitant global power, but hold markedly ambivalent attitudes toward developed nations (Arghiri, 1972; Jalle, 1968; Singh, 1983; Stavrianos, 1981). They seek a maximum of technological transfer, but with a minimum of "ideological contamination." Countries in this category include many that possess great wealth in natural resources. These countries have the means and desire to move rapidly into the modern world, but intend to do so strictly on *their* terms. Opportunities in IM countries extend across the full spectrum of low-to high-technology products and services, industrial and consumer.

TARGET MARKET EVALUATION

Opportunity analysis serves as a global screening device which identifies the most likely of market targets. Some MNCs having relatively narrow product lines may find their best opportunities in those nations pursuing one particular development course; others may see their product mixes to be potentially compatible with all modes.

Before the SBU(LDC) can decide whether, and how, to enter a given economy, more detailed evaluation is necessary. Both the substance and nuances of the development course must be discerned. This means a careful study of the history and tradition of the people, thorough analysis of political conditions and trends, and a genuine feel for the national aspiration. Thorough knowledge of the real and potential resources of a nation—material, cultural, and human—is needed.

Preferably, market target evaluation should be a continuous process. Sudden swerves in development course are a norm of third world countries. As an example of how the SBU(LDC) might handle this task, Caterpillar Tractor maintains a special department whose sole function is to "monitor the national pulse" of countries

throughout the world, to facilitate timely and intelligent response to
burgeoning opportunities and problems (Morgan, 1979).

PRODUCT STRATEGY

Some MNCs follow a policy of global product standardization, to
maximize economies of scale or to preserve worldwide image. In
the case of a product like Coca-Cola — simple, low-cost, and with
universal appeal — this policy might sensibly be extended into LDC
markets. For most MNCs, however, the great cultural and technological disparities between LDCs and developed countries make
product innovation and adaptation an especially important consideration. Within the constraints of corporate policy, the SBU(LDC)
must determine what products are to be offered, and what product
modifications are feasible and desirable, preferably on a market-by-
market basis.

Product strategies for LDC markets can range from offering
wholly new technological solutions, to making minor adaptations of
existing products. Figure 2 suggests four possible strategies,
ranked 1 to 4 on the basis of the level of commitment and challenge
represented.

Technological Innovation

At the high end of the scale, a firm can focus fundamental research and development on devising new technological solutions
suitable to LDC market needs. Such an approach would logically
relate especially to BN and AT countries, and might focus on such
basic areas as agriculture or energy. This strategy extends beyond

Figure 2. Product Strategies for LDC Markets

	INNOVATION	ADAPTATION
TECHNOLOGY	Devising new technological solutions 1	Adapting existing technologies 2
PRODUCTS	Developing new products 3	Adapting existing products 4

product development *per se*, and may be aimed at developing wholly new technological approaches suited to local customs, abilities, and temperaments. Technological innovation may take the form of new products to be sold, or processes to be introduced through licensing arrangements or partnerships with local enterprise.

The epitome of this strategy is illustrated by N.V. Philips, the Dutch electronics manufacturer, which maintains a special pilot plant for the sole purpose of devising new technologies in its areas of expertise that fit the market needs and production capabilities of various Third World countries.

Two approaches are open to a firm wishing to provide new technologies:

1. *Technological push.* This approach might aptly be termed, "technological solutions looking for social application." The idea is illustrated by the Dow Chemical Company's development of an inexpensive solar water stile that converts polluted, muddy, or toxic water to clean drinking water. With the technical process in hand, Dow contacted the Agency for International Development (AID). AID in turn was able to coordinate arrangements for a trial application of the process in Yemen.

2. *Technological pull.* The idea here is to study the needs and priorities of a country or region *before* attempting to develop a new technological solution. This approach has the advantage of early identification of on any potential user resistance to an innovative idea, as occurred when a firm introduced a box-type solar cooker made of cardboard in India, only to find that rural families would not make the modest investment for fear that its glass cover could too easily be broken by children.

As the foregoing examples suggest, technological innovation need not equate with sophisticated scientific research. More than this, it requires a change of thinking and approach. Whereas the usual technological orientation of industrial organizations is to maximize output and minimize cost, the more appropriate technologies for LDCs are those that maximize work, conserve energy, and employ indigenous resources.

Technological Adaptation

The focus of this strategy is to identify existing technologies that can be adapted to LDC needs.

Within the structure of industry, many firms find their strength in the ability to invent new and diversified applications of break-through technologies developed by industry research leaders. Such firms play a critical role in the dissemination of new generic technologies to every corner of industry, as in creating numerous applications of the microprocessor. This capability can readily be turned to Third World market applications.

As in technological innovation, the end result of technological adaptation may be products to be sold, or processes to be transferred through arrangements such as licensing. Concerning the latter, the economic interests of an organization may limit or preclude the transfer of technologies that have profit potential in primary markets. However, several approaches can be identified that involve only noncompeting technologies. For example:

1. *Research by-products*. In the course of their main research and development efforts, firms often discover by-product technologies that do not lead to products, for economic or other reasons. John Deere, for example, developed a scaled-down tractor for small farms, but decided not to produce it because the volume potential fell short of minimum requirements. Deere has licensed the design to a smaller firm that intends to market the product in Third World countries.

2. *Abandoned technologies*. As product life cycles unfold over time, numerous technologies fall into disuse. A huge volume of expired patents now exists. A backward search through this volume of ideas may identify many that have potential applications to countries seeking simpler technologies.

3. *Publicly available technology*. There exists an enormous amount of useful technology that appears in technical journals, arises from the practical experience of companies, or surfaces in technology symposiums. While such knowledge is in the public domain, it is underutilized by LDCs that typically lack both ready access to the information and the knowledge of how to convert it to productive activity.

Product Innovation

Product innovation is a middle-ground strategy, wherein new product designs are created specifically for LDC markets.

A starting point for a firm considering this approach is examination of the current product line, with a view toward simplification. For example, it may be possible to convert products that are electrically or fuel-powered to hand, foot, or horse-power. A case in point concerns pumps for lifting irrigation water. State-of-the-art pumps are diesel-powered, made of iron, and cost $1,500. One firm is working on the design of a manually-operated pump to be made of cheap, corrosion-resistant plastic that will cost only $100. As a hypothetical example, a manufacturer of sophisticated electronic products might consider resurrecting the design of a crystal radio set for Third World countries.

Product Adaptation

Toward the low end of the scale, existing products can be modified in ways that are neither fundamental nor dramatic, but which enhance their applicability to LDC markets. Key respects to be considered include brand name, labelling, usage instructions, packaging (especially possible secondary functions), colors, sizes, aesthetic aspects, constituents, and measurement units.

ENTRY STRATEGY

Overseas market entry options include (a) simple export, (b) contractual agreements such as licensing, (c) joint ventures, and (d) host-country manufacture. The SBU(LDC) must determine the most appropriate strategy for each target market; no single approach can be expected to yield optimal results in all LDC markets.

The options at either end of the above range are, in most cases, the least appropriate. Simple arms-length export minimizes risk, but also control and involvement. Host-country manufacture is an option that most MNCs would choose to employ only on a very selective basis, and then only after establishing market presence through one or more of the options requiring lower levels of investment and risk.

Contractual and joint venture arrangements are usually the preferred strategies for first-time entry in LDC markets. LDCs want the benefits foreign enterprise can provide, especially technology transfer; but they also want a significant measure of control over foreign investment. Commensurately, most LDCs favor partnership arrangements with special legal benefits. These typically cover such matters as approval procedures, guarantees against expropriation, profit transfer rights, tax exemptions, and remission of import duties.

Some LDCs require equity-sharing as a condition of entry, but even when this condition is not explicit, it is likely to be implicit. Bangladesh, for instance, used to be a profitable market for several major pharmaceutical firms. These companies resisted efforts of local entrepreneurs to participate more actively in some phase of the production and sale of medicinal drugs. Now, the market has been largely lost to a local physician who, with enthusiastic government support, managed to fabricate a viable native operation which makes and sells drugs at lower cost.

Regardless of political orientation or development mode, an animating characteristic of Third World thinking is to share responsibilities and rewards. The SBU(LDC) must take special care to demonstrate that an entry plan will stimulate the growth of local business, rather than competing against it. It may be possible to devise entry plans wherein locally-produced components are incorporated in the finished product, or where local firms share in the distribution and servicing functions. Somewhere along the line it should be possible to allow a measure of local input in decision-making. Even though the benefits may be indirect, the important point is that the plan of entry demonstrates concern with a positive impact on local business.

MARKETING PROGRAM

Commensurate with product and entry strategy, remaining elements of the marketing mix must be programmed. Price, distribution, and communication components need to be set.

1. *Price*. The price decision is a sensitive one. Host-country laws will sometimes impinge upon price-setting, and, in any event, it

may prove expeditious to allow the government a role in the pricing decision. Strategically, it may be found that there are alternative prices that would be forecast to return roughly equivalent profits, but with greatly differing ancillary effects. Such may be the case, for example, in comparing a skimming approach that would limit product availability to elite sectors as against a penetration approach that would extend availability to the mass market. It is desirable for the firm to allow the SBU(LDC) pricing latitude, and in general the latter should follow a variable cost pricing policy. Lesser returns may be acceptable in certain LDC markets where a strong market presence is desirable for overall strategic reasons.

2. *Distribution.* Distribution policies are likely to require adjustment from country to country as a function of middleman availability. Arranging for the distribution function may be worth much special thought by the SBU(LDC) for the reason that it offers the prime opportunity for linking local enterprise to the entry venture. Ways of accomplishing this goal are not limited simply to using existing distributor facilities, but include also the possibility of providing for the upgrading and training of distributors, and even initiating local entrepreneurship ventures to create new facilities.

3. *Communication.* In the communication area, corporate policy will dictate the extent to which global standardization of promotional themes is to be maintained. Within this constraint, the SBU(LDC) should strive for a maximum of fine-tuning to match local conditions.

One special opportunity for the SBU(LDC) is to employ the firm's communication power and skill in shaping more favorable attitudes toward MNC involvement in the Third World. It is an axiom of journalism that one plane crash is news, but 10,000 safe landings are not. Analogously, headlines have blared over MNC bribery scandals, while little has been said of the far more numerous instances of positive contributions. In short, MNCs suffer from a bad press. The irony is that free enterprise has perfected over the years the most powerful arsenal of tools and techniques known to mankind for influencing public attitudes. In designing promotional plans, the SBU(LDC) should consider objectives that go beyond mere stimulation of market demand. That is, the function of the

SBU(LDC) should be not only to sell products, but, equally important, to sell the MNC itself in the forum of world opinion.

IMPACT ANALYSIS

An important responsibility of the SBU(LDC) should be to evaluate the cultural, social, and economic ramifications of the firm's entry into each LDC market. In performing such impact analysis, a far-reaching perspective must be adopted.

Examples abound of MNC product introductions wherein dysfunctional side-effects were overlooked or ignored. Japanese firms introduced mechanical rice-hullers to Indonesia, and promptly put thousands of landless laborers out of work; subsequent protest riots led to hasty enactment of antiforeigner legislation. Nestle ignited a firestorm across the Third World when it introduced baby formula as a substitute for breast feeding.

The forces unleashed by technological innovation are often subtle and indirect, and the SBU(LDC) cannot be expected to foresee, let alone solve, all of them. It can, however, demonstrate concern and sensitivity through thoughtful impact analysis. Throughout the Third World a great web of nonprofit agencies work quietly to ameliorate the problems caused by rapid technological and cultural change. The SBU(LDC) can show a willingness to coordinate its marketing programs with the services of such agencies and appropriate bureaus of host-country governments.

CORPORATE IMPLEMENTATION
AND SUPPORT OF THE SBU(LDC)

Implementation of the SBU(LDC) concept must be tailored to the unique operating environment of each particular firm. MNCs differ widely both in general organization philosophy, as well as in specific organization structure. In some firms the business unit concept is well established, while in others separate divisions exist but are not explicitly recognized as distinct, autonomous units. Moreover, the specific organizational treatment of international operations varies from firm to firm. Some companies combine all such operations in a single division; others divide international responsibility among geographical or product units.

The essential concept of the SBU(LDC) could be adapted to all such organizational configurations. While implementation details would differ, the operational dimensions of the unit would be derived from thorough consideration of the following key issues:

1. *Scope of responsibility.* The market focus and boundaries of the SBU(LDC) have to be delineated by top management. It must be decided which regions or countries are to become the responsibility of the new unit. This decision may be relatively clear-cut for firms that presently have little or no involvement in Third World markets. For others, such as firms that have established significant trade relations with newly industrialized countries, the decision will be more complex. In instances such as the latter, the market focus of the SBU(LDC) might be confined to countries at lower levels of the development scale.

2. *Corporate interrelationships.* The working relationships between the SBU(LDC) and other organization components must be established. Generally, it might be expected that the SBU(LDC) would share corporate resources along with other SBUs, each drawing on the company pool of knowledge and services in areas such as marketing, manufacturing, marketing research, product planning, and engineering. However, the unique aspects of the SBU(LDC) almost certainly would require that it have its own internal capabilities in all or most such areas. For example, a firm's proprietary technical processes and engineering skills often would need to be adapted to LDC requirements, as in the case of devising appropriate technology solutions.

Coordination parameters need to be established to link the SBU (LDC) to other units of the organization involved in international operations. The scope of this problem is moderated by the fact that three-quarters of industrial nation merchandise exports presently go to other industrial nations. Potentially major overlaps would most commonly be expected with respect to nations at higher development levels; such cases can be solved by an upper management jurisdiction decision or a sharing of responsibility between the SBU(LDC) and other units.

3. *Staffing.* The distinctive mission and nontraditional perfor-

mance standards of the SBU(LDC) suggest the need for managers with special blends of experience, technical skills, and interests. Inasmuch as MNCs are predominantly headquartered in industrial nations, the new unit would constitute a logical center for the employment of nationals from various world regions at all managerial levels. Within the unit, personnel needs and opportunities would exist on a permanent or consulting basis for a variety of unconventional specialties such as cultural anthropology, linguistics, history, political science, sociology, and developmental economics.

4. *Corporate support.* As with any other business unit, the success of the SBU(LDC) would be proportionate to the measure of corporate support it receives. In the case of the SBU(LDC), such support must extend beyond resource allocations *per se.* It must include also the granting of unusual latitude in decision-making throughout the strategic planning process, as well as in the acceptance of performance criteria that are longer term and less stringently quantified.

Inasmuch as performance in LDC markets is likely to be an increasingly significant key to the long term viability of any firm with global operations, the ultimate rationalization for such support is, simply, the survival of the enterprise.

REFERENCES

Amin, S. (1974). *Acculturation on a World Scale: A Critique of the Theory of Underdevelopment*, New York: Monthly Review Press.

Arghiri, E. (1972). *Unequal Exchange: A Study of the Imperialism of Trade*, New York: Monthly Review Press.

Chipeta, C. (1981). *Indigenous Economics: A Cultural Approach.* New York: Exposition Press.

Ghai, D. P. (1977). *The Basic Needs Approach to Development.* Geneva: International Labour Organization.

Jain, S. C. (1984). *International Marketing Management.* Boston: Kent Publishing Co.

Jalle, P. (1968). *The Pillage of the Third World.* New York: Monthly Review Press.

Kotler, P. (1980). "Strategic Planning and the Marketing Process." *Business,* (May-June), 30, pp. 2-9.

Kraar, L. (1980, March 24). "Multinationals Get Smarter About Political Risks." *Fortune,* pp. 86-88.

Lisk, F. (1977). "Conventional Development Strategies and Basic Need Fulfillment." *International Labour Review*, (March), 68, pp. 175-191.

Mathieson, J. et al. (1981). *Basic Needs and the New International Order*. Washington: Overseas Development Council.

Morgan, L. L. (1979). "Challenges for Multinational Corporations." *Industrial Marketing Management*, (July), 8, pp. 187-191.

Oshima, H. T. (1977). "New Directions in Development Strategies." *Economic Development and Cultural Change*, (April), 25, pp. 555-579.

Pinches, C. R. (1977). "Economic Development: The Need for an Alternative Approach." *Economic Development and Cultural Change*, (October), 26, pp. 139-146.

Rizkallah, E. G. (1980). *Multiple Market Allocations: A Portfolio Approach*. Paper presented at the Academy of International Business Annual Meeting, New Orleans.

Schuh, G. E. (1986). *The United States and the Developing Countries: An Economic Perspective*, Washington: National Planning Association.

Schumacher, E. F. (1973). *Small Is Beautiful*. New York: Harper & Row.

Singh, V. H. (1983). *Technology Transfer and Economic Development: Models and Practices for Developing Countries*. Jersey City, NJ: Unz & Co.

Stavrianos, L. S. (1981). *Global Rift: The Third World Comes of Age*. New York: Morrow.

Streeten, P. (1977). "Changing Perceptions of Development." *Finance and Development*, (September), 14, pp. 14-16.

Szecsey, C. (1979). "Culturally Appropriate Technology." *Approtech*, 5, pp. 19-23.

U.S. Department of Commerce (1986). *Statistical Abstract of the U.S., 1986*. Washington, DC.

Waterlow, C. (1974). *Superpowers and Victims: The Outlook for World Community*. Englewood Cliffs, NJ: Prentice-Hall.

Wirada, H. J. (1983). "Toward a Nonethnocentric Theory of Development: Alternative Conceptions from the Third World." *Journal of Developing Areas*, (July), 7, pp. 48-59.

World Bank (1986). *World Development Report 1986*. New York: Oxford University Press.

Chapter 13

Incidence of Market Typologies and Pattern of Marketing Activity Performance in Selected African Countries

Kofi Q. Dadzie
Ishmael P. Akaah
Edward A. Riordan

SUMMARY. Although product-market and state control are offered as environmental variables that underlie the diversity of the market environment of the Third World, empirical assessment of their influence is lacking. This chapter therefore examines the incidence of product-market/state control market typologies in selected African countries when the two variables are coupled and also the extent to which marketing activity performance differs with respect to the product-market/state control market typologies. The study results suggest the existence of different product-market/state control market typologies in the countries studied and also differences in the pattern of marketing activity performance.

INTRODUCTION

Over the past decade, considerable literature attention has focused on marketing in developing or less developed countries (referred to hereafter as Third World countries) (Kaynak, 1982; Samli & Kaynak, 1984; Malhotra, 1986). This burgeoning literature has

This chapter was first published in the *Journal of Global Marketing*, Vol. 1(3), Spring 1988.

spanned a wide range of topics, including the role of marketing in the Third World and the organization of marketing strategy by Third World firms. Reflective of the literature is the acknowledgment that the market environment of the Third World differs from that of the industrialized countries (e.g., the U.S. and Western European countries).

While several environmental variables are believed to underlie the differences in market environment, two of these, product-market and state control, are offered as instrumental. The product-market variable pertains to whether the market environment under which Third World firms operate is that of a buyer's market (i.e., the demand for the firm's products/services is less than the supply) or that of a seller's market (i.e., the demand for the firm's products/services exceeds the supply). The state control variable pertains to the extent to which the marketing mix elements (i.e., price, promotion, product, and distribution) are controlled by the state or the government of the respective Third World country.

Although the influence of the two environmental variables (i.e., product-market and state control) on marketing strategy and/or tactics is widely acknowledged (Akaah, Riordan, & Dadzie, 1986; Bartels, 1983; Ross & McTavish, 1985), empirical assessment is lacking. Moreover, because many Third World countries are known to reflect sellers' type markets with high levels of state controls, the tendency in the literature is to treat Third World markets as if they are homogeneous in terms of product-market/state control environment. However, an examination of the socioeconomic environment of the Third World (*World Development Report,* 1984) suggests that Third World markets are far from homogeneous in terms of product-market/state control environment. Thus, to the extent that the product-market and state control variables are not collinear (e.g., the existence of a sellers' market environment is not contemporaneous with state control of the mix elements), one would expect some degree of heterogeneity in the product-market/state control environment of the Third World when the two environmental variables are coupled. This would in turn suggest the need for different marketing strategies by Third World firms, depending on the product-market/state control environment under which they operate (Cavusgil & Yavas, 1984).

The objective of the present paper is to explore, in the context of selected African countries, (1) the incidence of product-market/ state control market typologies when product-market and state control are coupled, and (2) the differences in marketing activity performance across product-market/state control market typologies. The paper should therefore provide the needed empirical evidence regarding the heterogeneity of product-market/state control environment and its influence on marketing activity performance in the Third World context.

LITERATURE REVIEW AND HYPOTHESES

As noted earlier, even though many Third World countries reflect a sellers' type market with relatively high levels of state controls compared to the Western industrialized countries, the markets of the Third World are far from homogeneous in terms of product-market/state control environment. With respect to product-market, Third World countries could be viewed as spanning the seller-buyer market continuum. Similarly, for state control, Third World countries could be viewed as spanning the controlled-uncontrolled continuum. Of course, since there is hardly a firm in the world (including those in the U.S. and Western European countries) that operates free of some degree of state controls, only the moderate-to-high end of the controlled-uncontrolled continuum is of practical relevance. If, for sake of empirical analysis, each of the variables is treated as dichotomous (i.e., sellers' versus buyers' market for product-market and moderately controlled versus highly controlled for state control), then their coupling yields four product-market/state control market typologies, namely: moderately controlled buyers' market, moderately controlled sellers' market, highly controlled buyers' market, and highly controlled sellers' market.

Moderately Controlled Buyers' Market

As the name suggests, a moderately controlled buyers' market reflects an environment where the mix elements are moderately controlled by the state and the demand for a firm's products/services is less than the supply. Thus, this market typology corresponds to the kind of market environment most firms in the industrialized countries (e.g., the U.S. and Western Europe) operate under. This market typology also underlies the organizing framework of the discipline (Bartels, 1983; Ross & McTavish, 1985). That is, the organizing framework of the discipline assumes a buyers' type market environment with minimal state controls and, thus, the ability of the marketing manager to manipulate the mix elements to achieve desired firm objectives (Kotler, 1984; Pride & Ferrell, 1985).

Moderately Controlled Sellers' Market

A moderately controlled sellers' market reflects an environment where the marketing mix elements are somewhat controlled by the state and the demand for a firm's products/services exceeds the supply, thus implying a shortage environment. To the extent that the shortages are short-lived and limited in focus, this corresponds to the petroleum-related shortages that characterized the U.S. in the 1970s. As the literature on "shortage" marketing indicates (e.g., Cravens, 1974; Kotler, 1974; Kotler & Levy, 1972; Papadopoulos, 1983), the shortage environment of this market typology demands a different marketing strategy than under a buyers' market environment.

Highly Controlled Buyers' Market

A highly controlled buyers' market pertains to an environment where the demand for a firm's products/services is less than the supply but the marketing mix elements are highly controlled by the state. This market typology is reflective of economies (e.g., of the Eastern bloc countries) that exhibit state control of the mix elements regardless of the ready availability of products/services. As Ross and McTavish (1985) have observed, the high level of state control that characterizes this market typology limits the marketing managers' ability to freely manipulate the marketing mix elements as assumed in traditional marketing conceptualizations.

Highly Controlled Sellers' Market

A highly controlled sellers' market reflects an environment where the demand for a firm's products/services exceeds the supply and the marketing mix elements are highly state-controlled. This market typology, as noted previously, is prototypical of the product-market/state control environment of many Third World countries. Unlike the short-lived petroleum-related shortages that characterized the U.S. in the 1970s (referred to earlier), the shortage environment of many Third World countries tends to be more prolonged and widespread in nature (Akaah, 1986). Since the literature on shortage marketing reflects experiences under an environment that was short-lived and limited in focus, and entailed minimal state controls, it remains to be demonstrated the extent to which marketing activity performance differs under a market environment where product/service shortages are prolonged and widespread, and also reflects a high level of state control of the mix variables.

Research Hypotheses

Deriving from the preceding discussion are two suppositions. The first is that the product-market/state control environment under which firms in the Third World operate is far from homogeneous in character. The second is that the utilization of marketing techniques would differ as a function of the product-market/state control environment under which firms in the Third World operate. As noted previously, empirical evidence is lacking regarding both suppositions. In view of this, the following two hypotheses were formulated and tested:

H1: The product-market/state control environment that characterizes the operations of firms in Africa is heterogeneous in character.

H2: The incidence and regularity of performance of marketing activities by firms in Africa differs as a function of the product-market/state control environment under which they operate.

METHODOLOGY

The Sample

To explore the study objectives, an English language questionnaire was developed and mailed to 565 marketing managers in five English-speaking African countries. The countries comprised Ghana, Nigeria, Kenya, Tanzania, and Zambia. The use of only English-speaking countries stemmed from the need to minimize the translation equivalence problem associated with cross-cultural research (Douglas & Craig, 1983).

The Owen's Directory (1982-1984) served as the sampling frame. This Directory contains the names and addresses of registered firms in each of the five countries. A stratified random sampling plan with country as stratum was used to select, on a proportional basis, firms from each of the five countries (as listed in the Gwen's Directory). The firms sampled represented approximately one percent of the total number of firms listed in the Directory for the five countries. To each of the sampled firms was mailed a questionnaire addressed to "The Marketing Manager." The cover letter that accompanied the questionnaire directed the recipient to pass it on to the individual in the firm with overall responsibility for marketing decisions in case he/she was not the one.

DATA COLLECTION AND INSTRUMENT

To help explore the differences in marketing activity performance across the four market typologies, respondents provided information regarding the extent to which their respective firms performed each of 40 marketing activities. The list of activities was culled from Pride and Ferrell (1985, p. 10) and was pretested to ensure clarity. The list spanned marketing information, marketing management, pricing, promotion, distribution, and product activities. The data on marketing activity performance were obtained via a Likert-type scale with descriptive anchors that ranged from "never performed" (coded 1), "performed 1-2 times a year" (coded 2), "performed 3-5 times a year" (coded 3), to "performed 6 or more times a year" (coded 4).

Additionally, respondents provided information about them-selves, their firms, and country of operation. The firm information pertained to industry category, nature of ownership, role of market-ing, size of firm, and the product-market environment under which their firms operated (i.e., whether a buyers' or a sellers' market). With respect to country of operation, respondents provided infor-mation regarding the nature of the economy of the country in which their firms operated and the extent of government control of the mix variables (i.e, price, product, promotion and distribution). The re-spondent information elicited included job title/position and respon-dents' organizational functions. The information regarding job title and organizational functions was used to assess whether respon-dents' questionnaire responses qualified for inclusion in the data analysis.

The data collection process spanned the spring/summer of 1985. Of the 565 questionnaires mailed, 188 usable responses were re-ceived — representing a 33% response rate. The country and firm profile of the respondents is summarized in Table 1. As the in-dustry breakdown indicates, the sample reflected the kinds of firms expected to perform marketing activities in the African context. The profile of the respondents in terms of job titles also reveals that most held marketing-related positions — thus implying their ability to de-scribe the extent to which their firms performed the marketing ac-tivities examined.

ANALYSIS AND RESULTS

Incidence of Market Typologies

To examine research hypothesis 1 (i.e., the heterogeneity of the product-market/state control environment under which firms in Af-rica operate), the firms in the study were classified into the four market typologies described previously. First, the firms were classi-fied into highly and moderately controlled categories. This classifi-cation was based on newspaper accounts and interviews with gov-ernment officials from the respective countries regarding the nature and extent of state control of marketing activities for the period covered by the study. Underlying the use of country as the classifi-

Table 1

COUNTRY AND FIRM PROFILE OF RESPONDENTS

I. Country Factors

    A. Country (per capita GNP)[a]

        1. Tanzania ($280)   17.0%
        2. Ghana ($360)   19.7%
        3. Kenya ($390)   17.6%
        4. Zambia ($640)   21.8%
        5. Nigeria ($860)   24.3%

    B. Product-Market[b]

        1. Buyers' market   28.9%
        2. Sellers' market   71.1%

    C. Economy Type[c]

        1. Market economy   16.0%
        2. Modified market economy 36.4%
        3. Economy of central command 48.4%

II. Corporate Factors

    D. Industry Category

        1. Manufacturing   38.3%
        2. Distributive trades   31.4%
        3. Transportation and service 20.2%
        4. Extractive and agriculture 10.1%

    E. Presence of Marketing Department

        1. Yes   75.2%
        2. No   24.8%

    F. Role of Marketing Function

        1. Not at all important   27.7%
        2. Somewhat important   33.5%
        3. Highly important   38.8%

    G. Nature of ownership

        1. Fully indigenous   53.3%
        2. Joint venture   33.2%
        3. Fully foreign   13.6%

    H. Corporate Size (number of
        employees)

        1. Small (under 100)   48.5%
        2. Medium (100-400)   22.7%
        3. Large (over 400)   28.8%

    I. Title of Respondent

        1. Marketing manager   42.5%
        2. Sales manager   27.9%
        3. General manager   15.0%
        4. Economist/accountant/
            financial director   14.6%

---

[a]Percentages are based on a sample of n=188. The distribution of respondents in terms of country corresponded to the underlying sample proportions.

[b]Operationalized in terms of whether the supply-demand environment for a firm's major products/services reflected a buyers' or a sellers' market.

[c]Based on respondents' assessment of state control of economic activities.

cation base was the rationale that the effect of state controls on business operations tends to be macro or country-wide in character. Based on the information gathered, the firms from Kenya, Nigeria, and Zambia were categorized as operating under a moderately controlled environment, and the firms from Ghana and Tanzania as operating under a highly controlled environment. As expected, the classification appeared quite consistent with the respondents' own assessment of the nature and extent of state control of the mix variables in their countries of operation.

Second, the firms were classified into sellers' and buyers' market categories. This classification was based on the respondents' evaluations of the product-market environment (i.e., buyers' or sellers') that characterized their firms' main products/services. The use of firm-based information as the classification base (as opposed to that of country) derived from the reasoning that the firms' product-markets would differ as a function of the supply-demand environment for their specific products/services more so than as a function of the overall economic picture of their respective countries. In this regard, classification on the basis of country (as in the case of state control) would serve to mask differences in product-market environment and, thus, its influence on marketing strategy or activity performance.

The cross-tabulation of the firms in terms of the product-market and state control categories yielded the marginal and cell frequencies summarized in Table 2. As the table indicates, 28.4% of the firms operated under a buyers' market environment and, the remaining 71.5%, under a sellers' market environment. For state control, 56.8% of the firms fell into the moderately controlled category and the remaining 43.2% into the highly controlled category. Of the four market typologies, the moderately controlled sellers' market typology reflected the highest incidence of firms (38.6%), followed by the highly controlled sellers' market typology (33.3%), the moderately controlled buyers' market typology (18.5%), and the highly controlled buyers' market typology (10.0%), respectively.

The chi-square test of independence of the product-market and state control variables yielded results that were not statistically significant (chi-square value of 2.04 at $p < .153$). This implied the lack of relationship between the product-market environment and state

Table 2

INCIDENCE OF PRODUCT-MARKET/STATE CONTROL MARKET TYPOLOGIES

| State Control | Product-Market [a,b] | | |
	Buyers' Market	Sellers' Market	Total
Moderately Controlled	Moderately Controlled Buyers' Market 34 (18.5)	Moderately Controlled Sellers' Market 70 (38.3)	104 (56.8)
Highly Controlled	Highly Controlled Buyers' Market 18 (10.0)	Highly Controlled Sellers' Market 61 (33.3)	79 (43.2)
Total	52 (28.4)	131 (71.5)	183 (100.0)

[a]Figures in parentheses refer to percentages.

[b]Figures exclude five respondents with missing values on the product-market variable.

control variables. In other words, state control of the mix variables is, for example, not necessarily contemporaneous with a sellers' market environment. The observed results probably stemmed from the classification method used (i.e., country-based for state control and firm-based for product-market) or from the fact that state control of marketing activities in African countries tend to derive from the political ideologies of governments more so than from the economic environment of countries. The overall results are interpretable as supporting research hypothesis 1.

Marketing Activity Performance Across Market Typologies

The examination of research hypothesis 2 (i.e., differences in marketing activity performance across product-market/state control environment) involved first utilizing the respondents' evaluations of the extent of their firms' performance of the 40 marketing activities in factor analysis to identify the subsets of underlying activities. Next, the subsets of activities identified (i.e., the extracted factors) were utilized in univariate and multivariate analysis of variance (ANOVAs and MANOVA). The extracted factors served as the dependent variables, and market typology as the independent variable in the ANOVAs and MANOVA.

A total of nine factors with eigenvalues of one or greater were extracted based on the factor analysis results. As noted, the nine factors were interpreted as reflecting the subsets of activities underlying the respondents' evaluations. On the basis of the pattern of the varimax-rotated factor loadings, the nine subsets of activities were named as follows:

Factor 1: Advertising and sales promotion
Factor 2: Marketing management
Factor 3: Channel design and evaluation
Factor 4: Pricing
Factor 5: Product design and testing
Factor 6: Marketing information
Factor 7: Transportation and inventory
Factor 8: Sales force management
Factor 9: Product/service warranty

Table 3 represents the factors and their varimax-rotated loadings. Not only is the pattern of factor loadings consistent with expectation but it is also reflective of how the activities are structured and/or presented in the literature (Pride & Ferrell, 1985).

Table 4 is a summary of the results of the ANOVAs and MANOVA. As the table indicates, the MANOVA F-value was highly significant ($p < .001$). This implied the existence of "overall" differences in marketing activity performance across the four market typologies. Examination of the univariate F-values shows that four of the subsets of activities, i.e., advertising and sales promotion (Factor 1), marketing management (Factor 2), channel design and evaluation (Factor 3), and pricing (Factor 4), contributed to the observed overall differences in marketing activity perfor-

Table 3

PATTERN OF VARIMAX-ROTATED LOADINGS FOR THE DERIVED ACTIVITY FACTORS

Marketing Activity	Advertising and Sales Promotion (1)	Marketing Management (2)	Channel Design and Evaluation (3)	Pricing (4)	Product Design and Testing (5)	Marketing Information (6)	Transportion and Inventory (7)	Salesforce Management (8)	Product/ Service Warranty (9)
Marketing Management Activities									
1. The establishment of marketing objectives.		.49							
2. The planning of marketing activities.		.68							
3. The coordination and integration of marketing activities.		.71							
4. The motivation of persons who implement marketing strategies or activities.		.72							
5. The evaluation and control of marketing activities.		.75							
Marketing Information Activities									
6. The design and conduct of marketing research activities.						.58			
7. The observation and analysis of consumer behavior (e.g., attitudes, preferences, loyalty patterns).						.75			
8. The analysis and interpretation of routinely collected marketing information (e.g., sales data).		.63							
9. The performance of market tests (e.g., test tests; brand recognition tests).						.70			
10. The provision of usable marketing information to managers for decision making.		.62							

Derived Activity Factors

Marketing Activity	Advertising and Sales Promotion (1)	Marketing Management (2)	Channel Design and Evaluation (3)	Pricing (4)	Product Design and Testing (5)	Marketing Information (6)	Transportion and Inventory (7)	Salesforce Management (8)	Product/Service Warranty (9)
Product/Service Activities									
11. The development, testing, and introduction of new products/services.					.67				
12. The modification of existing products/services.					.68				
13. The elimination of products/services that do not satisfy customers' desires.					.47				
14. The formulation of brand names and branding policies.					.56				
15. The preparation of product/service warranties and the establishment of procedures for fulfilling warranties.									.72
16. The planning of product/service packages (e.g., sizes, shapes, colors, designs).					.70				
Pricing Activities									
17. The analysis of competititors' prices.				.55					
18. The formulation of policies and methods for setting prices.				.78					
19. The actual setting of prices.				.70					
20. The determination of discounts for various categories of buyers.				.72					
21. The establishment of conditions and terms of sales.				.67					

Table 3 (Cont'd)

	Advertising and Sales Promotion (1)	Marketing Management (2)	Channel Design and Evaluation (3)	Pricing (4)	Product Design and Testing (5)	Marketing Information (6)	Transportion and Inventory (7)	Salesforce Management (8)	Product/Service Warranty (9)
Marketing Activity									
Distribution Activities									
22. The evaluation of various types of distribution channels.			.72						
23. The design of distribution channels.			.75						
24. The design and implementation of an effective program for dealer relations.			.43						
25. The establishment of distribution centers/outlets.			.69						
26. The formulation and implementation of procedures for efficient product/service handling.			.51						
27. The implementation of inventory controls.							.64		
28. The analysis of transportation methods.							.61		
29. The minimization of total distribution cost.							.74		
30. The analysis of possible locations for wholesale and retail outlets.			.60						
Promotion Activities									
31. The setting of promotional (e.g., advertising) objectives.	.75								
32. The determination of the major types of promotion (e.g., advertising, sales promotion, personal selling) to be used.	.66								
33. The selection and scheduling of advertising media.	.83								
34. The development of advertising messages.	.86								
35. The evaluation of advertising effectiveness.	.73								
36. The recruitment and training of salespersons.								.43	
37. The formulation of compensation programs for sales personnel.								.70	
38. The creation and development of sales territories.								.46	
39. The planning and implementation of sales promotion efforts (e.g., free samples, coupons, displays, sweepstakes, sales contests).	.52								
40. The preparation and dissemination of publicity releases.	.65								

Derived Activity Factors

Table 4

RESULTS OF ANOVAs AND MANOVA ON DERIVED ACTIVITY FACTORS

Derived Factor	F-Value (3,184)	p <
Univariate Tests		
Factor 1: Advertising and Sales Promotion	4.63	.004
Factor 2: Marketing Management	2.16	.094
Factor 3: Channel Design and Evaluation	4.01	.009
Factor 4: Pricing	3.69	.013
Factor 5: Product Design and Testing	1.26	.288
Factor 6: Marketing Information	.55	.652
Factor 7: Transportation and Inventory	.65	.564
Factor 8: Salesforce Management	1.43	.237
Factor 9: Product/Service Warranty	2.19	.648
Multivariate Test (Wilks' Criterion)[a]	2.19	.001

[a]Similar results, as reported here, were obtained for other MANOVA test-statistics (e.g., the Pillai's Trace).

mance. Each of the four subsets of activities yielded an F-value that was statistically significant (i.e., at the .10 level or better).

The group (typology) level means of the activities that comprised each of the four activity-subsets are presented in Table 5. The pattern of group level means indicates that the incidence and regularity of the respective activities' performance was highest for the firms operating under the moderately controlled buyers' market and lowest for the firms operating under the highly controlled sellers' market. However, for the firms operating under the moderately controlled sellers' and the highly controlled buyers' markets, the incidence and regularity of the respective activities' performance did not follow clearly discernible patterns. For some of the activities, the incidence and regularity of activity performance was higher for the firms operating under the moderately controlled sellers' market compared to the firms operating under the highly controlled buyers' market; for the other activities, the reverse pat-

Table 5

GROUP LEVEL MEANS ACROSS TYPOLOGIES FOR DERIVED FACTOR AND ACTIVITIES WITH SIGNIFICANT ANOVAs[a]

Derived Factor and Activities	Market Typology			
	Moderately Controlled Buyers' Market	Moderately Controlled Sellers' Market	Highly Controlled Buyers' Market	Highly Controlled Sellers' Market
Factor 1: Advertising and Sales Promotion				
31. The setting of promotional (e.g., advertising) objectives.	2.60	2.35	2.57	1.94
32. The determination of the major types of promotion (e.g., advertising, sales promotion, personal selling) to be used.	2.46	2.39	2.42	2.09
33. The selection and scheduling of advertising media.	2.40	2.32	2.11	1.73
34. The development of advertising messages.	2.43	2.39	2.26	1.84
35. The evaluation of advertising effectiveness.	2.27	2.23	1.95	1.69
Factor 2: Marketing Management				
1. The establishment of marketing objectives.	2.18	2.14	2.16	2.02
2. The planning of marketing activities.	2.57	2.35	2.42	2.15
3. The coordination and integration of marketing activities.	2.74	2.69	2.42	2.06
4. The motivation of persons who implement marketing strategies or activities.	2.80	2.27	2.11	2.00
5. The evaluation and control of marketing activities.	2.71	2.69	2.42	2.18
8. The analysis and interpretation of routinely collected marketing information (e.g., sales data).	3.09	2.89	3.00	2.59
10. The provision of usable marketing information to managers for decision making.	3.11	2.92	2.74	2.52

Factor 3: Channel Design and Evaluation

22. The evaluation of various types of distribution channels.	2.54	2.06	2.00	1.98
23. The design of distribution channels.	2.23	1.77	1.87	1.63
24. The design and implementation of an effective program for dealer relations.	2.17	1.83	1.84	1.79
25. The establishment of distribution centers/outlets.	2.26	1.99	1.87	1.68
26. The formulation and implementation of procedures for efficient product/service handling.	2.43	2.15	2.16	2.05
30. The analysis of possible locations for wholesale and retail outlets.	2.31	2.20	1.92	1.74

Factor 4: Pricing

17. The analysis of competitors' prices.	2.86	2.94	2.89	2.23
18. The formulation of policies and methods for setting prices.	2.51	2.46	2.47	2.19
19. The actual setting of prices.	2.74	2.63	2.42	2.23
20. The determination of discounts for various categories of buyers.	2.63	2.20	2.53	1.74
21. The establishment of conditions and terms of sales.	2.49	2.37	2.16	2.05

[a]On a 4-point scale that ranged from 1 = "never performed" to 4 = "performed 6 or more times a year."

257

tern of activity performance was observed. Thus, the results are to be interpreted as supporting research hypothesis 2.

CONCLUSION

Of the factors that underlie the diversity of the market environment of the Third World, two of these, product-market (i.e., sellers' versus buyers') and state control (i.e., moderately controlled versus highly controlled) are offered as instrumental in terms of their influence. However, empirical assessment of their influence is lacking. To provide the needed empirical evidence, the present study was organized. Specifically, this chapter explores the incidence of product-market/state control market typologies in selected African countries and the extent to which marketing activity performance differs as a function of the product-market/state control market environment.

Overall, the study results support the following conclusions:

1. The firms reflected in the study operate under a product-market/state control environment that is heterogeneous in character.
2. The product-market and state control variables are statistically independent — implying that state control of the mix variables is, for example, not necessarily synonymous with a sellers' market environment.
3. For the countries considered in the study, the predominant product-market/state control market typology is that of moderately controlled sellers' market, followed by the highly controlled sellers' market, the moderately controlled buyers' market, and the highly controlled buyers' market, respectively.
4. The incidence and regularity of marketing activity performance, particularly that of advertising and sales promotion, marketing management, channel design and evaluation, and pricing, varies as a function of the product-market/state control environment under which the firms in the study operate.

Because the discipline of marketing has evolved and been nurtured in the context of a buyer's market environment with minimal state controls (e.g., that of the U.S. and Western European countries), the widely held view is that the discipline's organizing framework lacks relevance in the Third World where the dominant market type is that of a sellers' market with moderate-to-high levels of state controls (Bartels, 1983; Dholakia, 1981; El-Sherbini, 1979; Ross & McTavish, 1985). While the study results support this viewpoint, they also indicate that the pattern of incidence and regularity of marketing activity performance defies unqualified generalizations.

Consistent with the literature, the study results support the predominance of a sellers' market environment with moderate-to-high levels of controls. The results also support the supposition that the organizing framework of the discipline is most pertinent under a buyers' market environment with minimal or moderate controls — assuming incidence and regularity of activity performance is any indicator of the discipline's pertinence. More specifically, the results indicate that the incidence and regularity of marketing activity performance is highest under a buyers' market environment with moderate levels of controls and lowest under a sellers' market environment with high levels of controls. Under a sellers' market environment with moderate levels of controls or a buyers' market environment with high levels of controls, the pattern of incidence and regularity of marketing activity performance is somewhat diffused, i.e., high for some activities and low for others. The implication therefore is that the planning and/or execution of marketing strategies in the African context should derive from the peculiarities of the product-market/state control environment under which firms operate.

In sum, the results of the present study shed light on the incidence of product-market/state control market typologies in the African context and the influence of the market typologies on the incidence and regularity of marketing activity performance. However, the one-shot nature of the present study implies the need for more empirical research. To enhance the generalizability of the findings from such research, it should span firms from continents other than Africa. Furthermore, such research could take the form of case studies of selected Third World firms. This would allow for a more detailed analysis of the pattern of marketing activity performance among Third World firms and the influence of environmental factors on Third World marketing practices.

REFERENCES

Akaah, I.P. (1986). Marketing Education in the Third World: Problems and Challenges, Working Paper, Wayne State University, Detroit, (October).
_____, Riordan, E.A. and Dadzie, K.Q. (1986). Applicability of Marketing Concepts and Management Activities in the Third World: An Empirical Investigation. Working Paper, Wayne State University, Detroit.
Bartels, R. (1983). "Is Marketing Defaulting Its Responsibilities?" *Journal of Marketing*, (Fall), 46, pp. 32-35.
Cavusgil, S.T. and Yavas, U. (1984). "Transfer of Management Know-How to Developing Countries: An Empirical Investigation." *Journal of Business Research*, 12, pp. 35-40.
Cravens, D.W. (1974). "Marketing Management in an Era of Shortages." *Business Horizons*, (February), pp. 79-85.
Dholakia, N. (1981). "The Future of Marketing in the Third World." In D.F. Mulvihil (Ed.) *Proceedings*: American Marketing Association, pp. 63-72.
Douglas, S.P. and Craig, C.S. (1983). *International Marketing Research*. NJ: Prentice-Hall, Inc.
El-Sherbini, A.A. (1979). "Behavioral Adjustments as Marketing Constraints on Economic Development." In G. Fisk et al. (Ed.) *Macromarketing Evolution of Thought*. Proceedings of the 4th Macromarketing Seminar, University of Colorado, Boulder, CO.
Kaynak, E. (1982). *Marketing in the Third World*. NY: Praeger Publishers, Inc.
Kotler, P. (1984). *Marketing Management: Analysis, Planning, and Control*. NJ: Prentice-Hall, Inc.
_____. (1974). "Marketing During Periods of Shortages." *Journal of Marketing*, (July), 38, pp. 20-29.
_____ and Levy, S.J. (1972). "Demarketing, Yes, Demarketing." *Harvard Business Review*, (November-December), pp. 74-80.
Malhotra, N.K. (1986). "Why Developing Societies Need Marketing Technology." *International Marketing Review*, (Spring), pp. 61-73.
Owen's Directory (1982-1984). *Owen's Commerce, Trade and International Register*, 886 High Road, Finchley, London, England.
Papadopoulos, N.G. (1983). "Shortage Marketing: A Comprehensive Framework." *Journal of the Academy of Marketing Science*, (Winter), 11, pp. 40-60.
Pride, W.M. and Ferrell, O.C. (1985). *Marketing: Basic Concepts and Decisions*. MA: Houghton-Mifflin Co.
Ross, C.A. and McTavish, R. (1985). "Marketing in The Third World: Educators' Views." Paper Presented at a Conference in Scotland (August).
Samili, A. and Kaynak, E. (1984). "Marketing Practices in Less-Developed Countries." *Journal of Business Research*, 12, pp. 5-18.
World Development Report (1984). World Bank, Washington, DC.

Chapter 14

Market Power vs. Marketing Prowess as Determinants of Company Performance in LDCs: The Case of Venezuela

Luis V. Domínguez

SUMMARY. Marketing scholars have argued that marketing has the potential to considerably increase productivity and quality of goods and services delivered by developing nations' marketing systems. But in order for this to occur it must be in the self-interest of entrepreneurs to adopt modem marketing practices. This need not be the case in the highly oligopolistic business structures of import substituting LDCs, where market power may be a more important determinant of success. The chapter tests this hypothesis in the context of Venezuela. The results suggest that market structures in LDCs offer limited incentive to the adoption of marketing, at least to the extent that self-interest is a crucial reason for adopting the marketing concept.

PURPOSE OF THE STUDY

Since Holton's (1953) and Drucker's (1954) pioneering works, many marketing writers have held the view that marketing modernization is an essential ingredient of economic development. In the

This chapter was first published in the *Journal of Global Marketing*, Vol. 2(2) 1988.

1960s and 1970s, Charles Slater and his colleagues were able to empirically demonstrate some of the beneficial effects of marketing modernization on income generation and economic progress in the food distribution sector (see Nason & White, 1982). Although their work's primary purpose was to develop policies at the institutional or "macro" level that would stimulate distribution efficiency, it was realized from the outset that sustained progress would require substantial changes in values and behavior of individual entrepreneurs.

More recently, marketing authors have been emphasizing the role of entrepreneurial initiative in less developed countries (LDCs). For example, Cundiff (1982, p. 16) has written ". . . marketing innovations and developments by individual entrepreneurs have had remarkable effects on the level of economic development of particular nations." He cites examples that illustrate how a climate that fosters individual initiative leads to significant improvements in marketing practices and distribution systems in LDCs. Clearly, however, the diffusion of modern marketing practices and organizational forms is predicated on the premise that such changes will pay off for the individual entrepreneur. That need not be the case. For example, studies by Ortiz-Buonafina (1987) and Kumcu and Kumcu (1987) report that traditional marketing institutions have outperformed "modern" ones in Guatemala and Turkey, respectively.

The purpose of this study is to test whether marketing does indeed pay off in the LDCs. Conditions brought about by underdevelopment itself and by policies of import substitution so widely prevalent in the developing world may render the adoption of marketing principles relatively less urgent or effective. It may indeed be not only feasible but also quite rational for a firm to attain success through market power rather than through marketing effort. The chapter first examines how this might occur, then posits specific hypotheses. Next the three key concepts of market power, marketing strategy, and market share are discussed. Description of the research design includes justification for choosing Venezuela as a test case. The chapter concludes with a discussion of implications of the results for public policy.

MARKETING AND INDUSTRIAL ENTERPRISE IN LDCs

Self-interest at the individual enterprise level has been a powerful motor in the evolution of social and economic systems, at a more aggregate level, since ancient times. For example, a study by Darian (1985) strongly suggests the importance of merchant classes in reshaping the ideology of classical India to conform with such goals as market expansion, facilitated distribution, and improved media of exchange. Understandably, distribution has been a focal point of research on marketing's role in economic development. Yet as Darian points out, important differences must be taken into account when analyzing contemporary problems of economic development:

> First, developing countries today are strongly influenced by their contact with more advanced countries. Secondly, developing countries are industrializing to some degree, and the role of marketing, in relation to production, changes with industrialization. In pre-industrial societies the craftsmen usually work under the dominance of the merchants. We can thus attribute the source of change to merchants and their marketing activities . . . In developing countries today modern manufacturing firms tend to incorporate the marketing function into the larger enterprise, and wholesalers and retailers have limited control over product decisions. (Darian, 1985, p. 25)

The lack of a research stream on the marketing behavior of industrial firms in LDCs constitutes an important gap in the literature. One simply cannot assume that the practices of modern marketing in developing nations will be successfully adopted, or that if they were, they would be effective.

Under import substitution policies that prevail in the developing world, manufacturers are granted generous tariff and nontariff protection, preferential access to public sector customers, and a variety of other benefits and privileges. In turn, governments resort to extensive regulation ranging from price controls to direct and indirect export restrictions when domestic supply is threatened. The distortions brought about by import substitution have been widely discussed in the economic literature (e.g., Todaro, 1985, pp. 409-20, Krueger, 1985, Balassa, 1980). Balassa has neatly summarized them:

> Countries applying inward-oriented industrial development strategies were further characterized by the prevalence of sellers' markets . . . The existence of sellers' markets provides little inducement for catering to the users' needs . . . Monopolies and oligopolies assumed importance, and the oligopolists often aimed at the maintenance of market shares while refraining from actions that would invoke retaliation. (Balassa, 1980, p. 520)

It is therefore plausible that market conditions brought about by underdevelopment and import substitution make adoption of modern marketing practices less urgent and effective. The question is whether marketing strategy is a significant determinant of a firm's success. If it is not, there may be little incentive to adopt the kinds of aggressive marketing strategies that have characterized marketing in today's developed market economies since the inception of the industrial revolution (Fullerton, 1988): opportunity-oriented analysis of customer needs, launching of new products, insistent promotion and advertising, extensive distribution, and price discounting and deals.

A study by Lecraw (1982, pp. 27-30) hints that a firm's profitability may depend on its attained market power as much as or perhaps more so on industry competitive structure than on its current marketing effort. His survey of 153 multinationals (MNCs) in the ASEAN countries found that the most significant determinants of firm ROI were the MNC's market share, the market shares held by the top three firms in its industry, and the (lack of) diversity of nationalities of MNCs in that industry — a proxy for how stable and predictable are the rules of competition in that industry. Those three measures were statistically significant predictors of firm ROI at the .05 level. In comparison, marketing intensity and R/D intensity (the latter partly a proxy for product development effort) were significant only at the .10 level.

Comparison of the relative effects of market power and marketing strategy as predictors of performance is therefore the key issue.

It is an important question given the high degree of concentration that exists in LDCs and the tendency of local investor groups to acquire controlling interests in a highly diversified portfolio of industries and businesses.

DETERMINANTS OF COMPANY PERFORMANCE

Marketing Strategy

Marketing strategy may be described holistically as a configuration of marketing tactics (e.g., market niching, cost leadership, push or pull oriented, etc.). The holistic approach, however, may lead to a considerable variety of marketing strategies (see O'Shaughnessy, 1984) and questions which strategies may be more aggressive or intensive. A reductionistic approach might be to simply measure total marketing expenditures as a percent of sales. However, such measures are difficult to isolate for single product lines of diversified firms and may be subject to underreporting in countries where governments may view marketing expenditures with a degree of suspicion as unproductive or inflationary. They also fail to capture the full texture of the firm's use of marketing tools.

A more practical approach and one more suited to the purpose of this chapter is to examine utilization of individual tactical elements of the marketing mix. These include product quality, relative price, incidence of promotional deals, and mode of coordination and control of channels of distribution.

Market Power

In the industrial organization literature, market power refers to the capacity of a firm to control supply and set prices. This power may accrue from a firm's position in a given industry and from its position in other industries (for a review of the evidence, see Scherer, 1980, Chapters 8 and 15). Market share is widely recognized as a measure of both market power and market structure; early entry is also an advantage frequently used by firms to consolidate their position and prevent successful new competition (Domínguez & Vanmarke, 1987).

A high level of industrial concentration has been a by-product of import substitution policies. This has been particularly true throughout most of Latin America, where import substitution has been pursued to a greater extent than in most other parts of the developing world (Balassa, 1980). Advantages in bargaining power with suppliers, customers, and governments, and superior technical resources available to MNCs and, to a lesser extent, to domestic groups[1] have been major determinants of competitive structure in many LDCs (e.g., Newfarmer, 1977).

Application of industrial organization concepts to marketing analysis requires some adjustments. Firstly, product markets, i.e., portions of one or more industries offering directly substitutable goods, rather than industries, are of primary interest to marketing (Buzzell, 1981). In that narrower context, a firm's market power would accrue from position attained in a given product market and that afforded by its position in other product markets. The former has been found to be a function of marketing strategy (e.g., Buzzell & Wiersema, 1981; Hagerty, Carman, & Russell, 1986). Secondly, whereas from an industrial organization vantage point market standing may represent attained market power, from that of the entrepreneur it is a telling sign of the firm's performance in the marketplace. For our purposes it is the latter that counts; the relevant issue is whether marketing savvy is as important to determining performance as is power attained elsewhere. For if it were, aggressive marketing would be in the entrepreneur's self-interest. Thus, in equation form, the firm's performance in product marketing may be described as:

$$R_{it} = f(P_{it}, A_{it}, D_{it}, C_{it}; MS_{Jt}): J = 1,2, \ldots ,n; J = i.$$

where the first four terms on the right side of the equation refer to price, advertising, distribution, and product content strategy indicators; the last term is a vector of market power indicators that includes market shares attained in other product-markets, and the firm's ties with MNCs and groups. Our concern is with the relative importance of the first set of predictors vs. market power.

It is difficult to set absolute boundaries between market power and the "pure" exercise of marketing strategy; for instance, marketing activities in other product markets may be considered a legitimate component of the firm's marketing strategy. Nevertheless, the question is whether a firm that successfully participates in other markets enjoys advantages, ceteris paribus, over single-line competitors by virtue of its greater influence over customers and intermediaries and its greater command of financial and technological resources. Given marketing's focus on competitors and customers, we shall focus on two sources of market power: (1) market position attained in other products markets and (2) ties with multinational corporations (MNCs) or groups that enhance access to financial, human, or technological resources.

Performance

Performance may be measured against key responsibility areas ranging from market standing, profitability, and productivity to human resources development and social responsibility (Drucker, 1954). Cash flow, return on investment, and market share are the most commonly used strategic planning criteria (see Abell & Hammond, 1979). Their measurement presents significant problems that are exacerbated in the context of analyzing the performance of individual products in LDCs. Firms may lack requisite information systems to estimate the profitability of individual products; estimates may be distorted by transfer price calculation; cost figures are subject to intercompany variations in the treatment of fixed costs; and of course, estimates of market share require a fairly precise idea of market size, something that is not always possible in LDCs.[2]

Analyses of the PIMS data base have repeatedly suggested that a difference of one share point translates into roughly half a percentage point in ROI (Buzzell, Gale, & Sultan, 1975; Gale, Heaney, & Swire, 1977). Recent studies have questioned this conclusion, suggesting instead that the contribution of market share to ROI is substantially smaller (Jacobson & Aaker, 1985). In any case, while market share may not be directly as powerful a determinant of profitability, it does represent a key dimension of performance:

... High market share, together with ROI, are indications that management has been following policies, whether by design or chance, that have proved to be successful. Market share can be used as an indicator of the effectiveness of current policies and suggestive of how these policies might be altered. (Jacobson & Aaker, 1985, p. 21)

Measurement of market share poses numerous conceptual as well as methodological difficulties in setting market boundaries. Despite methodological difficulties, however, it is essential that research on market performance in LDCs be encouraged, even if it means utilization of fairly crude measures, in order that welfare issues be discussed from an empirical rather than an ideologically laden, positivist perspective. Measures are explained in the following section.

SURVEY DESIGN

Venezuela was selected as a test case. It has been widely acknowledged that Latin American nations have pursued import substitution policies to a further extent than most other LDCs. Venezuela in particular has devoted much of its considerable oil income to pursue ambitious industrialization projects. As a result of its once highly overvalued currency and pent up demand, substantial tariff and nontariff barriers were erected to protect domestic industry. Considerable industrial concentration resulted (see Naim, 1984; Bitar & Troncoso, 1983). By 1981 Venezuela had registered one of the highest degrees of concentration of industrial production among large scale plants in Latin America (United Nations, 1982).

Thus, its substantial income base from oil exports has allowed it to travel further down the path of inward-oriented industrialization; its high degree of industry protection has caused it to have the kinds of oligopolistic market structures that give rise to the very debate whether marketing strategy will truly influence competitive advantage. It is a most suitable test case.

The data for this article were obtained from a cross-sectional survey of 69 manufacturing firms in Venezuela. They span 22 product markets ranging from highly competitive to highly monopolistic. At least one of the companies surveyed in each product-market had introduced a new product during 1976-81 that had significantly altered market shares or primary demand. Product markets were selected as to represent a balanced mix of MNCs, domestic groups, and firms affiliated with neither.[3]

The respondent in each firm was the executive identified by top management as having been responsible for marketing the specific product. The survey procedure is adapted from Kirpalani and Macintosh (1980). Two interviewers jointly questioned each respondent, utilizing a structure set of questions about the process of commercialization of the product in question; the interviewers independently filled out a set of scales and presented these to a moderator. Where discrepancies arose, the moderator called for a joint meeting. If this still did not resolve differences, the moderator recontacted the respondent. Finally, the ratings of companies' market position and market power were verified with experts on the particular industries. This method, although time consuming and cumbersome, ensures completed responses in cultures where people are unwilling or unable to find the time to respond to self-administered questionnaires.

Table A-I in the Appendix shows the scales used to measure market power and performance. Companies were classified according to their rank in market share position in the specific product-market, one of the most commonly employed measures of competitive structure and market position.[4] Because of the small sample size, the first three points on the scale corresponding to the smallest market shares were consolidated,[5] so that comparisons were made among three groups: market leader, runner-up, and the third through top eight competitors in a product-market. Appendix Table A-2 describes the marketing mix variables employed in the study.

RESULTS

The critical question is whether market power is a better predictor of market share than is marketing strategy. Three-group multiple discriminant analysis was employed for the tests. Because of the small number of observations in relation to the number of predictors, separate discriminant analyses were run for each construct, marketing strategy (Table 1) and market power (Table 2).

Table 1
DISCRIMINANT ANALYSIS RESULTS: MARKETING STRATEGY COMPARISONS

	Univariate F- ratios (v=2,v=66)	Standardized Discriminant Function Coefficients	
		Function 1	Function 2
Price relative to competitors	1.39	-.29	-.38
Quality relative to competitors	3.89[c]	.65	.21
Product line depth	1.41	-.12	.68
Incumbency	10.66[a]	.86	-.27
No. of Accounts	.91		
Key Account Program	1.12	.21	.65
Direct Sales	.38	-.16	-.55
Dedicated Distributor	1.06	-.40	.28
Exclusive Wholesaler	.67	-.28	-.18
Nonexclusive Wholesaler	.26		
Longest No. of steps	.44		
Sales Force Size	2.45		
Technical assistance	.20		
Promotional assistance	.35		
Setting and measuring advertising goals	.51		
Frequency of promotional discounts to the trade	1.10		
Frequency of promotional discounts to end users	1.66		

Overall Results:

Significance of Canonical Functions:

Function 1: X^2 = 24.28[b] ; df=16

Function 2: X^2 = 8.13 ; df= 7

F-ratio of distances between groups (v=8;v=59):

Top eight vs. top two   1.76

Top two vs. top one   2.80[b]

Top eight vs. top one   5.32[a]

Percent correctly classified: 64%

[a] $p<.001$ [b] $p<.01$ [c] $p<.05$

Table 2

DISCRIMINANT ANALYSIS RESULTS: MARKET POWER COMPARISONS

	Univariate F- ratios (v=2,v=66)	Standardized Discriminant Function Coefficients Function 1	Function 2
Organizational ties	3.75^c	.75	-.52
Position in other Product-markets (PMs)	3.01^c	.74	.02
Time of entry into Other PMs	3.92^c	.07	1.09
Product mix width	1.15	-.99	-.05
Product mix depth	1.61		

Overall Results:

Significance of canonical
    functions:

    Function 1: X^2 = 22.99^b ; df=8

    Function 2: x^2 = 7.66^c ; df=3

F-ratio of distances between groups (v_1 =4 ;v_2 =63):

    Top eight vs. top two   3.23^c

    Top two vs. top one   2.1.,4

    Top eight vs. top one   4.10^b

Percent correctly classified: 56.5%

---

^{a} p<.001 ^{b} p<.01 ^{c} p<.05

Comparisons of results will allow us to conclude which predictor is relatively more effective.

Each table shows univariate F-ratio tests of the null hypothesis that there are no statistically significant differences among market share groups for each predictor. Discriminant equations included all variables with multivariate F-ratios of 1.0 or higher, a rather low entry criterion used in order to include as complete as possible a set of indicators of each construct.

At the bottom of each table are two important indicators of the ability of each construct to explain market share differences. If the three market share groups are truly distinct, two discriminant functions are needed to set intergroup boundaries; therefore a critical test concerns how many discriminant functions are statistically significant. Secondly, F-ratio tests of pairwise differences will allow us to test whether the constructs effectively separate market share groups, say the market share leader from the second-highest share marketer.

Marketing Strategy

Univariate F-ratio tests found few differences in marketing strategy among market share categories. Indeed, the only statistically significant differences correspond to product quality ($p < .05$) and early entrance into a product-market ($p < .01$). The latter is interesting because it is perhaps the marketing decision that comes closest to also standing for market power. It is also nicely consistent with PIMS findings that market leadership (and high ROI) accrues to market quality leaders (Buzzell, Gale, & Sultan, 1975). Historically, MNCs have benefited from pioneering the establishment of large-scale manufacturing in the LDCs.

A similar statement might be made for product quality; the superior know-how and resources of MNCs facilitate their position as quality leaders. Sales force size was the only other, nearly significant correlate of market share ($p < .10$). In comparison, a comprehensive time-series study of the PIMS data base (Hagerty, Carman, & Russell, 1986) found sales force intensity the most significant determinant of market share, followed by price; quality and promotional effects were the least significant. The low importance of price in the present study is perhaps symptomatic of lack of vigorous competition, while the (marginal) effect of sales effort hints at the importance of market coverage.

Overall, the standardized discriminant function coefficients were smaller than those for market power (see Table 2), underscoring the low degree of differentiation in marketing strategy. Reaffirming the univariate tests, the largest standardized discriminant coefficients were those for product quality and incumbency. Only the first canonical function was statistically significant, indicating that marketing strategy differences fail to separate all three market share categories. Based on the F-ratios of pairwise comparisons, no significant differences were found between the marketing strategies of the top two and the top eight firms; i.e., their (weak) effect lies in separating the market leader from its closest rival.

MARKET POWER

There are several indications that market power differences (Table 2) were more defined than those due to marketing strategy. Both discriminant functions are statistically significant, indicating that important differences in market power distinguish the three market share groups. As stated earlier, the standardized discriminant function coefficients are higher than those seen in Table 1 for marketing strategy. The second discriminant function represents primarily the role of early entry into other product-markets, while the first represents organizational ties with MNCs and groups, position achieved in other product-markets, and *narrowness* of its number of product lines. Low-share competitors seem to have diversified to the greatest extent, whereas companies with strong market positions have been more successful through greater selectivity in their diversification efforts. This agrees with observations made by other researchers on the evolution of Venezuelan groups (Naim, 1984).

Although the three market share categories are significantly distinct, F-ratios indicate clear demarcation between market leader and the third-through-fourth market share positions, and between the latter and the runner-up. Market power is relatively less effective in separating the market leader from its closest challenger.

DISCUSSION

The evidence presented in this article cautions against highly optimistic assessments of the synergistic effects that have been assumed to exist between efforts to modernize industry and the adoption of aggressive marketing behavior that has characterized developed market economies. Import substituting experiments were designed to foster a nurturing environment for the nascent industries of LDCs by reducing the risk of decision making and isolating domestic industry from excessive competition. The process of modernization was expected to have been unidimensional in that the adoption of modern production technologies would work in unison with the adoption of modern management practices. While it was recognized that protectionist measures would lead to a temporary decrease in competition, it was also hoped that the door would be opened to the emergence of a highly entrepreneurial managerial class seeking new horizons of customer-oriented competition.

Instead, the data strongly indicate, at least in the case of Venezuela, that market power plays a major, more clearly identifiable, and stronger role than do individual marketing tactics. Marketing strategy does seem to play a (lesser) role: whereas market power differences distinguish the leaders from the also rans, they do not effectively separate the top share company from its closest challenger; that seems to be a distinction that is best accounted for by marketing strategy differences. But this is a rather limited role for marketing: as in every product-market there can be only one leader, this may not be enough of an incentive for other competitors to emulate its practices so long as the market can support the profitable operation of several players. Instead, the majority of firms in a market may prefer to engage in much more limited marketing effort.

Although marketing has a powerful conceptual argument to make to private enterprise in LDCs, the data from Venezuela furnish a less than compelling argument for truly innovative marketing experimentation in the sheltered world of import substitution. Until nations open their markets to more vigorous competition from abroad, domestic market environments do not encourage expansionistic, price-cutting, promotion-oriented marketing behavior. Indeed, evidence indicates that competitive structure is a major determinant of the extent of marketing activity in Venezuela; highly oligopolistic market structures have shown considerably less marketing activity, a result that is applicable to domestic as well as foreign firms.

Once more, the diffusion of marketing practices runs into obstacles rooted in the institutional make-up of the LDCs. In the case of the industrial sector the problems may prove to be even more formidable than those in the distributive sector.

NOTES

1. A group is constituted by enterprises owned partially or totally by one or more families, usually related by blood ties. Firms in a group are managed by family members or trusted associates. The group's holdings need not be related businesses and need not be managed according to portfolio principles.

2. For a review of measurement problems in LDCs, see Kaynak (1982), Chapter 4.

3. The distribution of market share positions was:

1:	Weak position in the product-market (PM)	3%
2:	One of the eight leading competitors in the PM	9%
3:	One of the four leading competitors in the PM	17%
4:	One of the two leading competitors in the PM	36%
5:	Undisputed PM leader	35%
		100%

4. Buzzell's (1981) analysis of market structure based on the PIMS data lends support to our use of market share ranks as adequate measures of market position. He concluded (p. 49): "Distributions of market shares of leading competitors in narrowly-defined product markets follows the same basic patterns that have been found in previous research on the size distributions of firms in more broadly-defined industries and in the economy as a whole."

5. After consolidation, only two firms in the smallest-share category were ranked below the top eight firms. See note 3.

REFERENCES

Abell, Derek F. and John S. Hammond. (1979). *Strategic Market Planning.* Englewood Cliffs, NJ: Prentice-Hall.

Balassa, Bela. (1980). "The Process of Industrial Development and Alternative Development Strategies." Princeton University, International Finance Section, Essays in International Finance No. 141, December; as reproduced in Meier (1984).

Bitar, Sergio and Troncoso. (1983). El Desafio Industrial de Venezuela, Caracas, Venezuela.

Buzzell, Robert D. (1981). "Are There 'Natural' Market Structures?" *Journal of Marketing,* 46 (Winter), pp. 42-51.

_____, Bradley T. Gale and Ralph G.M. Sultan. (1975). "Market Share – A Key to Profitability." *Harvard Business Review,* 73 (January-February), pp. 135-44.

_____ and Frederick D. Wiersema. (1981). "Modeling Changes in Market Share: A Cross Sectional Analysis." *Strategic Management Journal,* 2, pp. 27-52.

Cundiff, Edward W. (1982). "A Macromarketing Approach to Economic Development." *Journal of Marketing,* 2 (Spring), pp. 14-19.

Darian, Jean C. (1985). "Marketing and Economic Development: A Case Study from Classical India." *Journal of Macromarketing,* 5 (Spring), pp. 14-26.

Domínguez, Luis V. and Cristina Vanmarcke. (1987). "Market Structure and Marketing Behavior in LDCs: The Case of Venezuela." *Journal of Macromarketing,* 7 (Fall), pp. 4-16.

Drucker, Peter. (1954). *The Practice of Management.* New York: Harper & Row.

Fullerton, Ronald M. (1988). "How 'Modern' is Modern Marketing? Marketing's Evolution and the Myth of the 'Production Era'." *Journal of Marketing,* 52, pp. 4-13.

Gale, Bradley T., Donald F. Heaney and Donald S. Swire. (1977). "The Par ROI Report: Explanation and Commentary." Cambridge, MA: Strategic Planning Institute.

Hagerty, Michael R., James M. Carman and Gary J. Russell. (1986). "Estimating Elasticities with PIMS Data: Methodological Issues and Substantive Implications." Working paper, School of Business Administration, University of California, Berkeley.

Holton, Richard. (1953). "Market Structure and Economic Development." *Quarterly Journal of Economics* (August), pp. 348-9.

Jacobson, Robert and David A. Aaker. (1985). "Is Market Share All That It's Cracked Up to Be?." *Journal of Marketing,* 49 (Fall), pp. 11-22.

Kaynak, Erdener. (1982). *Marketing in the Third World.* New York: Praeger, Chapter 4.

Kirpalani, S.I. and N.B. Macintosh. (1980). "International Marketing Effectiveness of Technology-Oriented Small Firms." *Journal of International Business Studies,* 11 (Winter), pp. 81-90.

Krueger, Anne O. (1985). "Trade Policy as an Input to Development." *Economic Review, Papers and Proceedings,* May.

Kumcu, Erdogan and M. E. Kumcu. (1987). "Determinants of Food Retailing in Developing Economies: Some Empirical Evidence from Turkey." *Journal of Macromarketing,* 7 (Fall), pp. 26-40.

Lecraw, Donald J. (1982). "Performance of Transnational Corporations in Less Developed Countries." *Journal of International Business Studies,* 14 (Spring Summer), pp. 15-33.

Meier, Gerald M. (1984). *Leading Issues in Economic Development.* New York: Oxford University Press.

Naim, Moisés. (1984). "La Empresa Privada en Venezuela." in *El Caso Venezuela: Una Ilusión of Armonia,* ed. by Moisés Naím y Ramón Piñango, Caracas: Editorial IESA, pp. 152-83.

Nason, Robert W. and Phillip D. White. (1982). "The Visions of Charles Slater." *Journal of Macromarketing,* 1 (Fall), pp. 4-18.

Newfarmer, Richard S. (1977). "Multinational Conglomerates and the Economics of Dependent Development." Unpublished PhD dissertation, University of Wisconsin-Madison.

O'Shaughnessy, John. (1984). *Competitive Marketing.* Boston: George Allen & Unwin.

Ortiz-Buonafina, Marta. (1987). "The Economic Efficiency of Channels of Distribution in a Developing Society: The Case of the Guatemalan Retail Sector." *Journal of Macromarketing,* 7 (Fall) pp. 17-25.

Scherer, F. M. (1980). *Industrial Market Structure and Economic Performance.* Chicago: Rand McNally.

Todaro, Michael P. (1985). *Economic Development in the Third World.* New York: Longman.

United Nations (1982). *Statistical Yearbook for Latin America,* New York.

APPENDIX

Table A-1
MEASURES OF MARKET POWER AND MARKET POSITION

MARKET POWER

Organizational Ties
 1: Unaffiliated with Groups or MNCs
 2: Managed by a Group
 3: Managed by an MNC

Position in Other Product Markets (PMs)
 1: Does not participate in other PMs
 2: Weak position in other PMs
 3: Important competitor in at least one other PM
 4: Undisputed leader in at least one other PM

Time of Entry into Other Product Markets (PMs)
 1: Does not participate in other PMs
 2: Late entrant into other PMs
 3: One of the early entrants in at least one other PM
 4: Pioneered at least one other PM

Product Mix Width
 1: Does not participate in other PMs
 2: Participates only in related PMs (as to end user,
  need, or product technology)
 3: Participates in unrelated PMs

Product Mix Depth
 1: Does not participate in other PMs
 2: Sells only a limited assortment in each PM
 3: Sells a deep assortment in at least one other PM
 4: Sells a very complete assortment in all other PMs

PERFORMANCE

 1: Weak position in PM
 2: One of the eight leading competitors in the PM
 3: One of the four leading competitors in the PM
 4: One of the two leading competitors in the PM
 5: Undisputed PM leader

Table A-2
MARKETING STRATEGY DESCRIPTORS

Price relative to competitors
    1: Price leader
    2: Price parity
    3: Higher than the competition
Quality relative to competitors
    1: Lower quality typical of marginal producers
    2: Typical but below that of imports
    3: On par with imports
    4: Superior quality
Product line depth
    1: Single product
    2: Limited assortment
    3: Very complete assortment as to sizes, types, etc.
Incumbency
    1: Late entrant
    2: Early entrant
    3: First entrant
No. of Accounts
    1: Up to 100
    2: 101-1,000
    3: 1,001-3,000
    4: 3,001-6,000
    5: More than 6,000
Key Account Program
    1: Not used
    2: Program in use
Distribution System (to end users for intermediate goods; to retailers
for consumer goods):
Direct Sales
    1: No
    2: Yes for
Dedicated Distributor
    1: No
    2: Yes for
Exclusive Wholesaler
    1: No
    2: Yes for
Nonexclusive Wholesaler
    1: No
    2: Yes for
Longest No. of steps (no. of steps to end users for intermediate goods;
    to retailers for consumer goods.)
Sales Force Size
    1: No sales force
    2: Sales or marketing manager takes care of all sales
    3: Less than six salespeople
    4: 6-12 salespeople not counting general and regional sales mgrs.
    5: 13-24 salespeople not counting general and regional sales mgrs.
    6: Over 24 salespeople not counting general and regional sales mgrs.

Technical assistance offered to intermediaries and/or end users
    1: No
    2: Yes

Promotional assistance to intermediaries
    1: None offered
    2: Limited to printed materials, displays, etc.
    3: Special support services offered (e.g., missionary salespeople, demonstrators, etc.)
    4: Marketer must provide intermediaries their salesforce at point of sale

Setting and measuring advertising goals
    1: No specific goals set (e.g., % awareness)
    2: Specific goals set but not measured
    3: Measurement of specific goals

Frequency of promotional discounts to the trade
    1: Non utilized
    2: Infrequently utilized
    3: Frequently utilized

Frequency of promotional discounts to end users
    1: Non utilized
    2: Infrequently utilized
    3: Frequently utilized

Chapter 15

Strategy Development
for Manufactured Exports
of Third World Countries
to Developed Countries

Robert D. Schooler
Albert R. Wildt
Joseph M. Jones

SUMMARY. This chapter addresses the problem of developing consumer patronage in high income markets for the autonomous manufactured exports of Third World countries. Specifically, the focus is on overcoming consumer bias in high income markets against products of third world origin. Such bias exists; it has been established and tested in a twenty-year stream of research. This chapter extends that research and, more importantly, for the first time sets the problem in a real world, managerial context. The research presents an illustrative, hypothetical case, somewhat simplified but realistic. A new Mexican microwave oven is introduced into the U.S. market and positioned against competing U.S. brands. A multifactored marketing strategy is built from several levels of three strategic factors: price, warranty, and endorsement. The findings are promising and establish the following: (1) the power of the different strategic elements against consumer bias varies significantly, (2) the power of different multifactored strategies varies significantly, and (3) some multifactored strategies prove effective in overcoming consumer bias establishing competitive position against U.S. brands.

This chapter was first published in the *Journal of Global Marketing*, Vol. 1(1/2), Fall/Winter 1987.

INTRODUCTION

Third World countries are making concerted efforts to expand autonomous exports of manufactured goods to high income countries. This effort does not represent a rejection of the off-shore production facilities of foreign multinationals. The multinationals provide jobs and easy access to high income markets. Third World countries recognize the multinational contribution, but are uneasy with the multinational relationship. In the relationship the power is with the multinational. It is the multinational that controls technology, market access, and production location. The multinational can give jobs and take jobs away. Off-shore production facilities of multinationals just do not provide the security and reliability of autonomous exports from indigenous firms.

Some Third World countries have succeeded in establishing autonomous exports and consumer patronage in high income countries. Taiwan and Korea are examples. Unfortunately most Third World countries have neither patronage in, nor market access to, the highly competitive, difficult to penetrate, high income markets.

Third World access to high income markets has been facilitated through the General System of Preferences. However, preferential access does not easily translate into increased exports. Successful export expansion programs require a number of things, such as government incentives, reduced variance in product quality, increased reliability of delivery, and the matching of production capacity to market opportunities. Furthermore, even a well-structured and implemented export expansion program will confront a formidable set of market barriers in high income countries—the non-availability of channels, established consumption patterns, and strong trade names all constitute barriers to demand creation.

A particularly relevant market barrier is consumer bias on the basis of product origin. This is a barrier that often goes unrecognized and one not subject to negotiation. A comprehensive review of the literature on country of origin bias was published in 1982 (Bilkey & Nes).[1] The review established consumer bias on the basis of product origin as a general phenomenon, i.e., one applicable to consumer and industrial goods, to classes of products, to specific types of products, and to products from developing countries and products from advanced countries. The review established four points particularly relevant to this study: (1) consumer bias on the basis of product origin directly affects the acceptability of foreign products, (2) bias is particularly evident against the manufactured goods of developing countries, (3) the effect of bias on the purchase decision can be altered through circumventing strategies, and (4) the need is for multi-cue studies conforming to real life market conditions.

MARKETING STRATEGIES

Several marketing strategies designed to offset or overcome consumer bias have shown promise. Price concessions (Schooler & Wildt, 1968), regional labeling (Schooler & Sunoo, 1969) and association with prestigious retail outlets (Reierson, 1967) have proven effective in offsetting bias and making the foreign product more acceptable to the American consumer. However, there are two principal problems with the countervailing strategies suggested to date. First, some of the strategies, such as price reduction and regional labeling, present legal difficulties in the U.S. Second, the strategies have been unidimensional, i.e., they consider only a single element of the marketing mix. What is needed are countervailing strategies that are realistic and implementable, that is, strategies that have the qualities of marketing strategies implemented daily for domestic goods. The strategies should be multifaceted, combining several elements and offering several inducements, and the strategies must be legal, affordable and effective.

ROLE OF RESEARCH

Marketing research is an appropriate tool to aid in the formation of the needed strategies. Previous research brings us part way. It is known that there is consumer bias against products of certain foreign origins and that the bias problem is particularly acute against the manufactured goods of Third World countries. Furthermore, it is known how consumers react to a number of single inducements calculated to overcome negative consumer predispositions.

Now it is time to push on, to further develop export expansion strategies for developing countries. It should be noted that the issues involved are, or could be, equally relevant to sourcing strategies for firms in advanced countries. The objective is to develop an efficient and effective multidimensional strategy, a strategy in which individual inducements complement and support one another in offsetting or circumventing origin bias.

In constructing such strategies managers need to consider questions such as the following: What strategy elements can be used? Which ones seem appropriate in light of competitors' market positions? What is the cost and impact of individual "appropriate" elements? Which strategies or elements can the firm afford? What market response will the affordable combinations produce?

Research is needed to give the marketing manager the market response data to combine with the company resource data in building effective marketing strategies. It should be noted that the selection of elements to consider is made on the basis of experience, intuition, and previous research. There is no way to ensure that highly effective elements or highly effective combinations will not be overlooked.

DEVELOPING EFFECTIVE MARKETING STRATEGY

A research approach to building a multidimensional marketing strategy is illustrated below. This illustration is hypothetical and does not include all possible competitive brands or marketing mix elements, nor is it intended to be an exercise in rigorous technique. It is a description of an approach to the real problem of developing effective marketing strategies for autonomous exports of manufactured goods of Third World countries. The specific case involves a strategy in which price, warranty, and endorsement elements are mixed in various combinations in an attempt to win consumer patronage. The problem situation – the marketing of Mexican microwave ovens in the U.S. – is hypothetical, illustrative, and less complex than real world situations.

In this article no attention is given to the channel of distribution. It would be a mistake to conclude that the channel is not very important. To the contrary, a cooperative and efficient set of distributors is necessary to establish and maintain market position. However, channel considerations are beyond the scope of the issues addressed here.

Marketing Context

The product considered is a mini-microwave oven approximately one-third the capacity and one-fifth the weight of standard microwave ovens. The product was selected for several reasons. (1) It is a manufactured good, making it appropriate for the problem context considered. (2) It is a new extension of an existing product line, and as such, it possesses a high level of consumer familiarity with the product category but a low level of specific consumer knowledge. (3) The product is not yet in production, consequently verbal product descriptions are appropriate means of communicating with consumers. (4) Consumers perceive the product class to be characterized by a high degree of technical complexity. Complexity and unfamiliarity with the specific product create uncertainty and caution on the part of consumers. This heightens the salience of country of origin as a product cue.

The product is manufactured in Mexico, a newly industrialized Third World country and a neighbor to the U.S. Mexico's political stability has recently been questioned. Huge trade deficits, high inflation, and currency devaluations plague Mexico, and very high unemployment rates have produced social unrest. Mexico is a country that desperately needs to increase foreign exchange earnings through increased exports of manufactured goods. These factors combine to make Mexico an attractive choice for the country of origin in this illustration, though it should be noted that proximity to and familiarity with Mexico might affect, perhaps lower, the intensity of bias against Mexican products.

The product is to be sold in the U.S. under a Mexican brand name. The proposed marketing strategy combines many elements, but the three of primary interest are: price, warranty, and expert endorsement. Price is considered important because observed market behavior and previous research indicate its effectiveness in offsetting negative consumer predisposition based on the country of origin bias. Three levels of price are considered; (1) a parity price equal to the average price of the other comparable entries in the product category used in the study, (2) 90% of parity price, and (3) 80% of parity price.

Warranty and expert endorsement are also expected to affect consumers' evaluations and acceptance of the Mexican microwave oven. Two levels of warranty are considered: (1) a parity warranty roughly equivalent to the standard industry warranty of comparable product entries and (2) a superior warranty, significantly better than the parity warranty. Two levels of expert endorsement are considered: (1) no endorsement and (2) an endorsement of product quality by a consumer organization.

Market Research

Developing an effective marketing strategy requires identifying the most advantageous combination of the three marketing variables. Marketing research is used to estimate the impact of the selected levels of the three marketing factors on consumer brand choice under simulated competitive market conditions. The Mexican product is presented with twelve different marketing strategies (3 price levels, 2 warranty levels and 2 endorsement levels) to a sample of respondents representing the U.S. target market.

For this application a judgment, nonrandom, sample was drawn from the universe of interest, i.e., female consumers judged likely to purchase and use microwave ovens. Female respondents were recruited from civic, social and occupational organizations in a single midwest state. However, care was taken to assure representation from both rural and urban areas, and various socioeconomic groups. The final sample was slightly "up-scale" and heavy in white middle class respondents. Respondent median education level was high school graduate. Approximately half the respondents came from households in which the chief wage earner was in a white collar occupation, and approximately one-fourth were themselves the main wage earner of the household. Average household size was 2.75, median annual household income was greater than $25,000, and all respondents were over 18 years, with most between 25 and 64 years of age.

Interviews were conducted with all respondents from a single organization at a single group session at a location convenient to the organization's members. The researcher carefully explained the data collection procedure and the questionnaire forms. Respondents then completed individual self-administered questionnaires under controlled conditions which prohibited interaction among respondents.

Each respondent evaluated the twelve Mexican product offerings and three competing U.S. brands on product attractiveness (purchase preference) using an ordinal-valued ranking scale. In this illustration, Amana, General Electric, and Kenmore were selected as competing brands. In addition, each respondent evaluated the Mexican product she perceived as most attractive on ten product characteristics using seven-point scales.

Each respondent was given fifteen note cards. Twelve cards contained Mexican product descriptions and three cards contained American product descriptions. The descriptions included country of manufacture and information on six product attributes — the three factors of interest (price, warranty, and endorsement), and three other factors (size, cooking characteristics, and safety).[2] The latter three factors were held constant over all fifteen products. The descriptions of the American products were designed to represent the expected levels for those brands. Based on the product descriptions contained on the note cards, each respondent ranked the fifteen products according to purchase preference. Each respondent then evaluated selected product attributes[3] of her first choice Mexican product relative to the three American products using a set of ten semantic scales. Respondents also rated the importance of eight product characteristics,[4] and provided product usage and demographic information.

RESULTS

The competitive effectiveness of *each* of the twelve marketing strategies was evaluated by comparing the corresponding Mexican product with the three American products in a simulated four-brand market. Table 1 shows the preference share of each Mexican product when compared to the three American products. The Mexican microwave with the low price, the superior warranty, and the endorsement was the first choice of 24.1% of all respondents (sam-

TABLE 1. Preference Shares of Mexican Products in Simulated Four Brand Market

MEXICAN PRODUCT DESCRIPTION

PREFERENCE SHARE OF MEXICAN
PRODUCT IN FOUR BRAND MARKET

Price	Warranty	Endorsement	Total Sample (n=116)	Product Familiar* (n=85)
80% parity	superior	yes	24.1%**	23.5%
80% parity	superior	no	22.4%	21.2%
80% parity	parity	yes	10.3%	7.1%
80% parity	parity	no	7.8%	4.7%
90% parity	superior	yes	24.1%	23.5%
90% parity	superior	no	20.7%	20.0%
90% parity	parity	yes	9.5%	8.2%
90% parity	parity	no	6.0%	3.5%
parity	superior	yes	22.4%	21.2%
parity	superior	no	21.6%	20.0%
parity	parity	yes	8.6%	5.9%
parity	parity	no	3.4%	2.4%

*Respondents who currently have microwave oven or are considering purchasing one.

**Interpret as follows: 24.1% of respondents rated the Mexican product with low price, superior warranty, and endorsement higher than the three American brands - Amana, General Electric, and Kenmore - on overall product attractiveness.

ple size of 116) and 23.5% of product-familiar respondents (85 respondents with a microwave oven in their home or planning to purchase one) when choosing from the set of four products: Amana, General Electric, Kenmore, and Mexican. Likewise, the Mexican microwave with the low price, the superior warranty, and no endorsement was the choice of 22.4% of all respondents and 21.2% of product-familiar respondents, choosing one product from the set of four. The tabulated results suggest a strong impact for warranty and a lesser impact for endorsement and price. The absolute preference shares presented in Table 1 are influenced by the specific price, warranty and endorsement values assigned to the Mexican and American products and are not of great importance per se. The important issue in this study is the ability of the various attribute combinations to influence consumer evaluations.

To further assess the impact of the three factors, the preference share data from Table 1 were analyzed using ANOVA.[5] The results for the total sample, presented in Table 2, indicate that two strategy factors, warranty and endorsement, have a significant impact on consumer preference. An analysis of product-familiar respondents shows similar results for warranty and endorsement, but, in addition, indicates that price has a significant impact. Factor interactions were not indicated in either analysis.

Table 3 is derived directly from Table 1 and elaborates on the impact of each strategy factor by presenting the average preference share associated with each factor level independent of the other factors. Warranty emerges as the factor of greatest impact.

TABLE 2. Analysis of Variance of Preference Shares of Mexican Products*

SOURCE OF VARIATION	SUM OF SQUARES	DEGREES OF FREEDOM	MEAN SQUARE	F-RATIO
Price	8.0	2	4.0	2.4
Warranty	675.0	1	675.0	404.2**
Endorsement	21.3	1	21.3	12.8**
Error	11.7	7	1.7	
Total	716.0	11		

*Based on the total sample of 116 respondents. Data from the first column of Table 1.

**Greater than the tabulated F value at the .01 level.

NOTE: For the product familiar sample (results not reported here), the computed F for price is greater than the tabulated F at the .05 level and the computed F's for warranty and endorsement are greater than the tabulated F at the .01 level.

TABLE 3. Average Preference Shares for Mexican Products
for All Levels of Price, Warranty, and Endorsement

FACTOR	AVERAGE PREFERENCE SHARE	
	Total Sample (n=116)	Product Familiar* (n=85)
PRICE		
80% parity	16.2%**	14.1%
90% parity	15.1%	13.8%
parity	14.0%	12.4%
WARRANTY		
superior	22.6%	21.6%
parity	7.6%	5.3%
ENDORSEMENT		
yes	16.5%	14.9%
no	13.6%	12.0%

*Respondents who currently have a microwave oven or are considering purchasing one.

**Interpret as follows: 16.2% of all respondents indicated the Mexican product with low (80% parity) price was their most preferred product when compared to the three American brands. This value is averaged over the two warranty levels and the two endorsement levels, and is derived directly from Table 1.

For the total sample, the average preference share for the Mexican product with superior warranty (averaged over the three price levels and two endorsement levels) was 22.6% and for the average warranty only 7.6%, a difference of 15%. The impact of endorsement was much less than warranty, but greater than price.

Additional analysis of the data can provide information on which competitors are most affected by various combinations of strategy elements for the Mexican product. This can be done by examining preference shares for the American brands when confronted with the various Mexican product strategies. In this study, improving the Mexican product warranty had the greatest impact on U.S. consumer preference for the Amana microwave oven (the American brand with the best warranty), i.e., it lowered the preference share of Amana more than that for the other two American brands. Lowering the price of the Mexican product had the greatest impact on Kenmore, and including an endorsement affected both General Electric and Kenmore more than Amana. This type of analysis allows the manager to examine competitive subpatterns within the market.

Respondents choosing a Mexican oven first over all three American ovens were compared to those choosing any of the American ovens first. Data for the total sample and the product-familiar sample were similar and only results for the total sample are shown. Table 4 shows what one would expect: Respondents who preferred an American product rate the Mexican product a little worse than the American brands, and respondents who preferred the Mexican product rate it a little better than the American products. Both groups rate availability of service and ease of repair of the Mexican product to be worse than that of the American brands.

Table 5 shows far more agreement than disagreement on the importance of microwave characteristics to the two groups of respondents. The greatest divergence is on the importance of low price, with those preferring the Mexican product rating low price more important than those preferring an American brand. It should be noted that both groups rate availability of service and ease of repair as very important. No significant differences between the two groups on demographics variables (household size, education, home ownership, occupation of head of household, age and income) emerged. This was somewhat surprising.

IMPLICATIONS

The illustration provides both marketing (tactical) and business policy (strategic) implications. The marketing implications are based on the finding that multidimensional strategies can overcome consumer resistance based on product origin, and that the power of the individual strategy elements to overcome resistance can vary

TABLE 4. Evaluation of Most Preferred Mexican Product[a]

PRODUCT CHARACTERISTIC	AVERAGE RATINGS			RATING PROFILES[b]
	TOTAL SAMPLE	PREFER MEXICAN[c]	PREFER AMERICAN[d]	
safety[e]	3.9	4.6	3.7	1 2 3 4 5 6 7
durablity[e]	4.1	5.0	3.8	1 2 3 4 5 6 7
convenience of use[e]	3.8	4.4	3.6	1 2 3 4 5 6 7
ease of repair	3.0	3.6	2.8	1 2 3 4 5 6 7
optional features[e]	3.7	4.4	3.5	1 2 3 4 5 6 7
low price[e]	4.8	5.8	4.5	1 2 3 4 5 6 7
availability of service	2.8	2.8	2.8	1 2 3 4 5 6 7
even cooking[e]	3.8	4.3	3.7	1 2 3 4 5 6 7
warranty[e]	4.7	5.7	4.3	1 2 3 4 5 6 7
overall product quality[e]	3.9	4.8	3.7	1 2 3 4 5 6 7

a Based on total sample.
b Scale descriptions are: 1-much worse than the American brands, 4-same as the American brands, and 7-much better than the American brands. Profile designations are:— prefer Mexican and ---- prefer American.
c Respondents who preferred a Mexican product over the American products.
d Respondents who preferred an American product over all Mexican products.
e Difference between the "prefer Mexican" respondents and the "prefer American" respondents is statistically significant at the 0.05 level.

significantly. In considering the implications the reader is reminded that the findings are based on self-reported measures of product attractiveness (purchase intention), not on actual purchase behavior.

The first implication is that, where a particularly powerful strategic element exists, it may be desirable to build the marketing strategy around that element. In the illustration that powerful element is warranty. This does not mean that price and endorsement are unimportant and can be ignored. The implication is that price and en-

TABLE 5. Importance of Product Characteristics[a]

PRODUCT CHARACTERISTIC	AVERAGE RATINGS			RATING PROFILE[b]
	TOTAL SAMPLE	PREFER MEXICAN[c]	PREFER AMERICAN[d]	
safety[e]	6.7	6.9	6.6	1 2 3 4 5 6 7
durability	6.6	6.7	6.6	1 2 3 4 5 6 7
convenience	6.4	6.5	6.3	1 2 3 4 5 6 7
ease of repair	6.5	6.7	6.4	1 2 3 4 5 6 7
low price[e]	5.2	5.7	5.0	1 2 3 4 5 6 7
availability of service	6.6	6.7	6.6	1 2 3 4 5 6 7
warranty	6.6	6.8	6.5	1 2 3 4 5 6 7
overall product quality	6.5	6.6	6.5	1 2 3 4 5 6 7

a Based on total sample.
b Scale descriptions are: 1-not important and 7-extremely important. Profile designations are:
—— prefer Mexican and ---- prefer American.
c Respondents who preferred a Mexican product over the American products.
d Respondents who preferred an American product over all Mexican products.
e Difference between the "prefer Mexican" respondents and the "prefer American" respondents is statistically significant at the 0.05 level.

dorsement should be used in a way that complements and supplements a warranty strategy.

The second implication is that other factors, in the illustration cost considerations, combine with the favorable consumer response to make the warranty strategy even more attractive. With multidimensional strategies the marketing manager needs to balance the power of the individual elements against the type and level of individual element costs. In the illustration warranty represents a type of cost that Third World firms will find attractive. Warranty costs occur after the sale has produced revenue for the firm. For most Third World firms this type of cost is preferable to front-end costs that must be met before the sale of the product has produced revenue, for example advertising cost. The point is that once the power of the individual elements is known the manager can structure a marketing strategy based both on this information and the resources and capabilities of his firm.

The third implication requires a bit of caution, in fact, it is better considered an observation. When an element achieves a certain power level it can create a halo effect for the product. One could reasonably conclude from the illustration, though not prove, that the superior warranty did more than assure against repair expense, that it also persuaded consumers that the product was safe, durable, and of overall high quality. In such circumstances a strategy focused on the warranty is doubly attractive.

Now to the strategic implications of the illustration, the adoption of a warranty strategy requires the adoption of supporting decisions and actions throughout the firm. If a firm offers a superior warranty, it must produce a superior product. Otherwise warranty expense will run out of control. A superior product requires emphasis on quality inputs, process control, and a thorough inspection system. Another requirement of a warranty strategy is that the firm must emphasize and deliver service. High quality service must be readily available. Otherwise the power of the warranty will be dissipated by customer frustration and ill will. The strategic point is this: a firm should not adopt a marketing strategy unless it is prepared to adopt the required supporting policies elsewhere.

CONCLUSIONS

Conclusions are appropriate to both the case at hand and the broader problem of building marketing strategies for Third World autonomous exports to high income markets. First in the case of the Mexican microwave oven, the research indicates that the most promising strategy for the Mexican microwave in the U.S. market is a strategy offering a superior warranty, little if any price concession, and an expert endorsement if available at a reasonable cost.

At the broader level, it can be concluded that consumer bias against Third World manufactured goods is not an insurmountable barrier. Bias can be managed, even reversed, with carefully built and implemented marketing strategies. But the task must not be underestimated. The manager must not only create a strategy that overcomes bias; the strategy must be legal, affordable, and appropriate to the firm's resources and the competitive dynamics in the industry. The manager needs a feel for the market, and the intuition and sensitivity to identify and select the strategic elements to test. If he overlooks effective strategic elements, he will probably miss effective strategies.

That brings us to the contribution of this chapter: an uncomplicated, affordable, and implementable research approach to help the Third World marketing manager test the power of potential strategy elements and the power of multifactor strategies. Actually the approach does more than test and measure. The data produced provides insights and stimulates creative thinking which reduces the probability that the Third World marketing manager will overlook an effective strategy.

NOTES

1. An interesting addition to origin of goods research appeared in 1984 (Erickson, Johannson, and Chao) which concludes that the country of origin effect impacts beliefs, not attitudes.

2. For example, the low priced, superior warranty, endorsed Mexican product was described as possessing the following attributes:

- Made in Republic of Mexico
- Balanced wave cooking
- Underwriters Laboratories listed
- Usable oven volume: 0.6 cubic feet
- 10-year warranty on magnetron; 3-year on other parts and labor
- Endorsed as "Best Buy" by leading U.S. consumer group
- Price: $159

3. For a listing of the selected attributes refer to Table 4.

4. For a listing of the product characteristics refer to Table 5.

5. The data collection method employed is the same as that used in full-profile conjoint analysis. Using these data individual-level analyses could be preformed. However, in this context interest centers on the aggregate response to the marketing program and, therefore, an aggregate-level analysis was used.

REFERENCES

Bilkey, Warren, and Eric Nes. (1982). "Country of Origin Effects on Product Evaluations." *Journal of International Business Studies,* 13 (Spring-Summer), pp. 89-99.

Erickson, Gary, Johnny Johansson, and Paul Chao. (1976). "Image Variables in Multi-Attribute Product Evaluations: Country of Origin Effects." *Journal of Consumer Research,* 2 (November), pp. 694-99.

Reierson, Curtis C. (1967). "Attitude Changes Toward Foreign Products." *Journal of Marketing Research,* 4 (November), pp. 385-87.

Schooler, Robert D., and Don H. Sunoo. (1969). "Consumer Perceptions of International Products: Regional vs. National Labeling." *Social Science Quarterly,* 49 (March), pp. 886-90.

Schooler, Robert D., and Albert R. Wildt. (1968). "Elasticity of Product Bias." *Journal of Marketing Research, 5 (February),* pp. 78-81.

Chapter 16

What Can Third World Countries Learn from China?

Hans B. Thorelli

SUMMARY. Market socialism is a new hybrid among economic systems. Applied in an ad hoc fashion in Hungary, the huge-scale economic experimentation in the People's Republic of China, if allowed to continue, will first put to the test the basic concept of an open market within an economy of essentially publicly owned means of production. While each country should presumably adopt systems suited to local culture and resources, the PRC experience seems to offer Third World nations many worthwhile ideas.

INTRODUCTION

The socioeconomic experimentation in the People's Republic of China (PRC) in the last eight years is extraordinarily significant in many respects. It takes place in the most populous country in the world, accounting for some 25 percent of humanity. It is best interpreted as a unique attempt at combining socialism and liberalism. Returns thus far suggest that the experiments are highly successful in agriculture, at least moderately so in the distribution and services sectors, and promising in industry, especially with regard to consumer goods. All this is significant at a time when the classic development gospel practiced in a majority of Third World countries for

This chapter was first published in the *Journal of Global Marketing*, Vol. 1(1/2), Fall/Winter 1987.

at least 30 years is manifestly bankrupt. There is a tremendous need for new ideas and new approaches, such as those demonstrated in Japan, Taiwan, South Korea and Singapore in recent years and now, on an almost mind-boggling scale, in the PRC.

This chapter attempts briefly to summarize major implications of the PRC experiments for developing countries (DC) interested in learning from them. It is divided into three sections, dealing with accelerating and governing forces, cautions and constraints, and the transferability of the Chinese experience into different settings.

ACCELERATORS AND GOVERNORS

1. *Motivation is the key for us all as producers and consumers:* Man can be induced to contribute to a joint effort such as socioeconomic development in various ways. One is by brute force; the Cultural Revolution in the 1966-76 period in the PRC amply demonstrated the shortcomings of this technique. One can also be motivated by social, patriotic, religious, and altruistic appeals, which may be labeled "moral incentives." However, as observed by Xue Muquiao (1981) — famous economist and a guiding spirit in the PRC experiments — "it is essential to provide the working people material as well as moral incentives." There are also sources of personal satisfaction in addition to moral and material ones, such as love and camaraderie, acclaim, power and a certain style of life.

The "mix" of motivating factors emphasized varies considerably between societies. One way of looking at the problem of motivation is from an individual point of view. Among the roles that we all play the two most important are probably those of producer and consumer. Worker or manager, man as producer wants the joy of a good job, companionship, and a pleasant work environment. But a vital part of job satisfaction is material compensation, what one may call *money for value,* the value added to the product by the individual's contribution. While ostensibly taken into account in Marxist theory of labor value, this notion is clearly in contrast with that chronic socialist dogma, "from each according to his ability; to each according to his need." This thesis was incorporated in early PRC constitutions. Of critical importance to the understanding of the recent reforms is that the 1982 constitution of the PRC made a dramatic change in the last half of the dictum which now reads, "to each according to his *work*" (emphasis supplied). In the other role we want consumer satisfaction, based on free choice and *value for money*. Here again, a dramatic change in philosophy has taken place. Like other DC, the PRC before 1978 placed the consumer at the low end of national priorities. If not at the center of the stage, he is now pretty close to it, as will become clearer below. The rationale for this transformation is simple. The present leadership in China realizes that to be motivated as producers, most citizens must also be motivated as consumers.

2. *Open market sector stimulates competition and buyer's markets:* Total planning is typically associated with seller's markets. When a consumer product is in surplus it is generally of a less desirable variety. To move in the direction of the freedom of choice and value for money associated with buyer's markets, China has found it necessary to create a sizeable open market sector. The key characteristics of open markets are decentralized initiative and competition.

3. *Marketing is indispensable as stimulant and allocator:* Classic socialism looks at marketing with a jaundiced eye, seeing a tool of monopolist manipulation and bourgeois profiteering. Socialist doctrine stresses the physical "circulation" of goods produced at the behest of planners and managers presumably knowing better than consumers themselves what is good for them. By contrast, modern China has embraced marketing with considerable enthusiasm, realizing that it plays a dual and important role. In effect, marketing implements the division of labor and specialization without which progress is impossible (Thorelli, 1984). It does this by effecting transactions between buyers and sellers. In a competitive context marketing also affects the *future* division of labor as sellers giving better value are rewarded by greater sales.

Of perhaps even greater importance is marketing's role as a stimulant providing freedom of choice and value for money. It is essential to understand that marketing as a motivating force goes far beyond plain materialism. We buy books not for the paper, but for the thoughts. One buys a radio not for a kilo of electronics, but for the music, news, plays, — yes, sometimes even for the advertisements it may bring. Food is bought and consumed not just to fill the stomach, but for the enjoyment of its taste, of local and foreign cultures, and of social life as we break bread together. And the Chinese buys a bicycle not just for transport, but because it sets him free to enjoy nature, see new things, and yes, often to enjoy a degree of privacy difficult to obtain on public buses. In other words, PRC leaders have seen that marketing is indispensable not just to the accumulation of physical goods, but also to deliver individual styles of life in the middle of the mass production society around us.

4. *Public ownership, private property, and diversity in management:* The means of production as well as land are still in public or collective ownership to over ninety percent, and this may well obtain by 1990 as well. However, in agriculture, trade and services, and, to a smaller extent, in industry, productive organizations are now run by a diversity of manager types: individual and household entrepreneurs, partnerships, occasional stockholder-owned companies, cooperatives, collectives and municipal, provincial or state government operations. In many markets these various forms of management are competing with each other. Especially interesting is the kind of hybrid enterprise for which the state auctions off the managerial and profit-sharing rights to the highest private bidder or group of bidders, who in effect run the firm on good behavior.

With rising standards of living there is a vast increase in durable consumer goods, including housing in some cases, and in private property in general. The state has encouraged this development, and recently rights of inheritance have been strengthened.

5. *Agriculture comes first:* An outstanding characteristic of the Chinese reforms is the absolute priority given to agriculture in terms of both timing and effort. The essence of agricultural reform was the transformation of this huge sector from status to contract, or what is officially called the *responsibility system.* Under the new dispensation, individuals, households, groups of families, production teams and brigades may contract with collectives, state enterprises and other agencies for a certain minimum output, often more modest than previous quotas. Typically they have considerable freedom in specifying what they want to grow, husband, or produce. They are obliged to turn over their minimum output to the state at fixed prices as before, to pay state taxes, and to contribute to the collective's welfare fund. The contract may also provide for

charges for the use of any collective services or means of production. Sizeable increases in the minimum prices paid by the state for farm products have provided a strong practical incentive (Thorelli et al., 1986).

More recent is the emergence of a more modest number of so-called self-managing households, which may own some or all of their means of production short of whatever land they may till. Interestingly, members of some of these contractual units are free to invest money in them in addition to time, occasionally even in lieu of time. We should add that the agricultural reform recognized and included in the contract system "sideline occupations," such as fish-farming and brick-making, and more distantly related activity such as furniture and textile manufacturing or assembly work for urban firms. Designed to increase productivity and retain otherwise surplus labor in rural areas, these sideline occupations now employ an estimated 15 percent of rural labor.

Crucially significant are the rules governing the disposal of any farm surplus output beyond the agreed minimum. The contractor has three main options: to sell it to the state at a price usually higher than that set for the minimum output, to use it for home consumption (a popular means of providing previously unseen variety in diet), or to sell it in a nearby farmers' market. There are now well over 40,000 markets. As long as prices do not get out of hand they may be set freely. The markets are very popular, and are putting pressure on state food stores to become more customer-oriented.

Clearly, it took stamina to carry out an agricultural reform of these dimensions, considering that three-fourths of the Chinese population earns its living in agriculture and its sidelines. Although a policy of placing agriculture first is certainly called for in the majority of the Third World it will take even more political courage to launch there. Governments in these countries typically have made themselves dependent on the metropolitan population for support, perpetrating various policies of price control at the farm level and food price subsidies in the metropolitan area. Nevertheless, as food is a crucial concern in the Third World, agriculture *is* the logical place for new approaches to development. From an incentive point of view, farming also has the merit that the relationship between individual effort and output tends to be much more direct than in industry.

6. *Industry: consumer goods, decentralization, incentives:* To ensure that consumer demands are accommodated better, there has been a significant and determined shift in priorities from heavy to light industries. This again is clearly contrary to Soviet-type doctrine as well as the prevailing development orthodoxy. Of even greater potential importance is the application of the responsibility system philosophy in ever-larger segments of industry. Thus, "guidance planning" is being substituted for total planning in one branch of industry after the other with the aim that "mandatory planning" ultimately will be confined to defense and a handful of other critical industries.

In many industries obligatory quotas have been abolished altogether, and in others they have been reduced, all in favor of more open markets and decentralized decision making and entrepreneurship. In return for the self-management and marketing challenges thrown at them, firms have been given a new package of incentives. Earnings after taxes and interest (the cost of money now being explicitly recognized) are at the disposal of the enterprise, subject to overall guidelines which may vary from firm to firm. Typically, minimum shares of after-tax earnings are reserved for the welfare fund of the firm and for "capital accumulation," that is, reinvestment. The remainder is available for bonuses, where a major part is expected to be awarded on an individual basis. In principle, firms are expected to make a profit, managers unable to do so are at risk.

7. *Pricing system driven by cost and market demand:* It is difficult to imagine an open market sector in which prices are not allowed to move freely. The official view is that China is a country of "socialist planning with supplementary regulation by the market." In many areas, however, China's pricing system is still artificial from the point of view of production costs and/or world market prices. For example, the provision of adequate housing is an enormous challenge, and the government would like to enlist individual entrepreneurs in the effort. Yet it is difficult to attract private initiative in urban areas where for decades rents have been set at levels which have nothing to do with the cost of construction. In rural areas, where pricing is much freer and many farmers personally

participate in the building of their houses, residential construction is booming.

Prices have been decontrolled fully or partially in a great number of markets, and the policy is to continue this effort. Yet the fear of inflation and other political sensitivities apply definite brakes on the pace of pricing reform.

8. *Separate government and business—whether business is public or private:* As part of the policy of decentralizing economic activity, the PRC is making a determined effort to separate provincial and municipal government functions from those of business—regardless of type of enterprise management. Especially interesting in this respect is the abolishment of the commune system in favor of local government institutions more similar to those of Western countries. It is proving a bit more difficult to reduce the engagement of urban municipalities in their own businesses or in the activities of "independent" firms within their jurisdictions.

9. *Open door (at least ajar), recognize multinational companies:* The PRC has recognized the value of technology transfer by multinational corporations (MNC), somewhat contrary to socialist nationalism and traditional misgivings about foreign influence. Trade volume has multiplied in recent years, economic zones have been created, well over a thousand joint ventures have been formed, numerous Chinese enterprises are subcontractors to Western firms, and in some instances, MNCs have been granted the privilege of establishing wholly-owned subsidiaries in the PRC. China recently applied for membership in GATT, the very symbol of liberal, international trade philosophy.

To be sure, MNCs would like to see the PRC move a great deal further in opening up her markets and accepting greater managerial discretion from joint ventures and MNC subsidiaries. Her tight restrictions on consumer goods imports are also somewhat contradictory to the notion of freeing up consumer markets for incentive reasons. Nevertheless, the PRC is fast becoming a major international trader (Aharoni, 1977).

10. *Balanced development:* In effect, the PRC seems to be pursuing a policy of balanced development. In important respects this policy has been made explicit, as in the case of these dimensions:

light (consumer goods) and heavy (producer goods) industries;
rural and urban sectors;
short and long term;
socialist planning and regulation by the market;
buyers and sellers;
MNC and host country relations;
the role of self-interest and social responsibility in motivation.
(Collins & Holton, 1963; Chen, 1982; Drucker, 1958)

Not everyone will sympathize with what seems to be the Chinese concept of balance. Too, balance in one dimension may occasionally be obtainable only by sacrificing it in another, and, of course, like life itself, the balance keeps changing. It does, however, appear that in China balanced development is becoming a political philosophy rather than merely the exercising of pragmatic opportunism.

CAUTIONS AND CONSTRAINTS

1. *Inflation:* Any period of rapid development brings in its wake inflationary pressures. This is especially true in a society where prices have long been regimented and in critical markets have been based on sociopolitical rather than economic considerations. Although China has had her share of inflation it has not been accompanied by the social, political, and economic stress seen in many other countries, nor has it approached the rates recently experienced in many other Third World nations.

2. *Inequality in earnings:* The responsibility system and incentive and skills-based compensation systems will inevitably result in an uneven distribution of incomes and, in short order, in property. Chinese leaders have stated that their ambition is for all to get rich, but that for this goal to be met some will necessarily be richer sooner than others. This is indeed contrary to the classic socialist view that poverty is acceptable, as long as it is shared by all! It is natural that after 30 years of innumerable campaigns on the merit of income levelling there are quite a few letters to the editors of China dailies questioning the new philosophy. Meantime, there seems to be no doubt that the new philosophy is holding sway in the country.

Essential social welfare measures for those not able to earn a living wage in this philosophy will be taken by welfare funds of enterprises, by taxation, and by socially responsible individuals (the mutual obligations of family members and good neighbors, for example, are heavily stressed).

3. *Unemployment:* The problem of unemployment is typically associated with capitalist economies. Hidden unemployment is, however, also present in socialist countries. Interestingly, in China hundreds of thousands of city youths "waiting for assignment" have found opportunities for entrepreneurial profit or employment in the burgeoning open market establishments in retail trade and service, previously grossly underdimensioned in the country. The sideline occupations in rural areas have been another important means of avoiding potential unemployment problems. It is not yet clear, however, how China would resolve any structural unemployment problem which may emerge in the future. An inkling of problems yet to be faced was the failure of the Shenyang Explosion-Proof Equipment Factory in August, 1986, the first official bankruptcy in the PRC. It is not yet clear how this and other employment-threatening incidents will be handled in the future. Obviously, unemployment entails special hardship in a country still lacking a modern social security system.

4. *Establishment resistance:* Naturally, China's reforms have met with some resistance from various vested interests, including Maoist hardliners who have seen central and local government powers over the economy being drastically reduced. Vestiges of this resistance are still present. But then, of course, resistance to change is present in all human societies and organizations.

5. *Bribery:* Bribery is also present to varying degrees in all societies. The opportunities for corrupt behavior seem especially prevalent in countries where government and business are closely intertwined. This is still true in the PRC, and a number of local and provincial bribery scandals have been reported in the *Beijing Review.* As with any other DC, however, China can ill afford the luxury of bribery, whose chief characteristic is that it removes the cause-effect relationship between honest effort and results. Constant vigilance is necessary.

6. *Public enterprise to compete on equal terms:* It is exceedingly

important that competition between enterprises in the managed and open sectors be conducted *on an equal basis,* notwithstanding the difficulties in maintaining such a state of affairs. If favors are given managed-sector enterprise in the form of location, taxes, governmental purchases, import permits, etc., there is absolutely no way of evaluating the relative contribution of firms in the two sectors. Indeed, the giving of such privileges to public enterprises will merely foster empire building in the managed sector at the cost of flexibility and economic progress.

There are some signs that the significance of this elementary principle is not yet fully appreciated in the PRC.

7. *Consumer emancipation:* In most DC the consumer is the forgotten man, and consumer rights are typically not enforced, if indeed even recognized. "Let the buyer beware" is the rule in the seller's markets characteristic of these countries. Elsewhere we have developed a program of consumer protection, education, and information policy to enforce consumer rights (Thorelli, 1981, 1986). Consumer emancipation is needed not only because consumer rights are elementary *human* rights. Such emancipation is also a *necessary* (if not sufficient) prerequisite for the private sector to work like an open market. Open markets can function only when there is some semblance of equality of status between buyers and sellers.

The PRC has already begun a modest program of formalizing consumer rights. In addition, it is interesting to observe that Chinese middle class consumers apparently have a clearer view of what consumers rights should be than do their counterparts in Thailand (Thorelli, 1982).

8. *Nip cartelization and ossification in the bud:* The ultimate rationale for open markets is that they leave ample room for competition—without sacrificing constructive cooperation. Thus freedom of entry (and exit) is important. So is vigilance in counteracting undesirable restraints on competition, such as price cartels, output restricting, or market-sharing agreements. Ubiquitous in many DC based on "cryptocapitalism," at least a few such far-reaching attempts at eliminating competition have reared their ugly heads in the PRC. Such attempts at tampering with the open market should

be quenched at their inception, whether perpetrated by firms in the public or private sectors (or both).

9. *Proceed gradually, but do not lose systems view:* To attain balanced development it is imperative to keep the entire socioeconomic system constantly in mind. Yet the PRC experience teaches us that it is impossible to undertake all reforms at once. Agriculture was given top priority, industry followed and only very recently do we see a transformation in the pricing area. Still, it is true that the overall system has what the Germans would call *Gestalt*, meaning that partial reforms undertaken without regard for the total system may lead to suboptimization and counterproductive inconsistencies.

10. *Interaction of economic freedom with political:* It is our observation that consumer aspiration levels tend to grow (even exponentially) with degrees of economic development. This process may well increase the pressure for economic freedom and open markets, as will freer entry into markets and professions. (The process of freeing up the *labor* market has only really begun in the PRC.) If von Hayek was right in his proposition that there is a connection between political and economic freedom, we should expect to find increasing economic freedom to be accompanied by some degree of pressure for greater political freedom. Indeed, it may be that fear of such a connection is what ultimately ended the so-called Liberman experiments in the USSR during the 1960s (Thorelli, 1965).

Political leaders and development planners are wise to take into account the potential interaction of economic and political freedom. Certainly, for instance, a going back on economic freedoms to which people have become acculturated may be fraught with political danger (Kindra, 1984).

TRANSFERABILITY AND THE ECOLOGY
OF DEVELOPMENT

Deng Xiao Ping states that China aims to "build socialism with Chinese characteristics." In other words, the PRC wants to adapt socialist ideology to the environment and culture of China, rather than forcing the country to conform to orthodox (notably, Soviet-type) ideology.

Several Marxist-Leninist dogmas have been—or are being—abandoned or modified in the process of transformation from Maoism-Stalinism to Market Socialism:

1. "From each according to his ability, to each according to his need." A revolution in thinking was reflected in the substitution of "work" for "need" in the Constitution of the PRC.

2. "State or collective ownership of all means of production." This doctrine is the one *least* affected by the developments discussed here. Nevertheless, many small-scale vendors and craftsmen as well as family-size firms are permitted to own their own equipment. Too, many a farmer can now freely buy his own tractor and agricultural implements. A tiny percentage of productive enterprises are based on share ownership. Nevertheless, state or collective ownership of over 90 percent of the value of all means of production as well as land is the key socialist element in Market Socialism. The percentage of such ownership may decline, but not likely by many points.

   That individual entrepreneurs and a variety of other unorthodox organizations may be granted the *use* of state-owned means of production is, of course, another matter—and directly in line with Market Socialist thought.

3. "One individual employing another constitutes exploitation." This tired doctrine is daily yielding ground as youths and families start up their own firms and find it necessary to add hired hands in order to expand. While it is difficult to establish empirically just how many non-family employees are permitted in a private enterprise, it seems that in most cases it would not be advisable for an individual entrepreneur to expand beyond a dozen or so non-family employees.

4. "Thou shalt not resale for profit." In classic socialist thought, profit is the very symbol of exploitation. Under Market Socialism it is used as a benchmark of performance in both public and private enterprise.

5. "Service and distributive trades are demeaning and parasitical." This doctrine is yielding fast with the realization that marketing generally adds both value and motivation in the development process. Clearly, too, a variety of services are in-

dispensable in modern society. There is nothing demeaning about servicing another human being with professional skill and pride, no matter how modest the service may seem in "occupational prestige."

6. "Competition is wasteful – replace it with total planning." After 30 turbulent years whose only common denominator was the ambition to attain total planning, the PRC by 1978 appears to have learned that there are obvious limitations to such planning in complex modern societies. She also learned the highly significant lesson that it is difficult indeed to practice total planning over an extended period and sustain indispensable levels of popular motivation at the same time. On the other hand, competition clearly served as a motivational spur in many highly developed, or rapidly developing, countries. Thus was born the notion of "guidance planning with supplementary regulation by the market" which is – with the notion of public ownership of the principal means of production – the cornerstone of Market Socialist philosophy.

We are ready to generalize the Deng statement cited at the beginning of this section: each developing country should build a socioeconomic system based on its local culture and environment. Like Deng's own, this is an essentially *ecologic* view of development. Thus, many countries may not wish to follow directly in China's footsteps. Nevertheless, the PRC experience may well have some *universally* applicable characteristics for Third World countries (including those approaching the development challenge from a capitalist rather than socialist basis). These universals may include the following:

- for motivation, man needs personal as well as social, immediate as well as long-term, gratification;
- development calls for a viable open market sector. Viability has three connotations. First, the open sector must be large enough to be able to function reasonably independently of the managed sector and to make cost-and-market based pricing the norm rather than the exception. Second, consumer emancipation is called for, as open markets require a semblance of

equality between buyers and sellers. Third, the spirit of enterprise and competition is the very hallmark of open markets; don't-rock-the-boat cryptocapitalism is incompatible with such markets;
- the PRC experience suggests that public ownership of most means of production may not in itself be incompatible with open markets;
- in most DC agricultural reform should have priority over industrial;
- real development is balanced development.

We must conclude that PRC reforms initiated in 1978 provide a goldmine of ideas as Third World nations look for badly needed fresh approaches to socioeconomic development.

REFERENCES

Aharoni, Yair. (1977). *Marketing, Planning and Development*. Cambridge, MA: Ballinger.

Collins, N.R., and R.H. Holton. (1963). "Programming Changes in Marketing in Planned Economic Development." *Kyklos*, pp. 123-135.

Chen, Chu-Yuan. (1982). *China's Economic Development: Growth and Structural Change*. Boulder, CO: Westview.

Drucker, Peter F. (1958). "Marketing and Economic Development." *Journal of Marketing*, 22 (January), pp. 252-259.

Kindra, G.S., ed. (1984). *Marketing in Developing Countries.* London: Croom Helm.

Muquiao, Xue. (1981). *China's Socialist Economy*. Beijing: Foreign Language Press.

Thorelli, Hans B. (1965). "Libermanism is not Liberalism." *Business Horizons,* 8 (Summer), pp. 45-48.

_____. (1981). "Consumer Policy for the Third World." *Journal of Consumer Policy,* Vol. 3, 197-211.

_____. (1982). "Chinese Middle Class Consumers Look at Marketing Issues." in *Proceedings of the Academy of International Business,* pp. 743-756.

_____. (1983). "Concepts of Marketing: A Review, Preview, and Paradigm." in *The Marketing Concept: Perspectives and Viewpoints,* P. Varadarajan, ed., American Marketing Association Workshop, Texas A&M University.

_____. (1984). "The People's Republic of China—Test Case of Market Socialism." *Vital Speeches of the Day,* November 15, pp. 66-68.

_____. (1986). "Consumer Emancipation and Economic Development." Paper prepared for the International Conference on Marketing and Development, Istanbul, September 1-4, 1986.

_____, Fu Shenzhao and Gerald D. Sentell. (1986). "The Middle Class and the Marketplace: The PRC, Overseas Chinese and Thailand." in *Advances in International Marketing*, S. Tamer Cavusgil, ed., Greenwich, CT: JAI Press.

NOTE

English-speaking readers will find rich materials on socioeconomic as well as political and cultural developments in the PRC in the various foreign language editions of the weekly *Beijing Review* and the *China Daily,* also published in Beijing. The Asian editions of the London *Economist*, and *The Wall Street Journal* are also well worth consulting, as are the official English translations of the PRC state documents.

SECTION V:
MARKETING IN SOCIALIST
COUNTRIES

In this section, global marketing issues and approaches which pertain to Socialist countries of East Europe and the People's Republic of China, and marketing to developing countries of the Far East are explored conceptually and analytically.

In the first chapter Naor and Bod state that, under the Hungarian economic system following the 1968 reforms, central planning has relied increasingly on macroeconomic steering and regulation. Within this framework, innovative government-guided economic institution building has taken place, particularly since the mid-1970s.

This chapter presents a Hungarian development-stage model, leading from early post-World War II reconstruction and industrialization, through a post-1968 decision-making decentralization stage, to a structural decentralization stage. The focus of the article is on this third stage, from the mid-1970s to date, in which structural organizational decentralization and orientation types of changes, and institution building (such as those involving the introduction of entrepreneurship) are achieving increasing prominence. It is suggested that the Hungarian developmental experience, as outlined in the stages-model that is provided, is particularly appropriate for developing or medium-developed countries with weakly or nonfunctioning markets which attempt simultaneously to achieve or maintain Socialist equity principles regarding distribution, as is the case in Hungary. Hungary's experience may thus provide valuable developmental lessons for countries attempting to achieve such aims, regardless of their ideological orientation.

Negotiations with managers from diverse cultures are becoming an integral part of the international business dealings. In negotiating with the Chinese managers, American businessmen in most cases encounter difficulties due to their lack of understanding of the Chinese cultural system and the way business is done in China. The purpose of the chapter by Brunner and Koh is to ascertain the degree of understanding (or misunderstanding) between American and Chinese negotiators on issues germane to negotiating in China.

The successful global marketing of United States products and services calls for a critical understanding of the way business is conducted overseas. Basic to long-term trade and other business relationships between the U.S. and the People's Republic of China is the mutual understanding of how each party behaves before, during, and after contract negotiations. This research effort represents the first of its kind in an empirical investigation of the perceptions of negotiating behavior held by American and Chinese negotiators. Data were collected through a questionnaire which was mailed to 180 major Chinese organizations located in Beijing, Shanghai, Guangzhou, and Luoyong, and 150 American corporations who are primarily members of the National Council for United States-China Trade. An overall usable response rate of 47.9 percent was achieved (47.2 percent for the Chinese and 48.7 percent for the American respondents). This study focuses on 52 attitudinal statements of perceptions dealing with negotiating activities in China. A summary of t-test results comparing whether attitudes held by American and Chinese negotiators differed on each of the 52 statements is presented in a table.

According to the findings of this study, American and Chinese negotiators appear to agree on several of the formalities attached to the initial meeting, except on the issue of the letter of intent. The American and Chinese negotiators differed in their negotiating styles, especially on their perceptions concerning the need to be enthusiastic and patient. Great perceptual differences were observed between the respective negotiators on the use of criticism as a negotiating tool. The Chinese take a long-term view of the contractual agreement, and they tend to favor large well-known companies. Finally, it is helpful to understand "face" behavior as it is practiced by the Chinese. Hence, American businessmen must avoid actions which may cause the Chinese to lose face.

It is suggested by Hisrich and Peters that the importance of the long-term market possibilities of trade with China and the U.S.S.R. is increasingly recognized by U.S. manufacturers. The market potential of these two countries is significant, as each has a large population and geographic area including untapped resources. Current U.S.-Soviet and U.S.-China trade reflects both the potential of this trade by its growth and its sensitivity to the political environment by its volatility.

In order to maintain continued growth, it is important for manufacturers presently engaged in trade with either or both of these two countries to expand their activity; and for those others not presently involved, it is important that they be encouraged to begin trade with these countries. Knowing the value of establishing a long-term market area, manufacturers' trade with China involved a wide variety of products such as specialty chemicals, consumer goods, sporting goods, minerals, and raw materials. The U.S. government could facilitate an increase in this trade activity by developing a comprehensive trade policy and by providing more support, particularly in such areas as reducing the time needed to obtain an export license and assisting in advertising and public relations.

Although willing to varying degrees, non-trading manufacturing firms indicated that their lack of trade activity was due to concerns about the amount of time that would be required by senior management, the high initial investment needed, and financing of trade arrangements. Government assistance could also help alleviate some of these concerns for this group of firms. Seminars on financing alternatives, provision of marketing and distribution support, and hosting trade exhibits for interested manufacturing companies would reduce senior management time demands while helping to ensure successful market entry. Through these and other support efforts, trade can be increased between the U.S. and these two countries with a potential for a positive impact on the balance of trade and payments for the United States along with the usual benefits from trade for each country involved.

Today's China is a market with considerable potential for Western exporters. The chapter by Kirpalani and Robinson provides an overview of China as a market and reviews some relevant Canadian literature on the determinants of export success. It also reports the findings of a recent survey of successful Canadian exporters to China, suggesting some lessons which may be learned from analyses of those findings.

China's exports and imports, at $30 billion each, are three times greater than what they were in the mid-1970s. China's Five Year Plan (1986-1990) is targeted on transforming and enlarging a number of industrial sectors. A goal also is to upgrade the technology of enterprises. Further, China has become a fiercely competitive market.

The survey sample consisted of 33 successful Canadian exporters. Along with a clearly developed corporate mission and a commitment to exporting, top management effort, internal organizational structure and control of information were the most important factors for export success. Government assistance also turned out to be important.

Lessons to be learned are that small firms can be as successful as large ones, and that top management visits to status-conscious Chinese bureaucrats are a critical factor for success. Further, use of home-government operational and financial assistance services saves exporters considerable time and effort. Moreover, at headquarters, firms must designate one or more specific persons as responsible for the China market and must also employ at least one Chinese-speaking person. Exporters should try to deliver competitively priced product/services that are state-of-the-art technology, unique, or specialized. Chinese buyers and end users must be made fully aware of the product/services and the firm's capability in regard to delivery and training. Exporters should select a representative/agent with "guanki," or good personal connections. The most effective method of promotion in China is personal contact through trade shows, technical seminars, sales calls, and the sponsorship of buyers' visits to headquarters.

As China prepares to implement its eighth five-year plan (1991-1995), the possibilities for joint ventures (JVs) in China look better than ever. Knowles and Mathur discuss various strategic and negotiating factors that affect the formation of JVs in China. JVs in

China are particularly attractive due to access to raw materials, access to comparatively cheap labor, and access to numerically the world's largest consumer market. Strategic factors that need to be recognized are labor, materials, land and building, transfer of technology, external and internal markets, government regulations, transfer pricing, taxes, foreign personnel auditing procedures, and foreign exchange. Knowles and Mathur provide specific guidelines for negotiating favorable clauses for inclusion in the JV agreement. The authors explain how specific incentives for the Chinese JV partner can be negotiated so that JV products can be successfully sold in China.

The financing of the JV is partially a function of the desired level of equity held in the JV by each partner. The foreign partner generally contributes technology, machinery and working capital. There are certain advantages to financing through debt capital. The emerging financial markets in China can be viewed as one additional source of capital, while link financing is another source of debt capital.

China can be considered to provide a role model for other developing countries. Firms gaining experience in China may be able to transfer their learning to other developing countries. From a public policy viewpoint, countries that encourage China trade may be enhancing the abilities of their domestic firms to compete globally.

Chapter 17

Innovative State-Guided Economic Institution Building in Hungary — Some Developmental Lessons for Countries with Insufficiently Competitive Markets

Jacob Naor
Peter Akos Bod

SUMMARY. The Hungarian post-1968 experience provides some instructive examples of innovative government initiated and guided economic institution building. Such institution building appears suitable to an environment characterized by underdeveloped market conditions, and was designed to modernize the economy and increase its competitiveness, leading thereby to a society-wide raising of living standards. Several reform-based structural, organizational and orientational measures are presented, and their particular evolution in response to economic development needs, or economic policy orientations, is discussed. Special emphasis is laid throughout on the changing role of the state regarding economic development. A developmental-stages model of the Hungarian economy, to which these changes are related, is proposed. The Hungarian experience, as outlined in the model and in the related institutional changes, may well provide lessons for other countries attempting to achieve similar developmental goals under similar market conditions.

In Western economic development literature, economic development and market development appear traditionally to be closely

---

This chapter was first published in the *Journal of Global Marketing*, Vol. 2(1) 1988.

linked (see e.g., Bauer & Yamey, 1957; Friedman, 1962; Johnson, 1971; Little, 1982). It is certainly true that developed market economies with their sophisticated commodity, services, and financial institutions have provided to date some of the highest per capita consumption levels. However, economic history of nations in both East and West does not appear to have provided an exclusive route to what may be considered the "desired stage" of mass consumption. Indeed, even the definitions and conceptualizations of "market development" and of the "market" concept itself appear to vary substantially, leading in turn to differing developmental implications even in the case of countries that have chosen the "market" route.

The last two centuries have thus recorded varying attempts aimed at achieving economic development. For underdeveloped nations, there exists a permanent temptation to search for developmental shortcuts. Such search is the essence of most national planning attempts, not only in socialist countries but in economies on the "periphery" of world developments as well (Gerschenkron, 1966). The search for "better" ways to achieve rapid economic development continues thus to occupy a central place of importance, particularly in the radical "anti-market" development literature (Amin, 1974; Gunder Frank, 1967). The case of Hungary, a small, innovation bent, trade-dependent East-European country that has chosen a particular plan-and-market "blend," bridging in effect national planning and market-based systems, may therefore elicit broad professional interest.

Hungarian Economic Development post-World War II may be viewed, in general terms, as taking place either in the period prior to the watershed reforms of 1968, or in the period following the 1968 reforms. While the pre-reform development period involved rapid industrialization in the mold of a Soviet-style centrally planned economy, the post-1968 period saw the introduction of radical changes. It is on changes occurring during this period, in areas pertaining to structure, organization and orientation, and on the role of government in bringing about such changes, that this chapter will focus.

In particular, it will be argued that, under conditions of insufficiently competitive markets, changes of this kind, centrally planned and centrally "guided," were needed to permit some major shifts in economic policy orientation, as indicated in Table 1. Reform oriented changes, particularly those introduced since 1968, were thus designed to move the economy increasingly from a production orientation to a market orientation, stressing both domestic and foreign market needs. Both the macro structural environment, as well as the micro organizational and orientational environments of the

Table 1

Hungarian Development-Stages Model

Stages	Economic policy orientation	Characteristics
Stage I reconstruction, industrialization (1945 - 1968)	production	. priority investments in heavy industries . medium to low product quality . administratively determined distribution . specialized, monopolistic producers . exclusive public ownership . low priority assigned to exports
Stage II decision-making decentralization, monetarization, and "profit-ization" (1968-mid-70s)	"sales"	. rapidly increasing per capita consumption . increased attention to quality and consumer needs . market determined distribution of consumer goods, administratively determined distribution of basic services . elements of market competition . emerging small-scale private business . increasing foreign trade dependence
Stage III Structural and Organizational decentralization, introduction of entrepeneurship (mid-1970s to date)	market (inter-national and domestic)	. depletion of easily mobilizable resources . increased market orientation both as to goods and services . attention to structural and organizational innovations . increased price and non-price competition . increased intersectoral competition amongst state, co-op, private institutions . strong foreign trade dependence . introduction of entrepreneurial organizations

firm had to undergo significant changes to permit the meeting of such markets-related needs. The important role of centrally planned measures in stimulating the operation of market forces, "guiding" such stimulation carefully in the process, will be pointed out. Hungarian reformers felt such central measures to be essential if changes were to be implemented rapidly, effectively, and in harmony with national socioeconomic development goals. It is argued that, given the desire to maintain an economic system based on ideologically prescribed equity principles,[1] under conditions of weakly functioning or nonfunctioning markets, organizational, structural and orientational changes of the kind described here are vitally needed to achieve results akin to those met in highly developed market economies, provided that they be aimed specifically at raising *society-wide* living standards. The Hungarian experience could thus provide valuable lessons to developing countries in both East and West, aiming for a similarly targeted economic development under similar underdeveloped market conditions.

A DEVELOPMENT-STAGES MODEL OF THE HUNGARIAN ECONOMY

Hungarian post-World War II economic history has witnessed several major changes in economic policy, affecting in a fundamental way the structure and performance of the economy. A development path, progressing from concerns with supply to increasing concerns with demand, a nationwide, government guided, learning by experience process, has been characteristic of this period, which allows in turn the identification of some highly differentiated development stages.

A model indicating the major post-World War II developmental stages of the Hungarian economy is presented in Table 1. Although the identification of precise boundaries for any particular stage is open for debate, Hungarian and foreign students of Hungarian economic developments tend to agree that Hungarian economic developments may be seen as a three-stage process, as presented, taking place either in the pre-1968 period or in the period following the 1968 reforms (Bognar, 1985; Nyers, 1983; Hare, Radice, & Swain, 1981).

STAGE I:
RECONSTRUCTION AND INDUSTRIALIZATION
UNDER UNDEVELOPED MARKET CONDITIONS

The first stage of the development process, encompassing the two decades preceding the fundamental reforms of 1968, appears to be characteristically production oriented, taking place in an environment characterized by an extreme neglect, indeed suppression, of market forces. Following the Soviet example of rapid industrialization, Hungarian policy makers concentrated available resources on establishing a robust industrial base involving basic industries such as heavy machinery and engineering works, mining, chemical industries, and construction, in addition to efforts to modernize, along collective lines, the traditional agricultural sector.

It must be recalled, that the country had, prior to World War II, passed through an earlier industrialization phase which, unlike the situation in some other East-European socialist countries, had seen the establishment of some large export-oriented enterprises in Hungary (i.e., the GANZ enterprise producing cranes, engines, turbines, and power stations; TUNGSRAM in the electrical industry; PALMA [TAURUS] in the rubber industry; PICK and HERTZ in food processing; RICHTER in the pharmaceutical industry, etc.). Much of that had, however, seen severe war damage and was in dire need of reconstruction. To the credit of the rapid industrialization policy that followed, the first post-war years saw rapidly rising growth rates, as indicated in Table 2.

Economic growth rates may conceal significant developmental deficiencies, however. Thus, due to the exclusive emphasis ac-

Table 2

Annual Average Increase of Industrial Production in Hungary
Percentages

1951-55:	13.2
1956-60:	7.5
1961-65:	7.8
1966-70:	6.3
1971-75:	6.4
1976-80:	3.4
1981-85:	2.2

Source: Statisztikai Evkonyv, Statistical Yearbook, Budapest, 1985.

corded at that time to increases in the output of basic industrial
sectors, low priority had to be assigned to product quality, product
and process innovation, consumer needs and foreign market development considerations. In the absence of serious quality and demand constraints, growth statistics may clearly be but partial indicators of economic development. In addition, high growth rates, as
indicated in Table 2, did not prove to be lasting phenomena. As
pointed out by F. Janossy (1971), the high growth rates achieved in
the post-World War II period by Hungary must be viewed as part of
a post-war reconstruction pattern exhibited by many war-destroyed
economies, including those of Germany, Italy and Japan.

By the early sixties the reconstruction drive appeared to have lost
its original momentum. This may be seen in the slowdown exhibited by Hungarian industrial growth rates. The almost totally na-
tionalized Hungarian economy was now faced with challenges
which were similar in many respects to those of dynamic non-So-
cialist market economies. Participation in world trade in particular
appeared to be increasingly essential to continued rapid economic
development. As indicated in Table 3, Hungary's dependence
on foreign trade has indeed seen continued increases from the early
1950s to the mid-1980s. The problems faced in the post-reconstruction phase by Hungary may thus not be atypical. A production ori-

Table 3

Hungarian Foreign Trade

	Exports (As percent of GDP)	Imports (As percent of GDP)
1950	13.4	15.6
1955	16.8	18.4
1960	19.3	26.3
1965	27.4	34.6
1970	32.0	42.8
1975	37.2	45.5
1980	43.7	46.5
1984	48.0	41.0

Note: at constant 1981 prices

Source: Statisztikai Evkonyv, Statistical Yearbook, Budapest, 1985.

entation-based development appeared less and less suitable to meet newly emerging developmental challenges.

STAGE II:
DECISION-MAKING DECENTRALIZATION, MONETARIZATION AND "PROFITIZATION"

The realization of needed changes led to the introduction in 1968 of the so-called New Economic Mechanism (NEM) reform. This represented a centrally planned and guided[2] effort designed to move the economy rapidly to a post-reconstruction stage that would permit the economy to respond effectively to newly arising internal and external challenges. An extensive literature has emerged dealing with the characteristics and significance of the NEM (for example, Hare, Radice, & Swain, 1981; Bognar, 1985; Szamuely, 1984; Antal, 1981). As indicated by the proposed stages model, two important features characterize this developmental stage: the decentralization of decision making and monetarization, aimed at moving the economy increasingly from an exclusive emphasis on output to an emphasis on "saleable" output, i.e., sales.

In order to bring about a basic shift in enterprise managers' orientations, that would lead to increased attention to sales rather than output, the post-1968 decentralization saw changes designed to confer on productive enterprises increased decision making autonomy while retaining their state-owned character. The state essentially withdrew from day-to-day economic decision making, while retaining macro economic policy-making authority. Post-1968, Hungarian central planners stopped issuing production targets in physical terms to enterprise managers. The latter were increasingly on their own in defining market needs, working out production and distribution plans, making plant related investment decisions and the like. Such changes resulted indeed in rapid increases in consumption, undoubtedly due in no small measure to increased attention to the quality of goods, based on greater attention to consumer needs.

Economic "Monetarization," involving an increased reliance on transactions based on monetary and market relationships, may as well be seen to accompany decentralization in Hungary. Furthermore, individually arrived-at transactions between autonomous economic agents were carried out now increasingly with the aim of attaining profit and revenue related benefits independent of physical units calculations. Under the post-reform rules of the game, state-owned and cooperative business units had to show profits in order to finance desired capital formation, or hire labor and the like, all within the context of competition for resources and markets. A series of price reforms, freeing prices increasingly from central control, had been initiated starting in 1957, permitting enterprises to a growing extent to stress such newly developing market relationships.

In addition, increasing attention was being paid now to marketing research at the enterprise as well as at higher ministerial levels. Large institutes specializing in market research were formed for this purpose, providing a full range of services to enterprise or ministry clients. Knowledge of market needs and requirements was thus increasingly recognized as essential for the successful conduct of business operations.

STAGE III:
MARKET-ORIENTED STRUCTURAL,
ORGANIZATIONAL, AND ORIENTATIONAL CHANGES

While freeing economic units from overly burdensome central administration, additional steps were needed to change the nature of economic organizations. Changes were brought about in this stage through the utilization of a threefold approach involving the following: structural innovations or renovation (macro-decentralization measures), organizational changes (micro-decentralization measures), as well as orientational measures of a radical nature. It is on these changes, characteristic of Stage III of the proposed model, that this chapter will focus, arguing that, in the absence of sufficiently competitive markets, and given the requirement of *planned* economic development designed to bring about *society-wide* increases in living standards, such centrally initiated and guided measures[3] appeared needed to permit the emergence of an orientation that would be responsive to newly emerging internal and external market needs. It is argued that the Hungarian experience may well provide lessons for other countries attempting to achieve similar developmental goals under similar market conditions.

Structural Macro-Decentralization

The 1968 Economic Reform, aimed, amongst other things, at increasing the responsiveness of enterprises to market needs. Many of the previously strong formal linkages between state agencies and state-owned enterprises (SOEs) were then abruptly abolished. Economic planning emerged as a policy formation process in which central agencies and enterprises were assigned separate institutional goals: Macroeconomic targeting and profit-maximization, respectively. However, the increased autonomy and enlarged decision-making domain granted enterprises following the reform, saw little utilization immediately following the reform (Antal, 1981). The ability of the authorities to intervene remained strong, since top management at SOEs continued to be ministry-appointed and their activities continued to be evaluated by the supervising branch ministries.

Delaying the introduction of some presumably sensitive changes may have been deliberate, however. At the time of the introduction of the NEM, policy makers appeared to aim at minimizing excessive shocks that major reforms of this kind could be expected to bring about, shocks that may well have solidified opposition to the measures. For that reason, the prearranged program to split up large scale industrial and trade organizations, in monopoly (monopsony) situations, was delayed. The total number of enterprises continued to remain low, an inheritance of the socialist industrialization phase (Phase I of the model) and of the former highly centralized planning practices. (Fewer large scale enterprises were clearly easier to supervise from the planning center than would be the case with a larger number of enterprises.) Consequently, competition continued to remain weak, with large enterprises remaining in monopoly (oligopoly) situations. With insufficiently strong market incentives and threats, technical development and marketing efforts continued to lag. During the 1970s, it became increasingly clear that the large enterprises were able to efficiently block market competition within the state sector, while, not surprisingly, appearing increasingly unable to face foreign competition, as well as that of small scale private domestic businesses, in those cases where such competition was permitted. Major structural changes were clearly called for.

Some major steps taken in this direction involved the *deconcentration, demerger drive*, delayed in industry for reasons mentioned previously until 1981-83. This involved the splitting up of large, horizontal enterprises, which brought about finally a significant increase in the number of state and cooperatively owned enterprises (see Table 4).

Concomitant with the deconcentration drive, activity-related regulations of SOEs were changed as well, providing managements of SOEs much needed products-services related rights of diversification. They could henceforth form subsidiaries unrelated to the "product-profile" of the parent company. Such major structural reforms were clearly aimed at providing increased competitive pressures in domestic markets, making foreign transactions more attractive in the process.

Smaller enterprise size was expected to lead to increased managerial flexibility, greater attention to product innovation and an increasing orientation towards market needs and requirements, both domestic and international. Structural changes of this kind were considered essential *preconditions* to the emergence of what reformers expected would be a new managerial style that would be entrepreneurially oriented, and would result in the emergence of market-need responsive behavior. The dismantling of large-scale monopolistic organizations was deemed an essential first step in this direction.

Table 4

Number of non-private industrial organizations

(at the end of the year)

sector	1970	1980	1982	1985
state-owned enterprises	812	699	726	974
cooperatives	821	661	715	956

Source: Statisztikai Evkonyv, Statistical Yearbook, Budapest, 1985.

Organizational Micro-Decentralization

In order to create organizational preconditions for an entrepreneurially oriented management style at SOEs, internal, enterprise-centered, decentralization steps appeared needed. One of the most significant steps in this direction involved a new, state-introduced selection process of top enterprise managers. The right to nominate, appoint, and evaluate top managerial executives was indeed transferred, for most of the SOEs, from ministries to the enterprises themselves. Such reforms were apparently delayed until the previously mentioned demerger measures were well underway. As a result, depending on the size of the organization, the recent (1985) *Reform of Enterprise Management* provides the following three management forms for enterprises:

- Enterprise Councils (ECs) for large and medium sized SOEs
- General Assemblies for smaller enterprises
- Public Administration Control bodies for large scale utilities and select, strategically important large enterprises.

Briefly, enterprise councils, the focus of the decentralization effort, consist of management representatives and delegates of employees and workers. Nonmanagement representatives are elected for a five-year term, and, significantly, at least fifty percent of council seats are reserved for them. The remainder are occupied by management representatives, which partly serve exofficio, while others are appointed to the council by the director-general, who himself is appointed or dismissed by the council, in agreement with the appropriate supervising body (ministry, etc.) (Ministry of Finance, 1984, p. 26). As the interests of most council members lie in the profitable functioning of the firm, top management is expected to divert its attention and resources increasingly from attempts at gaining the "benevolence" of the authorities to the more desirable task of meeting market requirements.

Even greater "democratization" is provided for smaller enterprises. In these cases, an assembly of all employees elects the director-general, as well as an executive management, from among candidates either inside or outside the enterprise. Such grass-roots based self-administration was expected to provide the preconditions of a non-bureaucratic management style and bring about an increased identification with the firm by workers and management alike. It was expected that such changes, based on similar, extremely successful organizational changes introduced earlier in Hungarian agricultural and industrial cooperatives, would lead to similar results in industry, i.e., to the identification and exploitation of profitable market opportunities.

Lastly, the "public administration" category of enterprises included public utilities and large enterprises of national importance. At such enterprises the procedure of hiring and firing managers remained unchanged; i.e., in the hands of the supervising ministry. As an orientation based solely on profit could not be applied directly to enterprises of this kind, managerial motivation to meet plan-determined objectives in a resource-efficient manner continued to be based in this case on the traditional twin "levers" of financial incentives and direct administrative regulations.

As stated, organizational changes of this kind, similar in broad outline to earlier managerial reforms introduced in Yugoslavia, appeared needed, in the Hungarian context, to bring about desired changes in economic policy orientation. However, both the structural as well as the organizational changes indicated may well be seen as applicable as well to public sector enterprises beyond the confines of the East-bloc. Deconcentration, as a means of reducing bureaucratic tendencies, has indeed been employed on occasion in the public sector in Western economies, although less frequently than in the private sector. Similarly, organizational changes along the lines indicated in the preceding may see application, in one form or another, in economies of the "mixed" kind, a form that is often characteristic of many Western economies. Such "participatory" and "democratic" management may lead to a much needed increase in identification of managers and employees with their enterprises, while reducing the links between the enterprise and the state. This would tend to prod managers to rely less on state "guidance" or assistance, and more on market efforts.

Entrepreneurially Oriented Changes

While structural and organizational decentralization changes of the kind provided earlier were clearly recognized by Hungarian reformers as necessary, they were, at the same time, recognized as insufficient. Managements' orientations, its way of thinking and behaving, had to see some fundamental change that would find support from central authorities in order to achieve the aims of Phase III, as indicated in the economic development model. Thus, another important set of organizational-orientational innovative changes saw light in Hungary as of early 1982.[4] These were aimed at introducing specific environment-tailored entrepreneurial forms in both the private and public sectors of the economy (Miller & Lehoczky, 1984; Naor & Bod, 1986a). Numerous, newly developed organizational structures were then introduced with the basic aim of bringing about a more entrepreneurial, risk-taking style of management. A more detailed examination of some of these forms appears warranted, since they were designed to permit the achievement of the policy orientation of Phase III of the model, *without* destroying the existing structures of state-owned organizations.

Thus, *contractual-agreements*, or rental or lease arrangements, between state enterprises and private entrepreneurs were now introduced. Under such contracts, nonprofitable state-owned facilities, service units, or outlets might be offered for public bidding. Contracts were then concluded with the highest bidders for a maximum of five years. Under such agreements, private entrepreneurs paid a fixed annual fee to the sponsoring SOE that retained ownership, but enjoyed total freedom to organize the business within the broadly defined business policy of the parent enterprise. Entrepreneurs could now employ up to fifteen employees.

In practice, such lump sum rental fee arrangements forced the entrepreneurs to increase turnover and minimize labor cost. As a result, formerly nonprofitable state-owned units have more often than not registered healthy profits under this novel arrangement. Referring again to the third stage of the development-stages model, such operations may easily be shown to contribute to such desirable goals as increased market orientation, increased price and non-price competition, enhanced resource utilization, and the like. The innovative "grafting" of entrepreneurship onto the public enterprise, appears designed to "rejuvenate" the latter since the improved performance of the entrepreneurial unit could not fail to impact on the performance of the "parent" unit.

Autonomous In-Company Business-Work Partnerships

While contractual arrangements of the kind mentioned provided a much needed "external" graft of entrepreneurship to large state-owned enterprises, an "*internal*" (in-company) graft appeared needed as well. Thus, *employees* of sponsoring enterprises could now, for example, rent idle factory facilities or equipment, and run those after hours or on weekends, governed by specific contracts between the enterprise and the in-house partnership. The 1982 legislation authorized such partnerships within the public sector. An in-company partnership acts, therefore, in most cases, as an SOE-sponsored, highly specialized subcontractor. Such partnerships might sell their products/services either solely to the sponsoring enterprise or to other customers. In practice, most of the partnerships' business would be conducted with the parent enterprise.

Members of such partnerships differ significantly from workers doing simple overtime jobs for two important reasons. First, the work organization is totally up to the enterprising members who frequently fulfill tasks which are different from their position within the parent enterprise. Secondly, there are much needed elements of marketing and entrepreneurial activity involved, primarily in those externally oriented cases where contracts permit product/market choices to be made.

This innovative form of entrepreneurship, in particular, has achieved considerable dissemination, as indicated in Table 5. The number of those who wanted to join such partnerships increased rapidly in the year of introduction and has doubled annually since then. Recently, growth pertaining to this entrepreneurial form has slowed down somewhat. Nevertheless, the contribution of such partnerships towards enhanced market orientation may well be expected to have been considerable.

Table 5

Small scale business organizations

(at the end of the year)

	1982		1983		1984		1985	
	a	b	a	b	a	b	a	b
Contract-run retail outlets (or sub-units of enterprises)	5895	NA	9059	NA	10.769	NA	11.747	NA
Business-Work-Partnerships (In-Company)	2775	29.3	9192	98.0	17.337	196.0	23.165	262.9
Private-Work-Partnerships	2299	12.7	4831	25.4	7.346	42.5	9.312	60.5

a: Number of organizations
b: Number of participants (in thousands)
NA: Not available or not applicable

Source: Statisztikai Evkonyv, Statistical Yearbook, Budapest, 1985.

Private-Work Partnerships

In-company partnerships may at times decide to become independent and become private partnerships. The legal form involved had not been unknown in Hungary previously in certain professions (lawyers, contractors, teachers), and was now extended to such cases. Greater organizational flexibility was thus provided for. The new legislation authorized partnerships in various trades, just as under the in-house arrangement, combining partners up to a maximum of 30 persons. While the former organization would act within public sector enterprises, these partnerships would be of private character. In practice, however, most members retained their original, state-paid positions and assumed part time positions in such partnerships in addition to their regular work. One must clearly expect considerable "market-gap filling" types of activities from newly privatized organizations of this kind.

Legalized "Second-Economy" Related Activities

Since the early 1960s significant strata of entrepreneurially oriented Hungarian wage earners had been engaged in "moonlighting" activities of various sorts, such as car and home appliances maintenance, unlicensed taxi driving, animal husbandry, and the cultivation of household plots. In line with the entrepreneurial reforms touched upon, the government, in 1982, decided to strengthen its influence over the "second economy" by legalizing most of the activities involved. As an example, would-be private, part-time taxi drivers may now obtain licenses and registration at marginal cost, provided that the car is not older than six years, is in good condition, the name and address of the driver is prominently displayed, and a meter is provided. Illegal taxis have thus quickly disappeared in Hungary. Similar experiences have been chalked up in other trades and occupations. Market needs were clearly addressed here, bringing in addition greater competitive pressures to bear on existing cooperatively run or state-run organizations. It is interesting to note that "newly entering" part-time, private taxi drivers have shown a tendency to form autonomous professional associations, partial "cooperatives" in effect, in order to achieve economies of scale in servicing, maintenance, radio dispatch services, etc. Government initiated institution building is clearly evident here as well.

RECENT ENTREPRENEURSHIP-RELATED INFRASTRUCTURAL CHANGES

It may be instructive, at this point, to examine some of the latest, infrastructure-related changes pertaining to efforts to provide the newly introduced entrepreneurial forms some appropriate macroenvironmental conditions.

New Financing Instruments

Traditionally, budget allocations, subsidies and bank credits were, until 1983, the only financing instruments in Hungary. Since then, to provide for more effective capital distribution as well as enhanced scope for entrepreneurship, SOEs, municipalities, and cooperatives were given the right to issue bonds through banks. For that, such public sector agents had to obtain a prerequisite permit from the Ministry of Finance, since bonds of state-owned entities are guaranteed by the state. By the end of 1985 (excluding state bonds) such bonds issued amounted to 4.3 billion Forints, corresponding to about 2% of total annual investment in Hungary, and their volume was expected to increase. Banks have created a secondary market for bonds, and bond prices are published weekly. Since the spring of 1985, SOEs can, in addition, draw bills of exchange on banks, and banks discount and rediscount such bills. Entrepreneurial efforts of all kinds could thus draw on additional financial resources, openly traded, whose value, in the case of bonds, depended presumably on market performance.

Enterprise Assumption of Financial Responsibility

Public and private enterprises, under entrepreneurial conditions, may clearly on occasion run into financial difficulties endangering not only their own business viability but that of their customers as well. There has thus been a recognition of late of the need to institutionalize the financial settlement of corporate crises within public sector enterprises that have, since 1968, been forced to function on "business" principles. The 1970s and early 1980s saw indeed the liquidation of hundreds of medium to large scale cooperatives, thousands of small scale private businesses, but only a dozen large-scale SOEs, which the government presumably judged as being beyond rescue. The strengthening of market competition and the growing reluctance of the government to interfere in business affairs, even within the public sector, has led to an increasing number of such cases. The legislation thus issued, the Liquidation law (Fall 1986), was designed to safeguard the interests of stake holders in public and private firms. Under this law employees' claims to wages and salaries have priority under the liquidation process; other claims – including those of public agencies and banks – are to be met proportionally out of the mobilizable assets of the defaulted enterprise. Clearly, greater rewards as well as larger risks were now to be carried increasingly by economic units that saw structural as well as organizational decentralization, as well as an "infusion" of more entrepreneurially oriented management.

Early Introduction of Trading Houses

Finally, foreign trade could clearly not be expected to remain exempt from reform efforts involving decentralization efforts. The state monopoly of foreign trade has indeed gone through a profound evolution since the 1950s. The original concept had been built on the principle of monopoly-based specialized foreign trade companies. Under the NEM, since 1968, large industrial and agricultural enterprises and home trading chains could receive licenses to conduct foreign trade activities. At present (1986), the number of business units having such license exceeds 200, conducting approximately 20% of the total foreign trade (Berenyi, 1986). Since mid-1986, three state-owned foreign trading firms (Hungarotex, Konsumex, Transelektro) and one large cooperative chain (Skala-Coop) have been reorganized as trading houses, licensed to import and export *without branch restriction*. Furthermore, the state provided the trading houses substantial venture capital to enable them to organize export-destined production, set up joint ventures with foreign or domestic industrial enterprises, etc. These organizations have thus become increasingly entrepreneurially oriented, handling foreign-trade destined production, financing and distribution; a far cry indeed from the earlier, traditional foreign trade companies. It must be noted, however, that the trading-house concept is still at an early, experimental stage in Hungary at the present time. It will no doubt see further evolution and adaptation to the peculiar requirements of the domestic and foreign trade environments of Hungary. It is clear, however, that institution building, or "rebuilding," has been dealt with comprehensively by Hungarian reformers, and that the role of the state has been consistent: to initiate and guide developments, while, at the same time, encouraging and providing ample room for the unfolding of entrepreneurship.

CONCLUSIONS AND IMPLICATIONS

Under the post-1968 Hungarian economic system, central planning has relied increasingly on macro economic "steering and regulation." Production, sales, and much of capital formation were functions that were increasingly relegated, in principle and practice, to public and private (as well as mixed) enterprises. While political institutions, structures and values continue to assert that contemporary Hungary is a Socialist, collectivist society, the economic structure has evolved, in practice, into an interesting "blend" of planning cum market, albeit an insufficiently competitive market, that nevertheless requires increased attention to marketing research. It is that evolution that makes the Hungarian experience relevant to other developing countries with similar market structures.

The structural, organizational, and orientational arrangements that have evolved in Hungary appear to have been designed to move the economy increasingly from a "production" and "sales" orientation, to one geared towards the meeting of both domestic and foreign market needs. It may be too early to judge the success of such efforts, keeping in mind particularly the crushing effects of Hungary's large hard currency foreign debt, the repayment requirements of which effectively slowed down the much needed modernization of the economy. The evolution reviewed here offers, nevertheless, significant lessons as to the process and the institutional arrangements involved for other countries that face similar developmental tasks. It is argued that, in cases of mixed economies, structural, organizational, and orientational changes along the lines indicated here, to be adjusted and adapted in each case to the particular environment in question, may often be appropriate for "targeted" economic development, such as that instituted by Hungary. The Hungarian model thus appears appropriate for economies with some blend of market and planning that are intent on development that permits a simultaneous maintenance of an equitable income distribution structure.

Some particular lessons, regarding the role of the state in stimulating economic development under underdeveloped market conditions, that may be drawn from the experience provided, may be summarized as follows:

1. Efforts to modernize the economic structure should come from, and should be initiated by, those institutions that occupy a central place within the existing institutional structure. In centrally planned economies — and in most developing nations — this institution is the state. Particularly in those instances where development involves increases in the role of the private sector and, conse-

quently, the relative shrinkage of the public sector, effective and long-lasting changes cannot be reached given an unmotivated state machinery. The Hungarian experience indicates that there can be no real progress in the face of strong opposition from interests that hold central positions within the political structure. Indeed, change must come *from* that political structure. The modernization process has to involve profound changes in the role and orientation of precisely such decisive economic (and political) agents. The centrally initiated, and indeed centrally motivated, introduction of the profit motive into most of the public sector in Hungary, the decentralization of the day-to-day decision-making process from ministries to enterprise management, and the incorporation of various entrepreneurially oriented social strata into economic policy formation have all played, in our opinion, a decisive role in the successful implementation of Hungarian reforms designed to bring about a shift towards an orientation based on market needs.

2. The success of reform efforts of this kind appears to necessitate a profound *change of principles* — an example of which is provided by the introduction of a distinct, new orientation (the profit orientation) in Hungarian SOEs in 1968. An alternative strategy involving "small steps" can bear fruits only *after* major, qualitative changes have taken place. It appears that unless there is clear, and comprehensive, change of norms and orientations, which must of course be *appropriate* and *needed* in light of particular developmental stages, the forces that are detrimentally affected by the changes will inevitably try to restore the original status quo. (An example of that could be seen in Hungary in the early 1970s in connection with the worsening position of certain oversized, bureaucratic SOEs.) Another example is provided by the successful and highly popular introduction of entrepreneurship in Hungary. It was clearly appropriate and needed in the current stage of Hungarian economic development. As such, it may be considered a qualitative reform-related change of major proportions.

3. After changes in orientation have been implemented, the central agent in economic life — the state, in the context discussed above — has to be engaged, initially, in a detailed and continuous process of institution building. In Hungary, that activity characterizes the second and third phases of the post-1968 economic devel-

opment. At first, given a rapid state-induced industrialization process in the earlier stage, there appeared to be no immediate need to establish certain lacking market and exchange-related institutions. Following the reforms of 1968, those conditions changed rapidly, however, and both the concept of market-orientation as well as that of entrepreneurship have since been embraced wholeheartedly by Hungarian policy makers, who carefully designed and guided the institutional building process needed to implement such newly needed orientations.

4. A final critical development point: It is the state, given the experience at hand, that had (and has) to introduce or institutionalize market related entities. However, the state, following the Hungarian experience again, should withdraw to the extent possible, once the appropriate institutions have "taken hold," leaving the task of running most entrepreneurially oriented organizations to business agents. The continued "guidance" of the state is justified and needed, it appears, for some specific purposes only, such as the following; to provide macro-policy guidance to the economy; to mitigate the effects of insufficiently competitive market conditions due to excessive monopolization of production and distribution, through the kind of institution building detailed here; and lastly (for states subscribing to socialist principles), to ameliorate "undesirable" distributional market-effects, in line with egalitarian principles. Beyond that the state may presumably perceive its role as one of gradual withdrawal and self-diminution. This state-related self-constraint may constitute, possibly, the most difficult feature of an effective reform process. That this may be effectively achieved in practice however has been, and continues to be, demonstrated by the Hungarian experience.

NOTES

1. Socialist equity considerations, shared by a wide spectrum of "Socialist" countries whether in the East or West, and, discussed extensively elsewhere (Naor, 1986a), center, in principle, on a desire to maintain an egalitarian income and wealth distribution structure, based on the distributional principle of "to each according to his (work related) contribution," while providing at the same time adequate rewards for efficiency, based again on work and performance (Public Finance, 1984, p. 33).

2. Since 1968 Hungarian reformers have increasingly relied on "economic levers" (such as interest rates, prices, turn-over taxes, as well as administrative guidelines) to guide the economy, rather than on administrative "commands" that were characteristic of the reconstruction period.

3. Reference here will be to the highly instructive *role* of the government in bringing about desired changes. It would, in the Hungarian experience, introduce changes and then continue to *guide* institutional developments through the use of economic levers, *reducing* such guidance to the degree that market forces were judged to be sufficiently potent and able to substitute for administrative guidance. Such guidance would however not disappear altogether. *Some* administrative guidance would presumably be retained indefinitely, in order to ensure the continuation of an equitable income distribution process.

4. It is likely that reformers were conscious of the fact that a pool of *potential* entrepreneurs had to be in existence *prior* to the managerial reforms just alluded to. Hence, the indicated timing of these reform measures.

REFERENCES

Amin, S. (1974). *Accumulation on a World Scale* 2 vol., New York, London: Monthly Review Press, 1974.

Antal, L. (1983). "Historical Development of the Hungarian System of Economic Control and Management." *Acta Oeconomica*, Vol. 27/3-4.

Bauer, P.T. and Yamey, B. (1957). *The Economics of Underdeveloped Countries*. Chicago: The Free Press.

Berenyi, L. (1986). "The Organization of Foreign Trade in Hungary." *Hungarian Business Herald*, No. 1.

Bognar, J. (1985). "Evolution of Conception About Economic Policy and Control in Hungary in the Past Decades." *Acta Oeconomica*, Budapest, Vol. 34/3-4.

Friedman, M. (1962). *Capitalism and Freedom*. Chicago: The Free Press.

Gerschenkron, A. (1966). *Economic Backwardness in Historic Perspective*. Cambridge, MA, Harvard University Press.

Gunder, Frank A. (1967). *Capitalism and Underdevelopment in Latin America*. New York, London: Monthly Review Press.

Hare, P., Radice, H., and Swain, H. (eds.) (1981). *Hungary, A Decade of Economic Reform*. London: Longman.

Hirschman, A. (1958). *The Strategy of Economic Development*. New Haven: Yale.

Janossy, F. (1971). "Das Ende der Wirtschaftswunder-Erscheinung und Wesen der wirtschaftlichen Entwickulung," Frankfurt, Neue Kritik.

Johnson, H. (1971). "A Word to the Third World." *Encounter*, October.

Little, I. M. D. (1982). *Economic Development – Theory, Policy and International Relations.* New York: Basic Books.

Miller, R.L. and Lehoczky, Cs. K. (1984). "New Forms of Private Business in

Hungary: Some Economic and Social Implications." *Columbia Journal of World Business*, Vol. XIX. No. 4.

Naor, J. and Bod, P.A. (1986a). "Socialist Entrepreneurship in Hungary – Reconciling the Irreconcilables." *Columbia Journal of World Business*, Vol. XXI, No. 2, pp. 55-68, Summer.

Naor, J. and Bod, P.A. (1986b). "Some Economic Development Related Institutions Appropriated for Underdeveloped Market Conditions – The Hungarian Case." Proceedings of the International Conference on Marketing and Development, Istanbul, Turkey, Sept. 1-4, 1986.

Nyers, R. (1983). "Interrelation Between Policy and the Economic Reform in Hungary." *Journal of Comparative Economics*, 7.

Public Finance in Hungary. "Further Development of the Economic Control and Management System." Ministry of Finance, 1984, Budapest.

Szamuely, L. (1986). "The Second Wave of the Economic Mechanism Debate and the 1968 Reform in Hungary." *Acta Oeconomica*, Vol. 33/1-2.

Chapter 18

Negotiations in the People's Republic of China: An Empirical Survey of American and Chinese Negotiators' Perceptions and Practices

James A. Brunner
Anthony C. Koh

SUMMARY. The successful global marketing of United States products and services calls for a critical understanding of the way business is conducted overseas. Basic to long-term trade and other business relationships between the U.S. and the People's Republic of China is the mutual understanding of how each party behaves before, during, and after contract negotiations. This research effort represents the first of its kind in empirically investigating perceptions of negotiating behavior held by American and Chinese negotiators. The study investigated 52 attitudinal statements focused on negotiating activities and found more differences than similarities in views between U.S. and Chinese negotiators. Findings from this study should help to close this "perceptual gap of misunderstandings" and thus prove useful to both U.S. and Chinese businesspeople desiring to do business with each other.

INTRODUCTION

Napoleon described China as a "sleeping giant" and it appears to be awakening from its long sleep. In the past decade, Americans

This chapter was first published in the *Journal of Global Marketing*, Vol 2(1) 1988.

and other foreigners have initially viewed the People's Republic of China as a gigantic, untapped market potential with over a billion consumers. Many enthusiastically visited the country with the objective of opening its markets, but came away disillusioned for a variety of reasons. Some found that initial costs far exceeded their expectations; others found that risks were very real, and the payoffs less than anticipated; still others were frustrated by the Chinese bureaucracy — for example, having to deal with cumbersome custom policies and taxes. Perhaps, of more significance initially, is the lack of understanding of the Chinese cultural system and the way business is done in China.

China is being opened up for foreign trade and investments. In 1979, the total trade volume of China was U.S. $29.3 billion and this rose to $69.6 billion in 1985. By the end of 1985, $15.6 billion in foreign loans had been utilized, $4.6 billion for foreign direct investments had been made, and $1.3 billion in commercial credit agreements had been actually utilized. There have been more than 2,300 foreign joint ventures, 3,700 cooperative enterprises, and 120 fully-owned foreign enterprises established (Xie, 1987). Therefore, one can be reasonably optimistic that the "sleeping giant" has awakened. China desires to catch up with the rest of the world and wants to be in the forefront of the informational revolution now taking place (Hendryx, 1986).

Many authorities on Sino-American trade have endeavored to enlighten prospective businessmen concerning the peculiarities of Chinese negotiations (for example, see Harner, 1980; Hendryx, 1986; Pye, 1982, 1986; Terry, 1984; Wilson, 1979, 1981; Xie, 1987). American businessmen have been cautioned about the Chinese sensitivities to "face," "guanxi," the need to be extra patient, the long line of bureaucracy, the use of stalling tactics, the importance of using formal titles rather than first names, the critical need for pre-negotiating social get-togethers, post-contract behavior, and other similar Chinese negotiating practices or assumptions. While much has been written about these topics, one wonders whether American businessmen have learned from these studies and consequently have narrowed the "perceptual gap of misunderstandings" in doing business in China. In a similar vein, one would also think that Chinese businessmen have been learning about the American way of doing business. While the Americans view China as a vast, untapped market, likewise, the Chinese view the vast U.S. market as virtually untapped. Given these two parallel forces of "trying to understand each other," one wonders whether the East and West have finally met. Thus, the objective of this research effort is to empirically ascertain the degree of understanding (or misunderstanding) between American and Chinese negotiators on issues germane to negotiating activities in China. Where significant differences exist, then the findings from this study should prove to be useful to both American and Chinese businessmen desiring to do business together.

METHODOLOGY

Data were collected through a mail questionnaire mailed to 180 major Chinese organizations and corporations located in Beijing, Shanghai, Guangzhou, and Luoyong, and 150 American corporations who are primarily members of the National Council for United States-China Trade. All sample elements have conducted negotiations in China. The questionnaire was translated into Chinese and retranslated back into English. This chapter only focuses on 52 attitudinal statements dealing with perceptions about negotiating activities in China. A five-point Likert rating scale ranging from "1 = strongly agree" to "5 = strongly disagree" was used to measure the degree to which the Chinese and American negotiators agreed with each of the statements.

A total of 178 responses was received: 105 from the Chinese and 73 from the American corporations. However, 20 of the Chinese responses were excluded from the analysis as they were not answered appropriately for the research. Thus, an overall usable response rate of 47.9 percent was achieved (47.2 percent for the Chinese and 48.7 percent for the American respondents).

Two kinds of analyses are presented in Table 1: (1) the percentage of American and Chinese respondents who agreed (combination of those who "agree" or "strongly agree") compared to those who disagreed ("disagree" or "strongly disagree" combined), and (2) t-test analyses comparing whether mean attitudes on each of the

TABLE 1. Degree of Agreement with Attitudinal Statements by American and Chinese Negotiators

Attitudinal Statement	Percent American	
	Agree (N=73)	Disagree
A. The Initial Meeting and Agreement		
1. Prefer top official when starting negotiations.	63	30
2. The spirit of the Law of Intent of a contract is more important than its details.	34	58
3. Get initial agreement on general spirit before negotiating on specific details.	95	4
4. It is preferable to use formal titles rather than last names.	74	15
5. It is essential to have an interpreter for formal and informal negotiations.	84	11
6. Informal communications are as important as written documents.	33	61
7. One of the major benefits of negotiations is social activities such as dinners, sightseeing, etc.	30	60
B. Negotiating Styles		
8. One should be passive and not express enthusiasm.	29	53
9. Patience is a necessary negotiating skill.	100	0
10. The typical American businessman does not have the patience to negotiate skillfully.	67	23
C. Guanxi		
11. Emotional transactions are to be encouraged to bind parties together.	31	40
12. Chinese more than Americans try to create emotional ties with the other team.	34	55
13. Guanxi implies a special relationship and is to be encouraged.	54	8
14. Guanxi implies relationships which continue over a lengthy period of time on the same level though the parties may not communicate.	58	10
15. In a guanxi, the stronger party is more deeply obligated than the weaker one.	28	31

Percent Chinese (N=89)		Group Means		T-test	Views Compared**				
Agree	Disagree	American	Chinese	(p-level)	1	Am	Ch	Am	Ch
						2		3	
63	16	2.48	2.38	.583	X				
59	26	3.36	2.66	.000*				D	A
91	4	1.63	1.87	.060	X				
63	15	2.15	2.45	.050	X				
86	5	1.84	1.78	.709	X				
34	43	3.28	3.13	.351	X				
21	58	3.51	3.49	.944					
5	62	3.27	3.68	.004*		D	D+		
94	1	1.05	1.62	.000*		A+	A		
11	50	2.38	3.40	.000*				A	D
74	10	3.10	2.28	.000*				D	A
43	18	3.23	2.75	.003*				D	A
44	39	2.44	2.92	.001*		A+	A		
44	34	2.44	2.86	.004*		A+	A		
27	36	3.04	3.08	.769	X				

TABLE 1 (continued)

Attitudinal Statement	Percent American Agree (N=73)	Disagree
16. One of the objectives of negotiations is to cause one to feel strong and have a sense of obligation to the other.	18	65
17. In a guanxi relation one may be criticized if he does not meet his obligations to the other.	51	19
18. If one receives a gift or benefit from a guanxi partner, he need not feel a sense of indebtedness and need to reciprocate.	27	32
19. Essential to follow the rules of etiquette when negotiating.	90	4
20. One can raise one's reputation by helping others raise their self esteem.	89	3
21. Americans have more difficulty than Chinese in building up the self esteem of the other team of negotiators.	32	36
22. If one does not grant favors to a joint partner, he is not abiding by the spirit of their relationship.	22	53
D. The Use of Criticism		
23. One can positively influence another party by embarrassing him.	0	100
24. Criticism is generally expected while negotiating and one should not be upset about it.	58	31
25. Chinese are more concerned than Americans about being criticized about their actions.	83	6
26. If one makes a mistake, it should be pointed out to him because he will make concessions for it.	10	63
E. The Use of Stalling		
27. Americans use stalling techniques more than Chinese.	3	77
28. Negotiators frequently stall to give time for discussions with higher authorities.	89	5
29. Delaying and stalling adversely affect terms of contracts.	10	60

Percent		Group Means		T-test	Views Compared**					
Chinese					1	2		3		
Agree	Disagree	American	Chinese	(p-level)		Am	Ch	Am	Ch	
	(N=89)									
42	29	3.53	2.84	.000*				D	A	
36	21	2.63	2.85	.110	X					
51	37	3.03	2.82	.171	X					
88	6	1.75	1.97	.076	X					
82	2	1.97	2.05	.452	X					
10	28	3.08	3.16	.566	X					
38	35	3.38	2.89	.003*				D	A	
16	51	4.59	3.48	.000*		D+	D			
80	8	2.68	2.23	.002*		A	A+			
55	7	1.92	2.44	.000*		A+	A			
63	22	3.64	2.57	.000*				D	A	
17	40	4.22	3.27	.000*		D+	D			
57	15	1.89	2.53	.000*		A+	A			
53	19	3.53	2.62	.000*				D	A	

TABLE 1 (continued)

Attitudinal Statement	Percent American (N=73)	
	Agree	Disagree
F. Sharing Responsibilities and Authority of Negotiators		
30. Negotiating team leaders should accept sole responsibility for terms obtained rather than sharing with other members.	32	61
31. Lines of authority for Chinese negotiators are generally long.	81	9
32. Chinese negotiators have less authority than Americans in writing contracts.	78	11
G. Technology vs. Managerial Focus		
33. Americans should provide technology free of charge to Chinese and not expect to be paid for it.	3	96
34. Negotiators from more advanced countries should help the less advanced.	2	58
35. Most of China's modernization problems can be solved by advanced technology.	10	82
36. The absence of modern technology is more of a problem than the management methods used to operate Chinese enterprise in solving modernization problems.	3	90
H. Mutual Interests vs. Winner-Loser Outcome		
37. It is all right to make unreasonable demands in order to get modest concessions.	29	58
38. It is more important to be profitable than to benefit the modernization of the PRC to Chinese businessmen.	36	39
39. All business transactions produce a loser and a winner.	0	96
40. It is better to recognize mutual interests rather than making unreasonable demands to get concessions.	94	6
I. The Post-Contract Period		
41. Chinese negotiators believe that negotiating is an ongoing process and do not end when the agreement is reached.	79	14
42. Cancelling a contract should not lead to a breakdown of relations.	53	22
43. Negotiations may continue after a contract has been signed.	37	55

Marketing in Socialist Countries

Percent Chinese		Group Means		T-test	Views Compared**				
Agree	Disagree	American	Chinese	(p-level)	1	2 Am	2 Ch	3 Am	3 Ch
(N=89)									
87	8	3.39	2.09	.000*				D	A
73	10	2.04	2.24	.148	X				
66	21	2.14	2.47	.027*		A+	A		
24	36	4.65	3.11	.000*		D+	D		
65	23	3.73	2.42	.000*				D	A
44	30	4.07	2.81	.000*				D	A
31	35	4.19	3.03	.000*		D+	D		
12	71	3.42	3.74	.052	X				
46	30	3.07	2.86	.193	X				
80	8	4.47	2.09	.000*				D	A
97	3	1.58	1.67	.498	X				
81	17	2.08	2.27	.201	X				
46	21	2.60	2.73	.366	X				
56	36	3.26	2.84	.018*				D	A

TABLE 1 (continued)

Attitudinal Statement	Percent American	
	Agree	Disagree
	(N=73)	
J. The Chinese Negotiating Team		
44. Chinese negotiating teams change in size and personnel.	88	8
45. Chinese negotiating teams are generally larger than American teams.	95	1
46. Chinese technical specialists and representatives of end users of the product may participate aggressively in negotiations, but are not involved in the final writings of the agreement.	67	22
K. Other Negotiating Assumptions		
47. Reasonable to expect that initial contracts will not be profitable.	44	49
48. When establishing long-term relationships, it is better to select one company even though another may offer lower prices.	19	49
49. One must buy from large well-known companies to get the best quality in machinery and other products.	18	71
50. It is better to buy products with the latest technology to avoid criticism that they did not buy the best products.	22	64
51. One should be frank and admit shortcomings of products.	40	42
52. Generally desirable to reach agreement before a partner leaves the country.	56	32

Notes: *Significant at p<.05

  **Notations used in analyzing "Views Compared" between American and Chinese negotiators:

    1 = No differences in views between Americans and Chinese.
    2 = Intensity of agreement or disagreement differs.
    3 = Diametrically opposed in views.
    Am = Americans
    Ch = Chinese
    A = Agreed
    A+ = Agreed more
    D = Disagreed
    D+ = Disagreed more

Percent Chinese (N=89)		Group Means		T-test (p-level)	Views Compared**					
Agree	Disagree	American	Chinese		1	2		3		
						Am	Ch	Am	Ch	
37	24	1.89	2.86	.000*		A+	A			
66	7	1.75	2.33	.000*		A+	A			
62	25	2.50	2.55	.769	X					
58	29	3.11	2.65	.006*				D	A	
14	56	3.33	3.55	.136	X					
35	25	3.68	2.89	.000*				D	A	
21	42	3.47	3.67	.462	X					
82	8	3.04	2.02	.000*				D	A	
67	15	2.66	2.45	.157	X					

52 statements held by the American and Chinese groups differed significantly (at p < .05).

FINDINGS AND DISCUSSION

For the purpose of discussion, the 52 attitudinal statements concerning perceptions in American and Chinese negotiation styles and activities are grouped into 11 broad categories: (1) the initial meeting and agreement, (2) negotiating styles, (3) guanxi, (4) the use of criticism, (5) the use of stalling, (6) sharing responsibilities and authority of negotiators, (7) technology versus managerial focus, (8) mutual interests versus winner-loser outcome, (9) the post-contract period, (10) the Chinese negotiating team, and (11) other negotiating assumptions.

The Initial Meeting and Agreement

The study found that both the American and Chinese respondents (about two-thirds in each group) hold similar views that it would be preferable to send a top official to represent the company in the initial stages of the negotiation. This desire by both groups to send a top official rather than one from a lower rank indicates sincerity by both parties, and from the Chinese standpoint, gives them "face."[1] One way of "giving face" is to have a high level executive (typically the president or the CEO) initiate the negotiations. To do otherwise demeans the importance of the potential business venture and causes the Chinese to "lose face."

A stumbling block early in the negotiation process, however, focuses on the importance of the letter of intent. Only one-third of the American negotiators felt that the letter of intent was more important than its details, but almost 60 percent of the Chinese held this view. This significant difference (p < .05) in perception evolves from the emphasis the Chinese place on moralistic and ethical principles while the Americans stress legalistic implications (Pye, 1984). It is encouraging to note, however, that apart from the letter of intent, both groups overwhelmingly agreed that it was desirable to get an initial agreement on the general spirit of the contract before negotiating its specific details. Thus, early in the negotiation process, it may be advantageous to the American to focus on the general spirit of the contract rather than insist on a letter of intent to the law.

There appears to be a "meeting of the minds" on four other pre-negotiation activities: both Americans and Chinese agreed that it is preferable to use formal titles rather than address each other on a first-name basis; that it is desirable to have interpreters skilled in both languages; that it is not desirable to rely on informal communications (like word-of-mouth discussion or rumors); and that extensive social activities are not a major benefit of negotiations.

Negotiating Styles

There appears to be a great deal of disagreement between American and Chinese negotiators on negotiating styles. While both groups disagreed that "one should be passive and not express enthusiasm," it is surprising that the Chinese, who have been typified as being passive and modest, should disagree more intensively than the Americans on this issue. This is a significant divergence from expected behavior and suggests a change for the majority of these Chinese negotiators who now believe a more aggressive stance should be taken.

Both groups agree that patience is a necessary negotiating skill. On this matter, the Americans appear to agree with the statement more intensely than the Chinese. Concerning American patience in negotiating, the Chinese stated that the Americans do have patience, but the Americans felt otherwise! Apparently, either the Americans are putting too much emphasis on the importance of patience or the Chinese are "giving face" in evaluating the skill of the American; perhaps it is a combination of the two.

Guanxi

Guanxi refers to the intricate and pervasive network of personal relations which the Chinese cultivate with subtlety and imagination, and it is best described as the currency for getting things done and getting ahead in China (Harner, 1980). Pye (1982) noted that the Chinese endeavor to build close relationships which can lead to developing enduring ties, an objective the Chinese consider most important in negotiations. This study investigated 12 guanxi items, and the findings show that overall, the Americans appear to understand conceptually what guanxi behavior is all about. The Americans agreed with the Chinese that guanxi implies a special relationship which continues over a lengthy period of time, that one may be criticized if one does not meet one's obligations, that receiving a gift does not imply a sense of indebtedness, that it is essential to follow the rules of etiquette when negotiating, that helping another can raise one's own self-esteem, and that Americans do not face more difficulty in building up the self-esteem of another. However, the Americans and Chinese are diametrically opposed on these three guanxi practices: the Chinese agreed but the Americans disagreed that emotional ties are to be encouraged to bind parties together, that one of the objectives of negotiations is to cause one to feel strong and have a sense of obligation to the other, and that if one does not grant favors to a joint venture partner, one is not abiding by the spirit of their relationship. This study revealed that while the Americans are now beginning to understand what guanxi means and implies, they still find it "alien" to their own culture and do not agree with the extremes of the practice. Since the Chinese feel the responsibility of a guanxi more than the Americans, it follows that they will be offended if Americans fail to live up to their guanxi responsibilities; American negotiators must be aware of this potential source of disappointment as perceived by the Chinese.

The Use of Criticism

Sino-American observers have noted that the Chinese practice criticism as a negotiating tool. This study showed that substantial differences of opinion exist between Americans and Chinese on this issue. The Americans disagreed more intensely about the use of criticism as a means to influence the other party; however, the Chinese agreed more that criticism is expected while negotiating and one should not be upset by it. The two groups are diametrically opposite in views about the use of criticism in extracting concessions from the other party — the Chinese favoring but the Americans disagreeing with the practice.

The Use of Stalling

American and Chinese respondents have different views about the use of stalling. While both groups disagreed with the statement that "Americans use stalling techniques more than the Chinese," the Americans disagreed more intensely than the Chinese. On the other hand, while both groups agreed that "negotiators frequently stall to give time for discussions with higher authorities," the Americans agreed more strongly. Furthermore, the two groups hold divergent views concerning the effects of stalling on the terms of the contract: the Americans felt that the effects of stalling are not adverse, but the Chinese hold that the effects are adverse to the terms of the contract. This finding is surprising, for the popular notion is that Chinese view stalling as an acceptable practice in negotiation, the purpose of which is to give negotiators more time to revise their strategies or contact higher authorities to gain approval for tactical changes or modifications of the terms of the contract. By conferring with superiors frequently in order to get their approval it saves not only their "face" but the "face" of their superiors by obtaining prior acceptance of the terms being offered. On the other hand, the Americans appeared to hold a positive view of stalling and delaying tactics and tolerate this strategy, and presumably employ it also.

Sharing Responsibility and Authority of Negotiators

Both American and Chinese negotiators agreed that the lines of authority for Chinese negotiators are generally long. There is also agreement that Chinese negotiators have less authority than Americans in writing contracts, although the Americans appeared to agree more intensely with the statement than the Chinese. These findings support the general observation that the Chinese style of decision making is bureaucratic, thereby lengthening the time involved in negotiating with the Chinese.

The Americans and Chinese, however, held opposing views concerning the need to share responsibility with other team members for contractual terms obtained. A large majority (about 87 percent) of the Chinese negotiators felt that negotiating team leaders should accept the sole responsibility for terms obtained, but only one-third of the Americans held this view. This finding appears to contradict a perception expressed by Pye (1984) that the Chinese have a strong desire to protect themselves from possible criticisms and they prefer not to have this responsibility placed on the shoulders of any one individual.

Technology versus Managerial Focus

American businessmen have observed that oftentimes the Chinese want to obtain technology (such as software), but fail to place a monetary value upon it, thereby acknowledging the cost of its development. In brief, it is asserted that the Chinese believed that knowledge is to be shared (Hendryx, 1986). It is not surprising that almost all of the Americans disagreed strongly with the statement that "Americans should provide technology free of charge to the Chinese and not expect to be paid for it." However, only about one-third of the Chinese held this view; an analysis of the data showed that about 40 percent of the Chinese respondents chose to remain neutral on this subject. It would appear that the Chinese are not yet fully convinced that American technology should be paid for. In fact, in response to another similar question, two-thirds of the Chinese felt that negotiators from advanced countries should help the less advanced; only 2 percent of the Americans held this view.

Some Chinese assume that most of China's modernization problems can be solved by the use of advanced technology, while many Americans assert that while advanced technology will be beneficial, changes in the economic system as well as the adoption of modern management techniques are more essential. Some Sino experts maintain that an important approach for modernizing the manufacturing processes is the employment of modern management methods in Chinese enterprises, and these are the key to the solution rather than the use of modern technology. This study lends support to the perceptual difference between the Chinese and the Western world on the roles of technology and managerial expertise in economic development. Forty-four percent of the Chinese felt that China's modernization problems can be solved by advanced technology, but only 10 percent of the American negotiators agreed with the statement. In response to another similar question, 32 percent of the Chinese agreed that technology is more important than managerial techniques, but only 3 percent of the Americans held this view. Evidently, further investigation of the contributions of both of these approaches is essential and more education on the benefits of modern managerial practices is required before this approach to modernization can gain general acceptance in China.

Mutual Interests versus Winner-Loser Outcome

This study showed that both Americans and Chinese disagreed with the practice of making unreasonable demands in order to get modest concessions. The finding appears to contradict the observation by Pye (1982) that the Chinese use this technique to extract more favorable contractual terms. Even though some (12 percent of the Chinese respondents) may resort to this practice, this study revealed that it is not a common practice among the Chinese. In fact, an overwhelming majority of the Chinese (97 percent) and Americans (94 percent) agreed that it is better to recognize mutual interests rather than making unreasonable demands to get concessions.

However, in the Chinese calculus, there is an assumption that all business transactions produce a winner and a loser. All of the American negotiators disagreed with this perception. If this concept is interpreted that one may gain more than the other, then the one who receives less is a loser in the sense that he suffers a "loss of face." This concept differs from that held by Americans who stress mutual benefits being derived from negotiations.

As the PRC has a socialistic political system, it is generally assumed that the interests of the Chinese government (the country) are paramount in negotiating. Only 30 percent of the Chinese agreed with this view. Slightly less than half of the Chinese respondents felt that it is more important for the contract to benefit the businessmen than the modernization of the PRC.

The Post-Contract Period

Both American and Chinese respondents agreed that Chinese negotiators believe that negotiating is an ongoing process and does not end when the agreement is reached. This finding supports Pye's (1982) observation. They also felt that canceling a contract should not lead to a breakdown of relations. At this point, according to Pye (1982), both parties should continue to redefine their "mutual interests" and negotiate a new contract. The potential long-term gain far exceeds the frustrations of the short-term cancellation.

However, the Americans disagreed with the view held by the Chinese that negotiations may continue after a contract has been signed. This is frequently a point of frustration to American businessmen who believe that once a contract has been signed, the terms cannot be changed. The Chinese, however, do not share this view and continue to ask for modifications after signing the contract. This implies a lack of closure after a contract has been finalized, and is very frustrating to the Americans as it limits forward planning.

The Chinese Negotiating Team

While both the Americans and Chinese appeared to agree that the Chinese negotiating teams change in size and personnel, and that the Chinese teams are generally larger than the American teams, the Americans felt more strongly about these statements than the Chinese. It appears that the changing team-size and membership and relatively larger team-size in terms of number of personnel are common practices in China, so much so that the Chinese take them for granted. However, to the Americans, such practices are unusual and they take special note of them. Hendryx (1986) counseled that the Chinese teams are typically larger because they include specialists who are involved primarily for solving engineering problems. This observation is supported by this study as both the Americans and Chinese agreed that Chinese technical specialists and representatives of end-users of the product may participate aggressively in the negotiations. However, this study further showed that these individuals are not involved in the final writing of the specific details of the final contract. This supports the earlier finding that the numbers on the Chinese team change during the negotiation. Perhaps, the Chinese take the absence of the technical specialists in the phase in which the final contract is formalized and approved as providing them with an excuse to revise the contract after it has been signed. This would provide further support to the earlier finding that the Chinese have a penchant to view negotiations as an ongoing process even after the contract has been signed.

Other Negotiating Assumptions

Many American businessmen are endeavoring to form business relations in China with the objective of receiving favored treatment in the future. Some realistically recognize that in the short-run, initial efforts may not be profitable. There appears to be a difference in views between the Americans and Chinese concerning the time frame in which profits are expected. The Chinese agreed that it is reasonable to expect that the initial contracts may not be profitable, but the Americans disagreed. The Chinese appear to take a long-term view of the contractual relationships and feel that the initial contract will lay the basis for larger contracts later if goods and services involved are satisfactory. Interestingly, both groups agreed that it was inappropriate to establish a long-term relationship with only one company if another could meet the company's needs at a lower price. Thus, the common assumption that a Chinese enterprise will not switch suppliers if better offers are available elsewhere is not supported by this study.

One of the criticisms held by American businessmen about the Chinese is that they will purchase only from large, well-known companies. This is sometimes described as a penchant to buy only "the best" from the "number one" company (Pye, 1982). This study provides support to that observation in that the Chinese agree with that view; on the other hand, the Americans disagreed with the practice. However, both the Americans and Chinese disagreed with the practice of buying products with the latest technology in order to avoid criticism that they have not bought the best product. Apparently, in industrial buying, factors other than just technology play a critical role in the buying decision process; and this is recognized by both the American and Chinese respondents.

One issue facing American negotiators is the full disclosure of the strengths and weaknesses of their products. Typically, only those which are favorable are presented. There appears to be a difference of opinion between the Chinese and Americans on this practice: 40 percent of the Americans in contrast to 82 percent of the Chinese favored frankness and a willingness to identify the limitations of their products. Apparently, the Americans were aware of the possibility that if they mentioned the shortcomings of their products, this might arouse in the minds of the Chinese the thought that other defects might exist which were not mentioned. On the other hand, the Chinese were more willing to admit their products' limitations and would expect the Americans to do the same.

Finally, it was held by the majority of the respondents (67 percent of the Chinese and 56 percent of the Americans) that it is generally desirable to reach an agreement on a contract before the Americans leave China. While the majority of the Chinese agreed with this view, some Sino-American negotiating authorities have maintained that the Chinese tend to delay arriving at a final agreement by various tactics. Therefore, it behooves Americans to take steps to bring the contract into fruition, and shorten as much as possible the time spent on formulating the final agreement. One tactic has been the setting of a deadline for the departure from China and it has been an effective technique for accomplishing the objective (Hendryx, 1986).

CONCLUSION AND IMPLICATIONS FOR NEGOTIATING IN THE PRC

Of the 52 attitudinal statements examined, the American and Chinese negotiators shared similar views on 22 statements (or 42.3 percent), differed in the intensity of their agreement or disagreement on 14 statements (or 26.9 percent), and were diametrically opposed in perceptions on the remaining 16 statements (or 30.8 percent). (See t-tests of significance provided in the Table.) This study also provided either supporting evidence for or contradicted some commonly held perceptions concerning the Chinese way of doing business.

Based on the findings of this study, American and Chinese negotiators appeared to agree on several of the formalities attached to the initial meeting, except on the issue pertaining to the letter of intent. The Chinese felt that the spirit of the letter of intent was more important than the specific legalistic details. American businessmen must learn to appreciate this perception; however, to avoid future disagreements, U.S. negotiators must endeavor to develop agreements which clearly state the responsibilities of both parties.

The American and Chinese negotiators differed in their negotiating styles, especially on their perceptions concerning the need to be enthusiastic and patient. The respondents appeared to give deference to each other—the Americans appearing to want to be more patient and the Chinese appearing to show less patience than expected. But both groups agreed strongly that patience is a necessary negotiating skill. This is important because the Chinese are known to have a long line of authority, and negotiators must have the approval of their superiors. The Chinese bureaucracy is slow in reaching decisions.

The concept guanxi carries several dimensions. On some of these, the Americans and Chinese are in agreement; on others, differences in perceptions exist. For instance, this study showed that Americans and Chinese do not see eye-to-eye on the emotional basis for guanxi as practiced by the Chinese. Whether American negotiators like it or not, they should realize that the Chinese will offer friendship and endeavor to establish close ties with them. Great stress will be placed on building long-lasting friendships for the Chinese believe that a guanxi tie will bind both parties to an obligation to assist each other when requested to do so.

Great perceptual differences exist between American and Chinese negotiators on the use of criticism as a negotiating tool. The Chinese felt that criticism is a valid and useful tool in negotiations, and use it to gain concessions from the other party. Hence, their negotiating style may involve shaming and stubbornness. Perceptual differences also exist on the use of stalling as a negotiating technique. The Chinese felt that stalling will adversely affect the terms of the contract, but the Americans disagreed.

The American and Chinese negotiators hold differing views on the importance of technology and management expertise in modernization and economic development. The Chinese negotiators viewed advanced technology as more important than management expertise in economic development, but the Americans held opposing views. Thus, a push by the Americans in trying to sell modern management techniques to the Chinese may be regarded unfavorably by the Chinese.

The Chinese take a long-term view of the contractual arrangement and tend to favor large, well-known companies. However, the Chinese are aware that the political forces in China may change abruptly at any time and they feel that the decisions they make must be amenable to change. Hence, they view negotiations as an ongoing process, even though the contract has been signed and sealed. American negotiators must also realize that while the agreements concluded must be for the good of China, the Chinese are also motivated by profits.

Finally, it is helpful to understand "face" behavior as it is practiced by the Chinese. American businessmen must avoid actions which may cause the Chinese to lose face. Thus, Americans negotiating in China must learn to give praise when warranted, and recognize that the Chinese are oftentimes thin-skinned and may take offense if they sense they are being treated differently or are not receiving fair treatment in the negotiating process.

NOTE

1. This concept of "face," which is most perplexing to Americans, is perceived by the Chinese as one of the basic concepts of personal interaction. "Face behavior" is the process in China by which one gains and maintains status as well as moral reputation. The positive benefit is best described as "gained face" but has the negative connotation of "loss of face." This must be understood as it constitutes a most serious problem to the Chinese and they will go to great lengths to avoid it. Another perception of "face" refers to the attainment of reputation by hard work, skillful negotiation, and the ability of one to work well with others. It is attained also by the effective application of knowledge, personal judgement or by Communist Party affiliation and other government positions (Hu, 1944).

REFERENCES

Harner, Annie Lai. (1980). *Living and Working in the People's Republic of China*. Overseas Briefing Center, School of Area Studies, Foreign Service Institute, U.S. Department of State, Washington, DC.

Hendryx, Steven R. (1986). "The China Trade: Making the Deal Work." *Harvard Business Review*, (July-August).

Hu, Hsien Chin. (1944). "The Chinese Concept of Face." *American Anthropologist*, (January-March) Vol. 46.

Pye, Lucien W. (1982). *Chinese Commercial Negotiating Styles*. Cambridge: Olelgeschlager, Gunn, and Hain, Inc.

Pye, Lucien W. (1986). "The China Trade: Making the Deal." *Harvard Business Review*, (July-August).

Terry, Edith. (1984). *The Executive Guide to China,* New York: John Wiley & Sons, Inc.

Wilson, Richard, Sidney Greenblatt, and Amy Auerblatt Wilson (eds). (1979). *Value Change in Chinese Society*, New York: Praeger.

Wilson, Richard, Sidney Greenblatt, and Amy Auerblatt Wilson (eds). (1981). *Moral Behavior in Chinese Society*. New York: Praeger.

Xie, Ming-Gan. (1987). "China's Open-Door Policy and Sino-American Trade." *Business Horizons*, (July-August).

Chapter 19

Views of Trade Activity
with the Former Soviet Union and China
by U.S. Manufacturers

Robert D. Hisrich
Michael P. Peters

SUMMARY. Given the recent developments in China and the treaty activity between the U.S. and the U.S.S.R., it is important to understand the interest as well as the actual trade activity with these two countries. U.S. manufacturers that currently trade (as well as those that do not) with these countries were queried regarding their attitudes and interest in specific trade related activities. Based on an analysis and comparison of the results, the attitudes and trade activities are presented as well as the implications for the future.

Over the years the attitudes and research interests in East-West trade have varied with the level of trade activity and political parsimony between the U.S. and the particular controlled economy. This is especially true for U.S.-Soviet and U.S.-China trade than for any other trading partner. Each year certain events impact the stability of the trading relationship. Some of these events from 1982 through 1987 are highlighted in Table 1. As is reflected in these selected events, U.S.-Soviet and U.S.-China trade has gone from a very deteriorated condition in 1982 (due in part to Reagan's 1981 policies and sanctions) to a very positive situation in 1988 as a result of

This chapter was first published in the *Journal of Global Marketing*, Vol. 2(2) and reflects political and economic conditions in the former Soviet Union as they existed in 1988. It is presented here for its theoretical orientation and historical perspective.

Table 1

Selected Recent Major Events in East-West Trade

Year	Event
1982	Suspension of Poland's Most Favored National Status
	US-USSR trade deterioration due to Reagan's 1981 sanctions
	Change in USSR leadership
	First meeting of US-USSR Trade and Economic Council in 4 years
1983	US exports to China decrease due to trade retaliation and success of China's agricultural reforms
	Successful US-China Textile Agreement established
	US incurs a $54.3 million trade deficit
1984	Trade deficit decreases to $5.5 million due to wheat shipments to China
1985	US cuts Soviet fishing allocation in US waters in half
	Long term nuclear cooperation accord established between US and China
	Poland's debt restructured
1986	China joined Asian Development Bank
	Easing of US export license applications to export to USSR
	Protocal added to China trade treaty
	Loan commitment of $65.4 million to China from ExIM Bank for US exports to China
	China, Hungary, and Romania obtain Most Favored National Status
1987	US-USSR Nuclear Arms Reduction Agreement

the recent U.S.-Soviet nuclear arms agreement and U.S.-China accord.

The amount of the trade activity with a controlled economy, of course, reflects the political relations occurring at the time. U.S.-Soviet exports steadily increased from 1980 to $2,589 million in 1982 (see Table 2). Following a 20% decrease in 1983, these exports decreased steadily from a high of $3,282 million in 1984 until the slight upturn in 1987 to $1,480 million. Soviet imports exhibited a more turbulent yearly pattern at a much lower level reaching a high of only $408 million in 1987. The level of U.S.-China trade during the same eight-year period was much less volatile at a much higher level. While U.S. exports to China ranged from $3,749 million in 1980 to $3,497 million in 1987, imports increased from $1,039 million in 1980 to an all time high of $6,244 million in 1987, a significant increase (see Table 2).

BACKGROUND

The increasing level of East-West trade activity is reflected in the increase in research interest. The views of consumers, manufacturers, and banks regarding trade with China, the Soviet Union, and Eastern-bloc countries was the focus of three studies. The first one, focusing on consumer perceptions of products produced in controlled economies, indicated that there is a market in the U.S. with identifiable market segments willing to purchase products from particular countries (Hisrich, Peters, & Weinstein, 1981).

Manufacturers also varied in their views of trade with controlled economies (Hisrich & Peters, 1983). Firms not presently engaged in trade with Eastern Europe or the former U.S.S.R. felt that a lack of U.S. government support was a major problem. Additional problems included financing the trade arrangements and market unfamiliarity. The overwhelming reason given for engaging in East-West trade was long-term market access.

The third study examined the opinions and attitudes of financial institutions (Hisrich & Peters, 1985). A variety of services were provided by these banks: direct loans to foreign government or a central bank, quasi-government or private sector lending, commercial letters of credit, documentary collections, remittance of money

TABLE 2

East – West Trade
(Millions of U.S. $)

Exports	1980	1981	1982	1983	1984	1985	1986	(Jan.-Sept.) 1987
Albania	6.9	6.1	16.4	4.2	9.3	11.9	4.5	2.3
Bulgaria	160.7	258.1	106.4	65.4	44.1	103.5	96.5	58.3
China	3749.0	3598.6	2904.5	2163.2	2988.5	3796.2	3106.2	2373.3
Czechoslovakia	185.1	82.4	83.6	57.1	58.1	62.6	72.4	33.6
East Germany	477.4	295.6	222.7	139.0	135.8	72.3	67.9	41.9
Hungary	79.0	77.5	67.8	109.8	85.2	92.1	98.1	66.3
Poland	710.4	680.5	292.6	319.9	314.8	233.7	151.2	150.1
Romania	720.2	503.9	223.2	185.7	246.1	206.5	250.0	169.9
USSR	1509.7	2338.8	2589.0	2002.0	3282.7	2421.9	1247.5	1060.4
Total	7598.4	7771.5	6506.2	5046.3	7164.6	7000.7	5094.3	3956.1

Imports

Albania	10.7	34.0	2.8	3.5	2.2	3.0	3.1	1.5
Bulgaria	22.8	25.6	25.1	32.8	30.3	34.0	56.5	35.9
China	1039.2	1830.0	2215.9	2217.5	3040.4	3963.4	4770.9	4795.3
Czechoslovakia	61.1	67.2	61.5	62.8	84.2	75.0	85.1	59.7
East Germany	43.0	44.7	51.8	56.9	149.1	90.3	86.5	53.3
Hungary	104.3	127.9	133.2	154.6	220.1	216.6	225.1	204.6
Poland	414.9	359.9	212.9	190.6	215.7	217.0	232.6	219.4
Romania	310.6	559.4	339.1	512.8	896.7	881.3	753.9	538.8
USSR	431.2	357.4	228.8	341.1	556.1	406.9	558.2	292.7
Total	2347.8	3374.7	2929.2	3569.1	5192.6	5753.5	6685.4	6201.2

Sources: Report of the Congress and the Trade Policy Committee On Trade Between The United States and The Nonmarket Economy Countries, and The U.S. Department of Commerce.

transfer, and foreign exchange. Another general study focused on the various contractual arrangements and their aspects used in East-West trade (Kogut, 1986).

A final general study discussed the viability of trading with controlled economies and the opportunity to develop new business contacts and expand the international trade of the U.S. (Brandenburg, 1987). Specific controlled economies were addressed (U.S.S.R., Bulgaria, Czechoslovakia, German Democratic Republic, Hungary, Poland, and Rumania) in terms of a method for trading and their future prospects.

In addition to these general articles, much of the recent literature on East-West trade has focused on ventures in China due in part to the establishment of the Special Economic Zones (SEZs), the change in Chinese policy, and improved U.S.-China political relations. An examination of the SEZs, particularly Shenzhen, the most economically successful of the Chinese cities, indicates that SEZs are a "window" on Chinese policy as well as an experiment for foreign investment in a socialist Chinese economy (Wong, 1987).

Some of the specific problems of establishing a business in China were the focus of some articles in a special issue of the *Columbia Journal of World Business*. One of these articles presented an overview of business relations with China along with guidelines for U.S. doing business in China (Wang, 1986). Another article discussed the challenges for U.S. companies in China (Zamet & Bovarnick, 1986). These included: managing local work forces under the communist power structure and difficulty in living and working conditions for expatriate personnel. Insights on a technology transfer joint venture were presented in an article focusing on the Otis Elevator Company's formation of the Tianjin-Otis Joint Venture with particular emphasis on its negotiation and operations aspects (Hendryx, 1986). A final study focused on the problems and some keys to successfully doing business in China (Tai, 1988).

Further discussion of technology transfer centered on: the complex, changing export control system, the rapid changes that have occurred in the 1980s, and one problem area of East-West trade — nuclear trade (Ross, 1986). This area of nuclear trade and the implications for national security is further examined in an article focusing on China's need for foreign nuclear technology (Crane &

Suttmeier, 1986). Another specific area of trade with China — world food trade — is the focus of a study by Anderson and Tyers (1987). Focusing on the Chinese agricultural surplus of 1984 and 1985, the importance of China in world food trade in the future is presented even though agriculture is likely to become a smaller portion of the Chinese economy. Finally, an overview of entrepreneurship both before and after the Cultural Revolution and its implications for U.S.-China trade is the focus of a final article (Reeder, 1984).

Several studies also explored trade between the U.S. and specific Eastern European countries. Hungary and the establishment of private business within the socialist economic structure was the focus of two studies. One of these examined the background of the innovations, the new forms of economic organization and the socioeconomic issues raised by these new activities (Miller & Lehoczyke, 1984). The second study explored the emerging concept of socialist entrepreneurship concluding that there has been a successful introduction of entrepreneurship in Hungary (Naor & Bod, 1986).

A study exploring the joint ventures in Yugoslavia examined the opportunities and constraints facing Western multinational companies as well as the success factors in the various arrangements occurring (Artisien & Buckley, 1985). The role of transnational corporations in Eastern economies was found to be a significant factor in a study of Poland (Cieslik & Sosnowski, 1985).

Not surprisingly, given the strained political relations over the past seven years, there has been little interest in U.S.-Soviet trade. One research study on U.S.-Soviet trade focused on the trade activity following the Nixon-Brezhnev Summit of 1972 and discussed the prospects for the future (Goldman, 1985). However, more recently, numerous joint venture agreements are being planned or negotiated between the two countries. As is indicated in Table 3, these range from providing engineering management and building plants in the various industrial sectors (petrochemicals, sewing machines, herbicides, equipment, and diesel engines and components), to providing fast food (pizza restaurants). The fate of these joint ventures as well as the future of other U.S.-Soviet trade activities depends to a large extent on: (1) Gorbachev's ability to move the present Soviet centralized management system to a more democratic economic-based system; and (2) the attitudes, opinions, and

Table 3

Selected Joint Venture Agreements
between the United States
and the Soviet Union

U.S. Company	Aspects of Venture	Agreement Being Negotiated	Agreement Being Planned
Combustion Engineering	Providing engineering Management and Making equipment to upgrade industrial plants	X	
Pepsico	Open two Pizza Hut restaurants	X	
Occidental Petroleum	Build a petro chemical complex with Montedison, and Italian company	X	
SSMC	Build a plant to make sewing machines	X	

374

Company	Description		
Monsanto	Build a herbicide plant		X
Honeywell	Providing processing systems for chemical industry and designing plants	X	
Archer Daniels Midland	Ventures in chicken raising, grain storage, cooking oil, and soybean processing		
Dresser Industries	Build a plant to produce energy, mining, and construction equipment		
Cummins Engine	Build a plant to manufacture diesel engines or components		

Source: "Reforming the Soviet Economy", Business Week, December 7, 1987, p. 88.

375

concerns of the government, businesses, consumers, and financial institutions in the United States.

Given the problems with attitudes as well as currency, one mechanism for conducting East-West trade that is having increased usage is countertrade agreements. Countertrade agreements have taken several forms: barter, counterpurchase, offset, switch-trading, and buy-back. While in barter there is a straightforward exchange of goods for goods, a counterpurchase agreement modifies this arrangement by requiring the supplier (the U.S.) to a country (controlled economy) to buy a certain amount of goods for an amount sold. Offset is another form of a barter agreement where the seller agrees to use goods or services from the controlled economy buying in its final product.

Switch-trading, a more sophisticated form of barter, links several countries in a chain, allowing goods to be swapped more freely than could occur in a bilateral barter agreement. A final very popular form of bartering in selling capital equipment to a controlled economy is buy-back. Here, the selling company takes at least part of its payment for the equipment in the form of the product produced in the project. Often a countertrade agreement of one of these forms or another variation is the only way to trade with a controlled economy. Using a unique trade finance technique is especially helpful in exploiting trade opportunities with Eastern bloc countries (Barrett, 1987).

RESEARCH OBJECTIVES

This chapter focuses on one of these influencing factors — U.S. manufacturers — and provides an assessment of their participation as well as their attitudes and interest in trading with China and the U.S.S.R. Specifically, several issues were addressed: How willing are nontraders to begin trade relations with China or the U.S.S.R.? What is the level of satisfaction with trade support services provided by the U.S. government? What is the nature (type of transaction and level of satisfaction) of any existing trade activities? What types of products are generally purchased by U.S. firms? And, what factors in trade relations are of greatest concern?

RESEARCH METHODOLOGY

To provide answers to these questions a nationwide mail survey of 450 of the largest manufacturers in the U.S. was undertaken. The individual in either of these firms who was responsible for international affairs or marketing was sent a personal cover letter and questionnaire requesting their cooperation in the research undertaking. A self-addressed stamped envelope was provided for their convenience.

Of the 450 questionnaires sent, 140 usable responses were obtained. Of these 140 respondents, 50 were manufacturers presently involved in trade with either China or the U.S.S.R. The remaining 90 firms were not. Questions on attitudes toward trade with these countries were asked of all respondents regardless of any existing trade relationship.

FINDINGS

The findings of this research will be discussed in two sections. First, the attitudes and opinions of manufacturers not currently involved in any trade activity with China or the U.S.S.R. will be presented. This will be followed by information provided by those firms currently having business dealings with either or both of those countries.

Firms Not Currently Engaged in Trade

Manufacturers not currently engaged in trade with either of the two countries indicated a stronger interest in possibly trading with China than the U.S.S.R. While more than 76% of these firms indicated they would be interested or very interested in trading with China, only 51% had this degree of interest in trading with the U.S.S.R. Correspondingly, a complete unwillingness to trade with the U.S.S.R. was expressed by 29% of the respondents compared to only 11% expressing this degree of unwillingness for China. While the major reason for this negative attitude about trading with the U.S.S.R. was the existent political instability, recent reforms was the reason indicated for the willingness to trade with China.

Although never actually trading with either of these countries, the majority of the manufacturers had investigated the possibility. About 80% (71 of the 90 manufacturers not currently trading) indicated that they had carried out at least a limited investigation of establishing a trade relationship. Fifty-one firms had made contact with the U.S. government regarding participation in some type of trading activity. Of these, 24% indicated that they were very dissatisfied with the trade support services provided by the U.S. government. Bureaucracy, red tape, and lack of knowledge were the main reasons cited for this dissatisfaction. The majority of the others were only somewhat satisfied with the trade exhibits and the negotiation advice provided by the U.S. government.

There were some differences in factors considered most critical by U.S. manufacturers contemplating trade with either the U.S.S.R. or China. For trade with China, firms not currently involved in trade indicated that the time required by senior management was the most significant concern. Financing of trade arrangements and the high initial investment without assurance of return was also a concern in trading with either country. A notable difference in possible trade with the two countries was the lack of familiarity with the market in China. In spite of the more liberal attitudes within China, there is still uncertainty by U.S. manufacturers about the potential of the Chinese market. For the U.S.S.R., of more concern was the lack of protection of copyrights and patents than market needs and conditions.

T-tests on the weighted means were used to determine any significant difference between the countries on a number of selected factors critical in establishing trade relationships (see Table 4). Only three factors were statistically significant — high initial investment without assurance of return, time required of senior management, and loss of revenue from adverse American attitudes. The remaining factors were not viewed as being significantly different in trading with either country.

Each respondent was also asked to indicate their firm's attitude toward engaging in a number of trade relationships (importing, exporting, licensing, counterpurchases, or corporate schemes) with either of these two countries. Importing, exporting and licensing were considered as more desirable trading vehicles with China than

TABLE 4

WEIGHTED MEAN COMPARISONS OF FACTORS AFFECTING
TRADE BY FIRMS NOT CURRENTLY TRADING

FACTOR	Weighted Mean Values by Country	
	CHINA	USSR
Varying exchange rates	1.75	2.00
Financing of trade arrangements	3.23	3.37
Unfamiliarity with market	3.08	3.00
High initial investment without assurance of return	3.19	2.79[c]
Time required of senior management	3.30	2.38[a]
Language	2.39	2.05
Harassment of U.S. business by foreign government during political crises	2.12	2.48
Loss of revenue from adverse American attitudes toward trade with communist country	1.64	2.41[b]
Possibility of expropriation	1.85	1.75
Possibility of default	2.36	2.52
Lack of protection for U.S. copyrights and patents	2.69	2.68

a = significant at .01 level
b = significant at .05 level
c = significant at .10 level

with the U.S.S.R. No one felt that a licensing arrangement with the U.S.S.R. was very desirable. Subcontracting was not considered to be possible in the U.S.S.R. or China by most respondents. Joint ventures with China and the U.S.S.R. were regarded as more desirable than licensing, subcontracting, turnkey projects, or counterpurchase agreements. Counterpurchase agreements or coproduction schemes were the least desirable trade activity with either country.

Those not currently trading with China or the U.S.S.R. generally had a negative attitude toward purchasing specific products. Table 5 indicates the mean rating for each of 11 product types with a rating of 5 being very desirable. While mineral fuels and related products were the most acceptable products, live animal and tobacco were the least acceptable with mean ratings of 1.18 and 1.22 respectively. While clothing and textiles were more acceptable from China than the U.S.S.R., machinery (especially electrical) was more acceptable if manufactured in the U.S.S.R.

TABLE 5

MEAN RATINGS OF ATTITUDES OF PURCHASING
SPECIFIC PRODUCTS BY FIRMS NOT CURRENTLY TRADING

	Mean Ratings of Trading Area	
PRODUCT	CHINA	USSR
Food Products	1.58	1.57
Live Animals	1.21	1.26
Beverages	1.59	1.70
Tobacco	1.18	1.22
Inedible Crude Materials, except Fuels	1.76	1.83
Mineral Fuels and Related Products	1.90	1.96
Animal and Vegetable Oils and Fats	1.41	1.50
Machinery - Electric	1.63	1.80
Machinery - Nonelectric	1.61	1.68
Transport Equipment	1.62	1.75
Clothing and Textile	1.77	1.61
Other Manufactured Goods	1.82	1.71

Firms Currently Engaged in Trade

Fifty manufacturers indicated they were presently engaged in trade with either China, the U.S.S.R., or both. This group was queried in terms of the nature of their trade or business activities, reasons for trading, type and use of any products acquired, satisfaction with any service provided by the U.S. government, attitudes on factors important in trade relationships, and willingness to purchase a wide range of products.

Table 6 indicates the percentage of respondents involved with various types of trade activities. The most frequent activity was exporting to China (64%) which was significantly higher than exporting to the U.S.S.R. (44%). In fact, of the nine trade activities, seven were equal to or more frequently used in trading with China than with the U.S.S.R.

TABLE 6

TRADE ACTIVITIES BY COUNTRY

Of Those Currently Trading (N=50)

TRADE ACTIVITIES	PEOPLES' REPUBLIC OF CHINA	USSR
Import Only	8%	12%
Export Only	64	44
Import and Export (contracts not linked)	20	32
Licensing	20	20
Subcontracting	12	8
Joint Venture	16	8
Turnkey Project	12	12
Counter Purchase	16	8
Coproduction Schemes	8	4

When further queried regarding the level of satisfaction with the trade activity, respondents indicated an overall mean rating value of 3.19 for China and 3.42 for U.S.S.R. Firms only importing from China were primarily dissatisfied with the inconsistent quality of products as well as delivery problems. Respondents trading with China were generally satisfied with exporting (mean of 3.91). Counterpurchasing in China was rated lower (mean of 2.48), reflecting the substandard quality of goods, inability to meet schedules and the lack of coordination by government in the transactions experienced. While a number of manufacturers (25%) expressed significant dissatisfaction in exporting activities with the U.S.S.R., due in part to the political use of products, licensing was rated very high in trading with the country.

The establishment of long-term market areas was the major reason cited for trading with either country. Most of the manufacturers felt that both countries would continue to develop and become much more industry oriented. The untapped resources and the labor rates of the countries, particularly China, were the primary benefits envisioned in the future trading. Because of the potential of these countries, U.S. manufacturers were willing to endure less than adequate financial arrangements in the short-run in order to be in a position for returns in the long-run. Only those companies that had excess products and capacity in demand by the countries indicated short-term access to these markets as a primary reason for trading.

Trade with China involved such products as rosin, metals, special chemicals, consumer goods, sporting goods, minerals, raw materials, and chemicals. Most of the products were used by firms in their manufacturing process.

Machine tools, electronic parts, garments, chemicals, and raw materials were most likely to be involved in trade activities with the U.S.S.R. With the exception of garments (which were sold to a third party), these products were used in the manufacturing process by the U.S. firms.

While the overall level of satisfaction with the U.S. government services supporting trade with either country was low, it did vary significantly depending on the country involved. More satisfaction was expressed with the U.S. government support of trade with China (mean 3.4) than for the U.S.S.R. (mean 2.7). Major complaints included: the time to obtain an export license; lack of substance in public relations; lack of understanding of foreign trade policy; lack of clarity on embargoes; and superficial nature of support. The complaints did not concentrate in any particular industry sector. Some favorable comments centered around the trade show support by the trade council and help of attachés.

Table 7 provides a rating of concerns in trade with China and the U.S.S.R. by firms presently engaged in trade. The lack of protection for U.S. copyrights and patents was the greatest concern in trading with each country. While this concern at first glance appears somewhat inconsistent with companies rating licensing very high in trading with the U.S.S.R., it actually reflects the lack of knowledge and experience in East-West trade by the U.S. manufacturers responding. Time required of senior management and the financing of trade arrangements were also major concerns. Unfamiliarity with the market was more of a concern in China than with the U.S.S.R. which was also the case for nontrading manufacturers. Harassment

TABLE 7

FACTORS OF MOST CONCERN IN EACH TRADING AREA
BY FIRMS CURRENTLY TRADING

TRADING AREA	FACTORS IN ORDER OF CONCERN
China	- Lack of protection for U.S. copyrights and patents
	- Time required of senior management
	- Financing of trade arrangements
	- Unfamiliarity with market
USSR	- Lack of protection for U.S. copyrights and patents
	- Time required of senior management
	- Financing of trade arrangements
	- Harassment of U.S. business by foreign government during political crises

of U.S. business by a foreign government during political crisis was more of a concern in U.S.-Soviet trade.

Additional analysis of these factors was done using t-tests on the weighted means (see Table 8). For the two groups of firms, significant differences between China and the U.S.S.R. occurred in

TABLE 8

WEIGHTED MEAN COMPARISONS OF FACTORS AFFECTING
TRADE BY FIRMS CURRENTLY TRADING

	Weighted Mean Values by Country	
	CHINA	USSR
Varying exchange rates	1.85	1.90
Financing of Trade Arrangements	3.38	2.95[c]
Unfamiliarity with market	2.70	1.86[a]
High initial investment without assurance of return	2.68	2.26[c]
Time required of senior management	3.40	3.05
Language	2.10	1.50[c]
Harassment of U.S. business by foreign government during political crises	2.12	2.65[c]
Loss of revenue from adverse American attitudes toward trade with communist country	2.25	2.60
Possibility of expropriation	2.05	2.19
Possibility of default	1.79	1.94
Lack of protection for U.S. copyrights and patents	3.43	3.24

a = significant at .01 level
b = significant at .05 level
c = significant at .10 level

the areas of: financing of trade arrangements; unfamiliarity with market; high initial investment without assurance of return; and harassment of U.S. business by foreign government during political crisis.

Except for inedible crude materials (excluding fuels), mineral fuels, clothing, and textile goods from China, there was generally little interest in purchasing products from either country—a major problem in counterpurchase agreements. Both China and the U.S.S.R. were perceived as having little to offer in a countertrade agreement, which will, of course, be a strong deterrent to increased trade relationships in the future.

CONCLUSIONS

Since few of the manufacturers not currently involved in trade with China or the U.S.S.R. were completely unwilling to consider such trade activity, efforts should be made to facilitate this activity. First, good support services for this trade need to be provided by the U.S. government. The bureaucracy and red tape that some firms previously experienced when attempting to use U.S. government help needs to be replaced by knowledgeable helpful assistance. This assistance should help reduce the amount of time required by senior management—a concern of those manufacturers. The advice should particularly center around: alternative methods for financing the trade arrangement; good market information; and the negotiation strategy to be employed. Hosting trade exhibits combining several manufacturers in each country would be very beneficial, as would developing means for protecting copyrights and patents to the extent possible, and informing which Chinese or Russian products are best in countertrade agreements.

A low level of satisfaction with U.S. government services was also expressed by firms currently trading with either or both of the countries. Again, the government should support this trade activity by: shortening the time to obtain an export license; developing a comprehensive trade policy that is easily understood; assisting firms in advertising and public relations; and providing sound market information.

What does this mean for the future of U.S.-China and U.S.-Soviet trade activities? While this question generates a great deal of emotional and political response, the current findings, to the extent that they can be generalized, have important political, commercial, and educational implications. First, seminars that provide information on trade with China and the U.S.S.R., its benefits, problems, and procedures should be conducted. Firms in the United States should be made aware of the benefits and long-run payback of establishing trade relationships with these countries.

Second, there should be more emphasis on international business in colleges and universities. Specifically, time should be spent on the benefits, difficulties and procedures involved in trade with controlled economies in general and especially with these two countries. While the need to have this international component in management education has been acknowledged, its emphasis and substance in many schools is minimal if indeed existent.

Finally, more help needs to be provided in financing trade arrangements. Financial institutions need to be encouraged to provide the necessary capital and provide assistance in the various alternatives available to support the trade. This will probably need to be a cooperative effort with the U.S. government in the form of guarantees or other support.

It is evident that the importance, benefits, and problems of increased trade with China and the U.S.S.R. is not fully recognized by many manufacturing firms. Yet, improvement of the balance of payment, the strength of the U.S. dollar, and future markets for U.S. goods depends, in part, on increased support of trade with these countries by consumers, government, middlemen, manufacturers, and financial institutions. Improved attitudes and openness of these groups will significantly enhance the expansion of trade with China and the U.S.S.R. in future years.

REFERENCES

Anderson, K., & Tyers, R. (1987). "Economic Growth and Market Liberalization in China: Implications for Agricultural Trade." *The Developing Economies* (June), pp. 124-146.

Artisien, P. F. R., & Buckley, P. J. (1985). "Joint Ventures in Yugoslavia: Opportunities and Constraints. *Journal of International Business Studies*. (Spring), pp. 111-135.

Barrett, M. (1987). "East Bloc Counts on Counter Trade." *Euromoney* (September), 405, pp. 466-474.

Brandenberg, M. (1987). "Glasnost Spells Openness for East-West Trade." *Accountancy* (December), pp. 67-73.

Cieslik, J., & Sosnowski, B. (1985). "The Role of TNCs in Poland's East-West Trade." *Journal of International Business Studies* (Summer), pp. 121-137.

Crane, A. T., & Suttmeier, R. P. (1986). "Nuclear Trade with China." *The Columbia Journal of World Business* (Spring), pp. 35-40.

Goldman, M. I. (1985). "U.S.-Soviet Trade: What Went Wrong and What About the Future?" *The Columbia Journal of World Business* (Winter), pp. 45-48.

Hendryx, S. R. (1986). "Implementation of a Technology Transfer Joint Venture in the People's Republic of China: A Management Perspective." *The Columbia Journal of World Business* (Spring), pp. 57-66.

Hisrich, R. D., & Peters, M. P. (1985). "East-West Trade: An Assessment by U.S. Banks." *The Columbia Journal of World Business* (Spring), pp. 15-22.

Hisrich, R. D., & Peters, M. P. (1983). "East-West Trade: An Assessment by U.S. Manufacturers." *The Columbia Journal of World Business* (Winter), pp. 44-50.

Hisrich, R. D., Peters, M. P., & Weinstein, A. K. (1981). "East-West Trade: The View from the United States." *Journal of International Business Studies* (Winter), pp. 109-121.

Kogut, B. (1986). "On Developing Contracts to Guarantee Enforceability: Theory and Evidence from East-West Trade." *Journal of International Business Studies* (Spring), pp. 47-61.

Miller, R. L., & Lehoczyke, C. K. (1984). "New Forms of Private Business in Hungary: Some Economic and Social Implications." *The Columbia Journal of World Business* (Winter), pp. 47-52.

Naor, J., & Bod, P. (1986). "Socialist Entrepreneurship in Hungary: Reconciling the 'Irreconcilables.'" *The Columbia Journal of World Business* (Summer), pp. 55-68.

Reeder, J. A. (1984). "Entrepreneurship in the People's Republic of China." *The Columbia Journal of World Business* (Fall), pp. 43-51.

Ross, M. C. (1986). "China and the United States' Export Controls System." *The Columbia Journal of World Business* (Spring), pp. 27-33.

Tai, L. S. T. (1988). "Doing Business in the People's Republic of China: Some Keys to Success." *Management International Review* (February), pp. 5-9.

Wang, N. T. (1986). United States and China: Business Beyond Trade—An Overview." *The Columbia Journal of World Business* (Spring), pp. 3-11.

Wong, E. L. (1987). "Recent Developments in China's Special Economic Zones: Problems and Prognosis." *The Developing Economies* (March), pp. 73-85.

Zamet, J. M., & Bovarnick, M. E. (1986). "Employee Relations for Multinational Companies in China." *The Columbia Journal of World Business* (Spring), pp. 13-19.

Chapter 20

The China Market and Lessons from Successful Exporters

Vishnu H. Kirpalani
Wayne R. Robinson

SUMMARY. Today's China is a market with considerable potential for Western exporters. However, understanding the China market is difficult, and penetrating it requires a full commitment from top management. The China market is described and the findings from a survey of successful exporters is given. The survey results provide knowledge of the determinants of export success. Lessons to be learned from them are detailed. These should be useful to other exporters and governments.

The People's Republic of China (China) market is large, growing and relatively new to most outsiders. New because of China's recent "Open Door" policy which is turning that country towards more trade and investment from Japan and the West. The identification of the factors that contribute to export success in China is important for present and potential exporting firms, as well as for governments, with respect to their export support programs. This chapter reviews some relevant literature on the determinants of export success. It then provides an overview of today's China as a market, after which it reports the findings of a recent survey of successful Canadian exporters to China. Finally it suggests some

This chapter was first published in the *Journal of Global Marketing*, Vol. 2(4) 1989.

lessons that might be learned from analyses of those findings in the context of the China market.

In general four groups of variables have been identified as internal determinants of export behavior: managements' expectations, commitment to export marketing, firms' differential advantage, and the strength of managerial operations (Cavusgil & Nevin, 1981).

Planning for exports and the growth objectives of a firm have also been identified as important contributors to the export activities of firms (Walters, 1985). Reviewing export assistance from government agencies has also proved useful (Cavusgil, 1984). Other relevant variables are related to the differential advantage and marketing capability of firms. These are variables such as product quality (Malekzadeh, 1982) and pricing advantage (Rabino, 1980).

Two research studies in the Canadian context were deemed relevant. In a survey of Canadian and U.S. exporters concluded at the beginning of the 1980s (Kirpalani & Macintosh, 1980), the most powerful predictor of export success for the firm was found to be "managerial technology"—top management effort, internal organizational structure for exports, and control information. The factors emerging as next most important were marketing variables (promotional efforts, price/credit packages, and the quality of distribution channels). Production and manufacturing variables proved to be of lesser importance, and government assistance appeared to have little influence. Size was not important.

A 1985 study, by the Centre for International Business Studies at Dalhousie University for the Canadian Federal Department of External Affairs, of 27 companies that had won the Canada Export Award in 1983 and/or 1984 examined elements common to all these exporters. It concluded that "the most fundamental strength of the award winners is their people" (Rosson et al., 1985). As well as good people, these companies displayed a clear philosophy. Their corporate mission had been clearly developed and articulated, and included a commitment to exporting. These companies had also recognized the need and organized their operations so as to satisfy their target customers. Furthermore, these company strengths, people and philosophy, had been turned into success in exports as a result of sound action skills. These included the ability to locate and secure market niches, to design the right products and services, and to plan and implement an effective exporting campaign. The research studies indicated above were utilized in formulating this study.

The degree of success enjoyed by a firm in a particular market can be influenced favorably by the extent of its export marketing. This is evidenced by the adoption of a strategic approach with the focus on the customer segments and the environment, and its emphasis on method of market entry and strategic management. It is within this strategic concept that factors of success in exporting to China can be examined. Organization, planning, and control are also important, and in a Canadian context, the availability of government assistance and export financing can be significant in China. Let us first obtain a perspective on the China market.

CHINA: MARKET ENVIRONMENT, POTENTIAL, AND OPPORTUNITIES

China is a country with considerable potential. With over one billion people, it has nearly one-fourth of the world's population. China also possesses vast mineral wealth. It has a variety of coal deposits, large petroleum resources with low sulphur content, widely distributed iron-ore deposits, and many non-ferrous metals (Qu Wen, 1984). But China is still a developing country with a per capita GNP of only US $300 (World Development Report, 1985). The majority of the Chinese population are engaged in agriculture and 68% live in rural areas. Foreign trade used to be only about 7% of GNP, roughly $10 billion each of exports and imports. Today, however, its exports and imports are of the order of $30 billion each. This increase was the result of China's needed export revenues. Toward the end of the 1970s it became apparent to the Chinese leadership that the next stage of uplifting the economy would require continuous importation of proprietary technology and management expertise, notably from the West and Japan. China launched its drive toward modernization in 1978.

Effective Market Potential Assessment:
China

How should Canadian firms assess the market potential in China? A naive approach is to estimate demand based on population size, or population and current purchasing power (Stewart, 1985; Sokoloff & Lemoine, 1982). These factors alone however are not enough because developing economies can change rapidly. Assessment of a centrally planned economy requires an understanding of changes in the economic structure and resulting economic performance, economic policies and the business environment. In other words, a much more comprehensive approach is needed (Kirpalani & Xu Kuan, 1986).

Tremendous changes in market accessibility have taken place in China in recent years as the centralized economy gradually integrates more market mechanisms into the system in order to increase economic efficiency. These changes have had positive effects on economic performance and external trade. In the period 1980-1985, for example, China's total product grew on average by 11.3% and its foreign trade by 10.5% (*Beijing Review*, 1986).

Today, China's development strategy is focused on improving its external economic relations in order to attract capital, know-how and technology. The following are examples of some of China's recent economic policies that have eased market accessibility for Western firms:

- gradual decentralization has been taking place not only in the domestic economic sectors but also in the foreign trade sector (*Beijing Review*, 1985)
- China has opened its door to foreign investment, very little of which was previously permitted
- special economic zones have been granted more authority to trade independently with foreigners and accommodate foreign investors
- the Chinese domestic market has been partially opened to foreign joint ventures manufacturing products for consumption in China. Such products originally were regulated so that they could be sold only abroad (*Beijing Review*, 1984).

The vitalized Chinese economy has increased its ability to export both goods and services. According to Chinese statistics, the country's foreign exchange service income from tourism, and building and engineering services abroad, greatly exceeds expenses. Moreover, compared with the situation before 1978, when there was little direct foreign investment and foreign debt was minimal, the progress in attracting and employing foreign investment has been significant. During the 1979-1985 period, the volume of foreign loans reached US $20.3 billion, and the contract value of direct foreign investment totalled US $16.2 billion (*Beijing Review*, 1986).

The Changed Market Profile

China's consumers spend almost 60% of their incomes on food, and another 10-15% on clothing. Housing/rent expenditures are low in urban areas due to subsidization of urban housing. Consumption of durables in terms of numbers per household are in rank order — watches, bicycles, and radio sets. The attractiveness of inexpensive watches and radios is understandable; bicycles are the primary mode of passenger transportation and are also used to haul various materials. The television market is also growing phenomenally. There are already 85 television sets on average per 100 urban households (Taylor & Hardee, 1985). Most of the above goods are domestically produced. Close to 80% of China's imports consist of producer goods. The market for imported consumer goods, therefore, is limited and likely to remain so. International marketers should know how growth in the Chinese domestic market for consumer goods can create demand for producer goods, thus raising import demand for the latter products. Figure 1 depicts an example.

Marketing Opportunities in China

Opportunities in the Chinese market are growing. As the government moves toward more rapid economic development, new demand is created in infrastructure sectors of transport, communication and energy for imports, foreign investment, and various forms of international cooperation. Transportation in China mainly de-

FIGURE 1

ESTIMATED GROWTH IN FOOD CONSUMPTION AND
TOTAL PRODUCTION REQUIREMENTS: 1984-90

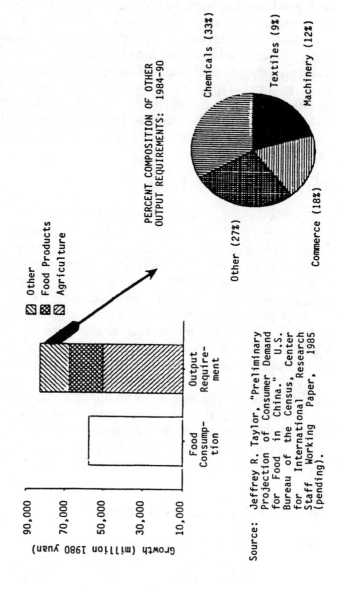

PERCENT COMPOSITION OF OTHER
OUTPUT REQUIREMENTS: 1984-90

Source: Jeffrey R. Taylor, "Preliminary
Projection of Consumer Demand
for Food in China." U.S.
Bureau of the Census, Center
for International Research
Staff Working Paper, 1985
(pending).

pends on the railway system. Rail freight volume today is 31.0 times greater than it was 30 years ago, while railway mileage has increased only 2.29 times, and the number of locomotives and wagons has increased only 2.50 times. The growth of railway carrying capacity is so far short of freight volume growth that some trunk railways can only meet 50-70 percent of their actual needs. The new Five-Year Plan (1986-1990) and a new research study titled "China in 2000" admit that by the end of 1990 the demand pressure on transport cannot be totally alleviated (Guojun, 1985). Furthermore, as China tends to diversify transport loads to all types of transportation, the need for trucks, ships and highway systems, and ports facilities will increase dramatically. In order to lay a solid transportation foundation for economic development, foreign investment in this sector must be given higher priority (*China Daily*, 1985).

There is also a big gap in the communication industry. A survey conducted in January 1983 indicated that only one person in every 200 in China has a phone. Only five other countries in the world have such a low number of telephones per capita (*Beijing Review*, 1984). Foreign technology and investment are desperately needed in this section. The lack of electricity generating capacity is another serious problem. The supply of power cannot meet the needs owing to the relatively low energy efficiency, the fast growing economy, and the low rate of growth of the energy industry. If new capacity is not developed quickly a serious energy supply shortage will occur by the year 2000 (*People's Daily*, 1985). In developing the power sector, the Chinese face serious financing problems because this industry requires enormous initial investment and has a long payback period. In the future, development of the power sector will stress the simultaneous development of thermal and hydro plants because of China's rich coal and hydraulic resources. Nuclear power plants may also be developed along the coast where coal and hydraulic resources are not available.

China's Five-Year Plan (1986-1990) is targeted on transforming and enlarging a number of industrial sectors. There will therefore be opportunities for international marketers in the following industries: machine building, electronics, metallurgy, chemicals, building materials, light industry, textiles, packaging, medical equipment, pharmaceutical, construction, agriculture, forestry, and animal husbandry. The Plan also focuses on some crucial new projects; large hydroelectric plants, nuclear power plants, strip-mining coal operations and harbors.

Upgrading the technology of enterprises presents another series of opportunities. Technological upgrading is needed in almost every sector of the Chinese economy, from high technology (such as the computer and aircraft industries) to ordinary technology (such as in food processing packaging) and managerial skills (such as hotel management and consulting). However, since China has only a limited amount of foreign exchange, they will have to buy technology on a selective basis. Accordingly, joint ventures, cooperative enterprises with foreign investors, and solely foreign-owned enterprises have been developed in the key project sectors of energy, railways, harbors, and raw and semi-finished materials (*Beijing Review*, 1986).

Constraints and Controls
in the China Market

While there are increasing opportunities in the Chinese market, it is not without some constraints. These are discussed below:

1. The centralized control over foreign economic affairs will be maintained. Although there are many relaxations in external economic relations and local governments have been granted some authority to do business with foreign firms, in practice, rather than directly intervening in foreign trade and investment, the government uses import and export licensing, and specialized import and export corporations and institutions, to monitor foreign economic activities and implement control and coordination.

2. The conservative foreign borrowing policy is impossible to change in the short term. The Chinese authorities are conservative in borrowing because they believe that China's export ability is not strong enough, while it is crucial to pay back any borrowing in order to preserve their independence of action. This attitude is steeped in history and the Communist approach. Most of China's exports are primary products such as grain, coal, oil, and other raw materials, whose prices fluctu-

ate very frequently in the international market. The other main exports, textile products and clothing, often face difficulties increasing their market shares because of protectionism in the world market.

In recent years, China's foreign trade has had a deficit every year, which has led to some concern for the Chinese government. If China's exports decrease due to changes in the international market, it is very likely that imports will be controlled sooner or later.

3. The infrastructure in China is relatively weak. It will take time to achieve improvement in sea and air ports, highway system, telephone system, and other public utilities.
4. Operational constraints exist. They result from cultural differences, geographic distance, bureaucracy, and management and technical skills. Without enough necessary preparation before arrival in China, operational problems may not be properly handled and could even lead to business failure.

The Changing China Market

There is no doubt that the nature of the Chinese market is changing. It has an increasing import capacity, new opportunities for foreign investors and improved market accessibility. But China's purchasing will remain highly correlated with its industrial growth sectors.

China has become a fiercely competitive market. Japan, the U.S., Hong Kong and West Germany are the largest exporters to China, with Canada ranking fifth. Japan's success in China is based on a corporate culture which recognizes the need for long-term commitments, the presence of over 250 trade officers throughout China, and a trading house capability that can deal with Chinese requirements for countertrade and commodity trade purchases in payment for export sales (Department of External Affairs, 1987).

Canada-China Trade

The composition of Canada-China trade has undergone major changes. Ten years ago fabricated products represented less than 27% of Canadian export sales to China; today that share has doubled. Technology intensive industrial products are also a major growth sector. Starting from a base of only $13 million in Canadian exports in 1983, sales of these products to China reached $305 million in 1986, a 23 fold increase (Chen, 1988). Canadian firms have recently won major contracts in the power sector, and continue to pursue projects in telecommunications, transportation, and agriculture. Much of this recent activity is partially a result of cooperative agreements with China that have resulted in established programs in areas ranging from agriculture to educational exchanges and medical research. Canadian government departments and agencies are actively promoting Canadian products and services in China.

Business organizations such as the Canada-China Trade Council have been created and the Canadian Chamber of Commerce is working in cooperation with the All China Federation of Industry and Commerce. Most of Canada's major banks have offices located in Beijing as do a growing number of large Canadian companies.

SURVEY OF SUCCESSFUL CANADIAN EXPORTERS TO CHINA

Sample and Questionnaire

The sample consisted of 33 successful Canadian exporters to China. Top management of thirty Canadian exporters known to have been successful in China were personally interviewed. The questionnaire responses of 26 of these companies were complete and thus useable. The questionnaire was also mailed to the top management of 70 other Canadian exporters known to have been trying to export to China. Of the 17 who replied, only seven reported success. This brought the total to 33 (26 + 7) successful exporters.

The sample firms constituted a fair cross-section of Canadian industry; 60% were manufacturers, 15% service companies, 12% consultants, and the others were trading companies sales agents/distributors. The industries they represented were mainly industrial products; with 33% from the petroleum and chemicals group, 18% from telecommunications, 18% from forest products, 12% from energy, and the rest spread across seven other sectors. Interestingly enough, a little over half the sample were small companies, having sales below $20 million. Also, the pull of the Pacific Rim evidenced itself by 51% of the firms being based in Alberta and British Columbia. Ontario firms were only 24% of the sample and the rest were divided between Quebec and Manitoba. All the firms had export experience.

The questionnaire focused on the firm's dealings with China and had three main sections. The first was concerned with general information about the firm. The second dealt with specific questions on the firm's export experience, knowledge of China, the marketing mix variables, export channels, and administrative arrangements for managing those export linkages. The third inquired about use of government assistance, financing methods and involvement with third parties. It also requested information on planning activities and perceived success factors.

FINDINGS

Management Variables and Government Assistance

The determinants of export success section indicated that top management effort, internal organizational structure and control information were very important, as were a clearly developed corporate mission and a commitment to exporting. The survey findings were a validation of the above. Government assistance also turned out to be important. This is understandable as regards a centrally controlled country like China.

Dedication and commitment to the China market were exemplified by the sample firms. China was stated to be one of their most important export markets by 64% of the firms, 42% included South and Southeast Asia, and 27% also listed the Pacific Rim. The many visits by most CEOs and other officers are shown in Table 1.

The reasons for these frequent visits by Canadian management to China varied from attending trade shows to conducting negotiations, sponsoring seminars and regular business visits. Much of their time was spent making contacts and gathering intelligence. Almost all the firms used the services of the Canadian government offices located in Beijing, Shanghai, and Hong Kong, 76% of these

TABLE 1

VISITS TO CHINA

Frequency of Visits to China by President or CEO	No. of Companies	% of Total
Never	3	9%
Once	7	23%
Occasional (2 - 5 times)	9	30%
Often (2 - 3 times/year)	6	20%
Very often (more than 3 times/year)	8	27%

Number of Other Officers in Company that have Visited China	No. of Companies	% of Total
1 - 5	18	55%
6 - 10	9	27%
11 - 15	2	6%
More than 15	4	12%

on a regular basis. Seventy percent of the respondents had participated in government-sponsored missions and trade fairs in China.

VISITS TO CHINA

Furthermore, 61% had utilized the Canadian government program for export market development (PEMD). Also, 48% stated that they sought advice from China specialists in the Department of External Affairs and most of these did this on a regular basis. Thus government assistance emerged as a very important factor as regards China. Moreover the Alberta firms believed that the provinces's government activities also contributed to their success. The Alberta government has had a long and active winning relationship with the Chinese province of Heilong Jiang and doubtless this has helped.

Many of the firms had tried to alter their internal organizational structures toward understanding the Chinese culture. Two-thirds of the firms employed at least one Chinese speaking person and 30% employed persons who had studied China in college or university. Thirty-nine percent of the firms had at least one employee at headquarters totally devoted to the Chinese market. With regard to control of information, almost all the firms exhibited detailed knowledge of the level of Chinese technology and the priority areas of China's present Five-Year Plan for which their products and services were suited.

Formal strategic planning activities for the China market were undertaken by 58% of the sample. In many of the firms surveyed decisions on activities in China were made at the very highest levels of the company. Negotiations with the Chinese in 42% of the cases were conducted by the CEO and for another 42% by a vice-president. Commitment to the China market was high. In the majority of the cases it had taken between one and four years to negotiate the first or most important contract.

Marketing Variables and Action Skills

Product/service was the most important marketing mix variable; 85% of the firms thought they were delivering state-of-the-art technology. Further, 81% felt their ability and willingness to provide training was important, and 70% felt that servicing and parts supply was critical to success.

When asked what they thought was the single greatest feature of their product/service from the Chinese buyer's perspective, technology, uniqueness of product and specialized nature scored high. Also, some believed it was their world class reputation. Only 9% thought they sold on price alone, and a further 3% believed their ability to offer a complete package was the main factor.

Price alone does not ensure success but coupled with product quality price can be critical. Almost all the firms priced competitively. In structuring a price for the China market most exporters considered all the elements the Chinese might expect to be included such as training, service and spare parts, and technology transfer. Negotiations with the Chinese often require several visits to China by top management. It is also frequently necessary to entertain Chinese visitors in Canada. Some of the interviewees indicated that if they had been aware of these costs, they would have structured their price differently.

The most prevalent export market entry channel to China is

through a representative/agent based in China, or Hong Kong. The Chinese concept of "guanxi," or personal connections, can be extremely important in choosing the right agent. The emphasis on personal relationships has always been a part of the Chinese system and as China modernizes and decentralizes some argue the concept of guanxi is becoming more widespread (Pye, 1982). A recent survey reported on how Chinese mid-level executives find new suppliers. One hundred percent of the executives contacted sources through old friends; 93% of them did this frequently, and 7% sometimes. In comparison only 19% frequently found suppliers through business directories and just 4% did this frequently through open bids.

Larger Canadian firms, 33% of the sample, had established offices in China or elsewhere in Asia to cover the China market. However, the costs of maintaining an office with a Canadian and one support staff in Beijing is estimated at $600,000 annually. A few firms used third parties based in the U.S., Japan, or in Canada. The use of consortia to penetrate the China market had been used by 27% of the firms and two-thirds of these indicated this approach was successful.

The favored promotional technique for most of the sample firms was face-to-face personal contact. Trade shows were attended by 58% of them and 52% regularly conducted technical seminars. Although 62% of the firms reported that they normally advertise in foreign markets, only 31% advertised in China. Moreover, much of what was termed advertising in China consisted of translation of sales brochures. Several of the executives interviewed indicated that the Chinese place a great deal of importance on personal contact and that once a personal relationship with the customer is established it is much easier to do business.

None of the respondents had any difficulties with payments from China. The credit terms and method of payment for their Chinese customers were identical to those offered to other foreign customers. But two firms had attempted countertrade and neither of them considered the transaction a success. With respect to forms of supportive financing, a few companies had been involved in World Bank contracts or with Canadian International Development Agency (CIDA) projects. A few others had utilized Canadian Export Development Corporation (EDC) financing.

LIMITATIONS OF THE STUDY

The universe of successful Canadian exporters to China is probably not much more than 100 companies. The representative of any Canadian exporter to China who arrives there is highly likely to make some contact with a Canadian Trade Commission Office. One of the authors had been a Trade Commissioner in China and accessed the total list of these exporters. Personal interviews were conducted with 30 of them and a mail questionnaire was sent to 70. Of the latter 17 responded. Thus close to 47% (30 + 17) of the universe responded and the actual sample comprised 33% (33). A limitation of the study is the small sample. A bigger sample obviously would have given more data. Whether it would have yielded very different results is a moot question.

There are basically no other limitations. This study has shown that there are common factors that have contributed to the success of Canadian exporters in China. Most of these fit in with those shown as important determinants of export success in more general previous studies.

LESSONS TO BE LEARNED

There are valuable lessons to be learned from the study for other firms involved in or intending to export to China.

1. Small firms can be as successful as large ones when exporting to China. But experience in exporting is important. If that experience has been gained in other parts of the Asia-Pacific region it is even more useful.
2. Top management effort is the most critical factor in achieving success. China is a very difficult and puzzling export market for Canadians, requiring a long-term commitment. Chinese bureaucrats are very status conscious and visits by top management can open many more doors than junior officers can.
3. Executives in charge of exports should make active use of the **extensive** Canadian government assistance services, both operational and financial. Use of these services will save exporters considerable time and effort in the information gather-

ing phase, help with finding their way through the Chinese bureaucracy, selecting representatives/agents and obtaining specific finance for market development and aid/conventional financing when necessary.

4. Exporters must structure their organization at headquarters so that one or more specific persons are designated as responsible for the China market.

5. Exporters should have at least one Chinese speaking person at headquarters in Canada. The impact of such person(s) would be very beneficial to the others in the organization who need to know and deal with the Chinese market.

6. Exporters should study the China government development plans in depth to ensure that their product/service is featured therein and will be in demand.

7. Exporters should try to deliver products/services that are state-of-the-art technology, unique, or specialized. They must also make certain that Chinese buyers and end-users are fully aware of the product/service technical qualities and the firm's capabilities in regard to delivery, training, and, where necessary, spare parts. Moreover, they must offer a competitive price.

8. Exporters should select a representative/agent with "guanxi," or good personal connections. To find the right person the exporter should consult with a Canadian trade commissioner, a Canadian chartered bank officer in the region, or other companies experienced in China. The agent should be utilized to identify opportunities, set up appropriate meetings, and act as advisor and interpreter of Chinese custom and law. Larger firms who can afford it should organize a local office in China.

9. The most effective method of promotion in China is personal face-to-face contact. This personal contact can be built up through trade shows, technical seminars, and direct sales calls on the appropriate Chinese government agencies and end-users. Sponsoring buyers' visits to Canada can also be useful. This personal contact and building of relationships is a very effective way to facilitate export success in China.

CONCLUSIONS

The similarity between China's development priorities and Canadian technological capabilities is striking. Sectors such as agriculture, energy, mining, and transportation figure prominently in China's development plans and are areas in which Canada has significant competitive advantage. This tends to make China a natural priority export market for many Canadian firms. There is also evidence to indicate that just being Canadian often gives a firm an edge over competition due to Canada's long standing friendly relations with China and the fact that Canada is not a superpower.

To be successful in China, Canadian firms must know China's Five-Year Plan and have a great deal of specific information on questions such as the suitability of their product/service, who are the Chinese buyers, who are the end-users, who is the competition and what are they selling, is one buying agency more important than another, and where are details on the industry available? China tends to be a very strange and mysterious place for most Westerners and Canadian government trade commissioners with experience can save exporters considerable time and effort in gathering information. Further, as regards China, the centrally planned hierarchic economy, the cultural and language barriers, and the enormous bureaucratic structure of decision making make it imperative for top management in exporting firms to make a significant commitment of time and effort in order to penetrate that market successfully.

REFERENCES

Beijing Review. (1986, April 14). "Ten Major SocioEconomic Changes," 29(15).

Beijing Review. (1985, January 7). "Chen Muhua Outline Tasks for 1985," 28(1).

Beijing Review. (1984, December 10). "Gin Mu on Policies for Coastal Cities," 27(50).

Cavusgil, S. Tamer (1986). "Differences Among Exporting Firms Based on Their Degree of Internalization." *Journal of Business Research*, 12(2), pp. 195-208.

Cavusgil, S. Tamer and Nevin, John R. (1981). "Internal Determinants of Export

Marketing Behaviour: An Empirical Investigation." *Journal of Marketing Research* (February) 18(1), pp. 114-119.

Chen, John (1988). "Canada's China Trade." *China Business Review*, (January-February).

China Daily. (1985, September 24).

Department of External Affairs. (1987, April). "General Briefing Material — People's Republic of China." Ottawa, Canada: Government of Canada.

Guojun, Yang. (1985, December 13), "Zhongwai Hesi Qiyie Qixian Jiang Yang Chang," *People's Daily* (overseas edition).

Kirpalani, V. H. and Macintosh, N. B. (1980). "International Marketing Effectiveness of Technology Oriented Small Firms." *Journal of International Business Studies*, (Winter), XI, 3, pp. 81-90.

Kirpalani, V. H. and Xu Kuan. (1986). "Effective International Market Potential Assessment: China," in Melanie Wallendorf and Paul Anderson (Eds.). *Advances in Consumer Research*, XIV (pp. 398-402). Seventeeth Annual Conference of the Association for Consumer Research held at Toronto, Ontario (October 16-19).

Malekzadeh, Ali R. (1982). "An Empirical Study of the Export Perceptions of California Manufacturers." Unpublished Dissertation, University of Utah.

People's Daily. Various issues.

Qu, Wen. (1984). *China: A General Survey*. Beijing: Foreign Language Press.

Rabino, Samuel. (1980). "An Examination of Barriers to Exporting Encountered by Small Manufacturing Companies." *Management International Review*, 20(1), pp. 67-73.

Rosson, P., Brooks, M., Kamath, D., and Patton, D. (1985). *Excellence in Exporting: Advice and Comments from Canada Export Award Winners*. Ottawa: Government of Canada, Department of External Affairs.

Sokoloff, Georges and Lemoine, Françoise. (1982). "China and the USSR: Limits to Trade with West." *Atlantic Papers*, 46, Paris, France: The Atlantic Institute for International Affairs.

Stewart, Sally. (1985). "One Billion Customers." *Asian Affairs*, (October), XVI, 111.

Taylor, Jeffrey R. and Hardee, Karen A. (1985). *Consumer Demand Factbook: China*. Washington, DC: U.S. Bureau of the Census; International Statistical Program Center and Center for International Research.

Walters, Peter G. (1985). "A Study of Planning for Export Operations." *International Marketing Review*, (Autumn) 2(3), pp. 74-81.

World Development Report (1985). New York: World Bank; Oxford University Press.

Chapter 21

Joint Venture Strategies
for Marketing in China

Lynette L. Knowles
Ike Mathur

SUMMARY. To date, joint ventures in China have offered much in potential but little in realized profits for foreign partners. Foreign partners need to negotiate terms such that they can readily and profitably market in China. Labor requirements, materials quality and supply sources, level of technology involved, the rewards for exporting, access to the Chinese market, government regulations, transfer pricing and other important factors need to be carefully negotiated before signing a joint venture contract. Financing the venture should take into consideration the emerging nature of the Chinese financial markets.

In 1984, China International Trust and Investment Corporation (CITIC) felt that the timing was ideally suitable to establish a cosmetics joint venture (JV) to meet China's great demand for cosmetics. It started discussions with a number of famous French cosmetics manufacturers, and found that all of them were interested in marketing in China but were reluctant to form a JV to do so. That is, until it contacted Parfums Jacques Bogart. After thirteen months of negotiations a JV agreement was signed to form Jacques Bogart China Co Ltd., which now manufactures lipstick, rouge, nail polish, perfumes, and other cosmetics in Nantong.[1] Jacques Bogart China is an example of how JVs can be successfully established in

This chapter was first published in the *Journal of Consumer Marketing*, Vol. 2(1) 1989.

China to service the Chinese market.[2] Unfortunately, such has not been the case with numerous other Chinese JVs that were enthusiastically formed, only to stagnate or cease operations later on.

The well-documented problems of JVs in China can be partially attributed to a lack of thorough understanding of the Chinese perspectives on JVs, and partially to a lack of giving full consideration to the strategic issues involved in starting a JV in China. While China has continued to emphasize self-reliance as a basis for Chinese society, it has also emphasized relationships with foreign firms based on "equality and mutual benefit." Employment creation, access to technology, modernization, and acquisition of foreign exchange are the major benefits that China expects to receive from its joint activities with foreign partners. An understanding of these and other Chinese perspectives is vital to the success of JVs.[3]

Strategic issues involved in starting a JV in China are discussed first in this chapter. The second section deals with negotiating factors. Some interesting alternatives for rewarding the servicing of foreign markets as well as the domestic market are discussed. The section on financing provides some alternatives to the traditional method where the Chinese partner provides the land and the building, and the foreign partner provides capital and technology. The fourth section examines managerial and public policy issues, while avenues for further research are explored in the last section.

STRATEGIC CONSIDERATIONS

As China prepares to implement its eighth five-year plan (1991-1995), the possibilities for JVs look better than ever (Xie, 1987). Both the Chinese vice-president of foreign economic relations and trade and the U.S. ambassador to China have commented on favorable Sino-American economic relations (Wang, 1988; Lord, 1988). The number of new JVs in China as well as China's exports and imports have been steadily increasing. In this environment, JVs constitute a viable strategy for marketing in China.

Foreign firms contemplating a JV in China are faced with a variety of problems that they do not face in their domestic endeavors. With the possible exception of firms based in Japan, foreign firms face a cultural environment quite different from that in their home countries.[4] The subtleties of a traditional culture whose roots go back thousands of years are difficult to understand for those coming from a Western culture.

The legal environment facing JV partners in China has a unique flavor. The Western manager, used to operating in a highly formalized, well-established and deterministic legal environment, suddenly finds out that not only are business laws nonexistent in China, but that the rules of the ball game seem to change periodically.

Chinese, besides being difficult to master, has nuances that can be interpreted only with high levels of familiarity with the language. The political environment is quite different from what one would encounter in the Western world. Communications between China and other countries can be a problem at times. Office operating expenses quite often can be higher in Beijing than in Chicago.

Despite these other constraints on operating in China, many firms want to form Chinese JVs because of their firm-specific advantages that can be readily transferred to China. Examples of firm-specific advantages include previous international experience, managerial skills, special promotional skills, brand names, research and development expertise, large firm size resulting in enhanced access to capital markets, and existence of oligopolies in the markets for the firm's products and patents. Some of these advantages can be and are exploited through licensing.

JVs in China become attractive when the above advantages complement advantages unique to locating in China. These location-specific advantages include access to raw materials, access to comparatively cheap labor, and access to numerically the world's largest consumer market.[5] Additional factors that influence the decision to form JVs in China include tax holidays for the profits of the JVs, the stability of the political environment in China, and China's limits on foreign goods imported for domestic consumption.

The potential for selling in the Chinese market is the dominant location-specific advantage. First, the size of the market is such that it cannot be ignored. Second, even if domestic sales volume is restricted it leads to brand name recognition, creating the potential for increased levels of sales in the future. Philip Knight, chairman of Nike, Inc., says that, "The trick is to get them to know Nike," (Ignatius, 1985, p. 34). Nike started selling its shoes in late 1985 in a Beijing department store. Despite a price tag that was equivalent to 10 days wages in China, the store was selling over a 100 pairs a day. Third, establishing oneself in the Chinese market at an early stage may serve to provide a competitive edge over home country competitors who may want to come into the Chinese market later. This rationale appears to be the primary one for attracting many overseas firms to China.

These factors have attracted to China many overseas firms who, in their haste to service the vast Chinese market, did not fully appreciate the Chinese perspectives, and thus have had to settle for negligible or low levels of profitability.

NEGOTIATING CONSIDERATIONS

An extensive sct of laws regulating business conduct and relations is nonexistent in China. The Chinese joint venture law, written in 1979, was designed to provide a framework for foreign investments in China. Many Western businesspeople failed to realize the lack of existence of a Chinese commercial code and thus did not include appropriate protective clauses in their JV agreements.

Recently, in response to complaints by foreign investors, China has implemented regulations designed to make JVs more attractive to foreigners. These regulations are designed to reduce bureaucratic red tape, labor costs, utility charges, and land-use fees. Despite these regulations, negotiating a JV agreement that provides sufficient safeguards for the foreign investor is essential.

Labor

One would expect that China would have adequate numbers of unskilled labor. However, skilled and semi-skilled workers may be in short supply. Foreign firms going into China should be willing to provide appropriate training to upgrade the skills levels of their workers. However, they should be aware that China assigns workers to JVs and quite often prefers to replace them every one to two years. While this may be beneficial for China in that trained workers are then available for Chinese firms, it creates a problem for JVs — having to train new workers all the time. One way to handle this would be to include a clause on worker turnover in the JV agreement.

In addition to laborers, foreign partners should be concerned about availability of clerical, supervisory, maintenance, management, and possibly sales personnel. The availability of some of these types of personnel is going to be governed by the JV agreement. To the extent possible, the foreign partner, in general, should be willing to utilize Chinese personnel in areas where local skill levels are appropriate. The issue of training key Chinese personnel at the foreign partner s non-Chinese operations should certainly be negotiated if it may have a positive impact on the operations of the JV.

Wages paid to Chinese workers have oftentimes been unilaterally established by the Chinese. The foreign partner should negotiate fair wages and include them in the JV agreement. The productivity level of Chinese workers should be kept in mind when negotiating wages.

China does not have much in the way of labor laws as is the case in Western countries. However, Chinese workers are provided a level of social benefits that is, in general, higher than in the Western world. A foreign firm in China would have to concern itself with a variety of factors related to work conditions and worker benefits. The hours to be worked, policies related to tardiness and absenteeism, and work breaks are of concern to the foreign partner. Foreign partners should be particularly concerned with having the latitude to replace or fire workers who are habitually tardy or absent.

Worker benefits such as health benefits, health clinics, sick leaves, vacations, pensions, housing, and day care centers, would generally be expected to be at least at the same level as those provided to workers in Chinese firms. The foreign partner may be willing to agree to providing a higher level of worker benefits if it serves to recruit outstanding workers and motivates them to achieve a high level of performance.

Materials

Local materials constitute an example of location-specific advantages that would attract a foreign investor to China. The foreign firm in China will seek assurances regarding the quality, quantity and prices of local raw materials. Many JV partners come from countries with well-established quality control procedures and are used to receiving high quality items. Their expectations regarding Chinese supply sources would be similar.

A steady supply of raw materials is assured if the supplier has sufficient warehouse capacity to smooth out the supply and demand cycles. Many Chinese businesses, due to a variety of factors, have a philosophy of producing for consumption. Either the JV partner or the local supplier would have to provide for sufficient warehousing capacity to assure a steady supply of materials. In this regard, the foreign partner would be interested in specifying delivery schedules in the materials purchase contracts.

Prices of raw materials are of prime concern to the JV partner because of their impact on the profitability of the venture. The foreign partner may insist on specifying a suitable pricing scheme for raw materials before even finalizing the JV.

The foreign partner would also have concerns about obtaining a steady supply of needed imported raw materials and parts. For countries with fully convertible currencies, obtaining imported raw materials is not a problem since the foreign currencies are readily available. However, this is an important issue in China since foreign exchange is a scarce resource and is allocated based on priorities established by the Chinese government. If the availability of imported parts is of critical importance to the venture, then the foreign partner may insist on an appropriate clause in the JV agreement regarding access to sufficient foreign exchange. The foreign partner would also want to assure itself that if materials are imported by a Chinese firm, rather than by the venture, that the prices would be nearly the same as if the venture imported the materials directly.

Land and Building

The Chinese partner would, in general, provide the land and building for the JV. The foreign partner may not have much choice in where the land is situated. However, the foreign partner would be concerned about assuring sufficient power and water. In the past, China has charged JVs considerably more for power and water than Chinese firms. Recent indications are that the Chinese will charge domestic firms and JVs the same rate for utilities. The foreign partner may want to stipulate this in the JV agreement.

The foreign partner would be interested in a dependable supply of power. If the power requirements of the JV cannot be met adequately with existing sources, then the foreign partner should explore the feasibility of generating its own power by specifying it in the JV agreement. Adequate supplies of power generation fuel such as oil or coal should be guaranteed before the start of the venture.

Western-type plant layouts generally specify a single story building because it is more efficient from an assembly viewpoint. The foreign partner may find that, due to space constraints, a single story building for the JV is not feasible. Higher operating costs associated with a multistory building would have to be accounted for in the JV agreement.

Transfer of Technology

The Chinese joint venture law specifies that the foreign partner utilize state of the art technology. Given that China has a large supply of workers and that wages are relatively low compared to Western standards, a natural question to arise is whether foreign partners have a serious interest in using high technology in the Chinese JVs.

The manufacturing experience of Western firms in Third World countries has been varied. Some have found that labor intensive production processes do not result in satisfactory products due to the skill levels of the workers. These firms have determined that utilizing high-technology production processes results in products of a higher, more uniform quality. Still other firms have found that high-technology production processes are not profitable because they require much larger production runs.

Research indicates that Western firms that have labor intensive production processes in their home countries can adapt their processes to the third world environment readily. Electronics firms that have a fair amount of labor intensity have proven to be adept at manufacturing in Third World countries.

In general, Western firms in China would prefer to utilize a level of technology that would enhance the profits of the JV. They would take into consideration factors such as tax incentives for using high technology, the existing capital intensity of their production processes, the adaptability of their production processes, the worker skill levels in China, Chinese regulations related to flexibility in adjusting the size of the JV's labor force, plant design, expected level of production, and China's desire for acquiring high technology.

External Markets

In general, China's preference is that JVs service the export markets so that more foreign exchange is earned by China. Obviously, with a population of one billion, the Chinese market has considerable appeal to foreign partners evaluating a potential JV. Thus, the foreign partner would definitely need to negotiate the mix between export sales and sales in China before entering into a JV agreement.

If some portion of the JV output is slated for export, the foreign partner will need to carefully define the export markets. Failure to do so may find the JV products competing directly with the foreign partner's products manufactured elsewhere. Quite often, the most desirable alternative is for the foreign partner to contract to purchase a portion of the output of the JV. This way issues related to marketing efforts, personal selling, foreign exchange risks, transfer pricing, trade discounts, and so on, do not result in friction between the JV partners.

Domestic Market

Selling the JV products in China is a major attraction for foreign partners. The Chinese partner should be in a position to contribute marketing know-how, provide channels of distribution, and provide personal and promotional selling efforts. The Chinese partner may be interested in negotiating two types of incentives that may pave the way for successfully selling JV products in China. The first would be a marketing fee paid to the Chinese partner for its marketing efforts in selling the products in China. This marketing fee would equal, say, five or seven percent of sales in China, would be part of the JV's operating expenses, and would be paid to the Chinese partner in addition to the profits distributed. Thus, the higher the sales level in China, the higher would be the returns to the Chinese partner.

The second incentive would be to pay the Chinese partner a management fee that is based on the ratio of the JV's output sold in China to its total output. This incentive would reward the Chinese partner for selling proportionally more of the JV's output in China. This management fee would be directly related to the mentioned ratio. A similar type of incentive could also be designed to provide additional returns to the foreign partner for increasing JV exports.

Government Regulations

Profits of a JV are greatly affected by host government regulations. In the past, foreign partners have complained that Chinese regulations have not been applied evenly and consistently. A JV partner pointed out in *Time* magazine that the two consecutive imports of the same materials were assessed two different tariffs, with the higher one being imposed on the second import shipment. When he complained, he was informed that if he wanted, the higher tariff could be imposed retroactively on the first shipment (*Time*, 1986, p. 56).

This incident, to a considerable extent, exemplifies the types of regulatory problems that foreign partners encounter in China. The foreign partners should try to establish the appropriate parameters for regulations as they apply to the JV. For a Western executive, this may sound odd, but not if one keeps in mind that China has little in the way of formal rules and regulations.

Tariffs and customs duties need to be established prior to signing the JV agreement. While this has not been a problem in the past, the foreign partner would be interested in establishing, or at least understanding, customs clearance procedures and delays. This would allow for maintaining adequate inventories of imported materials.

The foreign partner would also be interested in establishing basic rules governing exports of JV products. Any licenses or permissions needed should be assured during the negotiations process. China is not a signatory to world-wide copyright and patent laws. Thus, the foreign partner would be interested in maintaining the integrity of the patented items and processes that it provides the JV.

Transfer Pricing

Many foreign firms utilize transfer prices as a mechanism for adjusting their flow of funds in and out of different tax and sovereign jurisdictions. Western courts and laws have generally specified that transfer prices should reflect arm's length transactions. In many cases this simply means that prevailing market prices should be used as transfer prices. A complication arises if the goods in question are to be incorporated into another good being manufactured by the foreign partner and do not have external markets. In these cases transfer prices are subject to negotiation and should be part of the overall agreement.

Taxes

China does not have a comprehensive commercial code. Real estate and property taxes, local taxes, municipal taxes, regional taxes, inventory taxes, sales taxes, and other types of taxes need to be properly accounted for.

China now has regulations in place that cover the taxation of JV profits, and tax exemptions related to reinvested profits and to high technology. The foreign partner would be interested in specific identification of the tax rates and exemptions as applicable to its JV. Along the same lines, China now has tax laws that apply to earnings of foreign nationals working in China. These laws need to be recognized by the foreign partner because of the resulting effects on after-tax pay and employee motivation.

Foreign Personnel

The compensation for foreign personnel, their merit increases, bonuses, and fringe benefits need to be carefully considered. The foreign partner would have to provide a competitive package to either recruit new personnel for the JV, or transfer its own personnel to China. In many cases, Western compensation and personnel policies and procedures are not consonant with Chinese procedures. It may be that the JV may have to opt for dual procedures, one related to Chinese managers and one for foreign managers. The foreign partner would need to resolve these issues during the negotiations phase.

Housing, especially for Westerners, is in critical short supply in China. Many foreigners working in China have had to resort to living in hotels. This may be acceptable on a temporary basis, but foreign personnel based in China for extended time periods need to be provided with adequate housing. The foreign partner would need to negotiate on this point. Food, entertainment, health and hospitalization care, transportation, and communications to the home country are other areas of concern for foreign partners with China-based foreign personnel.

Foreign Exchange and Profit Repatriation

Access to foreign exchange and profit repatriation procedures should be incorporated into the JV agreement. In 1986, the Beijing Jeep Corporation, a joint venture of American Motors Corporation, halted production for a while and almost ended business because of its inability to access foreign exchange for buying parts in the United States. The Chinese government has issued assurances that adequate foreign exchange would be made available to JVs. However, the foreign partner may want some protection by building its foreign exchange requirements into the JV agreement.

Foreign partners would expect that transfer payments involving foreign exchange such as, for example, profits, royalties, licensing fees, management fees and so on, would be adequately protected in the JV agreement. If the foreign partner does not have the ability to repatriate these transfer payments, it cannot earn its expected profits. Thus, foreign partners should be especially concerned about obtaining adequate safeguards against inconvertibility of these payments.

Auditing Procedures

Auditing procedures are well established in Western countries. Auditing allows the foreign partner to determine that established policies and procedures are being followed and that the JV's cash flows are in keeping with expectations. The foreign partner would prefer to see appropriate auditing procedures in place. The selection of a suitable auditor and auditing on a timely basis are beneficial for both JV partners.

The foreign partner would also be interested in utilizing an established accounting procedure. The accounting procedure should be such that management is provided with relevant information for controlling the activities of the JV.

FINANCING CONSIDERATIONS

The JV is going to be financed through a variety of different options. The Chinese partner will generally contribute land and building. The foreign partner is expected to contribute equipment, technology and capital. Since the JV is only interested in acquiring the use of technology, the issue of licensing or contributing technology becomes a negotiating factor. From the foreign partner's viewpoint, licensing or contributing technology would be negotiated on the basis of the impact on returns.

Chinese firms generally expect that equipment will be contributed by the foreign partner. If the foreign partner does not have the proper equipment to contribute to the JV, then it is expected to increase its capital contribution so that the needed equipment can be purchased.

Foreign Partner Financing

The easiest method of financing is for the foreign partner to provide the capital needed to buy raw materials, pay wages, pay overhead expenses and maintain the necessary level of working capital. The capital contributed by the foreign partner increases its relative share of the JV. Thus, the foreign partner would have a proportionally larger share of the profits or losses.

Chinese Partner Financing

A second alternative is for the Chinese partner to provide a certain portion of the capital needs. For example, the Chinese partner may provide sufficient capital to meet inventory needs, while the foreign partner provides the remaining working capital needs.

The division of needed capital between the foreign and the Chinese partner would be dependent on their desired level of equity in the JV, their liquidity position, and their aversion to bearing risk. For example, the foreign partner may be reluctant to increase its equity in the JV by providing capital because it may feel that it may not be able to recover or repatriate its contributed capital if the venture is terminated or liquidated.

Equity and Debt Financing in China

For the first time since the revolution, China has allowed the organized trading of stocks, at a branch office of the Shanghai Trust and Investment Company. Demand for stocks has been far in excess of supply so far. Bonds are being traded in Shenyang. China has also opened stocks and bonds trading centers in cities such as Guangzhou, Wuhan, and Chongqing. Additionally, many companies have issued bonds and stocks, generally to their employees. Between 1984 and 1986, firms in the Guangdong province raised about $180 million by issuing bonds and stocks.

Another source of financing for a JV is to consider the feasibility of issuing bonds, or perhaps even stock, in China. The practical and legal aspects of this type of financing should become clearer over time. Initially, the bond and stock buyers might be the venture's employees. One of the side benefits of this type of financing might be increased efficiency in the JV.

Link Financing

Link financing, or back-to-back loans financing, is a mechanism for the foreign partner, or some other lending consortium, to provide funds to the JV indirectly. For example, a foreign partner is interested in debt financing for the JV and is willing to provide the funds as debt but not equity. It would deposit the amount of money involved with a cooperating bank. The bank then would lend an equivalent amount to the JV at a rate that is about two percentage points higher than the interest paid on the deposit by the foreign firm. The bank acts as an intermediary in funneling funds from the foreign partner to the JV.

Link financing permits the foreign partner to furnish needed funds to the JV in debt rather than equity. The foreign partner could, of course, lend money directly to the JV. Historically, however, countries have been less reluctant to interfere with the contractual debt cash flows to equity partners compared to similar flows to banks. Thus, link financing tends to reduce the risk level for foreign partners.

MANAGERIAL AND PUBLIC POLICY IMPLICATIONS

It is difficult for many Chinese to forget that China was under Japanese occupation during the 1930s and '40s. Chinese students in recent years have taken to marching periodically through Tian An Men Square to protest the "second occupation" by Japan, i.e., the marketing of Japanese goods in China. Yet, despite these negative sentiments, Japan is China's largest trading partner. Why the Japanese have been so successful in China, despite the local environment, is not a puzzle. The Japanese have been very adept at understanding and conforming to Chinese business customs, which range from the seating formalities at the traditional banquets to the *guanxi* system.[6] Attempts at understanding Chinese business customs hold the promise of significant payoffs for the patient firm.

Additionally, successful JVs are also dependent on recognizing the Chinese perspectives on JVs. For example, foreign firms that keep in mind China's need to create employment, or earn foreign exchange, will find that governmental agencies such as CITIC are very helpful in establishing JVs. Firms that are able to propose inland JVs, away from the coastal areas, would also encounter enthusiastic support from the Chinese government.

Thorelli (1987) states that the Chinese experimentation with its open door policies provides developing nations with many fresh ideas for increasing both economic output and consumer welfare. Kaynak (1986) develops the theme that marketing aids the economic development process through the creation of economic value and the improvement of the industrial and commercial bases of an economy. Combining the ideas of Thorelli and Kaynak provides interesting managerial and public policy implications.

It has been documented that many developing countries have high economic growth rates.[7] If Thorelli's arguments have merit, then these nations will start to implement their own versions of

China's open door policies. Firms that have gained experience in servicing the Chinese markets should then possess distinct advantages that would allow them to be highly successful as they establish themselves in these emerging markets in developing countries. Essentially, experience gained in China should strengthen the marketing competitiveness of firms globally.

From a public policy viewpoint, Western nations should provide all possible assistance to facilitate increased trade with China. To do so would enable their own firms to gain valuable experience in China in the expectation that this experience could be transferred to ventures in other developing countries. Regrettably, Western countries at times have shown a propensity for limiting China trade through a variety of mechanisms such as import controls, export restrictions, limitations on transfer of technology, nonconcessionary credit extension, and other protectionist policies. Restrictions of the type mentioned do not result in the development of economies, the strengthening of private sectors, higher political stability, and the resultant increase in the quality of life globally.

AVENUES FOR FURTHER RESEARCH

Sheth and Eshghi (1989) have conveniently summarized the general types of issues related to cross-cultural and international marketing research.[8] The focus of this section is on proposing some areas for further research related to marketing in China.

Indications are that the Chinese are very brand-conscious. The Kentucky Fried Chicken outlet on Tian An Men Square rings up daily sales that would be the envy of any KFC outlet in the U.S. Kodak, Fuji and other foreign filmmakers control over 70 percent of the color film market in China. Why? Raymond So, manager of J. Walter Thompson China, has the answer: "People in China are the most brand-conscious in the world."[9] Firms that own famous brand names appear to possess a natural advantage in marketing in China. A related research issue is whether brand names can be created to generate high appeal among the Chinese consumers.

Channels of distribution in China tend to be complicated and inefficient. Wholesalers will quite often not only sell competitive brands but also refuse to divulge inventory levels of their authorized brands. Moving goods to inland consumers is even more daunting. Coca Cola and Pepsi chose to do without a distribution network when they first started bottling in China. All they had to do was to wait for customers to bicycle to the production plants and buy their drinks. Over time though, both bottlers have developed excellent distribution networks. Coca Cola and Pepsi notwithstanding, distribution channels in China may very well continue to confound foreign marketers despite the research efforts that are destined for the area.

Motivating Chinese sales representatives to perform at their best levels constitutes a challenge for foreign marketers. Some JV partners report a decline in productivity once sales personnel reach their quotas. It may be that sales personnel are afraid that their quotas might be increased if they substantially exceed their quotas. Another reason may be that incentives such as banquets, plaques, medals and certificates may not be sufficient motivators to increase performance. The typical Western response of tying compensation to performance through a sales commission structure is deemed to be in conflict with socialistic values, and thus is illegal. Designing appropriate reward structures and motivating sales personnel in China are fertile areas for research.

Japanese firms, who view themselves as being in China for the long haul, have been very successful with preemptive advertising strategies in China. Whether the same strategies are equally successful for Western firms remains to be seen. Another approach that may work for Western firms is to test the effectiveness of instructive advertising. For example, a manufacturer of skin care products may find that advertisements explaining the proper care for chapped skin may increase brand awareness of its products. However, this conjecture has not been researched to date.

The evidence on the effectiveness of prizes, giveaways, coupons, and so on is very limited or nonexistent for the Chinese market. Lever Brothers promoted the introduction of its Shield brand of soap in China by asking consumers to guess the number of soap bars in a transparent container. With a color TV as the grand prize, the consumer response to this promotion was phenomenal. It may be that it will take the Chinese a few years before they show signs of becoming jaded shoppers as far as prizes, coupons, and giveaways are concerned. It may be a safe bet for firms to use these promotional approaches, but it may be even better to empirically verify their efficacy.

CONCLUSIONS

With the advent of the open door policy, China legislated the Joint Venture Law in 1979. Since then thousands of firms have negotiated JV agreements in China. Many of these JVs have yet to start operations. Others who have started operations have found profits to be illusory. Some of those who had counted on establishing themselves in the Chinese market through JVs have been bitterly disappointed. Some of those who had viewed China as a base for both Chinese sales and regional exports have been disappointed with the quality of the items produced for exports. Hindsight indicates that many foreign firms, in their euphoria of doing business in China, simply glossed over what should have been strategic considerations for them. Whether these firms can rectify their situations remains to be seen. However, they do provide precedents for what should be done in the future. This chapter has focused on the types of issues that a firm needs to address before signing a JV agreement.

A variety of strategic, negotiating, financing, managerial, public policy, and research issues are considered in this chapter. If the foreign firm is successful in negotiating to its satisfaction, then it has the potential for profits with its JV. But what about the firm that achieves only partially its negotiating objectives? One option is to sign the JV agreement, be reconciled to an extended period of "profitless prosperity," and hope for the best. The second option is to recognize that despite the efforts involved, the end results are not desirable and that the best alternative is to forego the particular JV opportunity. It may not be very palatable, but it may be the most suitable action.

NOTES

1. See "Consumer Goods J.V.: French to Promote Cosmetics in China," *Business China* (December 19, 1985), p. 185.
2. See Hendryx (1986a, 1986b) for some other examples of JVs in China.

3. See, for example, Wang (1984), Buxbaum, Joseph, and Reynolds (1982), MacLeod (1988), Pye (1982), and Campbell (1986) for discussions on the Chinese perspectives.

4. Grow (1986) has highlighted some of these cultural environment factors.

5. A moderating factor is that while China has the world's largest consumer market, its per capita income is that of a developing country.

6. The *guanxi* system is a complex mechanism for building interrelationships and interdependencies, which many Western managers find hard to understand and even harder to practice.

7. See, for example, Nalen (1986).

8. Kaynak (1986) has provided some additional insights into the problem of marketing research in developing countries.

9. "Laying the Foundation for the Great Mall of China," *Time* (January 25, 1988), p. 68.

REFERENCES

Buxbaum, David C., Joseph, C.E., and Reynolds, Paul D. (1982). *China Trade*, New York: Praeger Publishers.

Campbell, Nigel. (1986). *China Strategies: The Inside Story*. Manchester/Hong Kong: University of Manchester/University of Hong Kong.

Grow, Roy F. (1986). "Japanese and American Firms in China: Lessons of a New Market." *Columbia Journal of World Business* (Spring), pp. 49-55.

Hendryx, Steven R. (1986a). "Implementation of a Technology Transfer Joint Venture in the People's Republic of China: A Management Prospective." *Columbia Journal of World Business* (Spring), pp. 57-66.

Hendryx, Steven R. (1986b). "The China Trade: Making the Deal Work." *Harvard Business Review* (July-August), pp. 75,81-84.

Ignatius, Adi. (1985). "Sneaker-Maker Nike Eyes China's Two Billion Feet." *The Wall Street Journal* (December 11), p. 34.

Kaynak, Erdener. (1986). *Marketing and Economic Development*, New York: Praeger Publishers.

Lord, Winston. (1988). "Sino-U.S. Trade Cooperation Expands." *Beijing Review* (June 20-26), pp. 20-21.

MacLeod, Roderick. (1988). *China, Inc.* New York: Bantam Books.

Nalen, Craig A. (1986). "The Role of Private Investment in Third World Development." *Columbia Journal of World Business* (Twentieth Anniversary Issue), pp. 59-63.

Pye, Lucian W. (1982). *Chinese Commercial Negotiating Style*. Cambridge, MA: Oelgeschlager, Gunn & Hain.

Sheth, Jagdish, and Eshghi, Abdolreza. (1989). *Global Marketing Perspectives*. Cincinnati, OH: South-Western Publishing Co.

Thorelli, Hans B. (1987). "What Can Third World Countries Learn from China?" *Journal of Global Marketing* (Fall/Winter), pp. 69-83.

Time (1986, June 2). "Sweet is Turning to Sour." p. 56.

Wang, H.T. (1984). *China's Modernization and Transnational Corporations*. Lexington, MA: D.C. Heath and Company.

Wang, Pinqing. (1988). "Sino-U.S. Trade Cooperation Expands." *Beijing Review* (June 20-26), pp. 18-20.

Xie, Ming-gan. (1987). "China's Open Door Policy and Sino-American Trade." *Business Horizons* (July-August), pp. 10-15.

Index